Women in American Musical Theatre

*Essays on Composers, Lyricists,
Librettists, Arrangers, Choreographers,
Designers, Directors, Producers
and Performance Artists*

Edited by BUD COLEMAN
and JUDITH SEBESTA

McFarland & Company, Inc., Publishers
Jefferson, North Carolina, and London

LIBRARY OF CONGRESS CATALOGUING-IN-PUBLICATION DATA

Women in American Musical Theatre : essays on composers,
lyricists, librettists, arrangers, choreographers, designers,
directors, producers and performance artists / edited by Bud
Coleman and Judith A. Sebesta.
    p.   cm.
Includes bibliographical references and index.

ISBN 978-0-7864-3382-7
softcover : 50# alkaline paper ∞

1. Women musical theater producers and directors—United
States. 2. Women composers—United States. 3. Women
choreographers—United States. 4. Musical theater—United
States—History—20th century. I. Coleman, Bertram E.,
1956–   II. Sebesta, Judith, 1966–
ML82.W645   2008
792.6082'0973—dc22   2008009206

British Library cataloguing data are available

On the cover: Susan Stroman became the first woman in history to
win both the direction and choreography Tony Awards for her work
on *The Producers* (courtesy Susan Stroman); Matthew Broderick as
Leo Bloom and his dancing "Girls With Pearls" during the "I Wanna
Be A Producer" number (Photofest)

Manufactured in the United States of America

McFarland & Company, Inc., Publishers
Box 611, Jefferson, North Carolina 28640
www.mcfarlandpub.com

Acknowledgments

Editing an anthology of essays is a much more complex endeavor than we ever could have foreseen, as any editor likely knows. While we did not anticipate *how* complex, we also could not have imagined how rewarding working with our diligent authors could be. Therefore, we would like to thank, first and foremost, the authors who contributed to this volume. Their commitment to this project, as well as their patience throughout the process, inspired us as much as the work and lives of the women within these pages. As we assert in the Introduction, there exists a scholarly bias against musical theatre, and we are grateful to our authors for collaborating with us on our efforts to counteract that bias.

We also would like to thank the members of the Music Theatre/Dance Focus Group of the Association for Theatre in Higher Education. It was at an annual meeting of ATHE that we first conceived of this project, and our conversations were likely spurred by panels and discussions sponsored by this visionary, supportive group. Mary Jo Lodge, Michael Ellison, Helen Myers, Stephen Farrow, Korey Rothman, and Michael Garber, among many others, have joined us in exploring meaning in musicals, celebrating those who create them, learning better ways to teach about them, etc. To them we are most grateful.

Thank you as well to the photographers, artists, and individuals who generously contributed photographs so that our readers could put a face to the names of the amazing but often "invisible" women written about here.

Judith would like to thank her family, particularly her parents, Fred and Jean Sebesta, for all of their support throughout her academic career. My mother taught me about the quiet strength that can exist in many women; my father, an engineer, found a way to encourage my endeavors in theatre in spite of his complete lack of knowledge of and exposure to the field. I know that they wonder where I came from, but I could not have done this without them. My brother and sister-in-law, Stephen and Amy Sebesta, have been especially helpful with computer-related issues and have provided much-needed R & R. At the University of Arizona, Al Tucci, Jerry Dickey, Clare P. Rowe, Peter Beudert, Barbara McKean, and Laura McCammon were all supportive colleagues during the process of creating this book. Finally, I would like to thank my co-editor. Our collaboration produced not only this book but also a lasting friendship.

Bud would like to thank his family and friends for all of their encouragement through the various journeys of his life. My mother, a visual artist, dedicated her life to "children and art," decades before Sondheim coined the phrase. My father instilled in us a profound appreciation of the art of storytelling, as it is only by the telling of stories—whether in a theatre or around the kitchen table—that we know who we are and what we want to be. My partner in life and love, Rob Bein, has enriched my existence in so many ways, not the least of which are his two incredible sons: Joe and Sam. I am indebted to my many colleagues at the University of Colorado at Boulder—especially Jim Symons, Merrill Lessley, Oliver Gerland, and Sean Kelley—who have made UCB a rich artistic and academic home for me for many years. To my co-editor, words cannot begin to encompass my profound appreciation for our friendship and the enriching partnership which created this labor of love.

Judith and Bud would like to take this opportunity to acknowledge their deep appreciation for the exacting standards in editing and mentorship exhibited by the "dean" of theatre historians: Dr. Oscar G. Brockett.

Lyric Credits

Kiss Me, Kate
"Another Op'nin', Another Show"
Words and Music by Cole Porter
© 1949 by Cole Porter
Copyright renewed, assigned to John F. Wharton, Trustee of the Cole Porter Musical & Literary Property Trusts
Publication and Allied Rights assigned to Chappell & Co.
All Rights Reserved. Used by Permission

Blackbirds of 1928
"I Must Have That Man"
Words by Dorothy Fields
Music by Jimmy McHugh
© 1928 (Renewed) EMI Mills Music, Inc.
Rights for the Extended Renewal Term in the United States Controlled by Aldi Music Co. and Universal—MCA Music Publishing, a division of Universal Studios, Inc.
All Rights outside the United States Controlled by EMI Mills Music, Inc. (Publishing) and Alfred Publishing Co., Inc. (Print)
All Rights Reserved. Used by Permission

"I Can't Give You Anything But Love"
Words and music by Jimmy McHugh and
  Dorothy Fields
© 1928 (Renewed 1956) Cotton Club Publishing
and Aldi Music

All Rights for Cotton Club Publishing Controlled and Administered by EMI April Music Inc.
All Rights for ALDI Music Controlled and Administered by Happy Aspen Music LLC
All Rights Reserved International Copyright Secured Used by Permission © 1928 (Renewed) EMI Mills Music, Inc.
Rights for Extended Renewal Term in the United States controlled by Aldi Music Co. and Universal—MCA Music Publishing, a division of Universal Studios, Inc.
All rights outside the United State Controlled by EMI Mills Music, Inc. (Publishing) and Alfred Publishing Co., Inc. (Print)
All Rights Reserved. Used by Permission

Redhead
"My Girl Is Just Enough Woman for Me"
Words by Dorothy Fields
Music by Albert Hague
© 1958 (Renewed) Aldi Music Co. and
  Chappell & Co.
All Rights ReservedUsed By Permission

"Right Finger of My Left Hand"
Words by Dorothy Fields
Music by Albert Hague
© 1958 (Renewed) Aldi Music Co. & Chappell &
  Co.
All Rights Reserved. Used by Permission

Sweet Charity
"If My Friends Could See Me Now"
Music by Cy Coleman
Lyric by Dorothy Fields
© 1965, 1969 (Copyrights renewed) Notable
    Music Co., Inc. & Lida Enterprises, Inc.
    All Rights administered by WB Music Corp.
    All Rights Reserved. Used By Permission

"The Rhythm of Life"
Music by Cy Coleman
Lyrics by Dorothy Fields
© 1965, 1969 (Copyrights renewed) Notable
    Music Co., Inc. and Lida Enterprises, Inc.
    All rights administered by WB Music Corp.
    All Rights Reserved. Used by Permission

Eleanor (unproduced)
"The Women's Emancipation Proclamation"
Music by Cy Coleman
Lyrics by Dorothy Fields
    Used by permission of the Estate Cy Coleman,
    The David Lahm and Eliza Lahm Trusts, Lida
    Enterprises and Notable Music.

Title Unknown: "I Open My Eyes"
Music by Cy Coleman
Lyrics by Dorothy Fields
    Used by permission of the Estate Cy Coleman,
    The David Lahm and Eliza Lahm Trusts, Lida
    Enterprises and Notable Music.

Seesaw
"Nobody Does It Like Me"
Music by Cy Coleman
Lyrics by Dorothy Fields
© 1973 (Renewed) Notable Music Co., Inc.
    and Aldi Music Company
    All Rights administered by WB Music Corp.
    All Rights Reserved. Used by Permission

Billion Dollar Baby
"There I'd Be"
Lyrics by Betty Comden and Adolph Green
Music by Morton Gould
© 1945 (Renewed) Chappell & Co., Inc.
    All Rights Reserved. Used by Permission

Two on the Aisle
"Catch Our Act at the Met"
Lyrics by Betty Comden and Adolph Green
Music by Jule Styne
© 1959 (Renewed) WB Music Corp.
    All Rights Reserved. Used by Permission

Wonderful Town
"One Hundred Easy Ways to Lose a Man"
Music by Leonard Bernstein
Lyrics by Betty Comden and Adolph Green
    © 1953 (Renewed) Chappell & Co., Inc. and
    PolyGram International Music Publishing
    Ltd.

All rights administered by Chappell & Co., Inc.
All Rights Reserved. Used by Permission

Peter Pan
"Captain Hook's Waltz"
Lyric by Betty Comden and Adolph Green
Music by Jule Styne
© 1954, 1956 (Renewed) Betty Comden, Adolph
    Green and Jule Styne
    All Rights controlled by Edwin H. Morris &
    Company, a Division of MPL Music Publishing,
    Inc.
    All Rights Reserved

"Never Never Land"
Lyric by Betty Comden and Adolph Green
Music by Jule Styne
© 1954 (Renewed) Betty Comden, Adolph
    Green and Jule Styne
    All Rights controlled by Edwin H. Morris & Com-
    pany, A Division of MPL Music Publishing, Inc.
    All Rights Reserved

"I Won't Grow Up"
Lyric by Carolyn Leigh
Music by Mark Charlap
© 1954 (Renewed 1982) Carolyn Leigh and
    Mark Charlap
    All Rights Controlled by Edwin H. Morris &
    Company, a division of MPL Music Publishing,
    Inc. and Carwin Music Inc.
    All Rights Reserved
© 1954 (Renewed) Carolyn Leigh and Mark
    Charlap
    All Rights controlled by EMI Carwin Music,
    Inc. and Edwin H. Morris & Company, a division
    of MPL Communications, Inc.
    All Rights Reserved. Used by Permission

Bells Are Ringing
"It's a Simple Little System"
Lyrics by Betty Comden and Adolph Green
Music by Jule Styne
© 1956 (Renewed) Stratford Music Corporation
    All Rights Administered by Chappel & Co., Inc.
    All Rights Reserved. Used by Permission

Fade Out–Fade In
"You Musn't Feel Discouraged"
Lyrics by Betty Comden and Adolph Green
Music by Jule Styne
© 1964 (Renewed) Chappell & Co., Inc.
    All Rights Reserved. Used by Permission

On the Twentieth Century
"I've Got It All"
Music by Cy Coleman
Words by Betty Comden and Adolph Green
© 1978 Notable Music Co., Inc. and Betdolph
    Music Company
    All rights administered by WB Music Corp.
    All Rights Reserved. Used by Permission

A Doll's Life
"New Year's Eve"
Words by Betty Comden and Adolph Green
Music by Larry Grossman
© 1982 Warner-Tamerlane Publishing Corp., Fiddleback Music Publishing Co., Inc., Betdolph Music, Inc. and Revelation Music Publishing Corp.

All Rights on Behalf of Fiddleback Music Publishing Co., Inc. Administered by Warner-Tamerlane Publishing Corp.

All Rights on Behalf of Betdolph Music, Inc. and Revelation Music Publishing Corp. Administered by WB Music Corp.

All Rights Reserved. Used by Permission

The Will Rogers Follies
"Never Met a Man I Didn't Like"
Music by Cy Coleman
Lyrics by Betty Comden and Adolph Green
© 1991 Notable Music Co., Inc. and Betdolph Music Company

All rights Administered by WB Music Corp.
All Rights Reserved. Used by Permission

Wildcat
"Hey, Look Me Over"
Music by Cy Coleman
Lyrics by Carolyn Leigh
© 1960, 1961 (Renewed 1988, 1989) Notable Music Co., Inc. and EMI Carwin Catalog Inc.

All Rights on behalf of Notable Music Co., Inc. Administered by WB Music Corp.

Print Rights on behalf of EMI Carwin Catalog Inc. Administered by Alfred Publishing Co., Inc.

All Rights Reserved. Used by Permission

How Now, Dow Jones
"They Don't Make 'Em Like That Any More"
Lyrics by Carolyn Leigh
Music by Elmer Bernstein
© 1968 (Renewed) Carwin Music Inc.

All rights controlled and administered by EMI U Catalog Inc. (Publishing) and Alfred Publishing Co., Inc. (Print)

All Rights Reserved. Used by Permission

Gatsby (unproduced)
Title Unknown ("Bad bootleg hootch")
Lyrics by Carolyn Leigh
Music by Lee Pockriss

Reprinted with permission of the Leigh Estate

Smile
"Nightlife in Santa Rosa"
Lyrics by Carolyn Leigh
Music by Marvin Hamlisch

Reprinted with permission of the Leigh Estate

Title Unknown (**"For this I watched your overbite"**)
Lyrics by Carolyn Leigh
Music by Marvin Hamlisch

Reprinted with permission of the Leigh Estate

Seventh Heaven
"Sun at My Window, Love at My Door"
Words by Stella Unger
Music by Victor Young
© 1955 (Renewed) by WB Music Corp.

All Rights Reserved. Used by Permission

Ernest in Love
"Mr. Bunbury"
Lyrics by Anne Croswell
Music by Lee Pockriss

Reprinted with permission of Anne Croswell

Tovarich
"A Small Cartel"
Lyrics by Anne Croswell
Music by Lee Pockriss

Reprinted with permission of Anne Croswell

"It Used to Be"
Lyrics by Anne Croswell
Music by Lee Pockriss

Reprinted with permission of Anne Croswell

Songs and Stories from Moby Dick
"One White Whale"
By Laurie Anderson
© 2001 Difficult Music

Reprinted with permission of the author

Maytime
"Will You Remember"
By Rida Johnson Young and Sigmund Romberg
© 1917 by G. Schirmer, Inc. (ASCAP)

International Copyright Secured. All Rights Reserved
Reprinted by Permission

Naughty Marietta
"Ah! Sweet Mystery of Life"
English lyrics by Rida Johnson Young
French lyrics by Emilia Renaud
Music by Victor Herbert
© 1910 (Renewed) Warner Bros. Inc.

All Rights Reserved. Used by Permission

"I'm Falling in Love with Someone"
Lyrics by Rida Johnson Young
Music by Victor Herbert
© 1910 (Renewed) Warner Bros. Inc.

All Rights Reserved. Used By Permission

"Our America Gal"
Lyrics by Dorothy Fields

Used by permission of the Estate Cy Coleman, The David Lahm and Eliza Lahm Trusts, Lida Enterprises and Notable Music.

Excerpt from **Annie Get Your Gun**
Book by Herbert and Dorothy Fields
Music and Lyrics by Irving Berlin

Used by permission of The David Lahm and Eliza Lahm Trusts

Table of Contents

Introduction

Wherever I look, women are singled out, separated, distinguished
from their male colleagues by gender. Unfortunately, whatever
advances the women's movement has brought (and they have
been many and important), it has not erased the disparity
in most professional hierarchies between women and men and,
thus, not eliminated the need for separate considerations,
exhibitions, concerts, festivals, anthologies and theatres[....]
— Julia Miles, Women's Project & Productions[1]

Julie Taymor, Susan Stroman, Jeanine Tesori, Theoni Aldredge: these are
just a few names of prominent women creating musical theatre today. Increasingly, women find jobs directing, choreographing, writing, producing and
designing musicals in a variety of venues throughout America, both on and
Off Broadway and in regional, educational, and community theatre. Their work
builds on a history of women's contributions to the creation of musical theatre
throughout the twentieth century in America, from Anne Caldwell to Rida
Johnson Young to Patricia Zipprodt to Lynn Ahrens. That this most popular
of America's theatrical forms is a primarily male-created one is a common misconception, a misconception acknowledged by Mark W. Estrin in the *Oxford
Companion to Women's Writing*:

> Women writers have made a major collective contribution to the development
> of the American musical despite a body of evidence initially appearing to sug-
> gest otherwise. For in several significant respects, women's roles in the confus-
> ing collaborative process of American musical theater [...] *have* indeed been
> marginalized [author's emphasis].[2]

Feeding this misconception is the "body of evidence" mentioned by Estrin,
books on the history of musical theatre, which bear wide and deep holes within
their pages where narratives on the women of American musical theatre should
be. In *More Broadway Musicals: Since 1980*, Martin Gottfried writes, "On a
male-dominated Broadway, *The Secret Garden* was written by women (book and
lyrics by Marsha Norman, music by Lucy Simon) and it was directed by a
woman, Susan B. Schulman. The resulting musical was not only artistically
different but different in sensibility from traditionally 'tough' shows."[3] As

misguided as Gottfried's gendered assessment of *The Secret Garden* may be, the sad fact is that this statement is one of the rare considerations of the contributions of women in musical theatre. Most written histories of musical theatre discuss the work of female performers but make only a cursory nod to the work of its other female creators.

Only one choreographer/director and a handful of composers and lyricists are sometimes covered within the pages of these histories: Agnes de Mille, Dorothy Fields, Mary Rodgers, and Betty Comden. But finding information regarding other female creators can be difficult. None of the major works on the history of the musical theatre include sections on the contributions of women; most include considerable information on men who engaged in much less prolific careers than many women who are left out. Lehman Engel, in *The American Musical Theater: A Consideration* (1967), briefly explores the work of Comden, de Mille, Fields, Nancy Hamilton, Bella Spewack, and Kay Swift.[4] Kurt Ganzl's *Song and Dance* (1995) mentions Comden, Fields, Leigh, Carole Bayer Sager, Spewack, and Rida Johnson Young.[5] In Al Kasha and Joel Hirschhorn's *Notes on Broadway: Conversations with the Great Songwriters* (1985), only five of twenty-five interviews are with women.[6] And in Alan Jay Lerner's *The Musical Theatre: A Celebration* (1986), only Comden, de Mille, and Fields are celebrated.[7] Mark Steyn's *Broadway Babies Say Goodnight* (1997) does not discuss that many more women even though it was published eleven years after Lerner's book, and David Walsh and Len Platt in *Musical Theater and American Culture* (2003) find only de Mille worth mention.[8] John Bush Jones at least pauses several times in his book *Our Musicals, Ourselves* (2003) to consider what he terms "women's issues," briefly describing Eve Merriam's *The Club*, Gretchen Cryer and Nancy Ford's work, and even giving a nod to the 1970 show *Mod Donna*, which he calls "one of the rare New York musicals on or Off Broadway by an all female creative team."[9] In *The Rise and Fall of the Broadway Musical*, Mark N. Grant discusses the work of de Mille at some length, and he mentions such women as Cheryl Crawford, Trude Rittman, Hanya Holm, Albertina Rasch, Kathleen Marshall, Julie Taymor, and Susan Stroman, but beyond such efforts he does little better than his predecessors in truly exploring the work of women creators of musicals. (He does state the need for "some enterprising scholar" to "someday measure the exact yardage" of Rittman's—and Genevieve Pitot's—contributions to musicals. That measurement is, fortunately, taken in this volume.)[10] Jackson R. Bryer and Richard A. Davison's compilation, *The Art of the American Musical: Conversations with the Creators*, includes interviews with four women (Lynn Ahrens, Betty Comden, Kathleen Marshall, and Susan Stroman) out of a total of sixteen subjects.[11]

Since in the past twenty years a number of analytical works have focused more generally on the place of women in theatre, one might be hopeful that here would lie a goldmine of information on these unsung contributors. Books that recoup, analyze, and/or celebrate women's contributions to theatre throughout history would seem to be a perfect source for women's specific contributions to musical theatre. But unfortunately this has not been the case. Kathleen Betsko and Rachel Koenig's *Interviews with Contemporary Women Playwrights* (1987) includes only four writers who at that time were actively working in musical theatre: Gretchen Cryer, Eve Merriam, Ntozake Shange, and Megan Terry.[12] Sue Ellen Case's *Feminism and Theatre* (1988) briefly mentions Vinette Carroll, Ntozake Shange, and Ellen Stewart.[13] Jill Dolan's *The Feminist Spectator as Critic* (1988) gives cursory information on Karen Finley and Carmelita Tropicana, who work within an "alternative" musical form.[14] And one essay in Lynda Hart's *Making a Spectacle: Feminist Essays on Contemporary Women's Theatre* (1989) briefly discusses Ntozake Shange's views on black musicals.[15] *Women in American Theatre* (1987), edited by Helen Krich Chinoy and Linda Walsh Jenkins, provides the most extensive information, although the information given about fourteen women who have worked in musical theatre is not always specifically about their work in that genre.[16]

This historical dearth of information on women in *musical* theatre in books that focus on women in theatre in general might reflect a scholarly bias against this most popular of theatrical forms. One of the editors experienced this bias first-hand in graduate school when she was cautioned by advisors against writing a dissertation on musical theatre because it might not be marketable when she pursued publication. (The author capitulated.) Accordingly, although a number of works have treated the subject of musical theatre from a fairly traditional, almost "positivist" historical perspective, few have approached it theoretically or using a less "traditional" historical methodology, such as feminism, marxism, postmodernism, etc. Furthermore, journals on theatre, such as *The Drama Review, Theatre Journal, Theatre Survey* and *Theatre Topics*, have rarely included articles on musical theatre. And in *Theatre Journal* alone, which publishes both book and performance reviews, of 542 performance reviews published between 1997 and 2003, thirteen have been on musicals; of 454 book reviews during the same period, twelve have been of books on musical theatre. Whether or not this lack of attention to musical theatre reflected the lack of submissions of articles on the subject or the editors' lack of interest in essays is hard to say. And while it is impossible to ascertain if articles on musical theatre are rejected more often by editors than essays on "straight" or "legitimate" theatre, it is quantifiable that they have had less visibility than articles on non-musical theatre. This scholarly bias for spoken-word theatre is ironic given that audiences prefer musical theatre. During the twentieth century, eighty-six productions had a Broadway run of over 1000 performances; only twenty-six of them were non-musicals.

However, there does seem to be a shift away from this bias toward a more inclusive attitude toward the genre, reflected in books like D.A. Miller's *Place for Us: Essays on the Broadway Musical* (1998), John M. Clum's *Something for the Boys: Musical Theatre and Gay Culture* (1999), *Reading Stephen Sondheim*, edited by Sandhor Goodhart (2000), and Stacy Wolf's *A Problem Like Maria: Gender and Sexuality in the Musical* (2002).[17] Articles include Bruce McConachie's "Orientalism in the Musicals of Rodgers and Hammerstein," Andrea Most's "'You've Got to Be Carefully Taught': The Politics of Race in Rodgers and Hammerstein's *South Pacific*," and Stacy Wolf's "'Never Gonna Be a Man/Catch Me if You Can/I Won't Grow Up': A Lesbian Account of Mary Martin as Peter Pan," all in *Theatre Journal*.[18] Certainly the work delivered at panels sponsored by the Music Theatre/Dance Focus Group at the annual conference of the Association for Theatre in Higher Education each year, or in seminars at the annual meetings of the American Society for Theatre Research, suggests a keen interest in serious scholarly consideration of musical theatre.[19]

This anthology is an attempt to further this shift toward more serious scholarly consideration of musical theatre and to remedy the still-existent paucity of information on the American women who helped create it in the twentieth century. A few words about scope are perhaps necessary: first, we take a fairly broad view of the definition of musical theatre. Employing Robert Cohen's streamlined definition of musical theatre as "a theatre that employs a full singing score, usually accompanied by an orchestra and often dance as well," the majority of our essays examine musicals more "traditional" in form, following a genre that has developed over the past 150 years.[20] However, because women have sometimes been forced to work outside the boundaries of the mainstream theatre, we feel that it is important to include representative work being done by women that does not fit neatly within the genre of the traditional Broadway musical. Second, because a number of existing works highlight the contributions of female musical theatre performers, such as Fanny Brice, Mary Martin, Ethel Merman, Carol Channing, and Patti LuPone, among others, we have chosen to include essays that focus instead on the less-celebrated but equally important directors, designers, producers, choreographers, composers, lyricists, and others who more often than not combine these various roles. Third, although women certainly participate in the creation of musical theatre throughout the western world — and particularly in London on the West End — we have decided to focus on women whose careers have been situated primarily in America. Finally, this anthology concentrates on work done primarily within the twentieth century. This is not to suggest that the work of women in musical theatre suddenly began in 1901 or ended in 2000, but a single anthology simply does not permit the space to consider the contributions of women before this century or within the past couple of years. The authors hope that others will take up this torch to examine the women who laid the foundations for the work of the twentieth century and/or the increasing numbers of women who work to create musical theatre.

Similarly, it is not possible within one anthology to attempt a comprehensive overview of American women's vast contributions to musical theatre in the twentieth century. And it is important to avoid essentializing or generalizing about the work of women within musical theatre, as Gottfried does in his assessment of *The Secret Garden*. There is no one "female" form of musical theatre, no single way of working applicable to all women when they write, direct, design, produce, choreograph, or arrange. Therefore, *Women in American Musical Theatre* is meant to provide the reader a sampling, organized roughly chronologically, of the variety of work that women have done within this genre, and the variety of ways that they go about this work. The editors have encouraged the contributors, when possible, to describe and analyze the ways that being a woman has affected the processes, careers, and lives of the creators.

Korey R. Rothman focuses on the work of successful but historically neglected lyricists Rida Johnson Young, Anne Caldwell, and Dorothy Donnelly, examining similarities among their careers as well as reasons why women were so successful within operetta and early musical comedy. Barbara Means Fraser explores the work and lives of theatre luminaries Hallie Flanagan and Cheryl Crawford, particularly their contributions as producers of musical theatre during the Depression and beyond. Belying the notion that Agnes de Mille is the only female choreographer to have worked in the musical theatre, Anna Wheeler Gentry traces the image of the "showgirl" and the transformation of that image through the dance, choreography, and stage movement created by Anna Held, Albertina Rasch, Katherine Dunham, Hanya Holm, and June Taylor. Jennifer Jones Cavenaugh focuses on the significant but little-known work of Trude Rittman, a dance and choral arranger on nearly forty Broadway shows, as well as the work of dance arranger Genevieve Pitot. In order to recoup, better understand and celebrate their careers, Cavenaugh examines the "the deep-seated assumptions of male-privilege" in musical theatre that led to the women's virtual eradication from historical record. Gary Konas interrogates the notion that only "boys" write musical theatre through his examination of the lyrics and music of Dorothy Fields, Betty Comden, Carolyn Leigh, and Mary Rodgers. Utilizing interviews with artists when possible, Tish Dace provides an overview of the work of female designers on the musical stage, including lighting, costume, and scenic designers, and considers the reasons for the lack of women within the field of sound design. By focusing on the distinguished careers of producers Theresa Helburn, Jean Dalrymple, and Lucille Lortel, Bud Coleman explores the work of women who are in a double bind: working in a profession that, historically, has been both male dominated and underappreciated. Anne Fliotsos begins with a survey of numerical data on the number of women directing in various venues in the United States, highlighting the discrepancy between the number of men versus the number of women hired to direct professional musical productions. Then Fliotsos examines the careers of female directors of musical theatre arranged in a chronology of historical "waves" based on her data: Dorothy Raedler, Mary Hunter, Vida Hope, Lucia Victor, Vinnette Carroll, Sue Lawless, Julianne Boyd, Graciela Daniele, Susan Schulman, and Julie Taymor. Judith Sebesta compares the work of three women writing musicals during the height of the women's movement: Gretchen Cryer, Nancy Ford, and Elizabeth Swados. Their body of work reflects both a strident social consciousness and a search for unconventional forms and structures. Mary Jo Lodge looks at the increasing ubiquity of the female Director/Choreographer on Broadway, including Graciela Daniele, Patricia Birch, Lynne Taylor-Corbett, Ann Reinking, Susan Stroman, and Kathleen Marshall. Lodge's description and analysis of their careers is enhanced by interviews with a number of her subjects. Finally, Woodrow Hood questions the very definitions of music and theatre by examining the intersection of the two forms in the work of Laurie Anderson, Meredith Monk, and Diamanda Galas.

The American musical today is in a paradoxical state: on the one hand, it is arguably the most popular form of theatre in the United States today. On Broadway, during the 1990s, as much as 80 percent of the box-office take was from musicals, and between 1998 and 1999, more than twenty new musicals appeared on the Broadway stage, as opposed to only six new American plays.[21] At this writing, twenty-four musicals are playing on Broadway. Yet, it has become increasingly expensive to develop and mount a new musical, making revivals and musicals based on previously created, proven material (such as films) an appealing option for producers. Hence the number of new American musicals is decreasing, as are the opportunities for artists to hone their craft in the creation of new musicals. Furthermore, fears that non–American creators of musicals have co-opted what once was primarily an American form and are doing it better —fears fed by musicals such as *Cats* and *Les Miserables*— have reared their heads for the past two decades. As the number of American women directors/choreographers (Julie Taymor, Susan Stroman, Graciela Daniele, Lynn Taylor-Corbett, Tina Landau), designers (Heidi Ettinger, Natasha Katz, Peggy Eisenhower, Marjorie Kellogg), and producers (Rhoda Mayerson, Alecia Parker, Anita Waxman, Elizabeth Williams) has risen exponentially in the last decade of the twentieth century, it remains for the work of female composers, lyricists, and librettists to enjoy the same level of employment. This volume will explore this and other important issues concerning American musical theatre.

Notes

1. Julia Miles, "Year of the Woman?" *American Theatre* Sept. 1998: 19.
2. Mark W. Estrin, "Musicals," *Oxford Companion to Women's Writing* (Oxford: Oxford University Press, 1995) 592.
3. Martin Gottfried, *More Broadway Musicals: Since 1980* (New York: Abrams, 1991) 191.
4. Lehman Engel, *The American Musical Theater: A Consideration* (New York: CBS Records, 1967).
5. Kurt Ganzl, *Song and Dance* (New York: Smithmark, 1995).
6. Al Kasha and Joel Hirschhorn, *Notes on Broadway: Conversations with the Great Songwriters* (Chicago: Contemporary, 1985).
7. Alan Jay Lerner *The Musical Theatre: A Celebration* (New York: McGraw-Hill, 1986).

8. Mark Steyn, *Broadway Babies Say Goodnight: Musicals Then and Now* (New York: Routledge, 1997); David Walsh and Len Platt, *Musical Theater and American Culture* (Westport, CT: Praeger, 2003).

9. John Bush Jones, *Our Musicals, Ourselves: A Social History of the America Musical Theatre* (Hanover, NH: Brandeis University Press, 2003) 258.

10. Mark N. Grant, *The Rise and Fall of the Broadway Musical* (Boston: Northeastern University Press, 2004) 183.

11. Jackson R. Bryer and Richard A. Davison, *The Art of the American Musical: Conversations with the Creators* (New Brunswick, NJ: Rutgers University Press, 2005).

12. Kathleen Betsko and Rachel Koenig, *Interviews with Contemporary Women Playwrights* (New York: Morrow, 1987).

13. Sue-Ellen Case, *Feminism and Theatre* (New York: Routledge, 1988).

14. Jill Dolan, *The Feminist Spectator as Critic* (Ann Arbor: University of Michigan Press, 1988).

15. Lynda Hart, ed., *Making a Spectacle: Feminist Essays on Contemporary Women's Theatre* (Ann Arbor: University of Michigan Press, 1989).

16. Helen Krich Chinoy and Linda Walsh Jenkins, eds., *Women in American Theatre*, rev. ed. (New York: TCG, 1987).

17. D.A. Miller, *Place for Us: Essays on the Broadway Musical*, (Cambridge: Harvard University Press, 1998); John M. Clum, *Something for the Boys: Musical Theater and Gay Culture* (New York: Palgrave, 1999); Sandhor Goodhart, ed., *Reading Stephen Sondheim: A Collection of Critical Essays* (New York, Garland, 2000); Stacy Wolf, *A Problem Like Maria: Gender and Sexuality in the American Musical* (Ann Arbor: University of Michigan Press, 2002).

18. Bruce McConachie, "The Oriental Musicals of Rodgers and Hammerstein," *Theatre Journal* 46.3 (1994): 385–398; Andrea Most, "'You've Got to Be Carefully Taught': The Politics of Race in Rodgers and Hammerstein's *South Pacific*," *Theatre Journal* 52 (2000): 307–337; Stacy Wolf, "'Never Gonna Be a Man/Catch Me if You Can/I Won't Grow Up': A Lesbian Account of Mary Martin as Peter Pan," *Theatre Journal* 49.4 (1997): 493–509.

19. However, papers on musical theatre are rarely presented at *plenary* sessions during the ASTR conference. The November meetings of ASTR are divided into two formats, the more prestigious plenary sessions, where all attendees come together to hear three papers presented at each session, and seminars, in which attendees divide into numerous groups of scholars who have exchanged papers on a theme beforehand and then discuss them in the seminar.

20. Robert Cohen. *Theatre: Brief Version*, 5th ed. (Mountain View, CA: Mayfield, 2000) 255.

21. Cohen 256, 270.

"Will You Remember"

Female Lyricists of Operetta and Musical Comedy

Korey R. Rothman

> Sweetheart, sweetheart, sweetheart
> Will you love me ever?
> Will you remember this day?
> — Rida Johnson Young "Will You Remember"

The years between *The Black Crook* (1866), with its fortuitous joining of melodrama and leggy chorines, and *Oklahoma!* (1943), with its integrated song, dance, and plot, marked a fertile era for the nascent American musical theatre.[1] Unfortunately, though, historians of musical theatre often represent the period between these two musical milestones as a product of the creative efforts of a few outstanding men. These histories, however, belie the actual contributions of the women who were integral to America's incipient musical theatre. As the author of a 1917 article published in *The Literary Digest* points out:

> In song-writing, as in every other branch of business or profession, women are now pushing mere man very hard. They are said to be "putting over" the greater number of popular hits, many of them producing words, music, and orchestration.[2]

There were prolific female songwriters and many wrote lyrics for some of the most popular shows and performances between 1866 and 1943. Musical theatre historian Stanley Green asserted: "The creators of musical comedy in America are a body of men (and some women) who have consistently refused to do less than the best that was in them."[3] Considering the extensive contributions of female lyricists during musical theatre's embryonic period, their relegation to parenthetical references and footnotes is negligent.

The emphasis on the contributions of men in this period illuminates a disturbing trend in discussions of the musical: a tendency to erase women from the history of early twentieth century musical theatre.[4] Stanley Green's book, *The World of Musical Comedy: The Story of the American Musical Stage as Told Through the Careers of its Foremost Composers and Lyricists,* includes twenty-nine biographies of composers and lyricists— none of them women.[5] *The Poets of Tin Pan Alley: A History of America's Great Lyricists* lists ten lyricists, of which Dorothy Fields is the only woman.[6] *Word Crazy: Broadway Lyricists from Cohan to Sondheim* also includes only Dorothy Fields in its discussion of major lyricists.[7] In a survey sponsored by the Dramatist's Guild, twenty-five contemporary librettists, lyricists, and composers were asked to name their favorite Broadway lyricists. Again, Dorothy Fields was the only female lyricist mentioned from the early era.[8] The tendency to ignore early female lyricists occurs even among authors striving to reclaim female lyricists. A biography of Dorothy Fields apocryphally states: "As the only major-leagued woman songwriter of the golden age of American popular song and musical theatre, Dorothy Fields had been standing virtually alone among men for almost fifty years...."[9]

A review of histories of musical theatre seems to indicate that all female lyricists sprang from the head of Dorothy Fields. However, vaudevillians such as Nora Bayes and Elsie Janis earned popularity by performing songs with original lyrics and Nancy Hamilton and Agnes Morgan wrote songs for topical revues in "women-centered" venues before Fields was even born. In addition to these popular female lyricists, between 1866 and 1943 other female lyricists had active careers in vaudeville and revues, including Viola Shore Brothers, June Carroll, Rosetta and Vivian Duncan, Sylvia Fine (Kaye), Irene Franklin, Anna Held, Grace Henry, May Irwin, Blanche Merrill, Maude Nugent, Marion Sunshine, Helen Trix, and Ethel Waters.[10]

Although women lyricists worked in all forms of early musical theatre, they achieved the most success with operettas and musical comedies. In this period, Rida Johnson Young wrote the lyrics to *Maytime,* which, at 492 performances, was one of the most popular works of the World War I period. Anne Caldwell wrote lyrics to musical comedies that foreshadowed the integrated musical plays of Rodgers and Hammerstein. Dorothy Donnelly wrote the lyrics to two of the longest running musicals of the 1920s— *Blossom Time* (516 performances) and *The Student Prince* (608 performances). Dorothy Fields contributed "Lovely to Look At," "Sunny Side of the Street," and "I Can't Give you Anything But Love" to American popular song. Catherine Chisholm Cushing, Clare Kummer, Ann Ronell, Alma Sanders, and Zelda Sears also supplied lyrics to operettas, musical comedies, or both. Chronicling the professional trajectories of three especially successful (and often ignored) female lyricists of operetta and musical comedy — Rida Johnson Young, Anne Caldwell, and Dorothy Donnelly — will reveal commonalities in the careers of female lyricists and also help elucidate why women were particularly successful in these forms.[11]

Operetta and Musical Comedy

A fortuitous confluence of events led to the success of female lyricists in operetta and musical comedy. In the twenties, at the same time women were entering theatrical professions in unprecedented numbers, commercial theatre was in the midst of a boom. During this period, the forms of operetta and musical comedy reached the apogee of their popularity. Of the top-ten longest running shows of the twenties, nine were operettas or musical comedies.[12] Although operetta and musical comedies have formulaic similarities, they are different in tone and content. According to historian Gerald Bordman:

> What separated operetta and musical comedy were fundamental approaches, fundamental attitudes. At heart, operetta trafficked in a roseate, earnest romanticism, frequently transporting both its characters and its audiences to far-off, exotic lands and far-off, fondly remembered times. By contrast, musical comedy professed to take a jaundiced, cynical look at everyday and, more frequently than not, very contemporary foibles.[13]

Despite their divergent outlooks, in their own ways both operetta and musical comedy reflect the early twentieth-century *zeitgeist*. The 1920 census was the first to find the majority of Americans living in urban areas.[14] Musical comedies, such as *Very Good Eddie* (1915) and *No, No, Nanette* (1925), reflected the national obsession with urbanity. Although musicals often reflected the contemporary social environment, the whimsical jingoism of musical comedy offset the turbulence of a decade that found Americans recovering from World War I and experiencing the revival of the Ku Klux Klan, shifting gender roles, and labor and civil unrest. Changes in the operetta form also unveiled a rabid American nationalism. Staples of the late nineteenth-century American musical stage, operettas were generally translations of German or Austro-Hungarian works. Bordman notes that with the arrival of World War I there occurred "a national prejudice against anything connected to the Central Powers; even sauerkraut became liberty cabbage."[15] While maintaining the exotic locales, Cinderella stories, and Viennese sounds, American composers and lyricists adapted the form of the foreign operettas to suit the tastes of American audiences. A 1917 review of *Maytime* in *The New York Times* reveals this tendency to Americanize operetta:

> The musical success of last season in the German theatres was *Wie einst im Mai*. In view of the present international difference, this was thought to be unfitted in locale, and even in the nature of its music, to allied consumption. Rida Johnson Young took out the naturalization papers of the book, and though some violence is done to the probabilities and to local color, the hyphen has been, on the whole, very successfully eliminated.[16]

Conversely, but equally revealing, the reviewer of *Green Book Magazine* notes that *Maytime*

> is set down as the work of Rida Johnson Young and Sigmund Romberg. As a matter of fact, this is a bit of camouflage. The present unpopularity of Germans

serves as an excuse for crediting our own countrymen with accomplishments not properly theirs. Thus does questionable honesty masquerade as patriotism.[17]

Clearly, the development of "American" operetta required the skills of lyricists and librettists willing to traffic in adaptations of the romantic European form.[18]

Women in the American Theatre

Concurrent with the rising popularity of indigenous musical entertainment was the increasing prevalence of women in the public sphere. As Victorianism gave way to the twentieth century, educational opportunities for women expanded and opened a variety of professions previously closed to them. Technological developments that eased food preparation and cleaning aided some of the obligations of the home. Further, women's involvement in the work force, suffrage and other movements "elevated the popular concept of the liberated autonomous, self-expressive woman to levels unknown before."[19] This "New Woman" was especially prominent in the arts. An article written in 1917 for *New York World* asserts:

> One of the interesting features that instantly presents itself is the increasing number of women who year by year are enrolling in the ranks of playwrights. In no other season has the feminine pen, applied to the difficult art of writing for the stage, been so prolific or successful.[20]

In the early twentieth century, women were already established as actresses and beginning to thrive as playwrights and, more occasionally, as songwriters.

So it was that the post–World War I period was the most prolific decade for female lyricists, especially for those writing musicals and operettas. In the 1917 season, five musical comedies had lyrics or librettos by women. Of the fifty-one works with lyrics by women produced in the 1920s, thirty-one were musicals and operettas, most written by Young, Caldwell, and Donnelly — a triumvirate of women lyricists who typify the career trajectories of women working in operetta and musical comedy.[21]

Rida Johnson Young (c. 1875–1926)

Rida Johnson Young has been called "one of the most successful and prolific women dramatists of the early twentieth century."[22] She was also a prodigious lyricist, writing over thirty plays and musicals and the lyrics for more than five hundred songs. Like many female lyricists, Young entered theatre as a performer but eventually found songwriting and playwriting lucrative professions that funded her luxurious lifestyle.

asserts, "Romberg has written two very fine numbers. [...] 'The Same Silver Moon,' which carries the love theme, should become popular in no time."[62] In a favorable 1931 review of a revival of *Blossom Time*, a critic credits only the composer and producer: "Thanks to Sigmund Romberg's weaving of Shubert [Franz] melodies into the score of 'Blossom Time' it is the loveliest of Shubert [the producers] operettas."[63] However, although Romberg received much of the credit for *My Maryland*'s success, his recollection of their collaboration reveals how integral Donnelly was to the creation of the operetta:

Dorothy Donnelly — actor, lyricist, librettist, playwright, producer, and manager — found her greatest success as a lyricist in the early years of the twentieth century (courtesy Billy Rose Theatre Collection, The New York Public Library for the Performing Arts, Astor, Lenox and Tilden Foundations).

> We obtained the play *Barbara Frietchie*, on which it [*My Maryland*] is based, and read it several times. Then Miss Donnelly went to her country place on Long Island to write the scenario and arrange the music cues. These cues indicate the logical places in which to interpolate songs. Also, with each cue she wrote down a number of suggestions for the titles of songs. With some cues there were as many as twenty suggestions. I chose the ones I liked best and proceeded to compose the music. Usually, I wrote the opening phrase of the melody to fit the words of the title. [64]

Despite Donnelly's work, both the 1931 *Evening Post* and *New York Sun* reviews of the revival of *Blossom Time* ignored her lyrics and libretto and falsely credited Sigmund Romberg for the story.[65]

In addition to lyric and playwriting, Donnelly was a producer and manager. Active in a number of war organizations, she entertained troops in World War I, directed the Third Army stock company at Cobkentz and was vice-president of the Stage Women's War Relief. The S.W.W.R. was an organization that started in 1917 when seven female theatre professionals, including Rachel Crothers and Minnie Dupree, met to discuss possibilities for relief efforts in World War I.[66] In her 1920 address to the S.W.W.R., Donnelly said, "Entertainment is a large word, and, as we of the theatre know, a bird of many hues. But it happened to be oddly enough our particular job."[67] Through her career as an actor, lyricist, librettist, playwright, producer, and manager, Donnelly proved herself a multifaceted and successful entertainer — in all senses of the word.

"I Can't Give You Anything But Love"?

The similarities in the careers of Young, Caldwell, and Donnelly suggest patterns in female lyricists' employment in operettas and musical comedies. Like many other female lyricists, all three women began as performers and later moved to playwriting and lyric writing, achieving their greatest success in operettas and musical comedy. All three lyricists displayed cavalier attitudes toward their work and they publicly downplayed the value of their creative output.

Why female lyricists triumphed after World War I only to be forgotten is a historical enigma, but the solution may be located in the unique historical circumstance of that era. According to Lehman Engel, the dominant musical theatre forms of the post–World War I period, operetta and musical comedy, were "mythological in feeling and, of course, intensely romantic."[68] Women, perhaps, gained initial acceptance as lyric writers in this era because of the formal nature of the musical comedy and operetta, the nature of lyric writing, and the content of the genres. They flourished as songwriters for hire, writing formulaic lyrics for commercial theatre. Unfortunately, trends in the media's reportage of the activities of women in the theatre, the formal demands of operetta and musical comedy, and critical aspersions created a contemporary disregard for and historical erasure of the female lyricists.

Women, historically, have been identified as adept at writing romantic material. For example, the formal nature and romantic themes of sentimental, romance novels historically have made women desirable authors and, at times, men have published these types of writings under female pseudonyms.[69] Likewise, reviews clearly articulate the romantic and sentimental qualities invested in the forms of operetta and musicals. *Maytime* is "sentimental" and *My Maryland* is "a piece of sentiment, not a rollicking playboy affair."[70] *The Student Prince* is a "simple romantic story."[71] As if to stress the point, a reviewer rather redundantly describes *Maytime* as a "romance of delicate charm and poetic romance."[72] Perhaps because of the romantic lushness of operetta and musical comedy, producers considered the forms better suited to the feminine pen, a supposition that provided opportunities in which female lyric writers were not only acceptable, but even preferable to their male counterparts.

The rising popularity of American operetta in the 1920s brought with it a change in the nature of lyric writing in both operetta and musical comedy that may have further increased the prevalence of female lyricists during this period.

Timothy E. Scheurer writes that lyrics before the 1920s were "rich in popular iconography and they [rang] with an immediacy and contemporaneity...."[73] But in the 1920s and 1930s,

> The expressive range of popular song narrowed. Texts began dealing almost exclusively with personal emotions, almost never with events outside of the person. An increasingly large percentage of the most popular songs was concerned with one aspect or another of romantic love.[74]

Even before 1920, a correspondence course on songwriting published in 1917 instructed:

> If you will review all the great song successes of this year and of all the years that are past, you will come to the conclusion that without love there could be no popular song. [...] If your song is not founded on love, it is well to add this element. [...] If you have not love in your lyrics make haste to remedy the defect.[75]

Between 1920 and 1940, love was firmly entrenched in the lyrical vernacular and was the main topic of eighty-five percent of the songs written by both men and women.[76] Donnelly's lyrics for "Song of Love" in the popular *Blossom Time* are replete with the topic.[77] Young averred, "Love songs are the ones upon which writers depend for hits." Young's lyrics for "Ah! Sweet Mystery of Life" from *Naughty Marietta* certainly emphasized the operetta's obsession with love:

> Ah! Sweet Mystery of life at last I've found thee,
> Ah! I know at last the secret of it all;
> All the longing, seeking, striving, waiting, yearning,
> The burning hopes, the joy and idle tears that fall!
> For 'tis love, and love alone, the world is seeking;
> And 'tis love and love alone that can repay!
> 'Tis the answer, 'tis the end and all of living,
> For it is love alone that rules for aye![78]

Dorothy Fields, who began writing in the mid–1920s, claimed she used the word love more than 5,000 times in her songs.[79] Again, the romantic content of lyrics in this era perhaps made publishers more inclined towards female lyricists.

It seems further likely that lyrics and librettos were left to women because there was little glory in this aspect of the collaboration. Operetta and musical comedy in the era prior to the integrated musical combined "dialogue, music, lyrics, and dance in patchwork quilt fashion, leaving the slight unification of elements to ill-wrought books with slender plots."[80] Lehman Engel strongly asserts, "Until the 1930's, librettos for musical shows—with the qualified exception of Jerome Kern's *Show Boat*—not only were ineffectual and silly, they were expected to be."[81] Dorothy Fields averred that the advent of the integrated musical was "the first time that anybody realized that there was such a thing as lyrics. People used to sing anything—they'd sing because that was a song."[82] Even Oscar Hammerstein II suffered indignity as a lyricist. Show business legend has it that Dorothy Hammerstein, Oscar Hammerstein's wife, overheard someone speak of "Ol' Man River" as a "great Kern song." She interrupted, "I beg your pardon. But Jerome Kern wrote *dum dum dum da*; my husband wrote *ol' man river*."[83] Thus, women were allowed to work in the poorly regarded and undervalued areas of lyric and libretto writing. An anecdote from Clare Kummer's early career indicates that men in this era rarely entrusted women with "important" aspects of musical theatre, like composing:

> One day after a song just made itself, Miss [Clare] Kummer sighed resignedly and put on her bonnet. Leaving Brooklyn tremulously, perhaps we should say happily, the fledgling song writer went to the office of Alf Hayman in New York and expressed herself anxious to play the song for him.
> "No. Just read the first verse and chorus," he said. "You should not try to write music." Miss Kummer complied.
> "Good," exclaimed Hayman. "Now you go and find a man who knows how to write some good music for this and then come back again."
> "But listen to my music — it is just the thing for the verses," pleaded Miss Kummer.
> "Young lady," said Hayman sternly, "don't try to do so many things at once. Take my advice. Good morning."
> In three days Miss Kummer returned. She seated herself at the piano and played — her own music.
> "Ah! That's something like it. You see my child, my advice to you was worth something," remarked Hayman. His discomfiture can be imagined when he learned who the composer was.[84]

While music writing was considered an art, libretto and lyric writing were considered easily learned crafts and therefore could be left to women.

Women also may have been called upon to write in the forms of musical comedy and operetta because critics and the public often regarded women well-suited to the writing of popular pap. For example, a reviewer of the Anne Caldwell/Jerome Kern musical, *The Night Boat* (1920), wrote:

> Several current attractions were written by women and there are rumors that next season will see at least a dozen feminine offerings. To be sure, if one is to believe what is grudgingly told about these novelties, many of them are no more than fashionable trifles.[85]

Rida Johnson Young confirmed the critics' assertions:

> Just at present women writers are in the glory because frothy comedies and sentimental dramas enjoy preference over the stronger, more virile production of male writers. [...] When the war is over, this may change.[86]

Contrary to Young's proposition, however, women were not the only creators of banalities on the stage. Historians Kenneth W. Wheeler and Virginia Lee Lussier contend, "Many of these plays by women were irredeemable trash on par with most of the plays by men."[87] As a 1917 article in The *New York World* asserted:

> If plays by men have as a rule attained a higher importance than those by women it also is true that at the other end of the scale women do not write them as badly as some men.[88]

However, unlike their male counterparts, women playwrights and lyricists had a difficult time achieving recognition as artists. They were beleaguered by a public who "could not reconcile achievement with a modish gown and a pretty face" and critics who wrote that women authors "bubbled over continuously with aggravating, cynical, and facetious froth."[89]

New York critics were especially vocal in their condemnation of the lyrics and themes of operettas and musical comedies. A New York which had witnessed the experimental theatre of Elmer Rice, Sophie Treadwell, Eugene O'Neill and Susan Glaspell seemed to find the formulaic musical comedy and operetta unsophisticated and philistine. With unabashed snobbery, one New York reviewer balked at the operatic treacle and averred: "I find *My Maryland* a wee bit too unsavory for New Yorkers to swallow."[90] *Variety's* reviewer of *My Maryland* claimed New York theatergoers were too sophisticated for an operetta that "is just the sort of an operetta which is so unoriginal and so hokumey that it will not appeal to any theatrical sophisticate. Its audience will be the home folks and the occasional theatergoer."[91] Female lyricists flourished, however, writing words that were popular with producers and audiences. In their plays and lyrics, many seemed committed to Young's ideal: "What people want is an old story in a new dress."[92]

It is important to establish, however, that innovation was not the aspiration of many of the female lyricists and librettists. Many were simply hoping for financial success in the commercial theatre. As Young stated in 1910, "I am after the money."[93] Clare Kummer expressed similar sentiments. After writing and composing "Dearie" and selling millions of copies of the song, Kummer stated:

> I've struck the popular taste in songs, perhaps I can do the same in plays. I'm for the populace every time! If I can please the mass of people, instead of the few, I shall be happy. The masses are elemental.[94]

Young also claimed no aspiration to innovation. According to Young's interviewer, *Theatre* magazine's Helen Broeck:

> She wants to see a woman write THE GREAT AMERICAN PLAY. It is a perfectly impersonal ambition, however, for she has no aspiration towards giving the stage that masterpiece herself. [Broeck's emphasis][95]

Young confirmed, "I hope to putter in my garden and continue writing little plays that have no mission except to be clean and amusing."[96] Irrespective of their stated goals, reviewers often denounced female playwrights and lyricists for formulaic writing. For example, a review of Young's *Little Simplicity* (1918) calls it:

> Strictly Orthodox. It is concerned with nothing newer than the love of a man for a maid, and its three acts content themselves with separating the pair and bringing them together again.[97]

Audiences, however, enjoyed the predictable shenanigans in these plays, songs, musical comedies and operettas, and female lyricists reaped the profits.

Young, Donnelly, and Caldwell wrote to meet commercial demands and the content of their shows largely reflects the fact that operetta and musical comedies were produced for profits. For the most part, a musical had to have beautiful leading ladies and leggy chorines to compete with Florenz Ziegfeld's girlie extravaganzas. As Young asserted in 1920, "The people who come to the theatre want pretty leading ladies."[98] *My Maryland*, for example, transformed a historical figure, the elderly widow Barbara Fritchie, into a young Southern belle.[99] Further, an advertisement for *My Maryland* makes it clear that a major attraction in the show is "the hand-picked singing chorus of 60 pretty girls"; it also highlights the importance of the female form in the marketing of a show. Avant garde writers, such as Susan Glaspell, Rachel Crothers, and Sophie Tread-well, were experimenting with images of the "New Woman." Conversely, the writer of operetta and musical comedy relied heavily on the stock character of the ingenue. Although the form and content of operetta and musical comedy created a market for women writers, if women were to succeed in the medium they had to cater to the demands of producers, directors, and the public — demands that required them to recapitulate retrograde images of women on the stage.

Women lyricists, however, clearly flourished in the commercial musical theatre. Thus, their historical effacement is curious. To some degree, the lyricists were complicit in their own erasure, both in contemporaneous and historical perception. Many female lyricists consistently billed their works as mere trifles. Clare Kummer considered her money-making song "Dearie" "only a trifle when she wrote it,"[100] and Young divorced her work from the hint of any creative inspiration, deeming herself simply a "play manufacturer."[101] Caldwell seemed to indicate that lyrics were much easier to write than music when she reminisced about how she used to write music for her husband's lyrics: "My husband writes songs now and I write lyrics for them, rarely writing music at all any more, because I don't have time, being usually busy with other work."[102] Women may have minimized the significance of their work because the public expected humility of a woman working in the theatre.

It is also possible that female lyricists deliberately diminished the significance of their own work out of a knowledge that the media was not, for the most part, interested in women as theatre professionals. In the early part of the twentieth century articles about "lady playwrights" were often placed on the society page and the private personas of the female lyricists often overshadowed their professional output.[103] For example, rather than discussing the merits of her literary contributions, an article on *Maytime* describes how Young paralleled the events in the operetta by planting a tree on her Connecticut estate. A photographer traveled to Young's orchard to capture this publicity stunt.[104] Newspapers were also at hand when Young took dancing lessons or partied with undergraduates at Oxford.[105] Caldwell also scrambled for media attention for non-theatrical enterprises. One paper reported:

> Tiring of the verminy village vehicles of incalculable age that transported her from the station to the handsome O'Dea home, she bethought herself to show a public spirit and contribute something to the town industries by opening a taxicab garage. The garage was ACCO — her initials with the middle one doubled for euphony.[106]

At a luncheon in her honor, Anne Caldwell was asked what inspired her to name the heroine of *The Nest Egg* Hettie Gandy. Caldwell emphasized her own domesticity instead of her playwriting skill:

> The Gandy I took from the same source that has supplied the names of nearly all the stage characters that I have written — a seed catalogue. That's one advantage of living in the country and being a farmeress [sic].[107]

As if to highlight her gender, reporters took note of Dorothy Fields' habit of breaking up her morning and afternoon writing sessions with televised soap operas.[108] Articles on the songwriter also frequently mentioned Fields' collection of teapots.[109]

Feminine fripperies were also an important issue in contemporary discussion of female lyricists. Articles and interviews addressed Caldwell's physical appearance, beginning with her debut as a playwright. A newspaper reporter was surprised by Caldwell's appearance as a "gentle and genteel lady dressed all in black," an image that apparently contradicted the reporter's thoughts on how a female playwright should look.[110] Aware of public perceptions that a woman working in the glamorous world of theatre should appear glamorous, "like Maxine Elliot or Billie Burke,"[111] Caldwell confessed:

> Well, I have actually allowed my daughter's photograph to be published labeled as myself. Yes, she looked the part, I thought, so I decided it was the best thing to do.[112]

Likewise, newspapers frequently reported on Dorothy Fields' appearance. Reporters noted that Fields had an "aristocratic appearance [...] and impeccable taste in clothes." Fields even appears on the cover of a 1945 entertainment magazine, advertising *Fabulous* perfume with the quotation, "In 1872 no elegant lady would be safe in Central Park if she dared use even a drop of that tempestuous new perfume FABULOUS by CHARBERT."[113] The *New York Sunday News* emphasized:

> [Fields'] non-professional activities include much charitable work; frequent attendance at the opera, concerts, art shows; and keeping in touch with her children...[she is] just a fair cook, but phenomenal with needle and thread.[114]

Journalists were fascinated with the personal lives of the female lyricists, often disregarding their theatrical achievements.[115]

The works of female lyricists were overshadowed not only by their public personas, but also by the performers and music that usually took precedence over book and lyrics in operetta and musical comedy, where song and dance numbers were often showcases for the headliner. Young, for example, faced considerable challenges writing lyrics for *Naughty Marietta*, since the star, Italian performer Emma Trentini, did not speak fluent English.[116] Trentini's difficulty with English was highlighted by one reviewer's amazement: "Nothing could stop her [Trentini], not even words of four syllables."[117] In spite of favorable reviews, Trentini's ability with English limited Young to writing words that would not challenge the tongue. Likewise, Fred Stone, the frequent star of Caldwell's shows, often overshadowed her. One reviewer noted:

> It is difficult not to believe that Stone himself is responsible for the funny things he says. It is perhaps absurd to think it — but one does. One quite forgets poor, hardworking, worthy Anne Caldwell. Forgive us, Anne![118]

This review, however, was an exception. The credit for the women lyricist's material often went to the people speaking and singing the words.

In addition to showcasing performing talent, musical comedy and, especially operetta, emphasized music. When asked about her collaboration with Sigmund Romberg, Fields complained, "I could never hear one of my lyrics because the orchestra was so loud. Nothing is more annoying to an audience than to strain to hear the words."[119] In between the proverbial rock and hard place, the women were discouraged by producers from composing for operetta and musical comedy, forms that privileged music over lyrics. For *Naughty Marietta*, Young wrote:

> For I'm falling in love with someone
> Someone girl
> I'm falling in love with someone,
> Head awhirl;
> Yes! I'm falling in love with someone,
> Plain to see,
> I'm sure I could love some one madly,
> If someone would only love me![120]

These lyrics would seem to indicate that women lyricists were writing treacle that conformed to a form that gave music and performers precedence over sophisticated rhymes, witty lyrics and clever turns of phrase.

It is more likely that female lyricists of operettas and musical comedies have been forgotten because the notoriously sexist New York reviewers often deemed their lyrics middling and forgettable. A review of *Little Simplicity* calls "the book and lyrics of Rida Johnson Young [...] workmanlike, albeit far from inspired."[121] Another review states, "The music contributes more to the success of *Naughty Marietta* than the libretto does. [...] The book at the best was only a necessary evil."[122] A *Blossom Time* reviewer averred:

> It seems to this reviewer that the credit for the rescue of the old love story [...] goes in greater measure to Mr. Romberg than to Miss Donnelly, whose book,

while it serves the music as a sufficient vehicle, is notable rather for theatrical competence than for wit or taste.[123]

Critics also blamed Donnelly for problems with *My Maryland*:

> The trouble is book and comedy. There is nothing wrong with the music, for Romberg has written as fine an operetta score as I have head [sic] in aeons [sic]. The book is the trite shopworn war story thrown around the Barbara Frietchie incident, sprinkled with uniforms of the Blue and the Gray, and stirred from time to time by the American flag.[124]

A 1924 review in *The New York Time* asserted that *The Student Prince* "requires a minimum of dialogue and so clears the decks rapidly for the business of an operetta, which is music."[125] More recent opinion coincides with reviews from the period. In 1976 one critic proclaimed, "Rida Johnson Young's libretto has not stood the test of time," and in 1982 Douglas Watt wrote of Young's "two dimensional characters" which are only given life through Victor Herbert's music.[126]

One lyricist of musical comedy who fared well — both during her career and historically — was Dorothy Fields. In light of her enduring popular success, comparing Dorothy Fields to her female contemporaries may shed light on why other female lyricists have fallen into the historical abyss. Historians often praise Fields for her use of the colloquial and vernacular in shaping her lyrics.[127] For the revue *Blackbirds of 1928* she wrote the lyrics to "I Can't Give You Anything But Love":

> Gee, but it's tough to be broke, kid,
> It's not a joke, kid
> It's a curse;
> My luck is changing
> It's gotten
> From simply rotten
> To something worse.[128]

Like her contemporary, lyricist Lorenz Hart, Field's lyrics are full of colloquial phrasing and sophisticated rhyme structures. Fields talked often about the importance of finding the right words, not simply forcing lyrics into an ABAB rhyme structure. She stated:

> The thing is to get an idea into the lyric. Who cares about rhymes? Anyone can rhyme. My first rhyming dictionary was given to me by Cole Porter. He said, "You've got to stop this nonsense. Why knock yourself out trying to find the right words?"[129]

In contrast to Fields' method, Young rhymed shamelessly. She told an interviewer proudly, "I have just thought of a rhyme for 'caravan' and finished a lyric I have had on my mind for two days."[130] Young also said, "If I waited to capture the mood, I am afraid I should never write a word."[131] Like many of her male and female lyricist colleagues, Young employed formulaic lyrics and simple rhymes rather than inspired lyrics. Conversely, Fields rather prophetically asserted: "The point is that a good lyric writer has to inhale the idiom, not the cliché, of the moment. Those songs don't date."[132] Many rhymes in operettas and early musical comedies were of the moon/June variety and lyricists of musical comedy and operetta were often more rhymesters/rhymestresses than poets. Although the lyrics served an important function in the music and star-driven operettas and musical comedies—as well as providing steady income for their authors—the lack of innovation excludes them from the annals of great lyrics.

The nature of the lyrics should not, finally, negate the substantial achievement of the female lyricists of operetta and musical comedy. For one thing, these lyricists helped refute the popularly held notion that women have no sense of humor.[133] Critics finally recognized that a writer could be female and funny. One critic noted that Ann Caldwell "knows how to write a mighty pleasing libretto for a musical comedy, one that pokes a satirical witticism at an audience without leaving a scar. She knows what's timely and what will make us giggle."[134] A critic also praised the humor in Clare Kummer's musical comedy librettos and plays, saying:

> Her wit seems spontaneous and so your laughter is spontaneous. [...] She lures
> you, without any apparent intention, towards the commonplace, and then,
> with a sort of demure impishness, sweeps you off your feet into a gale of
> laughter, clean laughter, which makes the world a merry, irresponsible place in
> which one needs only a sense of humor.[135]

In 1941 a critic even noted, "Among the comic writers of a generation ago, none of the men [...] was able to reach the sheer delight of dialogue of Clare Kummer."[136]

Further, although none of these female lyricists subscribed to a specifically feminist agenda in their writing, some seemed to be aware of their responsibility to the women in the audience. In "Left All Alone Again Blues" from *The Night Boat*, Anne Caldwell creates lyrics for a disgruntled wife who laments being left alone at home while her husband goes out on the town. For this wife, marriage has robbed her of the good times she used to enjoy.[137]

Young did not write overtly strong female characters, but, rankled by images of women scrubbing and cooking, she once walked out on a movie she was watching. She asserted:

> The ideal heroine has long been a silly little thing, who does exactly as she is
> told. Flights of independence are put down as petulance. The woman of spirit
> has been caricatured as masculine and a freak.[138]

The female lyricists also recognized, and began to appeal to, a growing female audience. Young noted:

> The secret of success is merely to know what a million or so people would want
> in a song or play. [...] For one thing, I know a play cannot succeed if it doesn't

please women. And it's usually the woman [...] who suggests that they see a particular play.[139]

She went on to argue:

> I am supposed to write musical comedies which will please the "tired business man." But if they do not please the lady whom the tired businessman brings with him, the show will not last long.[140]

Female lyricists were mindful of the growing female theatre audience. Young warned, "We must be careful about making women ridiculous," because she felt women will not tolerate ridiculous portrayals of their gender on stage.[141]

Women also clearly found lyric writing a lucrative profession and many were able to achieve wealth and financial independence, becoming prominent professional women. After Clare Kummer's "Dearie" sold more than one million copies, she lamented, "[It] was really bad for my work, because I made so much money that I didn't have to do anything for some years."[142] Fields stated, "I do it because it's my chosen field and endeavor and it's very lucrative."[143] For many female lyricists, lyric writing was not a call from the muses: it was simply a way to earn a living. For example, when music publisher Irving Mills approached Fields to write a song about Ruth Elder, a woman preparing for a transatlantic flight, he provided Fields with the first two lines of "Our American Gal": "You took a notion to fly 'cross the ocean, Our American Gal!" Fields protested, "You just don't get a 'notion' to fly the ocean. Lindbergh has been the only one to do it up to now." But Fields went ahead and wrote the song with those lyrics, and earned fifty dollars for her efforts.[144] Rida Johnson Young used lyric writing to fund her preferred hobby: "Gardening is such an expensive hobby that it conduces one to a most pernicious activity in one's chosen profession in order to meet the financial obligations it imposes."[145] Although few of these female lyricists voiced lofty artistic intentions, their public financial successes in lyric writing may have encouraged other nascent female professionals, both in and outside of the theatre.

When female lyricists are remembered, they are often seen as anomalies in a profession dominated by men. Betty Comden said of Dorothy Fields, "She was the woman songwriter. [...] She did it all as the lone female amid the old-boy club of legends that gave us the American songbook."[146] Anne Caldwell's obituary identified her as, "A quiet woman little known to the public [...] one of the nation's leading musical comedy librettists and lyricists."[147] Newspapers called Ann Ronell "the nation's leading female songwriter."[148] Although several women wordsmiths achieved some degree of recognition on their own terms, historians have been reluctant to connect female lyricists and their collective contributions to the embryonic American musical theatre.

The female lyricists clearly struggled with gender inequality. Ann Ronell summarized the discrimination faced by women:

> But it was not so easy to get a hearing. There were many other people, with tunes at their finger tips, most of them boys. Girls were few in this keenly competitive field, and most of those in it at that time dropped out later.[149]

The perseverance and accomplishments of female lyricists are especially impressive in light of this struggle. There is a growing popular interest in women's contributions to popular song, as evidenced by a 1999 PBS special, *The Women of Tin Pan Alley*, and pianist Peter Mintun's recording of the works of early twentieth-century female songwriters, *Yours for a Song: Here's to the Ladies!* which came out that same year.[150] With continued exploration of the careers of female lyricists they may be restored to their rightful place in the history of the musical theatre. Then the inquiry implicit in Rida Johnson Young's lyrics to "Will You Remember" will be met with a resounding "yes!"

Notes

1. *The Black Crook* commonly marks the advent of musical theatre in America. Scholars, however, dispute whether *The Black Crook* is the beginning of American musical theatre. For an analysis of *The Black Crook's* position in the history of musical theatre see Julian Mates, "*The Black Crook* Myth," *Theatre Survey* 7 (May 1966): 31–43. *Oklahoma!* is commonly said to mark the beginning of the Golden Age of American musical theatre.

2. "Successful Women Songwriters," *The Literary Digest* 55.15 (13 October 1917): 87.

3. Stanley Green, *The World of Musical Comedy: The Story of the American Musical Stage as Told Through The Careers of its Foremost Composers and Lyricists* (New York: Ziff-Davis Publishing Co., 1960), viii.

4. The following examples establish a pattern that is fairly consistent throughout historical treatments of musical theatre. Even in more current histories of musical theatre, if female lyricists in the period from 1866 to 1943 are discussed, they are mentioned in conjunction with their male collaborators.

5. Green, *Musical Comedy*.

6. Philip Furia, *The Poets of Tin Pan Alley* (New York: Oxford University Press, 1990).

7. Thomas S. Hischak, *Word Crazy: Broadway Lyricists from Cohan to Sondheim* (New York: Praeger Publishers, 1991).

8. Otis L. Guernsey, Jr., ed., "Memorable Lyric Moments On Broadway Selected by Authors of Shows," in *Playwrights Lyricists Composers on Theatre* (New York: Dodd, Mead & Co., 1974) 104–126.

9. Deborah Grace Winer, *On the Sunny Side of the Street: The Life and Lyrics of Dorothy Fields*, with a preface by Betty Comden (New York: Schirmer Books, 1997) xv.

10. Many references to June Carroll occur under the name June Sillman. Rosetta and Vivian Duncan are better known as the Duncan Sisters. Sylvia Fine is often listed under Kaye, her married name. Alma Sanders is often referred to as Mrs. Monte Carlo. Marion Sunshine is at times listed as Marion Ijames.

11. Although Dorothy Fields was a popular and influential lyricist, she has been the only female lyricist from early musical theatre to achieve widespread recognition. The attention Fields has received limits the need for compensatory work about her in this chapter.

12. The longest running musical comedies and operettas were *The Student Prince* (608 performances), *Blossom Time* (592 performances), *Show Boat* (575 performances), *Sally* (570 performances), *Rose-Marie* (557 performances), *Good News!* (551 performances), *Sunny* (517 performances), *The Vagabond King* (511 performances), and *The New Moon* (509 performances). Ethan Mordden, *Make Believe: The Broadway Musical in the 1920s* (Oxford: Oxford University Press, 1997) 51.

132. Unidentified Clipping, Dorothy Fields, Clippings in the Theatre Collections, Performing Arts Research Center, New York Public Library, New York.

133. Shafer, *American Women Playwrights* 372.

134. Unidentified Clipping, Anne Caldwell, Clippings in the Theatre Collections, Performing Arts Research Center, New York Public Library, New York.

135. Unidentified Clipping, Clare Kummer, Clippings in the Theatre Collections, Performing Arts Research Center, New York Public Library, New York.

136. George Freedley and John A. Reeves, *A History of the Theatre* (New York: Crown, 1941) 586.

137. For a further discussion of the treatment of women in the plays of Caldwell, Kummer, and Young, see Coleman, "Gender Issues."

138. Quoted in Marion Weinstein, "Real Love for the Stage," *Kansas City Times* 10 September 1917, n. pag.; quoted in Shafer, *American Women Playwrights*, 207.

139. Bennett, "'Mother Machree'" n. pag.

140. Ibid.

141. Ibid.

142. Unidentified Newspaper Clipping, Clare Kummer, Clippings in the Theatre Collections, Performing Arts Research Center, New York Public Library, New York.

143. Unidentified Clipping, Dorothy Fields, Clippings in the Theatre Collections, Performing Arts Research Center, New York Public Library, New York.

144. Lardine, "Never at a Loss" 4.

145. Broeck, "Rida Johnson Young" n. pag.

146. Winer, *On the Sunny Side of the Street* xi.

147. "Anne Caldwell, 60, Librettist, Is Dead," *New York Times* 24 October 1936, 17:5.

148. Unidentified newspaper clipping, Ann Ronell, Clippings in the Theatre Collections, Performing Arts Research Center, New York Public Library, New York.

149. *The Christian Science Monitor* (Boston) 3 January 1955, Ann Ronell, Clippings in the Theatre Collections, Performing Arts Research Center, New York Public Library, New York.

150. Peter Mintun, *Yours for a Song: Here's to the Ladies!* Premier Recordings PRCD1065, 1999, CD.

Hallie Flanagan and Cheryl Crawford

Women Pioneer Producers of the 1930s

BARBARA MEANS FRASER

Hallie Flanagan and Cheryl Crawford shared a passion for the American musical theatre. Both women were producers contributing to American theatre history in distinctly different ways, and each made an impact on musical theatre. Shortly before these women arrived on the scene, the American theatre was in the midst of a renaissance. American theatre of the 1920s took two paths. Broadway belonged to the Shuberts and the Theatre Syndicate who produced dazzling entertainments for popular consumption, but it was also a time of change inspired by the art movements of Europe and the experimental plays of Eugene O'Neill. While the Shuberts and the Syndicate were commercial producers primarily interested in profit margins, theatre by the artistic producers as opposed to businessmen was revealed in the work of Provincetown Players, Washington Square Players, and the Theatre Guild. The more traditional Broadway producers used musical revues, operetta, and burlesque to garner impressive revenues, while the newer art theatres were more likely to present modern realism and expressionism. The theatre district was a wondrous and prosperous place of lavish spectacle, dramatic entertainment, and theatrical experimentation.

American theatre of the 1930s was a different place. American society was reeling in despair as the stock market crashed, crops shriveled into feed for grasshoppers, top soil blew away, farms were auctioned for taxes, unemployment lines grew, and hope diminished. America in the 1930s was not a time of opportunity and yet two women made a huge impact on the American theatre: Cheryl Crawford was one of the founders of the Group Theatre, and Hallie Flanagan became the Director of the Federal Theatre Project. Two of the most significant theatres in American theatre history were created in this decade, which in itself is miraculous in such an economically depressed time, but the fact that these two historically prestigious theatres were led by women is phenomenal. Crawford assimilated the best of what she learned working with one of Broadway's most shrewd producers, Lee Shubert, and blended it with the philosophy she developed in her work with many artistic theatre groups to challenge preexisting assumptions about the musical theatre. Flanagan brought forth her formidable education in social justice and theatre to accept the challenge of creating a venue for musical theatre (and other types of theatre) with federal support. Crawford and Flanagan not only penetrated the inner-circle of the Broadway theatre scene, but they contributed significantly by integrating art into the American musical theatre.

Cheryl Crawford and Hallie Flanagan both grew up in small midwestern American towns. Both attended small highly selective liberal arts colleges, both journeyed to the Soviet Union to study with Stanislavsky and Meyerhold, both were subpoenaed by HUAC, and both were extraordinary women making significant contributions in a "man's profession" in a male world. The 1930s in America only allowed success to a tiny few — minorities and women need not apply. Flanagan and Crawford carved their own opportunities and succeeded in contributing to the artistic enrichment of the American Theatre.

Hallie Flanagan

Crawford and Flanagan were establishing successful careers at the same time, but they approached the theatre world from two distinctly different directions. Whereas Crawford jumped immediately into the professional theatre world, Flanagan charted her course in academia.

Hallie Flanagan (*nee* Ferguson) was born and raised in the midwestern United States. After her birth in 1889 in South Dakota, her family moved to Omaha, Nebraska, finally settling in Grinnell, Iowa. This family decision played a significant role in the life of Hallie Flanagan. Flanagan's parents were drawn to Grinnell and Grinnell College because of the cultural advantages which would be available to their children. Her parents wanted each of their children to earn a college education, and they were also pleased when they saw that Hallie's early interest in playwriting was encouraged at Grinnell. A college education was not a common goal for America's youth of the time, and it was especially unusual for women.

Grinnell was a fine liberal arts college which encouraged its students to serve their community and to contribute to the betterment of society. Hallie Ferguson embraced this social justice philosophy and lived her life in its image. She was not the only student to be affected by Grinnell's ideology, as Harry Hopkins, who became Franklin Roosevelt's Vice President, and the Director of his WPA, attended the college; Hopkins began his association with Ferguson when they were students together at Grinnell.

Hallie Ferguson met and married Murray Flanagan in 1912, shortly after graduating from Grinnell. Her original plan was to pursue a teaching career, but a married woman could not hold a teaching position.[1] Not willing to sacrifice her career completely, she postponed her marriage a year, but then Murray prevailed, and Hallie entered married life. Hallie Flanagan, however, did not fit into a traditional married woman's role. She was not interested in cooking or other household chores, which caused strife in the marriage. Two years after she married Murray Flanagan, she became pregnant with their first child; at first she was thrilled, but she found motherhood as tedious as cooking and cleaning. Biographer Joanne Bentley explains that she missed the stimulation of students and could not help comparing her life with her husband's.[2] Although she supported her husband's work, she felt that her own talents were being wasted. Bentley suggests that Hallie Flanagan questioned the status quo by wondering, "Why did it always have to be the woman who tended the family and advanced the man's career? Why not the other way around?"[3] Their second child was born just as Hallie Flanagan had to face the beginning of her husband's fatal illness. Murray Flanagan was sent to a sanitarium in Colorado where he was diagnosed with tuberculoses.

At first Hallie Flanagan and the children moved back to Grinnell while her husband convalesced in Colorado, but at the end Flanagan left her children with their grandparents and went to be with her husband. Even while nursing her dying husband, Hallie could not stand to be idle. Unbeknownst to him, she found another woman in a similar situation and together they rented a space and taught private lessons in lace making. Flanagan managed to cover her expenses and divert her despair.

After Murray's death, Hallie Flanagan returned to her children in Grinnell and accepted a position teaching English to high school students. By the fall of 1920 she had joined the faculty at Grinnell College teaching freshman English. She became a member of a local chapter of the Drama League of America which rekindled her interest in playwriting. Their weekly meetings provoked lively discussions about theatre which led her to crave further study.

In 1922, Hallie Flanagan's older child, seven year old Jack, contracted meningitis for which there was no cure at the time. He died an agonizing death with his mother at his side. Her grief was intense. After Murray died she threw herself into work, but Jack's death had most probably brought back the pain she suppressed after Murray's death. She blamed herself for being a failure as mother and wife. Meanwhile, her younger son Frederic still needed his mother. Hallie's father penetrated her grief to remind her that those who remained needed life. Life must go forward.[4] For Hallie Flanagan, "forward" meant career.

Unaware of the implications of her temporary abandonment of Frederic, who had already lost a father and brother, Flanagan went to Chicago the summer after Jack's death to study with Alexander Dean and Irving Pichel. Dean and Pichel, pioneers in American stage directing, were producing modern plays controversial productions. However, two FTP musicals have become famous for the trouble they instigated.

No one is surprised when a play like *Ethiopia* causes the politicians to rise and take notice, but when musical theatre written for children becomes a target for admonishment, it causes one to pause. Under the direction of Elia Kazan, the FTP opened *Revolt of the Beavers*, by Oscar Saul and Louis Lantz, in 1937 to enthusiastic crowds of children and their parents.[14] The roller skating beavers wore lavishly colorful costumes and performed on technically inventive scenery full of imaginative tricks. John Randolf, an actor from the show, describes the throne on which the "King of the Beavers" sat:

> You know when you sit in a barber chair you can move the levers and go up and down and swing around? He [the King] had one of those, and they loved seeing it. [...] The chair was connected with a slide, so that when he wanted to go down and talk to anybody, he'd just press a lever and slide right down.[15]

Like many traditional stories, whether Robin Hood who steals from the rich and gives to the poor or Little Red Riding Hood who strays from the path, this fairy tale had a message. In *Revolt of the Beavers*, a "bad" greedy beaver forced the other beavers to work while he and his friends enjoyed themselves with ice cream and roller skates. When the "good" beaver complained that he was exiled (much like Robin Hood), he organized his friends to take over the bark business and share the ice cream.

The currents of the times were so electrified by fear of Communism that people were even scouring their fairy tales for Marxist philosophy, and they found it in Beaverland. Jack Renick, director of the Children's Theatre, believed the title was a problem: "If only they had given it a less provocative title, the play would have attracted no adverse attention."[16] Even though audiences loved it, the FTP was concerned about the political liability of *Revolt of the Beavers*. Ironically, the conservative Hearst *Journal-American* perceived a "harmless and pleasing fantasy for children,"[17] while Brooks Atkinson of *The New York Times* wrote: "Many children now unschooled in the technique of revolution now have an opportunity, at government expense, to improve their tender minds. Mother Goose is no longer a rhymed escapist. She has been studying Marx; Jack and Jill lead the class revolution."[18] Despite the show's popularity and its dazzling theatricality, FTP closed it after a month because the controversy surrounding it was too politically risky.

Revolt of the Beavers had created a lot of turmoil while the clearly political *Life and Death of an American*, another of FTP's musical theatre productions, was still running when Congress withdrew funding and terminated the Federal Theatre Project. *Life and Death of an American* is significant because it proved that artistic and socially challenging musical theatre could have commercial success on Broadway. George Sklar had originally written the play for the Theatre Union, but when it dissolved, FTP was eager to produce it. The music was written by Alex North and Earl Robinson. Robinson had previously worked on *Pins and Needles* with Harold Rome, and he had already written his most memorable songs, "Joe Hill" and "Abe Lincoln."[19]

In their book *Free, Adult, Uncensored*, O'Connor and Brolon compare *Life and Death of an American* to a living newspaper.[20] The subject matter was serious, the ending tragic, and a chorus of characters within the show introduces scenes, comments on the action, and becomes part of the crowd scenes in Brechtian style. Hallie Flanagan contends that Piscator (Brecht's early mentor and partner) considered *Life and Death of an American* to be the "most superb stage production he had seen in America."[21]

Life and Death of an American is certainly not typical musical theatre fare, and it still touched audiences deeply. The story is about Jerry, the first American born in the twentieth century. He comes from an impoverished family who wants the best for their boy. Jerry's dream of a college education is dashed when his father dies and he quits school to support his family. World War I provides Jerry with an opportunity to learn to fly, and after the war he works hard to achieve his slice of the American dream with an aviation drafting job. However, when the Depression comes, Jerry loses his job and is killed during a labor demonstration. This is the type of theatre that Hallie Flanagan encouraged: plays about Americans which challenged audiences to question their lives, their choices, and even their elected officials' decisions and values. Like many other FTP productions, this play was confrontational and challenging, and very "American."

Controversy occurred again when Marc Blitzstein's musical *The Cradle Will Rock* approached its New York opening. John Houseman, producer, and Orson Welles, director, were ready to open *The Cradle Will Rock* on June 16, 1937, when they received word from Washington that "because of cuts and reorganization" any new play, musical performance, or art gallery was prohibited from opening before July 1.[22] *The Cradle Will Rock* had paid for its costly rehearsal process and already sold 14,000 seats, so money was not the issue. In her book *Arena*, Hallie Flanagan states, "This was obviously censorship under a different guise."[23] Blitzstein's musical dealt with union organizing, at a time when John Lewis was trying to unionize the steel industry. The newspapers were full of stories about CIO (Congress of Industrial Organizations) sympathizers clogging the business districts to force factory and store closings as a protest for the arrest of picketers.

Flanagan requested an exception for *The Cradle Will Rock* since tickets were already sold, but the bureaucrats in Washington refused. Orson Welles traveled to Washington to appeal; he finally explained that if the FTP would not let them open the musical, then he and John Houseman would open it themselves. David Niles, head of WPA Information, responded, "In that case we would no longer be interested in it as a property."[24] The following morning, uniformed WPA officials locked the theatre and stood guard, preventing the technical crews from removing any props or scenery from the theatre, but that did not deter Wells and Houseman. Simplicity actually enhanced the musical, and the following day, Marc Blitzstein's *The Cradle Will Rock* was on the front page of all the newspapers. Welles and Houseman opened their new theatre company, The Mercury Theatre, with a hit. Hallie Flanagan was depressed about losing *The Cradle Will Rock* and Welles and Houseman, but she celebrated their new enterprise.[25]

Hallie Flanagan had lost Elmer Rice, John Houseman, and Orson Welles because of Washington politics. The censorship struggles began to discourage people from accepting positions with The Federal Theatre, and Harry Hopkins was pushing her for cuts. Flanagan moved her central operations from Washington D.C. into New York where she could also take personal direction of the New York region. Being able to focus on theatre for a time was refreshing, but the politics never went away.

After *The Cradle Will Rock* disappointment, Flanagan put her focus on the very ambitious creation of *One-third of a Nation*, a living newspaper which dealt with the conditions and people living in the slums of America. This successful play was adapted to each city's specific circumstances and played in Detroit, Cincinnati, Philadelphia, Hartford, New Orleans, Seattle, Portland, and San Francisco. Congressmen were quoted out of the Congressional Record, but some did not like to hear their words on the American stage. Eleanor Roosevelt felt that the play was extremely powerful; she told Hallie Flanagan that the play had "achieved something which will mean a tremendous amount in the future, socially, and in the education and growing-up of America [...] far more than any amount of speeches that Langdon Post or I, or even the President, might make."[26] Eleanor Roosevelt was right. Not only was the play powerful, it made powerful enemies.[27]

The FTP was America's first attempt to fund theatre so that it could reach Americans throughout the country. Many people saw live theatre for the first time because of federal funding. The FTP had theatres in thirty-two of the forty-eight states and the District of Columbia; 30,398,726 people attended 63,728 FTP productions between 1936 and 1939. In 1936, the FTP employed 12,372 people in twenty-five states.[28] Flanagan refers to a study done by Actor's Equity in 1937 which quotes Burgess Meredith as saying, "The entire enterprise [FTP] cost only 22 million or one half the price of a battleship."[29] The cost of the operation as of December 1937 was $46,207,779.00, the approximate "cost of one complete battleship."[30] Despite its positive impact on employment and the populace, the Federal Theatre Project was a popular target for anti–Roosevelt conservatives.

The House Committee on Un-American Activities (HUAC) was established in late May 1938 with Martin Dies, a conservative Democrat from Texas, as its chair. The conservative Democrats, largely, but not exclusively, Southern Democrats, strongly opposed Franklin Roosevelt. They were eager for the presidential primary elections in hope of defeating Roosevelt and running a conservative Democrat in the general election. Martin Dies believed, or pretended to believe, that "the crisis of the thirties had been caused by Communist conspirators and that the nation could be restored to normal only if this conspiracy was put down."[31] The Hearst newspapers had been saying the same thing for years. People who opposed Roosevelt's programs believed that unemployment was not the problem — Communism was the problem.

Hallie Flanagan was not interested in overthrowing the government and installing Communism. A proud American, a Congregationalist, and an Independent Democrat who supported Roosevelt, she was an idealist and believed in American democracy. She wanted the country to serve all Americans: black or white; rich or poor; urban or rural; Catholic, Protestant, or Jewish; Republican, Democrat, or Communist. She was interested in producing provocative artistic theatre which addressed social ills and challenged people to think. Flanagan did not operate through a single party's political agenda. If anything, she was too politically naive for her own good. Philip Barber, who had replaced Elmer Rice as head of the New York project, cautioned Hallie Flanagan against hiring Hazel Huffman because he "was sure she was a spy" for the "rightists in the local WPA office who wanted Flanagan replaced by a conservative."[32] Flanagan hired Huffman anyway for a secretarial position sorting mail. Huffman subsequently informed the Hearst press that Flanagan's mail was "incendiary, revolutionary, and seditious."[33] But Flanagan was even sorrier that Barber was right, when Hazel Huffman reported bizarre information and prejudiced hearsay as a prime witness before the House Committee on Un-American Activities.

Harry Hopkins and his WPA were popular targets for conservatives, and the FTP was their favorite. J. Parnell Thomas, a member of HUAC and later its chair, called the FTP "a link in the vast and unparalleled New Deal propaganda machine, and a branch of the Communist Party."[34] These attacks infuriated Flanagan and she was eager to appear before the committee and defend herself and the FTP, but WPA administrators did not want her to testify. By the time Martin Dies asked Hallie Flanagan to testify, serious damage had already been done. She was prepared to answer questions and clarify the many slanderous statements made by Hazel Huffman and the other disgruntled former employees of the Federal Theatre. However, HUAC controlled the agenda and seemed more interested in manipulating Flanagan into admitting Communist leanings than hearing what she had to offer the committee.

Congressman Starnes asked her questions about her book, *Shifting Scenes* (1928), which was written about the European theatre she studied during her Guggenheim Fellowship; Starnes was most interested in her praise of the Russian theatre. As discussed earlier, Flanagan went to the Soviet Union to meet Stanislavsky. The Committee members were either too artistically limited to understand that in spite of the Communist state in which he resided, Stanislavsky was the most renowned theatre director and acting teacher in the

world, or the Committee simply seized upon this opportunity to attack Flanagan. Congressman Starnes tried to imply some type of political agenda when
he asked: "Was she a member of a Russian organization?" "Was she a delegate
to anything?" The answer to both questions was "no."[35] Changing the subject,
Starnes referred to an article Flanagan had written in *Theatre Arts* about the
Federal Theatre. Starnes read the quotation, "They intend to make a social
structure without help of money, and this ambition alone invests their undertaking with a certain Marlowesque madness." Starnes then paused and asked,
"You are quoting from this Marlowe? Is he a Communist?"[36] The room erupted
in laughter, but Flanagan was not amused. This committee was playing politics with the lives of many artists who relied on the Federal Theatre to pay their
rent and feed their families. When the laughter eased, Flanagan replied, "I am
very sorry. I was quoting from Christopher Marlowe." Starnes probed, "Tell
us who this Marlowe is, so we can get the proper reference, because that is all
we want to do." Flanagan responded, "Put in the record, that Marlowe was the
greatest dramatist in the period immediately preceding Shakespeare."[37] After
a few more questions, the Committee took a recess for lunch. Once they realized what an intelligent, conscientious, thorough witness she was, they did not
allow her to continue. She appealed to Parnell Thomas, "If the committee isn't
convinced that neither I nor Federal Theatre is Communistic, I want to come
back this afternoon." Thomas responded, "We don't want you back. You're a
tough witness, and we're all worn out."[38] She offered her prepared statements,
but they were never accepted into the record.

After their six month investigation into the FTP, the Dies Committee
issued the following response.

> We are convinced that a rather large number of employees on the Federal The-
> atre project are either members of the Communist Party or are sympathetic
> with the Communist Party. It is also clear that certain employees felt under
> compulsion to join the Workers' Alliance in order to retain their jobs.[39]

This committee spent one morning trying to trick Flanagan into admitting that
the Federal Theatre was Communistic, which they did not accomplish, and
then would not allow her to make a statement in response to allegations made
against the FTP, most of which were based on hearsay. The papers branded her
"Hallie the Red Menace," and on June 14, 1939, Hallie Flanagan sat in the Senate Chamber and watched the United States Senate sentence to death the Federal Theatre: "No funds would be available for the Theatre after June 30, 1939."[40]
The Federal Theatre was finished, but Flanagan was not. She returned to academia and her family.

With financial assistance from a Rockefeller Grant and political assistance
from President Roosevelt, who arranged to have all of the FTP papers sent to
Vassar, Hallie Flanagan began writing her book, *Arena*. She divided her time
between writing, the Experimental Theatre at Vassar, and her family. She was
disillusioned by Washington politicians but began the transition of settling back

into a more relaxed routine when tragedy struck. Her husband, Philip, who had been so supportive and patient through all of her absence, died suddenly of a coronary thrombosis in February of 1940.[41] Her son Frederic was finishing college and had recently married, but Philip's children were still young: the twins, Jack and Joanne (now Bentley, author of *Hallie Flanagan: A Life in the American Theatre*) were twelve and their sister, Helen, was younger. Flanagan adopted Philip's children and kept the family together. She grieved Philip's death and questioned her four years away from him while she was dedicating herself to the Federal Theatre Project.

In 1942, Flanagan was offered a Dean's position at Smith College which promised her more money, the freedom to create her own theatre program, and an escape from Philip's constant absence. She moved herself and the children to Northampton where she continued her academic career. She wrote a Living Newspaper about the atomic age called $E = mc^2$ (1947) which was produced at Smith and then at ANTA (American National Theatre and Academy) in New York. But the same year she was diagnosed with Parkinson's disease. She had to shift her rhythms and reduce her stress and stop directing. In 1952, she retired and moved back to Poughkeepsie to be nearer to family.

Hallie Flanagan was a successful career woman who challenged traditional expectations regarding marriage and family. Her heart and drive were in her work while her children and husband took a secondary role. Hallie Flanagan did comprehend the pain of abandonment inflicted on her son, Frederic, and would have been devastated by his suicide which her family kept from her as she was nearing her own death. Motherhood may not have been her strength, according to today's standards, but she was an inspiring force in the American theatre. Perhaps saddest of all is that with all the family time she sacrificed to her career in the theatre, Hallie Flanagan felt that she had failed the FTP. In the final weeks before her death on 23 July 1969 she was haunted by HUAC. Friends witnessed her fitfully crying out defending herself against the accusations of Communism leveled at her thirty years earlier.

Hallie Flanagan's contributions to the American Theatre are obvious in her inspired direction of the Federal Theatre Project, but her legacy goes beyond that specific task. Her work with the FTP brought musical theatre (not just vaudeville and revues) to cities all across America. Flanagan gave opportunities to playwrights and composers to experiment with musical theatre within the context of the art movement. Artists were able to create musical theatre that had something significant to say. Once *The Cradle Will Rock, Revolt of the Beavers,* and *Life and Death of an American* succeeded, other commercial producers could see that message-driven musical theatre was a viable investment. Believing in the academic theories of George Pierce Baker, that audiences throughout America deserved high quality theatre, and that theatre should contain social justice issues and artistic expression, Flanagan took action to make these theoretical concepts become a reality within the American Theatre.

Cheryl Crawford

Cheryl Crawford did not have to fight the Federal government to do her job, and she did not have to worry about traditional family issues, but she was a woman trying to establish a career in a male dominated society during the worst economic conditions of our nation's history.

Like Hallie Flanagan, Cheryl Crawford had Midwestern roots. Crawford was born in 1902 into an upper-middle class family in Akron, Ohio. Her first successful encounter in a male world involved growing up the active leader of two younger brothers. "I had to do everything Alden and Newell did, and I had to do it better. I had to climb trees higher and bicycle faster [...] The three of us were very close and formed a strong phalanx in the neighborhood gang."[42] Her leadership, her courage, and her persistence even at that young age set the course. "We had dogs, cats, chickens and a half-horse brought from Texas, which we ingeniously named Tex. The day he threw me I knew I had to mount again because my brothers were watching, sibilantly whispering 'chicken, chicken' as I hesitated."[43] She showed no fear, she competed equally with all around her, and when she was thrown she "got right back on the horse." Crawford's childhood experiences of unstructured interpersonal socialization were rehearsal for the kind of business interaction at which she later excelled.

In 1921, she left Ohio and journeyed to New England to enroll at Smith College. College life was becoming accessible for more Americans in the 1920s, but certainly not common. For a woman to enter college in 1921 was exceptional, but to travel all the way to New England from her Midwestern roots took unusual courage. Cheryl Crawford was ready and eager for the journey. Following her junior year at Smith, she could not bear the thought of returning to Ohio for "another dull, quiet summer." Having read about George Cram Cook, Susan Glaspell, and Eugene O'Neill and their progressive and innovative group of theatre artists, the Provincetown Players, she decided to travel to Cape Cod, find a summer job, and work with them. The presumption of youth was alive and well within her.

Crawford arrived in Provincetown, found a room to rent, and began looking for the theatre. After a thorough search of the town, she stopped in an antique store to ask directions. "Good Lord! That theatre burned down several years ago," was the owner's reply.[44] She packed her trunk and was waiting for a boat when a casual conversation revealed to her that the Provincetown Players were in town trying to make arrangements for the summer. That's all she needed. She returned her trunk to her rented room and proceeded to find the theatre group. They invited her to join them for the summer. By that time, O'Neill and Cook were no longer with them, but Susan Glaspell was there, and Crawford was impressed that they had elected a woman as their president. Her summer on Cape Cod was full of merriment and theatre education. As autumn approached, Crawford was reluctant to leave Provincetown but clear about her long term goals. She returned to college to finish her degree so she could pursue a career in the professional theatre.

Whereas Flanagan pursued her theatrical career through academia, Crawford was eager to leave behind ivy covered walls and find her success in the professional theatre world. As graduation approached, Crawford discovered that the Theatre Guild had created an education branch. She interviewed with Theresa Helburn, another strong woman working successfully in the male dominated theatre world. Helburn began as a play reader for the Washington Square Players, became a board member and executive director of the Theatre Guild in the Twenties, added the Hollywood film industry to her credits in 1933, and became famous in New York in 1943 for "Helburn's Folly" when she produced Rodgers and Hammerstein's *Oklahoma!*[45] By the time Crawford met with Helburn she knew that she wanted to be a producer — not an actor and not a director. Helburn explained that the Theatre Guild school was for actors. Crawford was willing to train as an actor because she wanted to learn about the professional theatre. Helburn accepted her but warned that the Theatre Guild would weed out students that they felt were not serious about the professional theatre. This did not phase Crawford.

Following her year of education at the Theatre Guild, Cheryl Crawford began searching for a job as a stage manager. She went from office to office and received little encouragement. Crawford clarifies, "I was told that there had been only one woman stage manager in the professional theatre."[46] Producers did not want to hire women as stage managers, assistant stage managers or even as "water girls." Crawford claims, "Females were actresses or nothing, it seemed."[47]

Finally her connection with the Theatre Guild paid dividends. Theresa Helburn offered Crawford a part-time job as casting secretary. Crawford was desperate for work because parental support was not an option since they considered her career choice a frivolous one, and her money was almost gone. Despite her desperate situation, she negotiated for a better position. She was determined to prove herself as a stage manager. "I want to work backstage. [...] If I can be third assistant stage manager on your first fall production, I will be glad to work in the daytime and at night."[48] Helburn was stunned by her assertiveness, but she decided to take the risk.

She had the job, but that did not mean that she would not be tested. When *Porgy* opened at the Theatre Guild, Crawford was the assistant stage manager. The show was very successful and had a long run. In 1929, Crawford became production stage manager and took *Porgy* to London. Charles Cochran, maybe the most important London producer of the time, had made an arrangement with the Theatre Guild to produce *Porgy* at His Majesty's Theatre in the Haymarket. All was going well until Crawford spotted a stack of programs at the back of the theatre which read, "Charles Cochran presents *Porgy*."[49] She confronted the issue immediately, explaining that the Theatre Guild had not been credited. Cochran promised that the programs would be fixed by opening night. Whether it was an oversight or a misrepresentation is not clear, but when Crawford checked the program on opening night, the Theatre Guild still had not been credited. She knew that she could not return to New York without proper credit for the Theatre Guild, so she instructed the cast to stay in their dressing rooms until further notice, and then she waited. Twenty minutes after scheduled curtain time, Cochran went backstage. Crawford told him that the company could not perform until he made a curtain speech crediting the Theatre Guild. Cochran resisted, but in the end he made the speech and subsequently corrected the program.

Crawford's impressive contributions to the Theatre Guild were noticed by the board of directors as well as her peers. Her professional status with the board had risen considerably by 1931. Crawford was Helburn's choice to replace Helburn herself as executive director, but before that could happen, Crawford had become intrigued with Harold Clurman's dreams. A young Harold Clurman met Cheryl Crawford at the Theatre Guild where he was working as a "go-fer." He introduced her to Lee Strasberg, and the three of them founded the Group Theatre. Crawford's status with the Theatre Guild board, especially with Theresa Helburn, put her in a position to ask and receive initial financial support from the Theatre Guild for the early efforts of the Group Theatre. As Strasberg was involved with directing and acting training while Clurman established their artistic philosophy and eventually became a director, they left most of the producing responsibilities to Crawford. She found and developed scripts, she raised money, she brokered deals for food and housing, she took responsibility for all of the organizational details, and occasionally directed plays.

The Group Theatre was known for its development of "The Method," the Americanized version of Stanislavky's acting system. Lee Strasberg, having worked with Maria Ouspenskaya and Richard Boleslavsky, Stanislavsky disciples, was extremely excited about training actors. Crawford accompanied Harold Clurman on an extensive five week visit to the Soviet Union to meet with Constantin Stanislavsky and Vsevolod Meyerhold. Like Hallie Flanagan, Crawford was thrilled to visit The Moscow Art Theatre, which by the 1930s was the most famous and respected theatre in the world.

The Group Theatre would have been an impressive venture in any era, but, establishing this theatre and keeping it active for almost ten years during the midst of the Great Depression is all the more amazing. In the beginning years Crawford managed to feed and house the entire group of twenty-eight actors (plus spouses and children) while also securing finances to create theatre during America's worst economic climate.

Although the Group Theatre was known for its modern realism, Crawford was drawn to musicals. She developed the musical *Johnny Johnson* for the Group Theatre — working closely with composer Kurt Weill and playwright

Paul Green. Crawford confided, "This was the kind of work I really enjoyed, inspiring new works and being a part of their development."[50]

By 1937 the Group Theatre was having structural problems. Crawford constantly struggled to keep them solvent. The actors were questioning the leadership of the three directors, who were bickering among themselves. Members of the Group Theatre were upset with all three directors, but they seemed particularly judgmental of Crawford. According to Clurman:

> She's had six years of dirty jobs. We appreciate this, but she strikes us as a disappointed artist. She feels she is wasting her life, that she is a "martyr" to the Group, that without her the Group would fold in a minute and, worst of all, that no one appreciates her. She never stops trying to impress people with her own importance, the work she is doing, how what other people receive credit for doing is really her work. [...] We should get a business manager whom we really trust to take over these tasks. Cheryl's job lies in the creation of scripts like *Johnny Johnson* and tasks of general finance and promotion.[51]

It is difficult to assess the cause of the discontent. Was part of the judgment related to her being a woman? Was it related to Crawford being associated with the business part of the operation? In her history of the Group Theatre, Wendy Smith asserts that, given Crawford's treatment by her co-directors,

> her attitude was more than a little justified. Strasberg and Clurman had the arrogance of self-assured artists. They never did any work they didn't want to or felt they weren't suited for, and if their fellow directors or Group members didn't understand, that was too bad. Crawford spent her life taking care of the detail they disdained — raising money, making up budgets, getting the scenery built, renting the costumes. Had she been more confident of her own artistic abilities she might have had the courage to insist they find an administrator to deal with the odds and ends, but as it was she used her ceaseless round of caretaking activities as a means of asserting her value to the Group.[52]

The Group suspended its operations in 1937 to take a break before deciding their next course of action. While Clurman was out in Hollywood thinking about new structures, Cheryl Crawford decided to leave the Group and become an independent producer. Crawford produced a full range of theatrical productions, including several musicals. She was not as interested in musical comedy, however. She loved good literature and poetry and wanted to integrate drama with musical theatre; she was drawn to the music of Kurt Weill, George Gershwin, and Marc Blitzstein.

In 1940, Cheryl Crawford entered into an association with her attorney, John Wildberg, producing at Maplewood, a summer stock theatre in Maplewood, New Jersey, which had been abandoned. She wanted to end their third season with a big smash since they were closing the theatre due to gas rationing for the war effort. Crawford had seen the Theatre Guild's production of the Gershwins' *Porgy and Bess* when it was first produced in 1935; the Broadway production closed after only 124 performances, Crawford produced the second production of *Porgy and Bess* in 1942 with most of the same cast and the original conductor at Maplewood. Lee Shubert was impressed with the Crawford production, and with his support they moved it to the Shuberts' Majestic Theatre on Broadway for a long run of 286 performances, a national tour, and then two encore performances back in New York.

Producers expect to produce more failures than successes; therefore, when a show is successful, it must pay for the next few risks. Crawford, as in the case of most producers, usually did not put her own money into her projects, but she also did not see any profit until all the investors were paid back their initial investment. If a show was not financially profitable then Crawford did not make any money. The revival of *Porgy and Bess* continued to pay her bills through many subsequent projects.

Crawford was having more success with musicals than with her dramatic work so she approached Kurt Weill, with whom she had worked so successfully on *Johnny Johnson*, and they began another successful collaboration on *One Touch of Venus*. They secured Sid Perelman and Ogden Nash to write script and lyrics, Agnes de Mille to choreograph, Elia Kazan to direct, and Mary Martin to star. This show was a critical and financial success (567 performances) and proved to Crawford that *Porgy and Bess* was not just a fluke; she had established herself as a successful independent Broadway producer.

Following the success of *One Touch of Venus*, Margaret Webster convinced Crawford to produce Shakespeare's *The Tempest*. A hunger for the classics teamed her with Eva Le Gallienne and Webster to form the American Repertory Theatre. Among others, they produced Shakespeare's *Henry VIII*, Ibsen's *John Gabriel Borkman*, Shaw's *Androcles and the Lion*, and an adaptation by Le Gallienne of *Alice in Wonderland*, but ART had a short life. This classical repertory theatre was simply not financially viable in 1947. Crawford also managed to donate some of her time to the American National Theatre and Academy (ANTA) which had been chartered by Congress in 1935 but remained inactive until 1945–46 when the charter was activated "to extend the living theatre beyond its present limitations by bringing the best in the theatre to every state in the Union."[53] Crawford served as vice-president of the Board of Directors and encouraged the development of new plays and actors. She produced several plays for ANTA, including Brecht's *Galileo* and Ibsen's *Peer Gynt*, but neither had commercial success, and ultimately the theatre could not sustain itself.

While dabbling in the classics, Crawford continued to do what she did best: produce Broadway musicals. Her biggest and most famous producing success was *Brigadoon*, written by Alan Jay Lerner and Frederick Loewe. Other musicals would follow, some successful, some not: *Love Life* by Alan Jay Lerner and Kurt Weill; Marc Blitzstein's *Regina*, a musical adaptation of Lillian Hellman's *Little Foxes*; *Flahooley* by Yip Harburg, Fred Saide, and Sammy Fain; *Paint Your Wagon* by Lerner and Loewe; *Reuben, Reuben* by Marc Blitzstein; *Jennie* by Arthur Schwartz and Howard Dietz; *Chu Chem* by Ted Allen, Mitch Leigh, Jim Haines, and Jack Wohl; and *Celebration* by Harvey Schmidt and Tom Jones.

Cheryl Crawford also produced many plays that were not musicals, including four by Tennessee Williams: *The Rose Tattoo, Camino Real, Sweet Bird of Youth,* and *Period of Adjustment.* She also founded the Actor's Studio in 1947 with Elia Kazan and Bobby Lewis. (Although many people associate the Actor's Studio with Lee Strasberg, he did not become its director until 1951). All this time she never stopped producing musicals. The musical theatre was special to her:

> There's magic in a good musical. For me, the anticipation starts when the lights of the musicians' stands flick on in the pit, the violins tune softly and the trombones let out a few yelps. It grows as the conductor arrives and taps his baton for the overture to start. When there is no overture I feel cheated. I want music to make off with me, sweep me up into a special world.[54]

Cheryl Crawford's association with the Group Theatre was significant throughout her career. Because she worked with many of the Group Theatre's actors, directors and playwrights for years on other projects, she also received a subpoena to appear before the House Committee on Un-American Activities, chaired by J. Parnell Thomas, in 1957. Receiving a subpoena to appear before HUAC was certainly not a surprising occurrence considering the times and her associations. First of all her involvement with the Group Theatre made her suspicious. Some members of the Group Theatre probably had affiliations with the Communist Party during the 1930s when, in fact, the Communist Party was a legal party like the Democratic Party and the Republican Party. Secondly, Crawford, like Hallie Flanagan, went to the Soviet Union to meet Stanislavsky. Crawford's attorney managed to acquire a list of the suspicious behaviors for which she was being called. She was accused of being the following:

1. A faculty member of the National Training School of the New Theatre League.
2. A patron of the Manhattan Chapter of the Medical Bureau to aid Spanish Democracy.
3. A signer of an ad sponsored by the Committee for the First Amendment protesting the House Un-American Activities Committee.

She had also signed the following:

1. A telegram of greeting to the testimonial dinner for the Hollywood Ten by the Freedom from Fear Committee.
2. An open letter sponsored by the American Committee for Protection of Foreign Born.
3. A letter on behalf of Paul Robeson to *Nation* magazine regarding the Peekskill riots on September 17, 1949, which never appeared in the magazine.

Additionally,

1. She sponsored a committee to end Jim Crow in baseball.

2. She presented an award to Norman Corwin (whom she didn't know at the time) at an American Youth for Democracy dinner.[55]
3. She spoke at a conference of the National Council of American-Soviet Friendship where she lectured on Chekhov and Stanislavsky.[56]

This list is proof of a loyal patriot who cared about significant issues which specifically affect many marginalized Americans and generally affect all Americans. Most citizens would be proud to hold this resume.

Not on the list, but possibly another factor, might have been Cheryl Crawford's sexual orientation. Crawford was a lesbian in a homophobic and judgmental period. In her 1977 autobiography, she never mentions anything regarding her sexual preferences, which is not surprising given the generation in which she was raised. Evidence about Crawford's sexual orientation, however, is revealed in Wendy Smith's book about the Group Theatre. Smith refers to Crawford's long term relationship with Dorothy Patten, an actor with the Group Theatre.[57] Smith refers to a letter from Harold Clurman: "He sent regards to Dorothy Patten, whose liaison with Crawford was now an established and accepted relationship."[58] Despite her reticence to mention the relationship in her autobiography, it seems that Crawford was able to live openly within her theatre world. Nevertheless, Bobby Lewis, who was also a member of the Group Theatre, mentions her sexuality in passing during a judgmental moment about her involvement in the founding of the Actor's Studio:

> No, no. I'll tell you something about Cheryl. We were really not in her immediate circle. I don't think it's any secret that Cheryl was a lesbian and she had a lot of very good lesbian friends who were actors. Cheryl's lesbianism was very valuable. The rest of us didn't pal around with those girls—they were all society girls. [...] Cheryl was brought in by Kazan and me because we were lousy at business, and Cheryl was a very good businesswoman.[59]

Lewis was trying to discount Crawford's involvement in the founding of the Actor's Studio. His citing of her lesbianism as an "obvious" reason for their lack of personal association with her is an interesting reflection of either Lewis's or society's prejudices, or both. Describing an unfortunate business deal concerning Crawford's initial role as producer for *West Side Story*, Arthur Laurents uses her sexual orientation as he vents his negative feelings,

> She had the appearance and manner of a butch lesbian: short and stocky, mannish garb and hair, dry and humorless, an alert eye for a pretty, available girl [...] Neither her politics or her sexuality was ever mentioned by the theatre community; she was far too respected as a moral Christian New Englander to be either a socialist or a lesbian. Off the record, the theatre community was wrong all the way, with one exception: Cheryl was no socialist.[60]

These two "outings" are not as revealing about Crawford as that they portray a vengeance which shows people's general attitudes at the time.[61] If two artists and colleagues would use this piece of potentially damaging information against her, surely the committee would as well.

Crawford was fortunate because HUAC sent her a wire postponing her appearance indefinitely. How would she have handled the inquisition? "I hoped that I would behave as well as Lillian Hellman, even though I could not express myself with her memorable words"[62] No one knows until they face the situation, and Crawford felt great relief at never having to know. She was no doubt blacklisted, but since a producer does not work for other people there was no one to fire her. Whereas the blacklist was effective in Hollywood where producers caved to the pressure of the times, Broadway generally, and Crawford specifically, did not adhere to the rules of the blacklist. She continued to operate by the same hiring practices.

Given the opportunity, however, Crawford would probably have changed one of her hiring practices. In 1957, she agreed to accept Richard Chandler in an intern position believing his story that he came from a wealthy family and only wanted to learn from her. She was so pleased with his work that she eventually employed him and trusted him with her business accounts. He worked with her for twelve years before he disappeared, having concocted a sophisticated plan draining her bank accounts. If that was not sufficient, evidence suggests that he also tried, but thankfully failed, to poison her.[63] She produced a series of financial failures until 1970 when she managed to regain some financial security with the success of *Colette*, by Elinor Jones with songs by Schmidt and Jones, featuring Zoe Caldwell.

During her career Cheryl Crawford worked with four significant American theatre groups: Provincetown Players, Theatre Guild, Group Theatre, and The Actors Studio. For the Group and Actors Studio she was a founder — this in addition to her career as an independent producer. Although she had the insight to remount *Porgy and Bess*, and bring *Brigadoon* to life, Crawford like all producers missed seeing the financial and artistic possibilities in two landmark productions. "Who would want to see a play about an unhappy traveling salesman? Too depressing," was her assessment when presented with *Death of a Salesman*. Years later she also rejected *West Side Story*. Despite these two oversights, Crawford was a strong, vibrant, resourceful, intelligent woman who succeeded in a very competitive patriarchal society.

Cheryl Crawford and Hallie Flanagan were women who contributed significantly to American theatre. Each had her own cross to bear. Cheryl Crawford was a lesbian in an extremely homophobic period of American history. She guarded her privacy and charged into the profession with the confidence of a warring knight, earning her positions through hard work and persistence. People saw her value and sought her skills. She carved a place for herself in the theatre world and contributed well above and beyond any measured successful theatre career.

Not all the theatre units within the FTP blossomed equally within Hallie Flanagan's mission, but many artists were employed, and many Americans reaped the benefits by experiencing high quality live theatre. Flanagan's contribution was significant well beyond the individual quality of production. As more communities around the country received live theatre, many for the first time, the future of American theatre was being secured. Today, Americans have many healthy theatre communities outside of the New York City market; Hallie Flanagan was instrumental in achieving this reality.

These two women made significant contributions, but even more important, they helped pave the way for others who followed. Cheryl Crawford not only helped to develop a more sophisticated modern American musical, but she showed the American theatre that women could be successful as stage managers and as producers. She helped to open the door because she had faith in her own ability, a good solid work ethic, and the strength to persevere. Hallie Flanagan established the first federally funded theatre in America, helped establish academic theatre programs in three universities, and taught many young students who would enter the profession with the mission to create and expect high quality, socially conscious, relevant American theatre. She fought the good fight, and although in the end she lost the Federal Theatre, her dream for theatre produced in America from coast to coast has become a reality.

Notes

1. It was common policy among most school boards in the Midwest to employ only unmarried or widowed women as teachers. The idea of employing a second person in one household with public funds when men (or unmarried women) were in need was against public policy.

2. Joanne Bentley, *Hallie Flanagan: A Life in the Theatre* (New York: Alfred A. Knopf, 1988) 23.

3. Bentley 23.

4. Bentley 34.

5. Bentley 47.

6. Hallie Flanagan, "Theatre Experiment," *Theatre Arts* 13 (1929): 543.

7. Bentley xv–xvi.

8. Hallie Flanagan, *Arena* (New York: Duell, Slan and Pearce, 1943) 65–66.

9. Qtd. in John O'Connor and Lorraine Brown, eds., *Free, Adult, Uncensored* (Washington: New Republic, 1978) 138.

10. Qtd. in O'Connor and Brown 146.

11. Qtd. in O'Conner and Brown 146.

12. Flanagan, *Arena* 427.

13. Flanagan, *Arena* 381–435.

14. Tony Buttitta and Barry Witham, *Uncle Sam Presents: A Memoir of the Federal Theatre 1935–1939* (Philadelphia: University of Pennsylvania Press, 1982) 144–145.

15. Qtd. in John O'Connor and Lorraine Brown, eds., *Free, Adult, Uncensored* (Washington: New Republic, 1978) 196.

16. Qtd. in Jay Williams, *Stage Left* (New York: Scribners, 1974) 228.

17. Qtd. in Buttitta and Witham 145.

18. Qtd. in O'Connor 195.

19. Buttitta and Witham 194.

20. O'Connor 202.

21. Qtd. in O'Connor and Brown 202.

22. Flanagan, *Arena* 202.

23. Flanagan, *Arena* 202–203.

24. Qtd. in Flanagan, *Arena* 203.

25. Buttitta and Witham 148–149.
26. Qtd. in Flanagan, *Arena* 222.
27. At this time Langdon Post was the Tenement House Commissioner for New York City. He spoke to the cast following a performance and praised *One-Third of a Nation*: "This play, performed as it was tonight can do more to convert people to proper housing than all the shouting I have done in the past three years." Qtd. in Flanagan, *Arena* 221–222.
28. Flanagan, *Arena* 435.
29. Qtd. in Flanagan, *Arena* 436.
30. Flanagan, *Arena* 436.
31. Qtd. in Bentley 302.
32. Qtd. in Bentley 221.
33. Qtd. in Bentley 221.
34. Qtd. in Bentley 303.
35. Qtd. in Buttitta and Witham 200.
36. Qtd. in Buttitta and Witham 201.
37. Qtd. in Buttitta and Witham 202.
38. Qtd. in Buttitta and Witham 203.
39. Qtd. in Flanagan, *Arena* 347.
40. Flanagan, *Arena* 362
41. Bentley 355.
42. Cheryl Crawford, *One Naked Individual* (New York: Bobbs-Merrill Company, Inc., 1977) 8.
43. Crawford, *One* 8.
44. Qtd. in Crawford, *One* 20.
45. Williams 11, 104,183, 255.
46. Crawford, *One* 31.
47. Crawford, *One* 31.
48. Crawford, *One* 32.
49. Crawford, *One* 42.
50. Qtd. in Wendy Smith, *Real Life Drama: The Group Theatre and America, 1931–1940* (New York: Grove Weidenfeld, 1990) 262.
51. Harold Clurman, *The Fervent Years* (New York: Knopf, 1945) 195.
52. Smith 235.
53. Crawford, *One* 153.
54. Crawford, *One* 163.
55. Norman Corwin was a writer and producer for CBS Radio in the 1940s. Corwin, who wrote programs commemorating important events during World War II, was branded a Communist.
56. Crawford, *One* 255.
57. Smith 172.
58. Smith 172.
59. Mel Gussow, "First Things First: An Interview with Robert Lewis (1990–1997)," *American Theatre* 15:1 (January 1998) 27.
60. Arthur Laurents, *Original Story* (New York: Knopf, 2000) 325.
61. These outings are interesting in light of the fact that both Arthur Laurents and Bobby Lewis are/were gay. Homophobia and sexism are not necessarily limited to the heterosexual community. For more information regarding Crawford's sexual orientation, see Jay Plum, "Cheryl Crawford: One Not So Naked Individual," *Passing Performances: Queer Readings of Leading Players in American Theater History*, eds. Robert A. Schanke and Kim Marra (Ann Arbor: University of Michigan Press, 1998) 239–261.
62. Crawford, *One* 256. Crawford is referring to the famous letter that Hellman presented to the Committee in which she managed to refuse to name names of others without being charged with contempt of Congress or going to jail (she was, however, blacklisted). Hellman's risky choice is widely accepted as the turning point in public opinion against the HUAC. For more specific details see Hellman's book *Scoundrel Time* (Boston: Little, Brown and Co., 1976).
63. Crawford, *One* 257–260.

Twentieth-Century Women Choreographers

Refining and Redefining the Showgirl Image

ANNA WHEELER GENTRY

The contributions of women to dance, choreography, and stage movement within the genre of American musical theatre have often been either downplayed or ignored. Additionally, the experiences and artistic developments that influenced many of these women frequently escape recognition. Whether peripherally or directly, each of these women addressed here significantly affected the performing arts in ways that incorporated their personal experiences, professional affiliations, and cultural backgrounds with trends of the times, historic events, and developments in performance mediums. Anna Held and her collaborations with Florenz Ziegfeld, Albertina Rasch and her partnership with Dimitri Tiomkin, Katherine Dunham and her ethnological research, Hanya Holm and her analytical — and later philosophical — approach to dance and life, and June Taylor and her association with Jackie Gleason (and later Joe Robbie), all contributed to the development of dance presentation and choreography in twentieth-century American musical performance. These artists created a through-line in the transformation of the showgirl image from late nineteenth-century stage musicals and revues through twentieth-century film and television.

One of the earliest significant refinements in twentieth-century Broadway stage movement and showgirl characterization was introduced by dancer, singer, and cabaret performer Anna Held, the youngest born (18 March 1870) of a Polish-Catholic mother and a French-Jewish father, in Warsaw, Poland. Her career began in the music halls of London and thrived on the British Yiddish stage, but soon led to performances in clubs and cabarets of cities throughout Europe. As her success awarded her more sophisticated performance venues, Held maintained that she was from Paris, withholding her Jewish background for professional reasons. With a growing international reputation, her appearances attracted royalty and aristocrats, and inspired French painter Toulouse-Lautrec to make her the subject of two lithographs.

An impulsive decision to marry fifty-year-old South American gambler Maximo Carrera in 1894 preceded Held's career-move to the "City of Lights" where, in 1896, Florenz Ziegfeld introduced himself backstage after one of her shows. Ziegfeld, with an eye for talent and a charismatic ability to captivate ladies, was intrigued by Held's performances.[1] He offered her a contract abroad of $1500 per week for which she broke her 1896–97 contract at the *Folies-Bergère*.

Held, nearing bankruptcy, was being pursued by the French courts, who deemed her responsible for her husband's unpaid gambling debts. (Although she and her husband had separated, his Catholicism did not allow divorce, and thus the law asserted Held's 50/50 liability for her husband's debts.) She seized Ziegfeld's proposal to perform in New York, where success for a European female performer was all but guaranteed.[2] Furthermore, the offer was padded with an additional $4000 to assist her in clearing her husband's obligations. With that offer Ziegfeld succeeded in luring her to the New York stage.

Anna Held was her own creation. She was petite in stature with a tiny doll-like voice and had a great sense of comic timing, using with clever expertise her knowledge of language and diction (in Europe she had performed regularly in French, Yiddish, and Polish). Held made her triumphant American debut in *A Parlor Match* (1896)[3] at the Herald Square Theatre where she popped out of a cabinet, sang several songs, and vanished.[4] Subsequently, Ziegfeld managed her American engagements and produced seven Broadway musicals for her. In New York, she became known for her flirtatiousness, sexually alluring stage persona, and her "misbehaving eyes." Her rendition of "Won't You Come and Play Wiz Me?" (a song first introduced in *A Parlor Match*) became her trademark and thereafter she concluded each performance with this song. Curiously, Held never performed in an edition of the *Ziegfeld Follies* (although she did appear in a film short—another Ziegfeld first—during the 1910 *Follies*),[5] but with her as inspiration, Ziegfeld was able to create a perfect framework around which he built the format and dance structure of the *Ziegfeld Follies*. In that sense she was the first true "Ziegfeld Girl."

With *La Belle Époque* at its peak, Ziegfeld capitalized on a specific concept of feminine beauty and poise on stage. He expertly managed a flurry of commercial advertising featuring Anna Held, which intensified her image as an exotic woman of perfection. Held's legendary milk bath media event heralded that she bathed regularly in luxurious milk, which implied that the body—a thing of beauty—was of utmost importance. Many ladies of wealth and privilege sought out milk baths as a result of this publicity stunt. Her petite build, curvaceous figure (with the aid of a corset), and French accent were additionally beguiling, embodying turn-of-the-century female sexuality. Merchandise companies advertised Anna Held eye makeup, facial powders, and pomades, while the market was flooded with Anna Held corsets, and Anna Held cigars.[6]

As Ziegfeld's vision of the ideal chorus girl evolved, he conceived of a taller feminine stage image — a long-legged American beauty — while at the same time calling his chorus line the "Anna Held Girls" so as to still evoke the notion of French exoticism. Of the 1912 *Follies*, Robert Baral of *Variety* once wrote: "anything Frenchy seemed to spell class."[7] No longer would the girls in the chorus be referred to simply as chorus girls. Now they were "showgirls," bringing an air of untouchable, high-fashioned elegance to the stage. His showgirls were expected to mingle socially with the stylish and the wealthy, were trained in etiquette and charm, and possessed the ability to converse in any circle. Through Ziegfeld's vision of feminine (non-ethnic) beauty emerged the peremptory musical revue theme — to "Glorify the American Girl" — and the *Ziegfeld Follies* were born. Thus began the stage institution and cultural icon of the "Ziegfeld Girl," a phrase synonymous with glamour.[8]

In contrast to the elegance of the *Follies*, ragtime music inspired new movement on American dance floors during the Gay '90s and the first decade of the twentieth century. Animal-named dances such as the Turkey Trot, Monkey Glide, Chicken Scratch, and Bunny Hug swept ballrooms across the country. Vernacular dance was then elevated to the stage when Vernon (2 May 1887–15 February 1918) and Irene (7 April 1893–25 January 1969) Castle, after their 1912 success in Paris, popularized the Turkey Trot with their performance in the Broadway musical play *The Sunshine Girl* (1913).[9] "The Dancing Craze" phenomenon then followed, growing out of the couple's fresh interpretation of ragtime dances and new tangos, such as creating The Castle Walk as seen in *Watch Your Step* (1914). (The 1939 film biography *The Story of Vernon and Irene Castle* features Fred Astaire and Ginger Rogers in the title roles.)

The evolution of the chorus line is tightly interwoven with the appearance of dance within early musicals and revues. Although the long-running *The Black Crook* (1866) — originally a lackluster melodrama — became successful with the unpremeditated addition of a troupe of scantily clad French ballet dancers, not until the New York (all black) production of *The Creole Show* (1889) was a chorus of female dancers intentionally included in a musical. In a less music-oriented venue, Lydia Thompson and her British Blondes (parodied in the 1959 musical *Gypsy*) appeared in burlesques starting in 1868, after which phrases "Burlie-Q" or "leg show" were coined by theatrical producer Michael B. Leavitt.

The first female chorus lines on Broadway were headed by "dance directors" (as they were called) who were most often men with very little dance training. These early "choreographers" would seek out women with appealing looks and poise (rather than dance technique) when casting. A simple dance routine would be constructed based on eight to ten steps and often later recycled by re-costuming the chorus line for a different number: same movement,

Curvaceous (and corseted) showgirl Anna Held poses in an evening gown circa 1898 (courtesy Billy Rose Theatre Collection, The New York Public Library for the Performing Arts, Astor, Lenox and Tilden Foundations).

different apparel (a method parodied in the 1949 film *On the Town*, co-choreographed by Gene Kelly and Stanley Donen).

Ziegfeld successfully combined the vernacular and the sophisticated in his formula for successful entertainment. In 1907, Anna Held is credited with giving Ziegfeld the groundbreaking idea, suggesting a show with a variety format — based on the French revue from her experience in the *Folies-Bergère*—featuring a headliner who satirized society and the theatre. With that inspiration the impresario introduced opulent production numbers, farcical and topical sketches, comic personalities, a generous amount of songs, and ornately adorned showgirls to American audiences. Nearly every year from 1907 to 1931, he produced a series of extravagant musical revues featuring popular entertainers such as Norah Bayes, Bert Williams, Ed Wynn, Fanny Brice, W.C. Fields, Eddie Cantor, and Will Rogers, alongside his Ziegfeld Girls.

The qualifications to become a Ziegfeld Girl were to look gorgeous and to walk with confidence across the stage while wearing some of the most elaborate costumes ever conceived, often designed by Erté, surrounded by the spectacular sets of Joseph Urban, and staged by Florenz Ziegfeld or his protegé Busby Berkeley. The *Ziegfeld Follies* reigned supreme as popular theatrical entertainment and stimulated such competition as the Earl Carroll *Vanities,* George White's *Scandals,* the *Garrick Gaities, Greenwich Village Follies,* and Irving Berlin's *Music Box Revues.*

While some of the showgirls left the *Follies* after only a season or two, many others had careers launched by the *Follies.* Some of these women went on to further success, influencing a broad circle of performers to follow, while others simply capitalized on their Ziegfeld image. In essence, they maintained a certain style and beauty standard that evidenced itself in all areas of the ever-growing American entertainment industry, including Hollywood. Memorable Ziegfeld showgirls include: Marcelle Earle, a dancer whose portrait represented the *Ziegfeld Follies* in print for many years; Ann Pennington, who went on to star in films as early as 1916 and appeared as herself in the Ziegfeld biographical film *The Great Ziegfeld* (1936); Lillian Lorraine, who was a favored mistress to Ziegfeld during his common-law marriage to Anna Held and assured to be the inspiration for the tall, American-style revue girl;[10] Billie Burke (best remembered as "Glinda, the Good Witch of the North" in *The Wizard of Oz* (1939), who at the peak of her performing career became his second wife (1914) and provided an all–American demeanor and distance from Anna Held's European image, furthering the *Ziegfeld Follies* theme of "Glorifying the American Girl"; Marilyn Miller, who starred in the Ziegfeld production *Sally* (1920) which proved to be her vehicle to theatrical stardom; Billie Dove, who performed with the *Follies* (1919) as a specialty showgirl (best remembered for being loosely wrapped in a fringed shawl) later appeared in many Tom Mix westerns; Marion Davies, a dancer in the 1915 *Follies* whose film career was promoted (and bankrolled) by William Randolph Hearst, a prominent friend of Ziegfeld; dress salon model Kathleen Rose or simply "Dolores," as she was known, who became one of the most photographed Ziegfeld showgirls; and Paulette Goddard (whose name change from Marian Levy masked her Jewish heritage) who managed to launch her career as a Hollywood film star, as well as become a regular companion to George Gershwin.

When Held discovered in 1910 that Ziegfeld had set up Lillian Lorraine as his mistress, she returned to France where she worked tirelessly for the World War I war effort. In 1916 she returned to the American stage where she toured in the Shubert Brothers' (rival producers of Ziegfeld) production of *Follow Me* with a chorus of nine Anna Held Girls in addition to the thirty-four other dancers and showgirls. During this time her health declined and she eventually succumbed to cancer in 1918 at the age of 48.[11]

The concept of a dazzling ensemble of women moving glamorously about the stage spawned numerous concert dance groups, many of which were led by women. Some were inserted into Broadway stage productions and Hollywood films from the 1910s through the 1940s, including the Albertina Rasch Girls, the Goldwyn Girls, the Hanya Holm Dance Company, the Katherine Dunham Dance Company, the Rockettes, and the June Taylor Dancers. But within these new companies, even though beauty, glamour, and grace continued as fundamental elements, dance emerged as the focal point. As was the case with Held, the wide-reaching impact of Rasch, Holm, Dunham, and Taylor spread far beyond the dance medium. Through classical training and popular performance practice, in combination with creativity and ingenuity, each developed dance ensembles in their own choreographic style. This, in turn, influenced up-and-coming generations of dancers and choreographers, and broadened visual conceptualization and production values in live theatre, film, and television.

The prevalence of classical dance influences on the New York stage became apparent with Russian-born Michel Fokine. His standards were high, for among those who studied with him in Russia were Anna Pavlova, Tamara Karsavina, and Vaslav Nijinsky. Fokine came to America following a distinguished career with the *Ballets Russes* in Paris after his contract demands on Serge Diaghilev precipitated his leaving the company in 1914. He came to the United States and choreographed innovative (but traditional) ballets as early as 1919 for entertainments at the Hippodrome, where Albertina Rasch danced as a prima ballerina.

In understanding how ballet became a part of twentieth-century musical theatre, it is pivotal to comprehend the significance of Russian impressario Serge Diaghilev's influence on all who came after him. Diaghilev, founder of the *Ballets Russes*, had far-reaching influence as he nurtured choreographers (Michel Fokine, Vaclav Nijinsky, Léonide Massine, and George Balanchine among them) and transformed ballet into a modern and vital art form. His vision for the performing arts brought elaborate Russian themes to Paris thereby combining artistic concepts from east and west. His productions were beautiful, extravagant, groundbreaking, artistic, and of the highest quality. Even Vincent Minnelli, during his stint as designer for Radio City Music Hall, used Russian images—those of Leon Bakst and his work with the *Ballets Russes*—for his own design of a three-hundred-foot wide curtain for the 1931 *Vanities*.[12] Through the unique aesthetic of the *Ballet Russes*, Diaghilev supported and propelled the careers of many dancers, composers, designers, musicians, and choreographers.

On the vaudeville circuits many serious musicians and dancers performed alongside comedians, acrobats and variety acts of all sorts, and Rasch proved to be no exception. Albertina Rasch was born in Vienna in 1891, trained at Vienna's Imperial Ballet School, began performing at an early age, and made a life-changing decision to leave her Austrian homeland for New York City in 1910. With the combined knowledge of a vaudeville performer, *prima ballerina*, *première danseuse* for several opera companies, and dance director, she was uniquely poised to be the first to artistically integrate ballet into the American musical theatrical genre. Before she worked as a choreographer for Ziegfeld, the Shubert Brothers, or Metro Goldwyn Mayer, she first danced as a ballerina in shows at the Hippodrome and the Winter Garden, then for New York's Century Opera Company, American Opera Company, and the opera companies of Boston, Chicago, and Los Angeles (during an era in which there were no concert dance companies in the United States). When she returned from a 1916–17 vaudeville tour (on the bill with Sarah Bernhardt), Rasch formed the Albertina Rasch Girls, a highly disciplined, balletically-trained ensemble of women who performed *classique* ballet numbers.

With a proud demeanor and an independent flair, Rasch's dark hair and strong features added to her exotic quality and mystique. She met young Russian pianist Dimitri Tiomkin in 1925 and performed with him on his first American tour — on the vaudeville circuit — after which they were married.[13] Tiomkin introduced Rasch to a second love: Russian chocolates. She was so inspired by these delicate confections that she opened the Albertina Rasch Tea Room (the precursor to New York's infamous Russian Tea Room)—just months after her marriage—to serve authentic Russian chocolates.[14] Her colleagues affectionately thereafter referred to her as "the Tsarina."

Rasch and Tiomkin both made an early mark with George Gershwin's music. While on tour, in addition to meeting Gershwin, they also met Richard Rodgers and Jerome Kern who stimulated their interest in American popular song and American musical theatre. During those years Rasch had published a number of articles on the need for an American ballet, and indeed she achieved significant notoriety as the first to choreograph both George Gershwin's "Rhapsody in Blue" (inserted into Ziegfeld's 1929 production of *Show Girl* at the Hippodrome) and "An American in Paris" as ballets not long after they were composed. Tiomkin performed the French premiere of George Gershwin's "Concerto in F" in 1928 at L'Opera de Paris.

During the hey-day of the *Follies*, Albertina Rasch was the only woman to hold one of five main dance director positions. Rasch began choreographing for Florenz Ziegfeld in *American Revue* (1926) — known by two other names: *Palm Beach Nights* and *No Foolin'* — which opened in Palm Beach, Florida. After her work on the *Ziegfeld Follies of 1927* she was immediately booked to choreograph *Rio Rita* (1927), another Ziegfeld production, during which she organized the first Broadway musical appearance of the Albertina Rasch Girls. These were not Ziegfeld showgirls, but separately billed classically trained dancers. The production turned out to be the season's biggest musical success and inaugurated the Ziegfeld Theatre, the finest and most lavish Broadway theatre to date, specifically built for musical extravaganzas. Funded by William Randolph Hearst, the Joseph Urban–designed house was a masterpiece of *art déco*.

Rio Rita opened on 2 February 1927 with a stage overflowing with 100 of Ziegfeld's most beautiful women, including the toe-dancing Albertina Rasch Girls. In the first act Urban's design and Rasch's choreography moved away from both the swashbuckling story and visually rich colorings to present a contrasting piece: an elegant ballet done entirely in black and white. Audiences were drawn to these elements of theatrical contrast and ticket sales climbed. *Rio Rita* closed one week short of reaching the 500 performance mark, after which Rasch's classical balletic style became a significant presence on Broadway (predating the work of Balanchine and de Mille).

In the notable Broadway revue *Walk a Little Faster* (1932), Rasch featured the dance team of Dave and Dorothy Fitzgibbon. The production starred Beatrice Lillie, the comedy team of Clark and McCullough, and premiered the song "April in Paris."[15] Rasch's movement was augmented by the costumes of Staten Island–born Kiviette (née Yetta Kiviat), who was known for her designs of long, sleek women's gowns and formal men's attire. Kiviette's sophisticated costumes — at the height of the *art déco* period — provided the flowing look and sleekness called for in Rasch's elegant dances.[16] The look was Hollywoodesque, and clingy satin fabric accentuated Dorothy Fitzgibbon's every line in her movement. Kiviette costumed many Broadway productions: *Here's Howe!* (1928), *Girl Crazy* (1930), *Three's a Crowd* (1930), *The Cat and the Fiddle* (1931), *The Band Wagon* (1931), *Face the Music* (1932), *Walk a Little Faster* (1932), *Roberta* (1933), *Let 'Em Eat Cake* (1933), *Ziegfeld Follies of 1934* (1933), *Life Begins at 8:40* (1934), and *Between the Devil* (1937).

With a Russian-influenced creative team, *Walk a Little Faster* inaugurated the newly renamed St. James Theatre (formerly the Erlanger Theatre). Russian-born composer Vernon Duke, like ballet-master Michel Fokine, excelled as an artist in Paris during his stint with the *Ballets Russes*. This Broadway revue contained both pre-revolutionary Russian and post-revolutionary Soviet flairs: Vernon Duke's pre-revolutionary Kiev Conservatory training; Boris Aronson's (who apprenticed in Kiev with Russian designer Alexandra Exter) production conception and design; and S.J. Perelman's (whose parents were Russian immigrants) sketch for Bobby Clark parodying Josef Stalin.

Rasch was asked to replace Agnes de Mille — on what was to have been de Mille's debut as a Broadway choreographer for *Flying Colors* (1932) — when de Mille refused, after several rehearsal disasters, to come up with five new dances in five days.[17] Along with dance directors Bobby Connolly, Sammy Lee, Busby Berkeley, and Seymour Felix, Rasch was one of the busiest on Broadway during the latter portion of the 1920s and early 1930s, and the only woman among them.[18] While Richard Rodgers observed, "To be sure, Albertina Rasch had made a specialty of creating Broadway ballets,"[19] she was equally adept in other dance styles as she choreographed the dance teams of Buddy and Vilma Ebsen, Fred and Adele Astaire, and leading performers Mary Boland and Fred Mac-Murray.

With a keen sense of public taste, Rasch's complex routines drew on both ballet and American jazz. Rasch believed that old world knowledge of classical art forms could be combined creatively within a New World setting, that fine performances could be delivered in popular venues while appealing to the masses. She encouraged in women the ability to adopt a more stately grace on stage. One of her most renowned and devoted students was Jeanette MacDonald who immediately took to what Edward Baron Turk describes as Rasch's "demands for discipline, stamina, and consistency."[20] Rasch maintained dance studios in New York's Steinway Building on West Fifty-Seventh Street and in Los Angeles during the course of her career. In the studio she was known for her own brand of sarcasm, a thundering voice, and a pounding cane which emphasized rhythmic patterns for her dancers.

Rasch choreographed many promising young dancers in various Broadway productions from 1926–1941. Ballerina Tilly Losch danced Rasch's choreography in *The Band Wagon* (1931), along with young Fred and Adele Astaire, all of whom were exposed to her balletic style and meticulous technical instruction. American ballet dancer and teacher Ruby Asquith Christensen started out in vaudeville and worked with Rasch in *The Great Waltz*. Ann Hutchinson Guest — noted for her writing on dance notation and Labanotation — danced on Broadway from 1943 through 1950 during which time she worked with Albertina Rasch.[21]

When Rasch broadened her career and moved on to the Hollywood film industry, she choreographed *Hollywood Revue of 1929* (1929), *Rogue Song* (1930), *Broadway to Hollywood* (1933), *The Cat and the Fiddle* (1934), *The Merry Widow* (1934), *Rosalie* (1937), *Firefly* (1937), *The Girl of the Golden West* (1938), *Marie Antoinette* (1938), *Sweethearts* (1938), *The Great Waltz* (1938), and *Balalaika* (1939), many of which were produced by Metro-Goldwyn-Mayer. In Hollywood, the hand-picked Albertina Rasch Girls first emerged on film in *Angel Cake* (1931) and her film career blossomed thereafter. Her specialties—balletic spectacles and operettas, even those with dancing horses—often involved staging movement around a leading character and positioning the cameras for the shoot. She had great artistic control of the scenes she was given. As the only established female dance director in Hollywood, Rasch was all the more remarkable. She once admonished a journalist, "Will you please say that I am not the 2nd Pavlova, or the 3rd Genee, or the 4th Karsavina, or the 57th variety of anybody else? I am simply Albertina Rasch, 1st and last."[22]

When MGM hired Albertina Rasch in 1930 to assist in staging and choreographing several musical films, she was joined in California by her husband, Dimitri Tiomkin.[23] As a direct result of Rasch's contacts and influence, Tiomkin is recalled today for his extensive composing of Hollywood themes and scoring for films written during the 1950s and '60s. Tiomkin never intended for film music composition to become his career, but through his wife, he became one of the film industry's most prolific music directors and composers, writing over 250 film scores for some of the most successful screenplays ever produced. His songs include the Academy Award nominated "Green Leaves of Summer" (1961), while his outstanding film scores include *Lost Horizon* (1937), *Mr. Smith Goes to Washington* (1939), *It's a Wonderful Life* (1946), *High Noon* (1952), *Dial M for Murder* (1954), *Giant* (1956), *The Old Man and the Sea* (1958), *Rio Bravo* (1959), and *The Alamo* (1960).

While Rasch's European elegance was prevalent in pre–World War II musicals and revues, new forms of dance performance awaited in the wings. Katherine Dunham has straddled two worlds over the course of her lifetime: dance performance and ethnology studies. One of the first African-Americans to attend the University of Chicago, Dunham pioneered an authentically researched aboriginal conceptualization of movement.

Katherine Dunham was born in Glen Ellyn, Illinois, 22 June 1912. In her youth she studied with Mark Turbyfill, Ruth Page, and Russian Kamerny–trained modern dancer Ludmilla Speranzeva who put equal value on dance and acting technique. Dunham established her first dance studio in Chicago and founded Ballet Negre in 1931 (the first African-American ballet company in the United States) and the Negro Dance Group, which eventually developed into the Katherine Dunham Dance Company. Studio teaching allowed her to support herself while pursuing her education. Dunham first appeared publicly with her group at the Chicago Beaux Arts Theater in *A Negro Rhapsody,* and followed with her own appearance as a dancer with the Chicago Opera and at the 1933 Chicago World's Fair.

Dunham's fellowship from the Julius Rosenwald Fund afforded her the opportunity to travel to the West Indies to conduct field studies on the cultural pertinence of ritual dances, as part of her graduate research. Eighteen months experience living amongst the people of Jamaica, Martinique, Trinidad, and Haiti allowed her to observe secret rituals and dance rites, which led to the publication of groundbreaking scholarly essays and articles about her Caribbean observations (under the name of "K. Dunn").

In the late 1930s, Dunham chose to return to dance performance and marry theatrical designer John Pratt. Dunham first worked on Broadway assisting Gluck Sandor with his choreography for the ILGWU production of *Pins and Needles* in 1937. (She later provided the dances for the long-running version of *Pins and Needles* in 1940.) In January 1938 Dunham made her New York performance debut in *Tropics* and *Le Jazz Hot: From Haiti to Harlem,* for which she sported a bird cage on her head and a cigar in her mouth, a direct result of her anthropological research in the Caribbean where such accoutrements were standard for ladies circulating in seaport towns. Her work as a performer in New York was again seen in the revival of *The Emperor Jones* (1939) and in *Tropical Pinafore* (1939).

Noted for her humanistic approach and anthropological method, Dunham's creations were influenced by her Caribbean experience — augmented by a raw and natural authenticity — and provided a new, cutting-edge performance forum for African-American dancers and choreographers. Dunham's smooth and fluent choreography radiated beauty and femininity on stage with forceful yet subtle nuances. In October 1940 she was cast as seductive Georgia Brown in the John Latouche/Vernon Duke stage musical *Cabin in the Sky*. The all-black production was mounted to feature Ethel Waters, Todd Duncan, Katherine Dunham and the Katherine Dunham Dance Company. Although George Balanchine is often credited as choreographer, both movement and dance were a coordinated effort between Balanchine and Dunham.[24] She subsequently choreographed many Broadway musicals including *Tropical Revue* (1943), *Carib Song* (1945), *Bal Nègre* (1947), and *Caribbean Rhapsody* (1948).

Dunham's film work includes *Carnival of Rhythm* (1940), *Cabin in the Sky* (1942), *Star Spangled Rhythm* (1942), *Pardon My Sarong* (1942, for which she also provided the choreography), *Stormy Weather* (1943), *Casbah* (1948), *Botta e Risposta* (1950), *Mambo* (Italy, 1954), *Liebes Sender* (Germany, 1954), *Musica en la Noche* (Mexico, 1955), *Green Mansions* (1958), and *The Bible* (1964). It was these contributions to the film industry that later gained her induction into the Black Filmmakers Hall of Fame.

The Dunham School of Dance and Theatre was established in 1945 in New York City and offered courses in rhythm, voice, acting, dance, and dance ethnology. Students included Peter Gennaro, Chita Rivera, Eartha Kitt, Marlon Brando, and José Ferrer. Trained by Dunham, Alvin Ailey worked as a lead dancer in the E. Y. Harburg/Harold Arlen musical *Jamaica* (1957) and made his New York choreographic debut in 1958 at the 92nd Street Y founding the Alvin Ailey American Dance Theatre. Dunham's creative impact continued to emanate through the arts community, as she continued to broaden her scope of accomplishments to the operatic stage with *Aida* in 1963, when she became the first African-American to choreograph for the Metropolitan Opera. She then choreographed and directed Atlanta Opera's 1972 production of Scott Joplin's masterpiece *Treemonisha* (1908).

Katherine Dunham (center) with Roger Ohardieno and Tommy Gomez in the "Rara Tonga" number from *Tropical Revue*, 1943 (courtesy the Jerome Robbins Dance Division, The New York Public Library for the Performing Arts, Astor, Lenox and Tilden Foundations).

In 1967, Dunham joined the faculty of Southern Illinois University in Edwardsville, where she helped create a performing arts training center and establish a dance anthropology program. Moving her base of operation to East St. Louis in 1969, she founded a community-based arts education program. The Katherine Dunham Centers for the Arts and Humanities seek to provide metropolitan East St. Louis residents with an opportunity to witness and participate in all of the fine, performing and cultural arts. Among numerous honors, Katherine Dunham was awarded the Albert Schweitzer Music Award "for a life's work dedicated to music and devoted to humanity," and is the recipient of ten honorary doctorates.

Katherine Dunham celebrates performance as "a way of life" and is considered one of the founders of the anthropological dance movement. In the studio, Dunham espoused that head and neck rhythms were isolated from the rhythms and motion of both the abdomen and feet. Her style of dance extracted torso, arm, and foot movement from Africa and the Caribbean islands, while head and neck movements were derived from the Pacific. In performance she insisted on elaborate costuming and lighting to accompany her work. A fine illustration of both her choreography and dancing is preserved in the lengthy dance sequence of the film *Stormy Weather* (starring Lena Horne and Bill "Bojangles" Robinson), where Dunham performed as a soloist (surrounded by the Katherine Dunham Dance Company) in a ritualistic setting, with bold costumes and movements. As a dancer, choreographer, and scholar who revolutionized American dance, she explored roots of black dance and ritual by means of an innovative transformation of these ethnic traditions into an artistic choreographic medium. Her work with movement and its cultural origins awakened new possibilities in the American musical, paving the way for Broadway choreographers Jack Cole and Lester Wilson, among others.

Where Dunham fused Afro-Caribbean cultural ritualistic movement with Western ballet and modern dance for stage and film, a newly evolving modern dance vocabulary was popularized in American musical theatre through the work of Hanya Holm. Holm, whose original name was Johanna Eckert, was born in Worms-am-Rhein, Germany, 3 March 1893. Her studies in the 1920s were at the Hoch Conservatory and Dalcroze Institute. She continued her dance concentration with Mary Wigman (the leading modern dancer in Germany) in Dresden, the Mecca of modern expressionism in the arts.[25] The word "expressionism" references an era when a creative group of German artists forged the New Objectivity out of a search for social and psychological truths following World War I. Expressionism gave voice, in many art forms, to the anxieties and troubles of the times.

Holm began as a member of Wigman's first dance company (1921–1930) and became the principal instructor at the Mary Wigman Central Institute (1928–1931) in Dresden. After successful American tours of the Wigman Dance Company, international impresario Sol Hurok offered to finance a New York school in which Wigman could introduce her methods.

Holm, disillusioned and uncomfortable with Adolf Hitler's growing popularity in Germany, volunteered to teach at the new New York studio in 1931. After one year Hurok turned the Mary Wigman School in New York over to Holm, and in 1936 (due to American opposition to Germany and the Nazi regime) the name was changed to the Hanya Holm School of Dance. Holm's optimism and enthusiasm for American democracy versus Germany's current state of dark oppression made her the likely heir to Wigman's company in New York. Her concert pieces contained strong elements of social comment in the 1930s and 1940s, including *Trend* (1937) in which society triumphs over injustice, dictatorship, and money worship, emphasizing her view of the futility of war.

Holm became an American citizen in 1939 while continuing her career in New York. Among the many promising dancers and choreographers Holm trained were Bambi Lamb, Glen Tetley, Don Redlich, Valerie Bettis, Alwin Nikolais, Louise Kloepper, and Alvin Ailey. Holm's former students also include James Lipton, vice-president of the Actors Studio and host of *Inside the Actors Studio* on television's Bravo Network.

Holm's concepts were additionally broadened when she took her instruction to Mills College in Oakland, California (1932), the Perry-Mansfield Dance Camp in Steamboat Springs, Colorado (1934), the Bennington School of Dance in Vermont (1934), and Colorado College, in Colorado Springs (1941) where the Summer Ballet Intensive (a four-week program of instruction in classical ballet) continues to thrive in the twenty-first century.

During her early years, Holm's experimentation with the physical effects of gravity, momentum, and the principles of vibratory movement laid the foundation for her own dance philosophy where space played an integral part of movement. As a result of these analyses, her students were sometimes instructed to work a repetitious movement for hours until total exhaustion would allow a more natural and beautiful gesture. She formed the all-woman Hanya Holm Dance Company (1936–1944) and continued to tour her lecture-demonstrations throughout America, mostly to educational institutions. The dissolution of her dance company immediately after World War II marked the end of her performance career but a blossoming of her choreographic career.

Success as co-choreographer for *Ballet Ballads* (1948) at the Maxine Elliott Theatre Off Broadway led to the invitation to choreograph the Broadway premiere of *Kiss Me, Kate* (1948). Choreography for musical theatre became Holm's new hallmark in the dance world, and as she amplified the importance of written choreographic notation (Labanotation) in her studio, she became the first to copyright a professional dance by submitting to the Library of Congress her Labanotated score for *Kiss Me, Kate*. Other Broadway musical credits include *The Golden Fleece* (1941), *Blood Wedding* (1949), *The Liar* (1950), *Out of this World* (1950), *My Darlin' Aida* (1952), *The Golden Apple* (1954), *Reuben, Reuben* (1955, closed out of town), *My Fair Lady* (1956), *Christine* (1960), *Camelot* (1960), and *Anya* (1965). She also prepared the choreography and directed the Central City Opera premiere of Douglas Moore and John Latouche's *The Ballad of Baby Doe* (1956), as well as the Vancouver Opera production of *Orfeo ed Euridice* (1962). Holm's musical theatre work allowed individual dancers or characters to display purpose, providing a means for transitions in pace, mood, and style, while embracing folk and court dances, acrobatics, soft-shoe, jitterbug, modern, and classical ballet. With an organic quality, Hanya Holm's choreography impressively remained within the texture of each show.

The significance of Labanotation and its origins (traceable to the fifteenth century) cannot be overemphasized. The concept of modern dance notation first appeared in Bernard Klemm's book *Katechismus der Tanzkunst* published in Leipzig in 1855. Klemm made use of musical notes but did not devise a system of musical notation. Vladimir Stepanov, a student at the Imperial Dance Academy in St. Petersburg, Russia, devised and defended — but never advanced — his own dance notation system in 1893 after he traveled to Paris to study human anatomy and develop his ideas. It was at the Imperial Dance Academy that Nijinsky was first exposed to Stepanov's concepts, leading Nijinsky to begin creating his own system of notation in 1903 in St. Petersburg, improving on Stepanov's earlier work.[26] Although others have experimented and advanced dance notation, Stepanov's and Nijinsky's writings were the original concepts that facilitated Labanotation and Holm's breakthrough in copyrighting specific dance choreography in the United States.

As the performing arts evolved in America during the twentieth century, the formula for success for women varied greatly. Non-American cultural influences were introduced into the American dance medium through Anna Held's European (particularly Parisian) roots, Albertina Rasch's Russian connections, Katherine Dunham's Caribbean research, and Hanya Holm's German training. Each dance artist contributed broadly with their work as performers, choreographers, and business women. But American-born June Taylor drew her inspiration from the popular stateside sounds of emerging big bands.

Dance is frequently conceived around music, and musical styles determine the inspiration for many choreographers. The exciting sound of American big band jazz music in nightclubs and cabarets in the 1930s initiated a new jazz style within the dance medium. Born in 1918, June Taylor was brought up in the popular jazz dance genre, studying at the Merriel Abbott School in Chicago by the age of ten. In addition to their dance choreography, the Merriel Abbott Dancers[27] were an acrobatic precision team of women that integrated somersaults, handstands, Arabian rolls, and splits in split-second team work. There were several Merriel Abbott ensembles that toured simultaneously.

Taylor dropped out of high school after only three months and made her professional dance debut in the chorus of the George White *Scandals*, Chicago edition (1931). Following the *Scandals* she performed with the Merriel Abbott Dancers at Chicago's Palmer House (and then throughout the entire Hilton Hotel chain) in acrobatic, exhibition ballroom work, and variety entertainment centered around big bands and their vocalists. She traveled to Miami in 1933 for an engagement at the Miami Biltmore Hotel, after which she toured England as a dancer with the Ted Lewis Big Band.[28] In 1938 Taylor developed tuberculosis which forced her to take a two-year break from dancing. Upon reexamining her circumstances, she considered choreography instead of dancing as an occupation.

Much of June Taylor's career was built around the success of her ensemble, the June Taylor Dancers. As a choreographer she began to thrive in the early 1940s when she formed the June Taylor Dancers with six precision dancers. The group worked at local Chicago nightclubs, then opened in New York with the Duke Ellington Orchestra. That early acquaintance with Duke Ellington and his big band eventually inspired "The Duke" to compose "Take the A Train" in 1948 for the June Taylor Dancers.[29]

While Taylor began with a single ensemble, her studio grew into an empire of several touring groups in the 1940s, consisting of six different ensembles before she started in television in 1948. At one point, Taylor's groups were simultaneously performing in California, Kentucky, Florida, New York, and Canada. The June Taylor Dancers traveled to Miami Beach in 1945 for a year-long engagement at the Copacabana, on the bill with Kay Thompson, Danny Kaye, the Four Williams Brothers, and Sophie Tucker. The demand for her work in Miami prompted a year-long engagement at the Beachcomber, and she remained in Miami through 1948, during which time she married a theatrical lawyer and was invited to join in the creation of a show hosted by Ed Sullivan.

At a 1946 intermittent booking at the Chanticleer in Baltimore, June Taylor and Jackie Gleason crossed paths. Gleason had been booked in Baltimore at the last minute after he refused to go on at MGM's showcase in Manhattan as a guest star to Jimmy Dorsey and his band because of a contract dispute. It was this chance Baltimore engagement where Jackie Gleason first learned of the June Taylor Dancers and claimed that if he ever got a big hit, he wanted to hire that choreographer.

On *The Toast of the Town* (CBS, 1948) hosted by Ed Sullivan, June Taylor's ensemble made their television debut as The Toastettes. On *The Broadway Spotlight* (NBC, 1949) Taylor again crossed paths with Gleason, this time debuting as the June Taylor Television Dancers. In 1949 Gleason began hosting *Cavalcade of Stars*, which included one half-hour of showcase performances and one half-hour of character sketches. For each showcase portion he booked June Taylor's six dancers. When CBS negotiated a contract for *The Jackie Gleason Show* (1952–1959, 1962–1970), June Taylor — insisting on sixteen dancers now — became an integral part of that formula for success. Gleason had a portion of his leased Park Sheraton Hotel penthouses remodeled and redesigned as a dance studio, which included mirrors and bars (for Taylor and her dancers), alongside his luxurious suite, which included a large pool table and bars (for Gleason and his cronies).

In the wake of the success of *The Jackie Gleason Show* and the release of a number of romantic solo albums, Gleason tried his hand at composing for television (having had no training as a composer). His four-part tone poem *Tawny*—conceived as a dance piece — surprised the networks as the most extravagant television production number to date.

Gleason show conductor Ray Bloch assembled a fifty-five piece orchestra which Jackie rehearsed and conducted in performance, while June Taylor choreographed seventy-six dancers for the twenty-minute ballet. She auditioned dancers of various training and backgrounds with an eye for (at the time) the non-traditional: ballet dancers, jazz dancers, and African-American dancers. On twelve-inch black and white television sets, the 1953 viewing audience saw *Tawny*, shot with an unprecedented five cameras, one of which was directly overhead with a zoom lens for a kaleidoscope shot. Taylor always had input into the camera angles and logistics of the final product. In June Taylor's words, *Tawny* depicted "a beautiful girl who enticed Big Guy but always left him for Little Guy."[30]

Reviewers praised the production as superior television entertainment: "a poem for eye and ear."[31] Gleason went over budget for the production of the ballet and funded the excess out-of-pocket, but the expense paid off when the Capitol Records released soundtrack sold more than a million copies. This television production number had set a new precedent for the yet-young television medium.

In 1954, when Gleason returned from an European vacation, he decided to double the size of June Taylor's ensemble for the following season, from sixteen to thirty-two. The June Taylor Dancers were sometimes referred to as Gleason's showgirls — gorgeous, smiling, statuesque, leggy American showgirls — the Glea Girls.

When the show traveled by train to various locations, the dancers' quarters were absolutely off limits to the rest of the entourage. At the point where the drinking and partying became less contained, Gleason would signal Taylor to round up "the girls" to proceed back to their compartments. On the road, Taylor's role as choreographer and business woman included chaperone duties. As Ziegfeld insisted on certain social and behavioral attributes from his Ziegfeld Girls, Taylor also ran a strictly disciplined ensemble, maintaining a debutante-like aura both before and after hours with her dancers.

The June Taylor Dancers made Gleason's Saturday night television shows sparkle. His show openings became renowned with the assistance of the beautifully costumed women — adorning either side of the stage — surrounding Gleason for his entrance. Intermingled with segments of the Glea Girls escorting him around stage, bringing him coffee, and lighting his cigarettes, was a June Taylor signature tap, soft shoe, or jazz bit. Each dance piece on a Gleason show lasted approximately three minutes and featured the leggy beauties displaying their straight-line precision routines. Taylor often implemented overhead shots of circular formations — shades of Busby Berkeley — and according to James Bacon, became known as "the lady who owns Saturday night."

"The Jackie Gleason Show" found a new home base at the Miami Beach Civic Auditorium in 1964. Taylor was at first reluctant to move from New York City to the "Live, from Miami Beach!" location, thinking that Miami was too much of a vacationland to keep herself productive and motivated. She soon learned, however, that in Florida, her health was invigorated and her inspiration multiplied exponentially.

Taylor continued her televised success into the sports arena in 1977 when she was hired to streamline and choreograph the Dolphin Dolls. Joe Robbie, then owner of the National Football League's Miami Dolphins, contracted Taylor to give the group a more professional demeanor. Before Taylor arrived, the cheerleading squad consisted of 125 girls ranging from ages eight to eighteen. Under Taylor's guidance, an ensemble of thirty leggy (and athletic) beauties was chosen from over 300 women who auditioned for the newly named Dolphin Starbrites.[32]

The first Dolphin Starbrites wore one-piece bathing suits and go-go boots, as Taylor employed the use of a contemporary American showgirl image. The squad often cheered and danced on an end-zone stage in spectacular Broadway-style half-time shows. Taylor's design of the new Miami Dolphin Cheerleaders image also led, once again, to rules for behavior for the members of the ensemble, just as she had dictated for the June Taylor Dancers. Each cheerleader was to be gracious and kind, act like a lady, and maintain the exemplary image of the Miami Dolphins organization at all times. Entrepreneurial skills, and the ability to collaborate and astutely guide creative efforts in popular venues, continue to be the hallmark of June Taylor throughout her lengthy career.

Over several decades, June Taylor dominated television choreography through her work on "Toast of the Town" (1948–1949), "The Broadway Spotlight" (1949), "Cavalcade of Stars" (1949–1952), and "The Jackie Gleason Show" (1952–1959, 1962–1970) for which she received an Emmy Award for television excellence in 1954. Her career was then re-ignited through broadcast sports with reorganization of and fresh choreography for NFL's Miami Dolphin cheer squad (1977–1990). This restructuring of cheerleading as an athletic dance medium set new expectations for cheer squad performance that resonated throughout collegiate and professional athletic events.

A more contemporaneous example of the American showgirl pulled from the ranks of professional cheerleading is successful dancer/entertainer Paula Abdul. Abdul studied dance during her childhood and began with the Los Angeles Lakers basketball cheerleading squad. From her experience as a Laker Girl, she choreographed music videos for Janet Jackson, ZZ Top, Duran Duran, and the Pointer Sisters; film work includes staging the cheerleading sequences in the Academy Award winning film *American Beauty* (2000). While the stylized "cheerdance" movement may not be seen as directly associated with the American musical, it is an offspring of the evolution of theatrical dance, and highly influenced by the showgirl images established by Florenz Ziegfeld, Albertina Rasch, and June Taylor.

Variations on stylization rooted in ballet, modern, and jazz took their place on the twentieth-century theatrical stage. Cross-cultural influences and inspirations contributed greatly to the construction of this performance medium as we know it, particularly in the case of Held's Parisian air, Rasch's Russian influences, Dunham's Caribbean studies, Holm's German roots, and Taylor's all–American big band beginnings. Additionally, the image inspired by Anna Held, the balletic refinements contributed by Albertina Rasch, the African-American emphasis in Katherine Dunham's works, Hanya Holm's trend toward modernism, and June Taylor's pioneering of jazz dance in the television medium, helped to create the evolutionary substrata upon which dance in the American musical theatre venue has been built.

The showgirl stage personification has (in various forms) continued to reappear in Broadway musicals and revivals such as *Rose-Marie* (1924), *Rosalie* (1928), *Gentlemen Prefer Blondes* (1949, 1995), *Guys and Dolls* (1950, 1976, 1992), *Can-Can* (1953, 1981), *Cabaret* (1966, 1998), *A Chorus Line* (1975), *42nd Street* (1980, 2001), *La Cage Aux Folles* (1983), *The Will Rogers Follies* (1991), and *Crazy for You* (1992). In one of the most revived Broadway musicals, *Gypsy* (1959, 1974, 1989, 2003) tirelessly re-creates the chorus of ideal girls—Madame Rose and her Hollywood Blondes—as the fresh new vaudeville act that will launch success on the stage. "Glorifying the American Girl" is a phrase that appropriately establishes the through-line in the transformation of the showgirl image which has gracefully transferred from stage musicals, to film musicals, to television production numbers and athletic event entertainment. The showgirl has survived the test of time, but is best defined by the pioneering twentieth-century choreographers who stylized popular dance to an evolving fluency on the musical theatre stage.

Notes

1. Florenz Ziegfeld (15 March 1867–22 July 1932) was of German Lutheran extraction, in contrast to Held's Polish/French Jewish background.

2. Prior to Anna Held, successful European women performers such as Sarah Bernhardt, Jenny Lind, Julia Marlowe, and Helena Modjeska, and later the Dolly Sisters, made a great deal of money when they expanded their careers by performing in America.

3. A play in three acts with music, *A Parlor Match* had toured with great success ca. 1890s for about ten years, with new material and new performers added from town to town. (One of the songs introduced during the original run was "A Bicycle Built for Two.") Ziegfeld chose to produce a revival of the show in 1896, and recruited Anna Held from Paris for a small—but featured—role.

4. Eve Golden, *Anna Held and the birth of Ziegfeld's Broadway* (Lexington: University Press of Kentucky, 2000) 28–29.

5. Robert Baral, *Revue: The Great Broadway Period* (New York: Fleet, 1962) 48–49.

6. For specific details regarding the phenomenon of the Ziegfeld Girl, see Linda Mizejewski, *Ziegfeld Girl: Image and Icon in Culture and Cinema* (Durham, NC: Duke, 1999).

7. Baral 50.

8. Within the glamour of the female chorus, it was implied that an American beauty was defined by a light complexion. Anna Held never mentioned her true Jewish heritage in public and never explained her ability to speak Yiddish, fearing prejudice such as she had seen with the deadly pogroms of her youth in Poland. While she remained inactive with any religion during her lifetime, it was implied she was Catholic because of her first marriage to Carrera. See Golden 88–89.

9. *International Encyclopedia of Dance*, vol. 2, s.v. "Castle, Irene and Vernon," 79.

10. In the *Ziegfeld Follies of 1912*, Lillian Lorraine was featured to exemplify a new image in the Ziegfeld showgirl "representing the 20th-Century Girl," in contrast to the "pony" chorus. Gerald Bordman, *American Musical Theatre: A Chronicle* (New York: Oxford, 1978) 280.

11. Golden 202–214.

12. Vincente Minnelli, *I Remember It Well* (London: Angus & Robertson, 1975) 58.

13. Dimitri Tiomkin, *Please Don't Hate Me* (Garden City, NY: Doubleday, 1959) 125.

14. Tiomkin 167.

15. The revue *Walk a Little Faster* was the first full-length Broadway work for both lyricist E.Y. Harburg (né Erwin Yipsel Hochberg) and Russian-born composer Vernon Duke (né Vladimir Dukelsky).

16. Prior to *Walk a Little Faster*, Rasch and Kiviette (née Yetta Kiviat) had worked together on two other shows: *The Band Wagon* (1931) and *Face the Music* (1932). Kiviette's other Broadway productions included *Here's Howe!* (1928), *Girl Crazy* (1930), *Three's a Crowd* (1930), *The Cat and the Fiddle* (1931), *Roberta* (1933), *Let 'Em Eat Cake* (1933), *Ziegfeld Follies of 1934* (1933), *Life Begins at 8:40* (1934), and *Between the Devil* (1937).

17. *Flying Colors* ran for about 6 months on Broadway. Stanley Green, *Ring Bells! Sing Songs! Broadway Musicals of the 1930s* (New York: Galahad Books, 1971) 67.

18. Albertina Rasch's cumulative Broadway choreographic credits include: *Ziegfeld's American Revue* (1926), *Rufus le Maire's Affairs* (1927) with Jack Haskell, *Ziegfeld Follies* (1927), *Rio Rita* (1927) with Sammy Lee, *The Three Musketeers* (1928) a Ziegfeld production, *Show Girl* (1929) with Bobby Connolly, *Sons O' Guns* (1929) with Bobby Connolly, *Sari* (1930) a Viennese operetta, *Princess Charming* (1930), *Three's a Crowd* (1930), *The Wonder Bar* (1931) with John Pierce, *The Band Wagon* (1931), *Ziegfeld Follies* (1931) with Bobby Connolly, *Everybody's Welcome* (1931) with William Holbook, *The Cat and the Fiddle* (1931), *The Laugh Parade* (1931), *A Little Racketeer* (1932) with Jack Donohue, *Face the Music* (1932), *Flying Colors* (1932), *Walk a Little Faster* (1932), *Bohemian Girl* (1933), *The Great Waltz* (1934), *Jubilee* (1935), *Very Warm for May* (1939) with Harry Losee, and *Lady in the Dark* (1941).

19. Richard Rodgers, *Musical Stages* (New York: Random House, 1975) 175.

20. Edward Baron Turk, *Hollywood Diva: A Biography of Jeanette MacDonald* (Berkeley: University of California, 1998) 48.

21. Guest has analyzed written choreographic notation in both classical ballet and musical theatre. She is the author of an analysis of some of the earliest-known dance notation, that of Vaslav Nijinsky's *L'Après-midi d'un faune,* created and performed with Diaghilev's *Ballets Russes.* See Ann Hutchinson Guest, "Nijinsky's Dance Notation," in *L'Après-midi d'un Faune Vaslav Nijinsky 1912* (New York: Dance Horizons, 1983). Also see Larry Billman, *Film Choreographers and Dance Directors: An Illustrated Biographical Encyclopedia, with a History and Filmographies, 1893 through 1995* (Jefferson, NC: McFarland, 1997) s.v. "Albertina Rasch" and "Albertina Rasch Girls."

22. *Dance Magazine*, obituary, author unknown, November 1967: 5.

23. Tiomkin 153–155.

24. *Biographical Dictionary of Dance* (1982), s.v. "Katherine Dunham."

25. Expressionism, as a style, implies the use of distortion, exaggeration, symbolism and manifestation of emotions from within the human psyche, in an outward flow of primal energy. See Willi Apel, ed. *Harvard Dictionary of Music*, 2nd ed. (Cambridge, MA: Harvard University, 1972).

26. Ann Hutchinson Guest, "Nijinsky's Dance Notation," in *L'Après-midi d'un Faune Vaslav Nijinsky 1912* (New York: Dance Horizons, 1983) 117–130. Also see *International Encyclopedia of Dance v.4*, s.v. "Nijinsky, Vaslav," 645.

27. The top troupe of the Merriel Abbott Dancers can be seen in the films *Man About Town* (1939) and *Buck Benny Rides Again* (1940).

28. Ted Lewis was a big band leader, a clarinetist, and a true vaudevillian whose theme song was "When My Baby Smiles at Me." He always included in his act his favorite expression "Is everybody happy?" George T. Simon, *The Big Bands Songbook* (New York: Thomas Y. Crowell Co., 1975) 340–341.

29. Jane Wooldridge, "June Taylor" interview from *The Miami Herald* (Internet Edition, 1997).

30. W.J. Weatherby, *An Intimate Portrait of The Great One* (New York: Pharos Books, 1992) 91–92.

31. James Bacon, *How Sweet It Is: The Jackie Gleason Story* (New York: St. Martin's, 1985), 122.

32. Jane Wooldridge, "June Taylor" interview.

A Composer in Her Own Right

Arrangers, Musical Directors and Conductors

JENNIFER JONES CAVENAUGH

> Women were not welcome — we were appreciated because we got
> things done — but Agnes [de Mille] and I had a very tough
> time doing what men thought was their job. We had to battle our
> way through troubles, but Agnes was a very strong and resourceful
> woman; I guess in our own ways we were both strong women.
> — Trude Rittman

It is quite possible that you have never heard of Trude Rittman; but if you are one of the millions around the world who have enjoyed *The King and I, South Pacific,* or *My Fair Lady*, then you have heard Trude Rittman's music. A dance and choral arranger on nearly forty Broadway shows, Rittman wrote the ballet music, underscoring and intricate vocal harmonies for nearly all of the Rodgers and Hammerstein and Lerner and Loewe musicals. During the "golden age" of the American musical Rittman was revered by everyone in the business and, even today, young composers and veteran arrangers speak of her talents with awe. Yet if you look for her name in existing histories of musical theatre, or in the biographies of the male composers whose reputations benefited from her work and talent, you will look in vain. Another rarely mentioned woman dance arranger from the "golden age" was Genevieve Pitot, a New Orleans native who composed the dance arrangements for such landmark shows as *Kiss Me, Kate, Can-Can, Call Me Madam* and *Candide*. She too is rarely, if ever, mentioned in the existing histories of the American musical theatre.

Pitot and Rittman's exclusion from the historical record is due in part to the nature of an arranger's work. Broadway orchestrator and arranger Jonathan Tunick described the position of the arranger as someone who "lurks" in the background. "Producers and composers were a little embarrassed that we [arrangers] even existed. They are just as happy to appear before the public as a Bach or a Wagner."[1] Like the Wizard of Oz who warns his visitors to "pay no attention to the man behind the curtain," many of the male composers, who were often the producers of their own shows, had a vested interest in keeping their arranger's talent uncredited. In a rare newspaper article on Genevieve Pitot, Whitney Bolton quoted her as saying, "We are not exactly celebrated, they don't give us much publicity."[2] In that article, Bolton wrote:

> Most people know that for every musical there is an orchestrator, a talented man who takes music written by the composer and orchestrates it for the many kinds of instruments in the orchestra. A good orchestrator can make a score better than it really is, a bad one can ruin a score. But how many of you know that there is a composer behind the composer? Few. Even many who know all about musicals don't know that there is a composer who takes the original score early, and refashions it, shapes it, writes in, deletes, does all manner of things to make certain sections of the whole score danceable[...]The foremost on Broadway is a woman whose name probably will give you a blank look. You may never have heard of her, but 17 Broadway shows have been dancing hits because of Genevieve Pitot.[3]

Though the lack of public credit given to Pitot and Rittman by the male composers for whom they worked was partly due to the nature of the arranger's job, a significant part of their disappearance from the historical record can be attributed to their gender. This chapter has two aims: the first, to document and celebrate the contributions women musicians like Trude Rittman and Genevieve Pitot have made to American musical theatre; and the second, to examine the deep-seated assumptions of male-privilege in the professional musical theatre that makes the first aim necessary. Because Rittman was such a giant in the field and continues to exert an influence on composers and arrangers today the bulk of this chapter will focus on her career. She paved the way for many women who later were able to work on Broadway as musical directors, conductors and eventually as composers in their own right. Some of their stories will be interwoven with hers.

In order to appreciate Rittman's extraordinary skill it is important to explain the work she did. Most audience members assume that the composer of a musical has written every note they hear in the theatre, but very few Broadway composers are actually responsible for more than the song melodies and rhythms (and sometimes harmonies) in the musicals that bear their name. Unlike opera composers whose compositions include their orchestrations and choral arrangements, musical theatre composers will often turn over their melodies to other professional musicians who then write overtures, orchestrations, incidental accompaniments, dance music, and vocal arrangements.[4]

Arrangers write pages and pages of music from the thirty-two bars (or so) given to them by the show's composer.[5] Pitot described her work like this:

> First I listen to the original score[...]then I [take] the score home and begin improvising ... I take these ideas to [the choreographer] and we decide which could and could not be used by him and his dancers. These are not sitting down conferences. They are get up from the piano, hum the improvisation, do the skeletal forms of the choreography to the hums[...] When enough of those are useable they are then worked out in detail.[6]

Trude Rittman described how she would elaborate on the composer's melodies in order to create the dance arrangements and underscoring. Note that Rittman, a classically trained composer, assumes the gender of the Broadway composer to be male:

> I take his [the composer's] song, the essences, the song material, and start doing my own stuff. Very often it's hung onto a song, like what we call production numbers. You have to be very skillful and come up with oodles of different things. Expand, imagine, go away from it completely. Come back to it. Knit in the chorus. It is a major thing.[7]

Rittman's skill as a composer equaled, and often surpassed, that of the men for whom she worked, men whose names have become synonymous with American musical theatre, but at the time she was working, there were no women composers having their work produced on Broadway. In 1976 Rittman told an interviewer, "I was usually the only woman in all this professional creative stuff. There was rarely another lady sitting in these staff meetings. [...] And so I kind of say, it is of course and it is still to this day prejudice against women composers."[8] Jeanine Tesori, who was profiled in *American Theatre* (February 2000) as one of America's brightest young

Arranger and composer Trude Rittman's extensive contributions to the Golden Age of musical theatre have often been overlooked (courtesy Billy Rose Theatre Collection, The New York Public Library for the Performing Arts, Astor, Lenox and Tilden Foundations).

composers, was one of the few women composers whose work was produced in American musical theatre at the end of the twentieth century (*Twelfth Night*,[9] *Violet, Thoroughly Modern Millie*). Tesori feels that her situation was not that much different in the year 2000 from what Rittman described, and she notes that she is also often the only woman in musical production meetings. Tesori, who updated Rittman's dance arrangements for the 1990s Broadway revival of *The Sound of Music,* speaks with awe of her composition skills. "Trude had great craft, she was a true composer. Her work is symphonic, really, and her compositions stand the test of time, they show clear evidence of classical experience, the influence of Stravinsky and take-no-prisoner training."[10]

Both Pitot and Rittman were superb musicians, classically trained from an early age.[11] In speaking to those who either worked with Trude Rittman, or like Tesori, were inspired by her, one theme consistently emerges: Rittman's outstanding musicianship. Tunick calls her "one of the most skillful musicians I've ever met"[12] and her assistant Martha Johnson calls Rittman a "genius" and a "wunderkind."[13] Born and raised in Germany, Rittman entered a Conservatory at the age of six to study piano, and thus was classically trained in the rigorous European tradition. By the age of fourteen she had begun formal studies in composition with Ernst Toch. Recognizing her extraordinary talents, Toch recommended that she continue her studies in composition with Phillip Jarnach and her piano training with Edward Erdman at the Staatliche Hochschule für Musik in Cologne. Rittman earned an Artist's and a Teacher's diploma in both composition and piano at the age of twenty-one.

When she graduated, Rittman was one of Germany's most promising young composers, but the year was 1932 and life in that country was about to change radically. A German Jew, Rittman gave up a promising composition career when she fled the Nazis. "You see when I come I run from Hitler. I was four years on the go in Europe. I didn't quite know where to settle."[14] Though Rittman escaped the Nazis, her father was not so lucky: "My father took his own life under Hitler."[15] After teaching harmony and music theory in England, Rittman became an assistant to the distinguished conductor Hermann Scherchen in 1935 and began to compose ballets for the Kurt Joos School of the Dance. In the summer of 1937 she immigrated to the United States with very little money and no place to live. Like many German refugees, Rittman was offered help from the National Council of Jewish Women; it would not be the last time that women would provide Rittman with the financial and emotional support to do her work.

Rittman soon found work as a concert accompanist and pianist for the American Ballet Caravan and within a year she was made Musical Director of the company. During her time with American Ballet Caravan she worked with some of the country's brightest young composers—Aaron Copland, Elliot Carter, Virgil Thomson, Leonard Bernstein, and Marc Blitzstein—and in addition to playing and touring, she began to compose and arrange music for the company's new ballets. When American Ballet Caravan disbanded in 1941 Rittman became the concert accompanist for Agnes de Mille's small dance company. It was an historic moment for the American musical theatre when these two women combined talents for the first time.

Over her forty-year career Rittman worked with Broadway's best directors and choreographers, including Jerome Robbins, Hanya Holm, Josh Logan and Moss Hart, but Agnes de Mille was the only one of her collaborators to publicly acknowledge her debt to Rittman. Perhaps it was their close personal friendship outside of the rehearsal hall, or the fact that they were both talented women in a male-dominated profession, but these two women fought hard for each other and relied upon each other's talents to bring out their own best work. De Mille devotes an entire chapter to Rittman in her autobiography *And Promenade Home* (1956) and remarkably this tribute is the only written acknowledgment of Rittman's influence on the American musical theatre. In sharp contrast to many of Rittman's other collaborators who never mention her contributions, de Mille freely expresses her reliance on Rittman's talents:

> This gift for arranging and developing popular songs into dances and for underscoring scenes, dialogue and business is unique. Her unparalleled help in infusing variety and dramatic effectiveness into shows as well as into accompaniments is common knowledge on Broadway. [...] She is more than an arranger. I rely on her as on no one else in all departments of my work. I herewith make her the deepest reverence, and there are other choreographers, and the very best, bowing beside me. Several thousand dancers and all orchestrators and conductors rise to testify to the taste, good sense, musicality and creative force Trude Rittman brings to every show she touches, and the cheer and decorum she maintains in rehearsal.[16]

It was de Mille who first brought Trude Rittman to the Broadway stage in 1943 to work as rehearsal pianist for Kurt Weill's *One Touch of Venus*. Working as a rehearsal pianist was a step backward for an acclaimed European musician who had recently composed original ballets, but it was one of the few jobs, besides actress or dancer, open to women in professional musical theatre. Trude Rittman's long-time assistant, Martha Johnson, recalls that women were usually hired to play the eight to ten weeks of rehearsal, but when it came to the higher-paying, longer-running work of playing in the pit during the show it was always union men who were hired. "All these women could have made a living if after rehearsal we could have gone into the pit. The excuse given was always that the men had to support a family, but I had children to support as well."[17] According to music theorist and historian Jill Halstead, the gendering of the rehearsal pianists as female and the composer and performance pianist as male reflects a long held belief that women engage in music as a hobby or amateur interest while the professional world of the composer and performance pianist has been traditionally viewed as masculine.[18] It is significant then that neither Pitot nor Rittman were recognized as musicians by the Musicians local 802 union, the union of professional Broadway musicians.

I break with Rittman's story here for a moment to look at one of the women who benefited from Rittman's pioneering efforts. Karen Gustafson became the first woman to play piano in a Broadway orchestra pit for *The Vamp* (1955) starring Carol Channing.[19] Gustafson later became the first woman to conduct a Broadway orchestra when she took over for conductor Lehman Engel while he was on sick leave from *Destry Rides Again* (1959). In an interesting side note, Genevieve Pitot had done the dance arrangements for that show. Gustafson continued to conduct on Broadway stepping in as associate conductor on *Wildcat* (1960) and *The Gay Life* (1961). She told an interviewer that "there were misgivings among the men of *The Gay Life* orchestra when it was announced she would be associate conductor. But the misgivings vanished after her first performance, when a seasoned member of the orchestra said to her, 'You certainly surprised us.'"[20] Gustafson would later be the musical director for *Lost in the Stars* (1972) and *King of Hearts* (1978). Despite Gustafson's groundbreaking achievements as the first woman to play in the pit of a Broadway musical and the first woman to conduct on Broadway, newspaper coverage of her tended to downplay her musical accomplishments and focus on her feminine physique. In a 1961 article on Gustafson, John Chapman writes:

> If a tall beauty of a blond chooses the theatre for a career and makes the grade, odds are 12 to 7 that this doll will be in a musical comedy and up on the stage where people can look at her[...]however in *The Gay Life*[...]there is a lass of showgirl specifications who shows only the back of her head. She is Broadway's only woman musical comedy conductor, 5 feet 6, named Karen Gustafson. The only girl to have won the title of associate conductor on our stage.[21]

In spite of Gustafson's excellent musical credentials (years of classical music training and a position as a soloist with the Cincinnati Symphony Orchestra) this journalist describes her in the voyeuristic language of a peep show. Another journalist calls her "the pin-up girl of the pit band."[22] It would be hard to imagine one of the many distinguished male conductors being treated in this manner.

Gustafson may have had some success as a pit pianist and conductor in the 1950s and 1960s, but most women, including Trude Rittman and Genevieve Pitot, were still relegated to the rehearsal rooms and paid non-union wages. Some of the finest rehearsal pianists were women — Geraldine Schuster, Helen Lanfer and Norah Stevenson to name just a few — and de Mille wrote that "all the choreographers depended on them."[23] These women may also have been talented composers but we will never know; without job security or even a modest financial independence none of these women could afford the space or time required to compose their own music for the theatre.

Rittman, a classically trained composer, was hired as a rehearsal pianist but it did not take long for composers and choreographers to recognize her true talents. For her second musical (*Bloomergirl*) she was hired as the arranger of ballet music, again working with de Mille. One of de Mille's assistants, Dania Krupska, recalls that "Agnes and Trude didn't have to speak, each seemed to know what the other was thinking." She described the two women as being completely in tune with each other. "The music and the dance would come out as one."[24] Rittman described her relationship with de Mille as "intimate. A very close relationship. I knew very strongly what she was doing and she also reacted very strongly to me. We were both lyricists—lyrical."[25] De Mille always deferred to Rittman's musical judgments, and in her description of their working relationship she suggests that Rittman was able to create the perfect music for the dances almost effortlessly, as if by magic:

> Trude sat knitting and whistling between her teeth while I pushed people around the room. When an amount was blocked out she would go to the keyboard. Then she improvised melodic variations on the song tunes as we went along, playing full out, changing keys, modulating, developing a musical climax where the choreographic climax was shaping. "How would it be if we were to have two fives right here? And if I play three-four against your four-four? Don't change a count. You keep going. We come out together, you see? It gives a brilliance, a shimmer, no?"[26]

However, in a 1976 interview with Nancy Reynolds for the Dance Oral History Project at the New York Public Library, Rittman related her version of the creative process she shared with Agnes de Mille. Comparing the two women's description of creating the dances reveals that although both recall a strong collaboration, Rittman does not remember the music coming so effortlessly:

> You see we talk about it. Then she will go to her studio [...] and she will what she calls "fool around." She tries this and she tries that. I also improvise. Seeing what I am seeing I do this I do that. And then all of a sudden Agnes will scream, "Hold it! Hold it! That's it. Hold it. Don't lose it! Write it out!" And that is how it is. And it wouldn't be the first time she made me dive into a garbage can because I've already torn up something and she just dives after it. Then I start writing in earnest. Unhampered by anything.[27]

While de Mille portrays Rittman as possessing a brilliant improvisational talent, the composer herself recalls that the improvisation is only the first step in a long, difficult writing process. Rittman would watch and sketch all day at the piano during rehearsal and then go home and work most of the night in order to bring back a complete score the next day. Her perfectionism was legendary. Whenever de Mille or the dancers would say something was wonderful, Rittman would reply curtly: "It is not. I work it over tonight." She would take home her rehearsal scrawls and return with a fully scored arrangement—each count exactly as rehearsed.[28] Rittman was often the last to leave rehearsal and the first to arrive the next day. De Mille recalls coming into the theatre early one morning during *One Touch of Venus* and finding Trude working on the upright piano in the ladies lounge where she had already been hard at it for two hours.[29]

Rittman's energy seemed to be inexhaustible, but her perfectionism came at a cost. She suffered from terrible migraines and intense backaches and would often have a cot placed near the piano for those times when the pain became unbearable. A bottle of Excedrin was always on her piano next to the pencils and the five-lined music graph paper. Despite constant migraines, Rittman rarely looked after her own needs, but she always took care of de Mille and the dancers. "It was always Trude who raised the dead, comforted the sick, counseled the forlorn and who found out and informed me of what I should know in order to help. She was big sister, mother, school mistress and scoutmaster."[30] One can hardly imagine Fritz Loewe or Richard Rodgers comforting a singer, bringing tea to the conductor or lending a sympathetic ear to a forlorn actor.

In addition to her musical contributions to de Mille's work, Rittman seemed to function as a mentor to the famous choreographer. De Mille recalls:

> She was stern and demanding, but the hope and solace and patience that woman could summon when everyone else had stamped out disappointed was why some of us were able to weather our jobs. I cannot number the times she has cleared the hall, brought me tea, or taken me to dinner and then returned to work quietly all night, if need be. The sane musicianly counsel she supplies, the expert eye, the humor and the large background experience which reaches into the best Europe could teach and embraces all forms and styles—*these are at the disposal of every colleague who will listen*—as well as her courage. And let no one underestimate what courage it takes to make an innovation in the commercial theatre[31] [author's emphasis].

A final caveat in de Mille's tribute to her collaborator reveals the fact that not everyone was able to appreciate Rittman's expertise or accept her musical advice. In a 1999 biography of Richard Rodgers, Ethan Mordden's only mention of Rittman comes when he describes Rodgers' frustration with her use of her own original music in many of her dance arrangements: "'It's not Rittman and Hammerstein,' Rodgers would tell her. 'It's Rodgers and Hammerstein.'"[32] Genevieve Pitot was well aware that she was there to serve the show's composers and not inject her own musical vision into the dance arrangements. In a 1959 interview Pitot was asked if there was anything she needed to guard against in her work. She replied, "There certainly is. The intrusion of one's own personality, musically speaking. You have to understand that you are writing to project this quality and mood of the dance, and that the audience is not there to hear YOU but to feel the character and spirit of the show. Nor are you to intrude yourself on the original composer's own music" [Pitot's emphasis].[33]

Rittman was not as comfortable as Pitot appeared to be in relinquishing her own musical voice to the show's composer. Some of Rittman's most stunning work was done for Richard Rodgers, but their relationship was not always an easy one. Rittman always spoke of Rodgers with a guarded respect but others were more frank about the tensions between the two composers. In a phone interview, Bruce Pomahac, Director of Music for the Rodgers & Hammerstein Organization, remembered when the organization's Executive Director

Ted Chapin tried to track down Trude Rittman in 1992. When Chapin called Agnes de Mille, she had said, "If you're going to talk to Trude Rittman you'd better have something to say to her because Rodgers stole her soul."[34] Though Rittman always maintained that Rodgers could have written anything she had if he had not been so busy producing the Rodgers and Hammerstein productions, much of Rodgers music was greatly enhanced by Trude Rittman's musicianship. In an interview she described her complex relationship with the famous composer.

> I am not a great friend of Richard Rodgers. I've done six shows with him and so I know him quite well. But I'd say this. He hands over the show and says "Do." He writes the songs. That's it. And gets out. And when it is a question of choral numbers—first of all I usually do the choral stuff too, the arrangements—but I also open these songs to enormous things.[35]

One of Rittman's most stunning compositional achievements is the ballet from *The King and I*, "The Small House of Uncle Thomas," which she worked on with a young choreographer named Jerome Robbins. With the exception of a short variation of "Hello Young Lovers" played underneath the ice skating scene, the entire score is original music by Rittman. She and Robbins were creating something entirely new for the commercial theatre. "It was only with percussion. Very little otherwise. And it was something quite different from anything else. [...] It was an enormous experience for me. I must say, because no one had ever seen such a percussion orchestra assembled."[36] As she had with de Mille, Rittman worked side by side with Robbins to create what is for many *The King and I*'s most memorable scene. "There was a point it was very difficult, but it was an enormous challenge for both of us. [...] He kept saying. 'We are like a very old couple going up a steep hill. One is pushing the other.'"[37] In his autobiography *Musical Stages*, Richard Rodgers praises Jerome Robbins for his vision and talent in creating "The Small House of Uncle Thomas," but Trude Rittman's contribution of nearly twenty minutes of original music is never even mentioned. By omitting her name, Rodgers tacitly takes credit for Rittman's music. "Rodgers was very appreciative of my work but he wouldn't let it out — wouldn't do anything to let it slip from his, what is the word ... glory."[38] For many years the scores of the Rodgers and Hammerstein musicals did not even have Trude Rittman's name on them. It was not until Rodgers died in 1979 that his daughter, composer Mary Rodgers, convinced the Rodgers & Hammerstein Organization to print Rittman's name on the music she had composed and arranged.

Though ballets and dance numbers such as "The Small House of Uncle Thomas" are clear examples of Rittman compositions that were absorbed in Rodgers' score, much of her work for Rodgers and Hammerstein is harder to isolate because it is so intricately woven into the fabric of the musical. The glorious choral arrangements in *The Sound of Music* are Rittman's, as is the dramatic and provocative underscoring in *South Pacific*. Michael Rafter, the

Musical Director on the 1990s Rodgers and Hammerstein Broadway revivals of *The King and I* and *The Sound of Music*, testifies to the power and timelessness of Rittman's compositions. "When you think of the amount of the score of *The Sound of Music* that is in vocal arrangements— it's a huge part of that score and the underscoring to *South Pacific* is vital to the piece. It drives the sentiment."[39] When Rafter recently tried to adapt the score for a benefit choral performance he found that it was nearly impossible to cut any underscoring because Rittman's music was perfectly integrated into the dramatic action; any change in the text disrupted her intricate composition and detracted from the emotional progression of the scene.

The underscoring to *South Pacific* is certainly one of Rittman's most skillful compositions. As she had with de Mille and Robbins, she worked side by side with *South Pacific*'s director Josh Logan during rehearsals. It was one of the most enjoyable collaborations of her career.

> There we really worked together as if we were married to each other. It's the closest relationship I've ever had because he had a sense of music, but completely unschooled. But he had an enormous feeling for the musical theatre. I think it was implanted in him by Stanislavsky. His greatest experience in life was as a young man when he came to Russia and he saw what Stanislavsky did with his operas. [...] and *South Pacific* was really done from that point of view. We worked on that score together until it was one unit.[40]

It is striking that the woman who received so little recognition for her contributions to Rodgers' work was so quick to share credit for the power of her composition with Logan. Though in his autobiography Josh Logan describes Rittman as a "superb German-born composer, orchestrator and arranger" he does not indicate the extent or importance of her contributions to *South Pacific*.[41] He certainly does not describe their collaboration with the joy and respect that Rittman does.

With *South Pacific* Rittman had expanded her role beyond a dance and choral arranger who relies on the composer's melodies. She was now creating original music that, though not sung, was inextricably linked to the progression of the musical's storyline. A new title had to be found for her, and in 1949 she received the first Playbill credit for Musical Continuity, a title that had to be created for Rittman to describe all the things she did on a production. Rittman's assistant, Martha Johnson, described her as the person who sewed a show together, but composer Jeanine Tesori thinks that the image of a seamstress is inadequate to describe Rittman's talents and contribution: "A seamstress works with pieces that are already there and simply puts them together. Trude created the very fabric of the music."[42]

Not all composers were as difficult to work with as Richard Rodgers, and Rittman had very satisfying collaborations with both Jule Styne and Frederick (Fritz) Loewe. If Agnes de Mille was Rittman's closest choreographic collaborator, her most important musical relationship was with her compatriot composer Fritz Loewe. She worked on every one of his musicals including classics such as *Brigadoon* (1947), *Paint Your Wagon* (1952), *My Fair Lady* (1956), and *Camelot* (1961); the two musicians had great respect for each other's talents. Rittman described Loewe as a virtuoso pianist and an inspired musician: "Fritz is a musician how they come very rarely these days."[43] Their working relationship was completely different from the one she had had with Rodgers. Whereas Rodgers would hand her the melodic themes and then go off to other tasks, Loewe and Rittman would work side by side. Often he would play and she would record whatever he was improvising. According to Rittman, "He had a wealth of melodic invention. A wealth. A very lazy wealth."[44] She likened her role to that of a looking glass in which Loewe could observe and perfect his own work: "I'm like a mirror, like a reflector and it is of course marvelous. Because somebody listens and observes and watches and says, 'I think you could do that much more beautifully.' I wish I had such a reflector myself."[45] A composer of her talents should have had such a reflector in which to perfect her own work, but Trude Rittman was always cast in the supporting role.

Loewe was a close personal friend, and, as a fellow German, they enjoyed speaking in "code" with each other. Rittman was known for leaving little notes in German on her scores since several of the Broadway conductors had also emigrated from Germany. At the bottom of "The Small House of Uncle Thomas" score is a small note in German that translated reads: "Thank God it's over!" Loewe seemed more eager than Rodgers to collaborate with Rittman, and Martha Johnson describes the excitement of watching them work together on *Camelot*. "It was the highlight of my career. To witness the wittiness of Lerner, the lyricism of Loewe and Trude as musical consultant and collaborator was watching history being made!" But even within this supportive relationship there were some heartbreaking compromises. At one point Rittman had composed a gorgeous dance arrangement for *Paint Your Wagon* using the tune of "Another Autumn." When the song was cut from the show, Loewe insisted that the dance arrangement be based on a tune still in the show and the entire arrangement had to be dumped.[46] At times Rittman would express the frustration she felt at having her own compositions always in service to someone else's vision. Rittman described her complicated relationship with Loewe's lyricist, Alan Jay (Alvin) Lerner:

> Since very often ballets or dances or even underscoring are connected with the ins and outs into the very songs you are doing, you are in touch always. It is a ticklish, delicate thing. It has to be right. Alvin usually has very distinctive ideas about how to go into a song. How to approach it. [...] Where to come in with the music. And of course I do too, and sometimes we don't see eye to eye on this. So it has obviously to "va bien" between two people or three people or four people. That makes work in the theatre difficult. [...] And some people get irritated or high strung under pressure.[47]

Perhaps Rittman survived the pressures and tensions of collaboration in the musical theatre by maintaining the diplomatic demeanor of a person who was only visiting this strange world. "I have an easy way of getting along with people but I always, I must say I do not live in this world. I just work there. After the show is done I close the door and it is forgotten. [...] I love the theatre. It gives me to this day a thrill. But I cannot live in this atmosphere of over-heated ... I cannot, I cannot. It is not my character. It is not my nature."[48] When I asked Trude Rittman which of her compositions was her favorite, she replied that she loved the work that came from early on in her pre-theatre days, but she hadn't heard it in years. "I would like to have continued my own compositions, but I had to support myself."[49] The male composers who hired Trude Rittman were able to amass small fortunes because they owned a piece of each show, but Rittman was paid on a show by show basis and never earned any royalties for her compositions. Had she received compensation commensurate with her contributions as a vocal and dance arranger she would have had the financial and professional freedom to write her own compositions for the theatre, the symphony hall or the ballet. But, as composer Jeanine Tesori has said so succinctly, "When your hands are at the piano, it's not freedom."[50] Perhaps as an acknowledgment of his debt to her, Fritz Loewe left Rittman a generous bequest upon his death. When Richard Rodgers died, his daughter Mary Rodgers convinced the Rodgers & Hammerstein Organization to pay Rittman a monthly royalty check for, as Rittman calls it, "the whole caboodle."[51] Rodgers had seen Trude Rittman's extraordinary talent first hand. As a composer herself she could appreciate the importance of Rittman's contribution to the Rodgers and Hammerstein canon. In honoring the financial debt Richard Rodgers owed Trude Rittman perhaps Mary Rodgers was acknowledging her own debt to Rittman for paving the way for women to be Broadway composers in their own right.

Rittman was an extraordinary composer, and although she did not get public recognition for her work, there is no doubt that she was a major influence on the American musical theatre. One wonders how many young women would have been inspired to compose if they had known a woman had written the glorious choral arrangements in *The Sound of Music* or the breathtaking ballet in *The King and I.* One cannot help but speculate if Trude Rittman had been as much of a household name as Richard Rodgers would it have been easier for young women to enter the male-dominated field of the Broadway musical? Music historian Jill Halstead writes in *The Woman Composer: Creativity and the Gendered Politics of Musical Composition,* "The most obvious way of suppressing awareness and encouragement of female creativity is by denying its existence. Although it is now clear that women have participated in music as composers throughout history and across cultures, the term composer has usually been understood to denote a male creator."[52] The absorption of Trude Rittman's breathtaking compositions into the scores of male composers makes it more difficult for young women to claim their rightful place as composers in the musical theatre. Agnes de Mille described the power of sexist expectations when she wrote:

It matters not a whit how you educate a girl, what techniques or attitudes you teach her. If she knows that her men will not welcome her talents she is going to proceed timidly. Put any gifted child at the keyboard, train her, and exhort her six hours a day. But let it be borne in on her that there never has been in recorded music a first-rate female composer, that no man will consider her work without condescension, and, worst of all, that within herself she may provoke conflicts that she cannot hope to surmount, and you may get results, but they won't be Beethoven.[53]

Trude Rittman was an important role model for many women like Margaret Harris, Karen Gustafson, and Mary Rodgers who sought careers as composers, conductors, arrangers and musical directors: Elizabeth (Fermgen) Williams, the rehearsal pianist for *Sunset Boulevard* and *Miss Saigon* and replacement Assistant Conductor for *Les Miserables* and the revival of *Dreamgirls* who later moved into a producing career; Liza Redfield, the Musical Director of *Charlie and Algernon* and *Good News*; Yolanda Segovia, the replacement conductor for *Aida* and the original Musical Director of *Dreamgirls*; Linda Twine, the Musical Director of *A Year With Frog and Toad* and Musical Director and Conductor of *Jelly's Last Jam* and *Big River*; and of course Jeanine Tesori, one of Broadway's most sought after composers and arrangers today. Tesori considers Trude Rittman a personal heroine and a "theatre treasure." She says, "We need to uncover the lives of women who have been lost to us, women like Trude, the early writers. These women were taught not to break a code but out came their talent anyway! They didn't get to claim it for their own, it was in the service of a male composer, that's what so painful."[54]

During an early *South Pacific* rehearsal Mary Martin lost control of a cartwheel and flew off the stage into the orchestra pit. Everyone rushed to help her up and, shaken but unhurt, Martin returned to the stage to continue the rehearsal. It was several minutes before Oscar Hammerstein noticed that Rittman was slumped over the piano, unconscious, knocked out cold by Martin's fall.[55] This story seems the perfect metaphor for the career of Trude Rittman who was one of the women, behind the men, who made the American musical. The image of her lying stretched out across the piano keys evokes her exhaustive work ethic; the fact that no one noticed she was hurt until well after the star had been taken care of reflects the shameful invisibility of this remarkable composer, orchestrator and arranger.

Agnes de Mille once said that Rittman would fight for everyone but herself. It is telling that those who have championed Trude Rittman are other women, many of whom also struggled to succeed in a male dominated profession. Agnes de Mille, Mary Rodgers, and Jeanine Tesori have each, in their own way, fought to bring Rittman the financial and professional compensation she so richly deserves. It remains for young women today to build on the foundation so painstakingly laid by Trude Rittman and make their own extraordinary music.[56]

Notes

1. Jonathan Tunick, telephone interview, 30 May 2000. Tunick actually won the first Tony Award for Orchestration (not awarded until 1997) for his work on Maury Yeston's *Titanic*.
2. Genevieve Pitot, qtd. in Whitney Bolton, "Genevieve Pitot Backs Composer. Makes Musical Scores Danceable," *Monday Telegraph* 18 June 1959, n.pag. In the Billy Rose Theatre Collection of the New York Public Library.
3. Bolton, n.pag.
4. Arthur Sullivan, Victor Herbert, George Gershwin, Leonard Bernstein and Andrew Lloyd Webber occasionally did/do their own arrangements.
5. But at least one composer was not so eager to hand over all of the arrangements to another composer. There is a wonderful anecdote about Jule Styne who was working with Rittman on *Gentlemen Prefer Blondes*. As Agnes de Mille's assistant Dania Krupska tells it, Styne wanted very much to write one of the dance arrangements for the show and bemoaned the fact that "no one thinks I can compose, everyone thinks I'm a song writer!" At the time Rittman was ill and was glad not to have to write another scherzo and so Styne composed a dance arrangement that was eventually used in the show. He also composed some dance music for *The Red Shoes*. Dania Krupska, telephone interview, 16 May 2000.
6. Pitot, qtd. in Bolton, n.pag.
7. Trude Rittman, qtd in Nancy Reynolds, "Interview with Trude Rittman" for the Oral History Project, Dance Collection New York Public Library, 9 December 1976, transcript, 35.
8. Rittman, qtd in Reynolds 61.
9. This was incidental music for a production of *Twelfth Night*, not a musical version of the play. Tesori was, however, nominated for a Tony for Best Score for her work on this production.
10. Jeanine Tesori, telephone interview, 1 July 2000.
11. Many of the women who would follow in their footsteps had extensive experience with the classical repertoire, often from an early age. For example, Margaret Rozesarian Harris, the first African-American woman conductor and musical director on Broadway (*Hair, Raisin* and *Two Gentlemen of Verona*) gave her first concert at the age of three and later trained at Julliard. In the course of her career she was a guest conductor with the Chicago, St. Louis, Minneapolis, San Diego and Detroit Symphony Orchestras.
12. Jonathan Tunick, telephone interview, 30 May 2000.
13. Martha Johnson, telephone interview, 10 May 2000.
14. Rittman, qtd. in Reynolds 2.
15. Trude Rittman, telephone interview, 15 July 2000.
16. Agnes de Mille, *And Promenade Home* (Boston: Little Brown and Company, 1956) 68.
17. Martha Johnson, telephone interview, 10 May 2000
18. Jill Halstead, *The Woman Composer: Creativity and the Gendered Politics of Musical Composition* (Aldershot: Ashgate Publishing Limited, 1997) 30.
19. John Chapman, "She Runs The Show," *Sunday News* 17 December 1961, 2:16.
20. Robert Wahls, "Leader of the Band," *New York Daily News* 14 May 1967, n.pag. Billy Rose Theatre Collection of the New York Public Library.
21. Chapman 2:16.
22. Wahls n.pag.
23. Agnes de Mille, *Dance to the Piper* (New York: Bantham, 1952) 199.
24. Dania Krupska, telephone interview, 16 May 2000.
25. Rittman qtd. in Reynolds 31.
26. de Mille, *And Promenade Home* 62–3.
27. Rittman qtd in Reynolds 32.
28. Rittman qtd. in de Mille, *And Promenade Home* 63.
29. de Mille, *And Promenade Home* 108.
30. de Mille, *And Promenade Home* 64.
31. de Mille, *And Promenade Home* 69.
32. Richard Rodgers, qtd. in Ethan Mordden, *Rodgers & Hammerstein* (New York: Harry N. Abrams, Inc. Publishers, 1999) 142.

33. Qtd. in Bolton n.pag.

34. Agnes de Mille, qtd. in telephone interview with Bruce Pomahac, 1 May 2000.

35. Rittman, qtd. in Reynolds 55.

36. Rittman, qtd. in Reynolds 43.

37. Rittman, qtd in Reynolds 44.

38. Trude Rittman, telephone interview, 15 July 2000.

39. Michael Rafter, telephone interview, 1 July 2000.

40. Rittman, qtd in Reynolds 54.

41. Joshua Logan, *My Up and Down, In and Out Life* (New York: Delacourt Press, 1976) 229–234.

42. Jeanine Tesori, telephone interview, 1 July 2000.

43. Rittman, qtd. in Reynolds 59.

44. Rittman, qtd. in Reynolds 59.

45. Rittman, qtd. in Reynolds 59.

46. Martha Johnson, telephone interview, 10 May 2000.

47. Rittman, qtd. in Reynolds 61.

48. Rittman, qtd. in Reynolds 56.

49. Trude Rittman, telephone interview, 15 July 2000.

50. Jeanine Tesori, telephone interview, 1 July 2000.

51. Trude Rittman, telephone interview, 15 July 2000.

52. Halstead 140

53. de Mille, and Promenade Home 218

54. Jeanine Tesori, telephone interview, 1 July 2000.

55. de Mille, *And Promenade Home* 66. This story is also found in Meryle Secrest's *Somewhere For Me: A Biography of Richard Rodgers* (New York: Knopf Publishers, 2001) 290.

56. Editors' note: Rittman died at the age of ninety-six in March 2005.

Working with the Boys

Women Who Wrote Musicals in the Golden Age

GARY KONAS

Creating a musical is an intimately collaborative pursuit that usually involves ego-stroking, head-scratching, and Alka-Seltzer. Theatrical lore is full of apocryphal tales of the out-of-town tryout in Philly, Boston, or Baltimo', where, according to the Cole Porter song, things "couldn't be worse."[1] At this point the producer cries out from the rear of the dimly lit theatre, "Where are the boys? We need a new song!" "The boys"— perhaps Rodgers and Hart, Lerner and Loewe, or Strouse and Adams— huddle with the director, receive instructions to enliven a dead spot in the show, then retire to the men's lounge downstairs, where they create a brilliant new melody and lyric in one hour. A show that seemed destined to be DOA in NYC becomes a smash.

Whether this scenario represents reality or romantic myth, the musical theatre has nonetheless been predominantly a medium in which "boys" work, argue, and collaborate. It is therefore natural to wonder whether/how introducing a woman into the songwriting mix affects the workings of the entire creative team. No doubt "the kids" would need to find a more suitable working space than the men's lavatory, but is there a recognizable woman's sound in a musical? Or was playwright Rachel Crothers correct when she stated in 1912, "Drama is drama [...] what difference does it make whether women or men are working on it?"[2] Even if Crothers' assertion extends to musical theatre, the most talented female writers tend to be less known than their male counterparts. This may be partly attributable to the fact that most wrote either lyrics or libretti, while the composer — usually male — has tended to garner more attention and a bigger "name." After all, show tunes are routinely "covered" in instrumental recordings, whereas books and lyrics have rarely been recited by themselves.

The discussion in this chapter will be confined — somewhat arbitrarily — to those women who grew up in the "Golden Age" when the best show tunes were big-band staples and hit songs. (Judith Sebesta's essay discusses women who began their careers after 1960.) Our exploration of the female side of the street — namely Broadway — begins in the 1920s. Although early in the twentieth century women wrote occasionally in musical theatre, one of the first females to reach prominence in the field — if only briefly — was Anne Caldwell, who collaborated with Vincent Youmans during the 1920s. (See Korey Rothman's essay in this volume for a detailed discussion of Caldwell.)

Dorothy Donnelly's name may not draw much recognition today, but she contributed solidly to 1920s musical theatre. As well as writing *Hello, Lola* with William Kinnell (1926), she wrote lyrics for four Sigmund Romberg operettas: *Blossom Time* (1921), *The Student Prince* (1924), *My Maryland* (1927; book and lyrics), and *My Princess* (1927). These shows yielded such popular numbers as "Serenade," "Drinking Song," and "Deep in My Heart, Dear." She died at the age of 48 shortly after her last show opened. Although Donnelly was certainly successful, her career was rather brief, and her lyrics adhere to the operetta tradition of overtly metaphoric expressions of love. They therefore sound more like nineteenth-century poetry than the energetic Jazz Age discourse of the innovative women who followed, so that it becomes difficult to trace a line of influence from Donnelly to the women who used words to create fresher images. For this modern style, the role model is another Dorothy.

She Had Refinement: Dorothy Fields

Dorothy Fields's father, the famous comedian/producer Lew Fields, did not think that show business was a fit profession for a lady and actively discouraged her from following anywhere near his footsteps. "But I'm not a lady," she protested, "I'm your daughter!" Fortunately, she ignored his advice and, during a long career as a lyricist and librettist, became the role model for all songwriting daughters who followed her.

Born on 15 July 1905, Dorothy Fields achieved early success as a Broadway lyricist in 1928.[3] Fields contributed steadily to the musical theatre over the next 45 years. Of the eight shows she wrote with Jimmy McHugh, the first one — *Lew Leslie's Blackbirds of 1928* — is most noteworthy, for it was not only a hit, but one for which the two collaborators wrote the entire score. They contributed one or two songs to most of their other shows. (See Appendix 1 for a complete listing of Fields's stage shows.)

With 518 performances on Broadway, *Blackbirds* was one of the more popular all-black revues of the decade. It yielded two big hits, "I Can't Give You Anything But Love"[4] and "Doin' the New Lowdown." Fields also wrote a lyric for "I Must Have That Man" that lyricist Sammy Cahn deemed perfect.[5] It combines simple diction with intertwined rhyme to achieve an authentic blues sound:

> I'm like a oven that's cryin' for heat,
> He treats me awful each time that we meet,
> It's just unlawful how that boy can cheat,
> But I must have that man![6]

Overall this was an impressive first Broadway effort, even though Fields would soon yearn to write a book musical instead of contributing isolated songs to revues.[7]

Before she would get that opportunity, however, she left Broadway for several years to turn out a string of film musicals with Jimmy McHugh and Jerome Kern, including the Astaire/Rogers hits *Roberta* (1935) and *Swing Time* (1936). These films produced several standards, including "On the Sunny Side of the Street" and an Oscar winner, "The Way You Look Tonight." When she returned to New York, it was to write with a new collaborator, Arthur Schwartz, a former attorney who had written the outstanding 1931 revue *The Band Wagon* with Howard Dietz. Yet his first show with Fields, *Stars in Your Eyes* (1939; 127 performances) was lackluster, even though the audience saw rising stars in Ethel Merman and Jimmy Durante. The original plot about leftist politics was gradually diluted into a standard love story.[8]

During World War II Dorothy teamed with her brother Herbert to write libretti for three popular Cole Porter musicals, all produced by the flamboyant Mike Todd. *Let's Face It* (1941; 547 performances) was notable for providing Danny Kaye's follow-up role to his star-making turn in *Lady in the Dark* earlier that year. Herbert had already written libretti for several Vinton Freedley–produced shows, and when Freedley suggested he find a collaborator, he chose sister Dorothy.[9] The plot, involving three wives who take up with soldiers in order to test their husbands' faithfulness, was evidently inspired by a *Variety* story on real-life women "anxious to build Army morale by inviting personable privates to their homes for week-ends."[10] The show's long run may have been at least partly attributable to its war-related theme and charismatic star. *New York Times* critic Brooks Atkinson approved of the libretto: "Taking an old remainder, once known as 'Cradle Snatchers,' Herbert and Dorothy Fields have run it up into an impudent knockabout book that keeps all the performers congenially at work."[11]

According to one source, the idea for *Something for the Boys* (1943) came from Dorothy when she "read a story about a defense-factory worker who became a radio receiving set through carborundum in his fillings. To Miss Fields, the idea had Ethel Merman's name all over it." Merman's character, Blossom, and her two cousins inherit a 4000-acre Texas ranch located near a military unit on maneuvers. When an inheritance lawyer asks Blossom how soon she can get down to Texas, she replies, "I'm a little crowded for cash just now, but the minute they finish that pipeline, they can shoot me through with the oil."[12]

The third show, *Mexican Hayride* (1944; 481 performances), was a Bobby Clark vehicle in which the comedian played, as described by *New York Times* critic Lewis Nichols, "a numbers racketeer who is on the lam in Mexico City, a story which allows for a lot of good will between sister republics—and doesn't get in the way of the actors."[13] In an extraordinary coincidence, his bullfighting sister-in-law (!) recognizes him in the stands during her performance and angrily throws a bull's ear at him. Complications ensue. Nichols noted that the Fieldses "usually can keep a story far enough ahead that the actors do not stumble over its recumbent form."[14]

Dorothy's next project would be Sigmund Romberg's final show. After a career of writing songs for 50 revues and operettas (four of them with Dorothy Donnelly), Romberg tried a "musical play" with *Up in Central Park* (1945; 500+ performances), which Mike Todd opened in the Century Theatre, adjacent to Central Park. Dorothy and Herbert constructed a romance between a muckraking journalist attacking Boss Tweed and the daughter of one of Tweed's political minions. The score does resemble Romberg's earnest operettas of the 1920s, but the only song remembered today is "[We'll be] Close As Pages in a Book."[15] Although the title presents a cozily romantic simile, overall the song contains awkward lines which are unworthy of Fields's imagination.[16]

Her inspiration soon returned, though, when the idea of "Ethel Merman as Annie Oakley" suddenly came to her. "It was the only time in my life an idea came absolutely from God."[17] *Annie Get Your Gun* opened in 1946, delighting audiences for 1147 performances.[18] Although the show's star and hit-filled Irving Berlin score certainly accounted for much of its popularity, Herbert and Dorothy's contribution was also fine. It introduced a variety of characters efficiently and kept propelling the story toward the next memorable song.[19] For example, when Annie meets fellow sharpshooter Frank Butler, the libretto conveys their mutual attraction and competitiveness efficiently:

> ANNIE: [...] I don't shoot like a girl. I shoot like a man.
>
> FRANK: Pretty set on yourself, ain't you?
>
> ANNIE: 'Bout that I am. (Wilts again as she turns to Frank) But soon's I try to shine up to folks, (she tries to shine up to him) I'm gawky as a scrub oak. (Fishing) Ain't I?
>
> FRANK: Oh I don't know. I seen worse than you.

He actually admits to liking her but complains, "You're not enough woman for me," i.e., not feminine enough.[20] This guarded conversation leads naturally into two Berlin songs that flesh out their respective thoughts: "The Girl That I Marry" and "You Can't Get a Man with a Gun." From a feminist perspective, the theme is problematic, as Annie *does* get her man with a gun — by intentionally losing her climactic shooting contest with Frank. It should be noted that this outcome paralleled the recent return of Rosie the Riveter and all her co-workers to their kitchens, after their G.I. husbands returned home victorious.

In the wake of this phenomenal success, Fields's next musical, *Arms and the Girl* (1950; 134 performances) failed to come close to *Annie*'s success, despite featuring another independent, spunky female character, this one participating in the Revolutionary War. Brooks Atkinson said that the "spy-and-lover story [...] is not conspicuous for originality. In craftsmanship and point of view it is closer to 'The Student Prince' than [the Fieldses] probably intended."[21] Nor was he impressed with the plot device of bundling, which elicited "titillated snickers over one of the minor household customs of our practical ancestors."[22] The score by Morton Gould and Dorothy yielded no memorable songs, although Pearl Bailey, playing an escaped slave, had two numbers that showcased her talent. As in *Blackbirds*, Fields showed an ability to write intelligent lyrics in a black idiom.

As 1951 approached, Fields was midway through her theatrical career. She had gone through several winning streaks, including revues with McHugh, films with Kern, and musical comedies with Porter. In her remaining 23 years, she would complete five more shows (two each with Schwartz and Cy Coleman), four of which would rank among her finest works. The first of these, *A Tree Grows in Brooklyn* (1951; 270 performances), struggled to compete against such blockbusters as *Guys and Dolls* and *The King and I* (not to mention such holdovers as *South Pacific* and *Kiss Me, Kate*). Betty Smith's *roman à clef* of a girl Francie and her loving but alcoholic father Johnny was adapted first as a 1945 film, then as a musical by Smith and George Abbott.[23] In the latter version, however, the emphasis shifted to Johnny, who is doomed to failure by drink, and his patient wife Katie, with Francie not appearing until Act II. As has been noted, this story of a ne'er-do-well who dies,

Dorothy Fields enjoyed a long, successful career as a lyricist and librettist (courtesy the David Lahm Archive).

leaving a wife and daughter behind, bears similarities to *Carousel*,[24] without duplicating its success. But like the rarely revived *House of Flowers* and *The Golden Apple*, *A Tree Grows in Brooklyn*, which included Shirley Booth in the cast as Cissy, is a 1950s treasure with a great score that continues to attract admirers primarily through its original cast album. The lyrics provide a sparkling showcase for Fields's ready wit and ability to write clear, believable lines for inarticulate characters.[25]

By the Beautiful Sea (1954), also written with Schwartz and starring Booth, suffers by comparison with *Tree*, even though the original productions ran an equal number of performances. The time period is similar, as is the setting — Coney Island. Booth's character, Lottie, falls in love with one of her roomers; in perhaps the show's best number, "Alone Too Long," he confesses that he is rusty in romance. He expresses simply his fears over kissing her, mainly in monosyllabic words, a technique which conveys the character's awkward sincerity. Elsewhere, however, the score lacked the inspiration of the pair's work three years earlier.

Although both of these shows with Schwartz were built around a charismatic female star, neither strayed far from 1950s traditional values of women depending on sometimes-undependable men.[26] In her next show, *Redhead* (1959; 455 performances), Fields wrote lyrics and co-wrote the book for another female star, Gwen Verdon.[27] *Redhead* was yet another period piece, this time taking place in 1907 London. The plot involved apparitions and a wax museum and was loosely based on Jack the Ripper. (Yes, it *is* a musical comedy.) Interestingly, Fields wrote the liner notes for the original cast album, in which she offered an "unprejudiced" comment on the show: "It's absolutely great! Could anyone be more objective than that?"[28] Protagonist Essie has never had a date, and she longs for a husband: "The Right Finger of My Left Hand / Is the lonesomest place in town":

> You'd think someone quarantined it,
> It's a sort of a no-man's land.
> Oh wouldn't I swoon if some afternoon
> I found a small gold band
> On the light finger, the white finger,
> The right finger of my lone left hand.

The end rhyme in alternating lines is supplemented by internal rhymes that show off Fields's verbal skills.

After her first date with Tom, he sings "My Girl Is Just Enough Woman for Me,"[29] a lilting song with a rather sexist, albeit clever, lyric:

> She's so feminine, she clings so well,
> She wears all those silly, frilly things so well,
> Her posterior, superior.

A manuscript draft is even more explicit, containing the lines, "My girl's wonderful!/ Unbeatable/ Like peaches and cream/ This dream is eatable!"[30] The latter two lines were crossed out, presumably by Fields.

In the end Essie and Tom try to mediate their differences in "I'll Try," in which each says the other deserves a great partner. Yet traditional gender roles manage to sneak into their peppy duet, as Tom promises to tell Essie where he has spent nights he does not come home. He also pledges to do his part in producing a baby.

As Fields admits, "This record cannot demonstrate the superb direction and choreography of Bob Fosse"[31] (nor does it illuminate the suspenseful elements of the plot); indeed, *Redhead* is remembered today primarily for Fosse's staging and Verdon's performance. Yet even if the show is remembered primarily for its star and director, the score repays repeated listenings, because Fields presents an old-fashioned romance with evocative lyrics.

Seven years passed before Fields returned to Broadway, writing lyrics for another Fosse/Verdon hit, *Sweet Charity* (1966; 608 performances). The show remains popular today, partly because of the score's freshness, as well as some solid comedy by librettist Neil Simon. Although the protagonist Charity Hope Valentine suffers from masochistic tendencies toward the men in her life, she shows her independent, optimistic spirit when she sings "If My Friends Could See Me Now," "Traipsing 'round this/ Million-dollar chicken coop"—i.e., the closet of a famous movie director's hotel room.[32]

Even though Charity is a dance-hall hostess who has been around the floor a few times, she has the same insecurities that most of us have. Stuck in an elevator with the shy, claustrophobic Oscar, she sings "I'm the Bravest Individual" to fortify his (and her) courage.[33] Later, Oscar takes Charity to a meeting at his "church of the month." "The Rhythm of Life" is an effective song because on one level it lampoons the Hippie-inspired religions that emerged during the 1960s, while also genuinely seducing the audience with its hypnotic chant that repeats key words:

> And the rhythm of life
> Is a powerful beat,
> Puts a tingle in your fingers
> And a tingle in your feet,
> Rhythm in your bedroom,
> Rhythm in the street.
> Yes, the rhythm of life
> Is a powerful beat![34]

Once again Fields repeats key words, this time to mesmerize the listener with a lyrical chant (supported by Coleman's syncopated melody). Although romance develops between the two, Oscar can neither forgive nor forget Charity's past, and they part in a bittersweet, believable ending.

At age 61, Fields revealed in *Sweet Charity* a hip, youthful side that meshed well with the jazz sophistication of her young collaborator, Cy Coleman. Her output may have been trailing off in quantity, but not in quality. Although another seven years would pass before they reached Broadway again, Fields and

Coleman were busily working in 1970 on a musical biography of Eleanor Roosevelt. It appears that Fields and Coleman wrote a nearly complete score for the unproduced *Eleanor*, including several evocative lyrics. In "The Women's Emancipation Proclamation," FDR argues passionately for women's suffrage:

> We will not *bend* or bow!
> We'll chain ourselves to buildings!
> We'll march! We'll go to jail!
> But the Women's Emancipation Movement
> Will prevail![35]

In a quieter moment, Eleanor assesses her looks and her prospects with Franklin:

> I open my eyes [...]
> What do I see?
> One foolish face belonging to me [...]
> What a wonderful waste of time
> Love can be.[36]

The lyric rings true with what we know about Eleanor, the public figure who would marry her charismatic but sexually uninterested cousin. If any lyricist was qualified to speak for the most admired woman in postwar America, it was Dorothy Fields. Unfortunately, this was not to be; for whatever reason, the project was never completed.

Instead, Fields and Coleman had one final Broadway fling together with *Seesaw* (1973; 296 performances). Like *Sweet Charity*, this show was controlled by a strong director/choreographer (Michael Bennett), and it featured a romance between a quirky young woman and an ultimately unavailable man. Village denizen Gittel Mosca seems a mismatch for Jerry Ryan; after all, he is a WASP lawyer from Omaha, and she's a Jewish dancer who's a klutz, as she makes clear in the charming "Nobody Does It Like Me":

> If there's a wrong bell I ring it
> A wrong note I sing it
> Nobody does it like me
> If there's a problem I duck it
> I don't solve it I just muck it up [...]
> And so I try to be a lady
> I'm no lady, I'm a fraud
> When I talk like I'm a lady
> What I sound like is a broad.[37]

The monosyllabic rhymes are consistent with Gittel's lack of sophistication; moreover, a slight melodic pause before "muck" might lead the listener to expect a more explicit rhyme for "duck." Throughout the song the lyricist manages to wink confidently at us while remaining sympathetic to the insecure character singing the song.

In another song, Jerry finds her "A Lovable Lunatic"—though he never says "I love you" until the closing scene, when he leaves Gittel to return to his estranged wife. Gittel is devastated, but as the curtain descends she under-stands in the title song that love does indeed have the ups and downs of a see-saw, and it's a game that only works with two persons. The lyric draws upon the writer's half century of accumulated experience and wisdom.

On 28 March 1974, one year after *Seesaw* opened, Dorothy Fields died in New York. She leaves behind a series of memorable protagonists. They tend to cling to men who will eventually hurt them, but they survive. Fields touched audiences and influenced songwriting women — as well as men — who followed her. For example, in the mid 1940s she invited Frank Loesser to join her back-stage at *Up in Central Park*. At the time he was, as he described it, "on my way to becoming the most highly paid songwriter in film." She nevertheless admon-ished him, "Frankie, you must get into show business."[38] He took her advice and wrote *Guys and Dolls*, among other great musicals, becoming a mentor to young theatrical songwriters himself. Just as Frances Marion showed in the 1910s that a woman could write screenplays along with the best men in Holly-wood, Fields was a Broadway professional who gained the respect of her male collaborators. She definitely had refinement.

Lucky to Be Me: Betty Comden

Any discussion of Betty Comden must begin with the disclaimer that she has been joined at the pen with Adolph Green for over 60 years, which makes it impossible to separate her contributions to musical theatre from those of her partner. We can only review their considerable body of work and assume that half of it came from Comden. Betty Cohen was born in Brooklyn in 1917[39] and graduated with a Bachelor of Science in drama from New York University in 1938. Later that year she formed The Revuers, a nightclub act, with Green, Judith Tuvim (Judy Holliday), Al Hammer, and John Frank.[40]

Even though Comden and Green (hereafter, C&G) have been savvy writer/performers and practically define the term "show-business veterans" (having collaborated during seven decades of the twentieth century), their work has meshed with the classical world too. Most notably, they wrote two of their most successful shows with Leonard Bernstein. It should be noted, too, that three of their other collaborators— Jules Styne, Morton Gould, and Cy Coleman — were classically trained pianists who started as child prodigies before pursuing pop-ular music. This collective interest in highbrow culture has, as we shall see, often been reflected in their musicals. More obviously, C&G shows and films tend to take place in the big city (usually New York, sometimes Los Angeles), and some aspect of show business is often a theme in their work.

See Appendix 2 for a complete list of Comden and Green's stage musicals. In addition to completing the 18 musicals listed, they have written many film musicals, and they worked on several uncompleted projects, including *Straws in the Wind* (Coleman; workshop production), *The Singing Ghost* (Styne), *Skin of Our Teeth* (Bernstein), *Sunset Blvd.*, and *Tucker.*

On the Town (1944; 463 performances) represents C&G's Broadway debut as both lyricists and performers. It is a male-oriented show, as three sailors on leave have one day to absorb as many of the sights, sounds, and women of "New York, New York, a hell of a town" as possible. Ozzie (Green) meets anthropologist Claire de Loon (Comden), who admires his "sub-super-dolicocephalic" head. The latter's name is, of course, a loony homonym of Debussy's famous work. Chip is picked up (literally and figuratively) by cabby Hildy, whose full name, Brunhilde Esterhazy, evokes the memories of both Wagner's *Walküre* and Haydn's patron. She aggressively attempts to seduce the naïve sailor in "My Place," which refers to numerous New York attractions, past and present. (The fast-paced "list song" would become a C&G staple.)

The plot centers on Gabey's search for Ivy Smith, a.k.a. Miss Turnstiles, with whose picture he has fallen in love. Although the musical-comedy conventions are followed by having Gabey ultimately winning over Ivy, the fact that the sailors must return to their ship without knowing whether they will ever see their women again creates a bittersweet ending. Two of the best songs in the score, "Lonely Town" and "Lucky to Be Me," counterbalance the silliness of the plot and lend wistful substance to the show, making it more than World War II escapist fare.[41] The talents of Broadway newcomers Bernstein, Comden & Green, and director/choreographer Jerome Robbins combined to make *On the Town* a historically notable musical. In 1998, a New York Encores! concert staging of the show proved so popular that George C. Wolfe and the New York Shakespeare Festival mounted a full-scale Broadway revival, which surprisingly failed.

C&G's next two shows fell well short of *On the Town*'s success. In *Billion Dollar Baby* (1945; 220 performances) they collaborated with Morton Gould, who, like Leonard Bernstein, was known primarily as a classical music composer, pianist, and conductor.[42] In this musical, the main character, Maribelle, is a newly crowned Miss New York from Staten Island. The Miss America pageant — which she loses — receives a satirical treatment reminiscent of the contests shown in Carolyn Leigh's *Smile* (see below). Maribelle reveals her pseudo-sophistication and avarice when she sings that

> [...] when I win I will be
> The wife of some romantic French Marquis
> I'll live in several chateaus [sic]
> And I'll have a flock of gigolos
> And everyone will wish they were me.[43]

While Maribelle may be a bit dull-witted, the rhymes are anything but. The juxtaposition of a mispronounced "chateaux" and "gigolos" would impress the most experienced wordsmith.

The plot of C&G's original libretto involves a bootlegger and an honest suitor, as well as a dance marathon. Act I ends with "A Lovely Girl," which would be a sweet song, except that a character is shot dead offstage during the number. Also, despite such sincerely titled songs as "Dreams Come True," "Speaking of Pals," and "I'm Sure of Your Love," C&G subvert the standard musical-comedy pattern by having Maribelle choose the wealthy Montague over nice-guy Rocky. The show has a darkly comic ending too. Just as Maribelle and Montague marry, the stock market crashes, wiping him out. Blissfully unaware, Maribelle throws bracelets to her wedding guests, and the curtain comes down with Montague madly scrambling to stop her.

Even though Jerome Robbins supplied an energetic "Charleston" dance,[44] *Billion Dollar Baby* failed to sustain a long run. As Alice Robinson points out, "Some of the critics called the social-climbing heroine a female Pal Joey."[45] Perhaps critics and audiences in 1945 were unwilling to embrace a she-heel lead character, just as *Pal Joey* (1940) was initially reviled because of its unsympathetic protagonist Joey Evans, only to gain popularity a decade later. In 1980, Comden described the musical as being "a *succes d'estime*, which means it didn't run very long," while Green felt that, by combining a dark theme with entertainment, the show had a lasting effect on producer/director Hal Prince.[46]

Though not a hit, *Billion Dollar Baby* was *South Pacific* compared to *Bonanza Bound!* (1947; closed in Philadelphia), for which MGM stalwart Saul Chaplin wrote the music. The 1898 Alaska Gold Rush plot involved shady commerce, social climbing, and show business (with Green playing a touring vaudevillian named Leonardo Da Vinci), all of which are characteristic C&G concerns. Comden explains that the song "Inspiration," which describes the women behind several great men, is one "we might have written a little differently today. But after all, we all know that behind every great and famous man, you must always look for the little woman who's really responsible for the whole thing." For example, when Rimsky-Korsakov is unable to come up with a musical idea, his wife suggests that he relax and look at the trees, flowers, and bees in the back yard. This advice inspires him to write "Flight of the Bumble Bee."[47]

The pair fared somewhat better in 1951 with their revue *Two on the Aisle* (281 performances). Most notably, this show marked the first of nine collaborations with Jule Styne. Probably the most amusing song, and one exploiting the songwriters' interest in mixing highbrow music with show biz, was "Catch Our Act at the Met." The lyric quotes a headline assessing a production of *Der Fledermaus* at the Metropolitan Opera: "*Variety* says, 'Mouse Packs House'"; Donizetti is referred to as "Don Ameche," and so on.

After nine years of moderate-at-best success on Broadway following *On the Town*, the pair was no doubt eager to collaborate again with their old friend Leonard Bernstein on *Wonderful Town* (1953; 559 performances), even though they were given only four weeks to write the score. This hit, which tells the story of sisters Ruth and Eileen moving from Ohio to Greenwich Village, gave Betty Comden her best opportunity to date to express herself as a woman. The star was brash, talented Rosalind Russell, who was uniquely qualified to sell such songs as "One Hundred Easy Ways To Lose":

> He takes you to a baseball game,
> You sit knee to knee —
> He says, "The next man up at bat will bunt, you'll see."
> Don't say, "Oooh, what's a bunt? This game's too hard for little me."
> *(Spoken)*
> Just say "Bunt? Are you nuts?!! With no outs and two men on base, and a
> left-handed batter coming up, you'll walk right into a triple play just like
> it happened in the fifth game of the World Series in 1923."
> *(Sung)*
> That's a sure way to lose a man.[48]

The song depicts Ruth's free-speaking urges that must be suppressed if she is ever to catch a husband in the Big Apple. Like *On the Town, Wonderful Town* is as much about "the town" (New York) as its newcomers, but in this case the women remain independent and conquer the city, not just a man.

C&G's next assignment was the complete opposite of *Wonderful Town*: it originated in California, the action took place in Never Never Land, the star was demure rather than brassy, and ten songs had already been written by other songwriters. The show, *Peter Pan* (1954; 149 performances) began with out-of-town problems in San Francisco. Styne and C&G were summoned[49] to write songs to supplement those by neophytes Carolyn Leigh and Moose Charlap (see Leigh below). C&G contributed an enchanting song, "Never, Never Land" ("It's not on any chart/ You must find it with your heart"), which established the proper mood early in the show, while also giving the show a comic edge with such songs as "Captain Hook's Waltz":

> Who's the swiniest swine in the world?
> Captain Hook, Captain Hook. [...]
> What a prize, what a joy,
> Mrs. Hook's little baby boy,
> The scourge of the sea, just little old me,
> Captain Hook!

The alliteration and rhymes accentuate the sweet/sour contrast in Hook's self-image. "Never, Never Land," the place where "You can never, never grow old," speaks well for Comden, whose 60-plus-year career on stage and screen reminds one of the ageless boy (always played by a woman) Peter.[50]

Two years later C&G were reunited with another old friend, Judy Holliday. C&G and Jule Styne wrote the score for *Bells are Ringing* (924 performances), in which Holliday played an answering-service operator, Ella Peterson, who cares about her clients — especially procrastinating playwright Jeff Moss. Besides two big hit songs, "Just in Time" and "The Party's Over," the score included a couple of amusing songs. "It's a Simple Little System" describes a code in which thuggish bookies use composers' names that correspond to race tracks: e.g., "Beethoven" for "Belmont Park." The song ends with a surefire

Betty Comden, pictured *sans* frequent collaborator Adolph Green, began her career as a performer but made her mark primarily as a lyricist and librettist (courtesy Billy Rose Theatre Collection, The New York Public Library for the Performing Arts, Astor, Lenox and Tilden Foundations).

laugh. "What is Handel?" the bookie asks. The chorus responds with a *Messiah* chant: "Hialeah! Hialeah!"[51] Once again, C&G put a PDQ Bach spin on the classics. In a list song, "Drop That Name," oh-so-sophisticated partygoers cite every celebrity known to 1956 culture, while unpolished Ella can only cite "Rin-Tin-Tin." In the end she discovers that Jeff loves the real her, not the disguised Melisande she pretended to be. The show combined a fresh storyline with a solid score and ran nearly as long as C&G's previous four shows combined.

In 1957 the pair returned to writing lyrics only, this time in *Say, Darling* (333 performances), an adaptation of Richard Bissell's novel of the same title. The plot — yet another show-biz saga — involved the author's experience in adapting a previous novel, *7½ Cents*, into the musical *The Pajama Game*. The show for which C&G and Styne supplied songs was therefore a musical play about the making of a musical, adapted from a novel about the making of another musical based on another novel! Various characters represented such thinly disguised personalities as Bobby Griffith, Hal Prince, George Abbott, Janis Paige, and a composite of Adler and Ross. The script was co-written by Bissell's wife Marian, which is noteworthy because the plot details the married author's real-life infidelity with the star of the *Pajama Game*–like musical.

The score is difficult to evaluate out of context, given that some of the songs were intentionally bad and the RCA original cast album was fully orchestrated, whereas in the show only two onstage rehearsal pianos were used. Although *Say, Darling* had a respectable run, it is virtually forgotten today. Still, anyone interested in show-business intrigue should read Bissell's novel and imagine how C&G's songs would fit in. Several, including "Dance Only with Me," "The River Song," and "Try to Love Me," somehow sound like standards, even though they are not.

C&G and Styne followed this unusual experience by writing a straightforward star-vehicle musical comedy, *Do Re Mi* (1960; 400 performances). Phil Silvers played no-goodnik Hubie Cram, with Nancy Walker as his long-suffering wife Kay. The plot, yet another show-business-and-underworld concoction, involved a get-rich-quick scheme with juke boxes. It was based on a novella by Garson Kanin, who wrote the libretto.[52] "Make Someone Happy" became an instant standard, but the score includes an impressive string of solid tunes. Although not frequently produced in recent years, a 1999 Encores! concert performance in New York was very well received and released on compact disc.[53]

The following year C&G returned to writing book, as well as lyrics, to Styne's music, in *Subways Are for Sleeping* (1961, 205 performances). This was probably unfortunate. Had Abe Burrows (librettist for *Guys and Dolls* and *How to Succeed in Business*) been persuaded to write the libretto, he might have found a way to adapt Edmund G. Love's book about New York's homeless denizens into an effective musical. More likely, the material was best left as a series of prose vignettes. Instead, reluctant librettists C&G devised a romance between a homeless former businessman and a successful magazine writer.

According to biographer Alice M. Robinson, audiences were more interested in the subplot between a man who mooches meals from friends and a woman who wears only a towel to make it harder for hotel management to evict her.[54] The score included a few good tunes along with a fine lyric for "How Can You Describe a Face?" Styne's complex, shifting harmonies add emotional impact to the lyric's graceful imagery as it struggles to describe an indescribable face. Overall, however, *Subways* is not among C&G's better efforts.

In their next show the three partners returned to the formula of *Do Re Mi* (show business, comedy, star vehicle) with *Fade Out–Fade In* (1964; 271 performances). Like C&G's classic film *Singin' in the Rain* (1952), this show poked fun at Hollywood. Perhaps because the collaborators had previous experience in this area, their storytelling seems more confident than it did in *Subways*. In its portrait of the appropriately named usher Hope who is picked for stardom — through mistaken identity — by a movie mogul, *Fade Out* satirizes such 1930s Hollywood stereotypes as egotistical stars, nepo- or more accurately *nephew*tism (six of them!), and corporate backstabbing, as well as psychoanalysis.

The fast-paced story was punctuated by lively numbers — including a list song about renamed actors (e.g., Archie Leach to Cary Grant) — well suited to the star, Carol Burnett. "Call Me Savage" lists vamps from Lorelei to Mata Hari that the timid Hope tries in vain to emulate. Burnett also performed a memorable Shirley Temple impersonation in "You Mustn't Feel Discouraged" ("There's always one step further down you can go"). Eventually the egotist is demoted from star to tour guide, Hope marries the good nephew, and everything seems great. But the show ends with Hope leaving an impression of her face at Grauman's Chinese; as the curtain descends, she is unable to extricate herself from the wet cement. Does she suffocate, thus proving that Hollywood smothers all hope? Ironically, the show, which received good reviews, choked on its own success, as the irreplaceable Burnett missed too many performances, then became pregnant when the show re-opened after a hiatus. It closed prematurely.

At this point in their career, Comden and Green had written ten book musicals in twenty years. Half of the shows were set at least one generation in the past, and the present-day plots in the others hewed closely to the white, middle-class experience of the audience. In 1967, C&G, along with Jule Styne and librettist Arthur Laurents, tried something new by writing about a black heroine in *Hallelujah, Baby!* (293 performances). Young singer Leslie Uggams was cast as Georgina; she and three other characters lived through the century without aging.[55] Each episode shows Georgina striving to become a success while dealing with racism in America. The inevitable question, however, is how four affluent Jews could present the African-American experience authentically in words, music, and dance to a largely white audience. As historians Cecil Smith and Glenn Litton put it, "The submerged rage and open, raw despair of blues, jazz, gospel, and spirituals were missing from a score that was strictly Tin Pan Alley."[56] In fairness, the title song does attempt to present rhythmic, hand-clapping gospel, albeit filtered through a Broadway sensibility. Overall, the score is traditional C&G/Styne show biz. For example, one might assume that the song "Being Good (Isn't Good Enough)" would be an indictment of unequal treatment of blacks in America, but the lyric, which relies on flight images, presents a nonspecific message about striving to succeed. While the title hints at a fundamental problem of being black in America, the song fails to develop the theme effectively.

Although the show won the Tony Award for Best Musical, Robinson points out that most reviews were negative, even hostile.[57] In 1995, Comden stated that "it was a difficult show — a very tough thing to handle." She described the musical as "a combination of a personal story, sort of a vaudeville, and the history. Some of it's very entertaining."[58] If Comden had any desire to make a feminist statement in this score, it went largely unrecognized. No doubt Lena Horne, the original choice to star, would have accentuated the race and gender issues in the show, whereas Uggams was at that time a talented but young television singer. It seems most likely that Comden and her colleagues were trying to write a topical show without straying from what they thought would please a predominantly white audience.

C&G returned to a firmer footing in *Applause* (1970; 840 performances), their adaptation of the ultimate backstage film *All About Eve* (1950). They came into the project late to replace an unsatisfactory libretto; the score was by Charles Strouse and Lee Adams. The pair had a daunting task: to adapt one of the most brilliantly written films of all time, with Lauren Bacall stepping into Bette Davis's shoes as Margo Channing. Fortunately, the libretto retains the edge of Joseph Mankiewicz's screenplay. Referring to her conniving understudy Eve, C&G have Margo remark, "Isn't she a treasure? [...] I think I'll bury her!"[59] When the playwright Buzz exclaims, "You empty-headed, conceited bass fiddle! You're just a body and a voice! Don't ever forget — I'm the brain!," Margo replies, "Till the autopsy, there's no proof!"[60] Comden's assessment of her experience in *Applause* echoes that of the audience: "That was fun."[61] Although the show followed a strong woman competing in a man's world, it ends with Margo telling her lover Bill she's glad that Eve stole a starring role from her. "If it weren't for her, I would have lost you. *(Looking out to the front with a happy grin, and calling)* Eve! You four-star bitch! Thank you!"[62] Having a man is "something greater" for her than retaining the stardom she has worked 25 years to build. Feminists and dedicated professionals everywhere might be uneasy with this position.

In 1995, Comden commented succinctly on *Lorelei* (1974; 320 performances): "I don't want to talk about 'Lorelei.' Those are my thoughts."[63] The show was a reworking of *Gentlemen Prefer Blondes* (1949; see Loos below). C&G wrote four new songs[64] that were mixed in with Styne and Leo Robin's reshuffled *Gentlemen* score, with Carol Channing reprising her 1949 role of Lorelei Lee. The original *Gentlemen* was an effective musical (as demonstrated in a 1995 Broadway revival) that should have been left alone.

Although four years passed before their return to Broadway with *On the Twentieth Century* (1978; 460 performances), Comden would later fondly recall, "I love the score. [...] The score is almost like a comic opera. I'm very proud of that show."[65] The score spoofs operetta and even grand opera throughout, giving C&G a great opportunity to play out their highbrow proclivities within yet another show-business setting.[66] Their new collaborator was Cy Coleman, heretofore known mainly for jazz and pop scores, including two earlier shows with Carolyn Leigh.[67] A reworking of the Hecht/MacArthur play of the same title, the musical presented the mutual manipulations of an egotistical film star and an over-the-top theatrical producer sharing a train ride to New York. Lily and Oscar play like Jeanette MacDonald and Nelson Eddy's evil twins, warbling through heavily ironic spins on operetta, grand opera, and art songs. In "Never," punctuated by sopranic leaps, movie star Lily refuses to consider appearing in Oscar's new play. The argument continues in "I've Got It All," in which Oscar rebuts that claim by Lily with an indictment of phony, lowbrow Hollywood that contains some of C&G's most brilliant internal rhymes:

> Your reputation's soiled, a billion shopgirls ape you,
> Nightly nationwide, a billion farmhands rape you. [...]
> Cheesy, sleazy Hollywood,
> Pitiful city full of celluloid slime,
> Ermine vested, vermin infested,
> Home of freaks and sheiks and geeks
> And celluloid crime.[68]

This is one of the funniest lyrics of 1970s Broadway, thanks to the hyperbolic curse "a billion farmhands rape you" and rhymes as garish as the town it mocks: "ermine/vermin" is an ironic pairing worthy of Sondheim. As a result Oscar's jealousy neutralizes his venom toward Lily.[69] By contrast, "Our Private World," a lovely barcarolle whose romantic byplay summons "Ah! Sweet Mystery of Life," provides layers of irony to an essentially unromantic musical. *On the Twentieth Century* allowed C&G to draw upon their lifelong interest in show business, the movies, classical music, and opera. It has received at least one Off Broadway revival and deserves to become one of the pair's more enduring works.

Their next project, *A Doll's Life* (1982; 5 performances), was built upon a classic of world drama. C&G, along with composer Larry Grossman, wrote a musical drama that tried to answer the oft-asked question about Ibsen's *A Doll's House*: What happens after Nora leaves her husband Torvald and slams the door? The creators, including director Hal Prince, chose to frame their historical story by a present-day rehearsal of *A Doll's House*, with the actors reappearing in the story of Nora's post-walkout life. Nora goes through several menial jobs, reading during breaks and absorbing ideas about women's rights. She sees what life is like outside her home. In "New Year's Eve," for example, she learns about marriage from a male viewpoint by serving affluent diners who toast their wives at home:

To her heart, to her soul, to her face like a troll,
That is looming at home New Year's Eve. [...]
Here's to the season opera box,
Here's to the bedroom door she locks,
Here's to the bills that never cease,
Here's to the girl I call my niece.[70]

The lyric alternates amusingly between reputable images and less savory ones to comment on nineteenth-century male attitudes toward marriage and infidelity.

Yet Nora too abandons fidelity during her journey of self-discovery. When the owner of the cannery she has picketed asks her to return home with him, she accepts and becomes his mistress. This, however, is mainly a business decision: through judicious pawning and saving, she eventually buys her own company. Eventually Nora returns to her husband and children as a successful, independent woman. After an awkward reunion, Torvald concludes by saying, "Sit down, Nora, we must talk," leaving this work with some of the ambiguity of the ending of Ibsen's play, which similarly begins with Nora saying "Sit down, Torvald, we must talk."

A Doll's Life received uniformly poor reviews and closed quickly, though not before being videotaped. In a pre-curtain speech, Green said, "It's a show we're very proud of. I know this show isn't over; it's just the beginning." No doubt Comden felt, as Robinson says, "especially close to the idea" of adopting Ibsen's protofeminist Nora Torvald.[71] After all, she was one of a handful of respected women in her field during a time that most women acted more like the pre-enlightened Nora. The result was nevertheless an uncompelling musical, due in no small part to Prince's excessively dark staging.[72]

After *A Doll's Life*, C&G must have felt that their next stage work, *Singin' in the Rain* (1985; 367 performances) represented a creative step backward in their career. The adaptation of their great musical film (with songs by Nacio Herb Brown and Arthur Freed) was first staged in London. This 1983 stage version had been turned into a star vehicle for Tommy Steele. Songs by other songwriters were interpolated, including Gershwin's "Fascinating Rhythm," Fields's "I Can't Give You Anything But Love," and Cole Porter's "Be a Clown." The latter replaced "Make 'em Laugh," Brown and Freed's near-clone of "Clown" they had written for the film. To rework the show for an American audience, C&G were engaged to restore their original script. But according to Robinson, director Twyla Tharp—heretofore known only as a ballet choreographer—blocked any attempts to stray from the film version, as she wanted to reproduce it exactly on stage.[73] In any event, the show nearly closed on opening night but survived for ten months through an effective advertising campaign. The show's greatest attraction may have been an actual rainstorm onstage.

If *The Will Rogers Follies, A Life in Revue* (1991; 982 performances) turns out to be C&G's final musical, it will serve as an appropriate valedictory. The show is as bright and hopeful as *A Doll's Life* was dark and brooding. This is not to say that Peter Stone's book or Cy Coleman's score are sappy. Indeed, Wiley Post (with whom Rogers died in a 1935 plane crash) appears periodically to remind us of the protagonist's untimely end. C&G began the project by writing "Never Met a Man I Didn't Like"; Comden states that "we felt pretty exhilarated, when that song came out the way it did."[74] Even though much of the song consists of spoken dialog, the lyric efficiently introduces a man who likes everyone equally, whether he be "High-falutin' gent or Bowery bum."[75]

Will introduces us to his woman Betty Blake, who is portrayed in "My Big Mistake" as the typically ignored "woman behind the man." It may be foolish to love such a public figure, but she realizes she loves her mistake. The song has melodic leaps and falls to match Betty's moods. Another song, "No Man Left for Me," tries to be a blues lament, but it sounds too cheerful to make us pity or empathize with Betty. Despite these marital moments, the show is clearly yet another paean to show biz that C&G do so well. Ultimately, their contribution to the work's success, though important, was just one among several. *The Will Rogers Follies* is really director/choreographer Tommy Tune's creation, with everyone else involved supporting his vision.

Most likely American theatre will never see another partnership remotely approaching that of Comden and Green for longevity or consistency. They have taken audiences inside the theatre, Hollywood, and the neighborhoods of New York. Time after time, they have played with the classics and created characters — both male and female — striving to succeed in a world that lacks class. As a bonus, C&G were also accomplished performers. Not only did they appear in several stage musicals and films, they also performed "and then we wrote"–type concerts, which they called "Parties." The author can attest that no one could sing C&G songs like Betty and Adolph, even though the latter was often more enthusiastic than on-pitch. Their "Party" renditions of their songs rival those of their original cast members.

If Comden cannot be hailed as a feminist icon of the musical theatre, she has succeeded, to borrow a Fred Ebb line, as "one of the girls who's one of the boys," or at least a woman who proved herself the equal of any of the men she worked with. She and Adolph Green collaborated for sixty years, a Ripkenesque streak that is unlikely to be broken. The venerable team of Kander and Ebb, for example, would have had to write together for another 25 years to wrest the longevity record from The Kids.

I've Got Your Number: Carolyn Leigh

Although Carolyn Leigh's theatrical career was not nearly as lengthy or prodigious as Dorothy Fields's or Betty Comden's, her lyrics are equally vigorous. They reveal a sharp mind and generous yet unsentimental heart. Born on

21 August 1926 in New York City, she began writing verse as a child. After graduating from New York University, she wrote for a radio station and an advertising agency, while also learning the craft of songwriting.

Leigh soon achieved success as a pop song lyricist in 1951 when Rosemary Clooney recorded "I'm Waiting For You," and two years later "Young At Heart" became a huge Sinatra hit. On the basis of this song, Broadway legend Mary Martin had Leigh and fellow neophyte Mark "Moose" Charlap hired to write the score for *Peter Pan*. They composed several songs for Martin that expressed the exuberance of childhood (whether temporary or perpetual), including "I've Gotta Crow," "I'm Flying," and "I Won't Grow Up." The latter speaks, with a mix of simplicity and subtle sophistication, for many people who balk at forfeiting their freedom to the adult world:

> If growing up means it would be
> Beneath my dignity to climb a tree,
> I'll never grow up, [...]
> I don't want to grow up,
> I don't want to wear a tie
> And a serious expression,
> In the middle of July.[76]

Even though Leigh's first stage work was admirable,[77] director/choreographer Jerome Robbins summoned Betty Comden, Adolph Green, and Jule Styne during San Francisco tryouts to write additional songs (see Comden above). Several Leigh/Charlap songs were cut, including the lovely "It's What You Believe In," which contains provocative thoughts about the power of faith and a positive attitude. Yet the song balances dichotomies ("distressing"/"blessing")("storms"/"shimmering world") so it invokes a hopeful attitude without sappiness, à la Hammerstein.[78] Think of it as "You'll Never Fly Alone."

Despite the fantasy theme of *Peter Pan*, this experience provided Leigh a real-world introduction to the business of Broadway.[79] During the next six years, Leigh wrote popular songs with several collaborators—most notably, Cy Coleman ("Witchcraft")—as well as a few television musicals. She and Philip Springer also contributed two songs to *Ziegfeld Follies of 1957* and one to *Shoestring '57*. Leigh and Coleman planned to write a musical adaptation of the W. Somerset Maugham novel *Rain*, and according to Barry Kleinbort, their pop hit "You Fascinate Me So," which was included in the 1958 Off Broadway revue *Demi-Dozen*, was intended for *Rain*'s tropical vamp Sadie Thompson.[80] The pair also auditioned unsuccessfully to write the score for *Gypsy*, an assignment which went to Jule Styne and Stephen Sondheim (substituting for Styne's frequent collaborators Comden and Green).

In December 1960 Leigh and Coleman finally made it to Broadway together with the star vehicle *Wildcat* (172 performances). Their star was TV's equivalent of Ethel Merman, but without the vocal talent: Lucille Ball. The show, about a boastful oil prospector named Wildcat with her eye on an unwilling romantic prospect, included "Hey, Look Me Over," which became a standard. The lyric demonstrates Leigh's sassy optimism as Wildcat tries to inspire her lame sister Janie:

> Hey, look me over, lend me an ear;
> Fresh out of clover, mortgaged up to here.
> But don't pass the plate, folks, don't pass the cup;
> I figure whenever you're down and out, the only way is up.[81]

These economical lines are full of metaphorical allusions: "clover" refers to luck, "pass the plate/cup" to charity, and so on.

Elsewhere, however, the score — involving a spunky, assertive 1912 frontier heroine — seems reminiscent of other period musicals with strong female characters. For example, "You're a Liar" bears similarities to *Annie Get Your Gun*'s "Anything You Can Do," while "What Takes My Fancy" sounds like something out of *The Unsinkable Molly Brown*.[82] The show nevertheless allowed Leigh to write songs about an independent woman beating men at their own games (oil drilling, sex) on their turf. As in *Peter Pan*, the lyricist also showed a softer side — in this case, writing "That's What I Want for Janie," in which Wildcat ponders how earnings from just one productive oil well might allow her sister to walk.

Wildcat led thirteen months later to Leigh and Coleman's second — and final — musical together, *Little Me* (1962; 257 performances). This story of Belle Schlumpfert, a woman from "The Other Side of the Tracks" who goes through seven men in search of "wealth, culture and social position," yielded several hit songs, including "Real Live Girl" and "I've Got Your Number." The show was intended as a *tour de force* for Sid Caesar, who played all seven male characters. However, in addition to the farcical plot and comic songs, the score includes one poignant song for the survivor Belle, who has finally become a "Poor Little Hollywood Star." Coleman's melancholy harmony under Leigh's subtly rhymed lyrics helps convey Belle's mood, as in the closing song "Here's to Us." Here again Coleman's harmony, alternating between major and minor mode, matches the character's ambivalence about life expressed in Leigh's lyrics.

Nearly twenty years later the show was revived on Broadway,[83] with some revisions to address the 1962 critics' dissatisfaction that "the show had no heart or sympathy for its characters."[84] The new version expired after just 36 performances, but Leigh left behind a wonderfully upbeat new lyric in "I Wanna Be Yours," creating amusing, fresh images out of clichés and pop culture references, a technique that in lesser hands could sound amateurish.[85]

During those intervening two decades Leigh worked on a dozen new musicals,[86] only one of which would reach Broadway: *How Now, Dow Jones* (1967; 220 performances). This improbably titled work, for which Leigh had the original idea, involves two female friends. Kate, "the Voice of Dow Jones," is perpetually engaged to a businessman who says he will marry her when the stock index reaches 1,000. One day she finds herself falsely announcing that milestone, which causes chaos on Wall Street. Stock Exchange tour guide Cynthia's problem is that she's a kept woman whose Sugar Daddy never finds the time to claim his conjugal reward. In the end, both the American economy and female virtue are saved.

The show's hit song "Step to the Rear" was, like "Hey, Look Me Over," a rousing anthem to confidence. Although the plot was silly, the score included some pointed lyrics and dazzling internal rhymes. For example, "They Don't Make Them Like That Any More" lampooned libido-sapping Big Business in a jazzy waltz:

> In this big so-called city of fun,
> It's a notion conceived by a nun,
> That each goggle-eyed goon of a budding tycoon
> Is a latent Attila the Hun.
> Oh they kiss you goodnight at the door,
> Oozing Standard and Poor from each pore,
> But the beast is deceased who would go to the mat,
> They don't make them like that any more.[87]

The lyric is impressive not just for its clever rhymes (e.g., fun/nun/Hun), but also for the phrasing leading up to each rhyme. For instance, "conceived by a nun" delights because neither big-city fun nor conception would normally be associated with a holy woman. Overall, if *How Now* did anything to advance the cause of 1960s feminism, it was to remind the audience that modern women want more attention and (gasp!) even sex.

Leigh continued to write for the theatre, although little of her later work would reach theatregoers. A few of her projects, however, deserve at least passing mention. After *How Now*, she spent considerable time during 1969–70 on *Gatsby*, which David Merrick eventually produced as a film without an original score. Surviving lyrics of a dozen songs show that her work was not the show's problem. Leigh's verbal virtuosity perfectly evokes the mood of F. Scott Fitzgerald's Jazz Age. In the following song, assertive "b" alliteration of the first lines gives way to a vividly drunken image of being poured into a jazz-wailing sax:

> Bad bootleg hooch is the scratch for my itch
> Burns like a bitch
> But it loosens the clay
> So pour me
> Right into a saxophone.
> Let me wail
> Let me moan
> As long as I go insane
> Numb my brain
> Jazz my pain away.[88]

In 1977–78 Leigh worked with Morton Gould on *Enter Juliet*, an uncompleted musical based, like Fields's *Sweet Charity*, on a Fellini film.[89] An outwardly happy wife is inwardly dissatisfied — in particular she suspects her husband of infidelity. Yet the song "Without Him" expresses the ambivalence of a wife who is dependent on her philandering husband. She has cause to accuse him and leave him, but where would that leave *her*? No doubt many women have been similarly torn, ultimately deciding it is better not to query their husbands and deal with the heartbreaking answer.

Leigh's final semi-completed project was *Smile*, with music by Marvin Hamlisch. The show was sort of *A Chorus Line* for small-town beauty-pageant contestants, with songs revealing each girl's desires and personality. After Leigh's death the project was produced on Broadway in 1986 with lyrics by Howard Ashman. The consistently negative reviews repeatedly mentioned an uneasy mixed attitude of affection and derision toward its subject. Leigh's unused lyrics show a more consistently tough edge that might have served better. Her sarcastic description of the contest's host "city" in "Nightlife in Santa Rosa" provides just one example:

> Santa Rosa sun goes down
> There's nothin' but the flushin' of the chemical johns
> From seven thousand mobile homes
> Night life in Santa Rosa
> Is sit in the tub
> And applaud if the bubble bath foams.[90]

Like Fields, Leigh was able to inhabit the minds of lower-class characters very unlike herself. But she could also empathize with middle-class characters' concerns, including parental sacrifice:

> For this I watched your overbite
> And cut your supply of Good Humors
> For this I scrimped on pow'r and light
> And thought about taking in roomers.[91]

Once again Leigh employs offbeat rhymes to convey sentiment without lapsing into sentimentality. Sadly, on 19 November 1983, just a few months after writing these lyrics, Leigh died of a heart attack. She leaves behind a body of work waiting to be more fully appreciated.

In discussing her craft, Leigh said, "Words used to tickle or paint pictures are my favorite toys." She also explained that

> [r]hymes have a reason. [...] most of the time, people hearing your lyrics are only barely listening to them. So the writer, in self defense, gets sneaky. He knows that the human ear, once conditioned to a sound, will maybe then let the brain get around to absorbing the meaning.

Leigh's fresh rhymes certainly do work their witchcraft on the listener's brain. As for her being a female working in musical theatre, she added,

> I've never felt that gender was important to the writing of lyrics or the writing of anything else for that matter. Just look at the great recipes men write. [...]

But a woman writing about and for a woman has the advantage of a constant intimacy, to say nothing of fascination with the subject.[92]

Looking back on Leigh's output, we do not hear the sort of romantic excess or sentimentality that one might stereotypically label "feminine." Her style is more akin to that of such emotionally restrained yet honest poets as Denise Levertov or Adrienne Rich. We discern in Leigh's work an intimate knowledge of women, whether they be outsiders, social climbers, mistresses, or wives. Aside from *Little Me* and *Peter Pan*, little of her stage work is likely to be heard again in its original context, but for those who admire smart lyrics that tickle the ear and paint a mental picture, Carolyn Leigh's got your number.

Brief Takes: A Medley of Other Writers

What follows is meant to be a generous sampling of women who wrote for musicals, some of whom were better known in other creative areas. It is by no means a comprehensive listing of every woman who contributed to the "Golden Age" of the Broadway musical.

Kay Swift was best known as the composer of the score for *Fine and Dandy* (1930) and its popular title song. The previous year "Can't We Be Friends?" (*The Little Show*, 1929) also enjoyed popularity. In 1952 Swift wrote words and music for the one-woman show *Paris '90* starring Cornelia Otis Skinner, a series of short monologues leading into such songs as "Champs Elysées Polka" and "Lady on a Tandem Bicycle." Ultimately Swift may be best remembered as a member of George Gershwin's inner circle who helped reconstruct some of his scores decades after his death.

Alberta Nichols, with her husband Mann Holiner, wrote songs for 1931's *Rhapsody in Black* (to which Dorothy Fields also contributed), including "What's Keeping My Prince Charming?" and "You Can't Stop Me From Loving You" for Ethel Waters.[93] They also wrote several songs for *Blackbirds of 1933–34*.

Legendary show-business personality Anita Loos wrote a number of memoirs, novels, and screenplays. Most notably, she created the character of Lorelei Lee, whose best friends were diamonds, in *Gentlemen Prefer Blondes: The Illuminating Diary of a Professional Lady* (1925). In 1949 Loos (pronounced "Lohs") wrote the libretto for the Jule Styne–Leo Robin musical adaptation, which in 1974 would be revised as *Lorelei* with new lyrics by Comden and Green (see above). Loos also wrote the book for *The Amazing Adele*, a musical which closed in Boston in 1955.

Two literary figures should also be noted here in passing. Gertrude Stein was best known for her prose and poetry, but she did write two famous operas with Virgil Thomson. *Four Saints in Three Acts* opened on Broadway in 1934, while *The Mother of Us All* premiered at Columbia University one year after

her 1946 death. In 1967, Al Carmines constructed an Off Off Broadway show from Stein's words titled *In Circles*; three years later Ann Sternberg performed similar duties for *Gertrude Stein's First Reader*. In 1960, Nobel Prize–winning novelist Pearl Buck wrote the book for *Christine*, with score by Sammy Fain and Paul Francis Webster. The plot involved an unsuccessful romance between an Irish woman and an East Indian doctor; although the show lasted just 12 performances, Columbia released an original cast album.

Sam and Bella Spewack were celebrated newspaper reporters (Bella had found and interviewed the woman claiming to be Grand Duchess Anastasia Romanov) before they began to collaborate on plays. They wrote their first libretto for Cole Porter's *Leave It to Me* (1938). The husband-and-wife team exploited their globetrotting journalistic experience by concocting this story of a reluctant American ambassador to the Soviet Union who, assisted by a newspaper reporter who also wants him out, tries various stunts to get himself recalled. None of their attempts at career sabotage work until the ambassador begins promoting pacifism and equality among nations.

The Spewacks' only other libretto, also for Porter, was a blockbuster: *Kiss Me, Kate* (1948; 1030 performances). The verbal sparring between two divorced stars rang true, as did the echoes of Shakespeare's *Taming of the Shrew*. The dialog blended seamlessly with Cole Porter's songs. The 1999 Broadway revival, which remained true in its fashion to the original, sparkled and became an instant hit.

Stella Unger wrote lyrics and co-wrote the book for one musical, 1955's *Seventh Heaven*, with music by Victor Young. The romantic Parisian story of street walker Helen and street cleaner Chico had gone from a 1922 play to a 1927 Oscar-winning silent film, then a sound film, and finally a Broadway musical that lasted 44 performances. In "Sun at my Window, Love at my Door," Chico sings to Helen,

> I never felt keener,
> The grass is much greener,
> The sky is tantalizingly blue.
> Let's tell all the fellas
> We don't need umbrellas,
> The sun's all around me
> When I'm around you.[94]

While some of the lyrics are mildly interesting (especially when a youthful Chita Rivera sings as a racy prostitute in "Camille, Collette, Fifi"), the original material may have been better left as a silent movie.

Jean Kerr was a well-known humorist/writer who, along with her husband, respected newspaper critic Walter Kerr, co-wrote book and lyrics for 1958's *Goldilocks*. Leroy Anderson, prominent composer of symphonic tone poems, wrote his only Broadway score for this show.[95] The Kerrs, singly and together, had previous experience in several plays, and they had written lyrics for 1949's *Touch and Go*, with music by Jay Gorney. *Goldilocks* boasted considerable creative talent, as well as a star in Don Ameche, yet could only manage 161 performances. Although the book has been labeled "heavy-handed,"[96] the libretto and score include entertaining verbal duels between sleazy silent-film director Max and his unwilling star Maggie. The juxtaposition of seemingly incongruous words and phrases in the lyrics of such songs as "No One'll Ever Love You" from *Goldilocks* express the same sort of gleeful sarcasm that Jean Kerr made famous in such books as *The Grass is Always Greener Over the Septic Tank*. *Goldilocks* was given a New York concert staging in 2000. Perhaps one day it will have a chance to succeed in a full revival.[97]

In 1959, Fran Landesman wrote the lyrics for *The Nervous Set*, with book co-written by her husband Jay (based on his novel) and music by Tommy Wolf. The plot involved a romantic and cultural clash between the Beat life of Greenwich Village and the more conservative uptown culture. The show, transplanted from St. Louis to Broadway by the Landesmans, is noteworthy chiefly for having its score preserved on a Columbia original cast album produced by the legendary Goddard Lieberson. Without the album (recently remastered on compact disc), the show's excellent song "The Ballad of the Sad Young Men" might never have become an audition and cabaret-act favorite.[98]

Isobel Lennart was a screenwriter who should be mentioned briefly for having written the libretto for Barbra Streisand's first starring role, *Funny Girl* (1964). Lennart's story of Fanny Brice may have been somewhat fictionalized, but it brought the comedienne back to life for new generations of people when she might otherwise have faded into show-business lore.

Anne Croswell's first stage show, *Ernest in Love*, played Off Broadway in 1960 but is still fondly remembered, largely due to its delightful original cast album. Lee Pockriss wrote the music to Croswell's book and lyrics in this adaptation of Oscar Wilde's *The Importance of Being Earnest*. Adding songs to a perfect play would seem to be superfluous,[99] yet several of the numbers nicely underscore Wilde's wit. For example, "A Handbag Is Not a Proper Mother" takes Lady Bracknell's objection to Jack's orphan background and turns it into a three-minute delight. The songs, about such mundane subjects as hats and muffins, somehow compress the plot while preserving Wilde's satire, so that one feels the original play has not been compromised.[100] Rhyme can also underscore wit, as it does when Jack and Algernon toast the latter's fictional friend in the 6/8 romp "Mr. Bunbury":

> Fellows can have a lark,
> A dallying in the park,
> A girl is an easy mark with Mr. Bunbury [...]
> So you can have an escapade
> With dairy maids and marmalade,
> And you can have an episode
> With London ladies à la mode,
> We offer a hearty toast to Mr. Bunbury.

Croswell and Pockriss made it to Broadway three years later with *Tovarich* (264 performances), starring Vivien Leigh. Six months after it opened, "Leigh left the show in a state of emotional collapse,"[101] which probably hastened its demise. The score has its pleasant moments, and even though the show takes place in the 1920s, "A Small Cartel" seems to prophesy the 1991 Gulf War:

> If the stock takes a dip
> We can call a friend aboard a battleship,
> Start a war, very small,
> Then sit back and read the writing on the wall:
> Oil up, 18 points, hurrah. [...]

Another jaundiced view of the world is depicted in "It Used to Be," a rhythmic number in which Russians reminisce about their Motherland under the Czar:

> Christmas bells and mistletoe,
> Droskeys gliding to and fro,
> Peasants freezing in the snow,
> That's how it used to be.
> People dancing everywhere,
> Gypsy music in the air,
> Executions in the Square,
> That's how it used to be.

The lyric exploits the time-honored "triple": a list of three items, with the joke contained in the third. The triple rhyme accentuates the dark humor. As with *Earnest*, in *Tovarich* Croswell and Pockriss do best with upbeat, satiric songs.

In 1968 Croswell wrote the lyrics to Pockriss's music for *I'm Solomon*. This musical about the biblical king and his look-alike commoner lasted one week on Broadway. More recently, Croswell and Pockriss wrote *Conrack* (based on the Jon Voight film), which has been produced in New York (1987) and Washington D.C. (1992).

A Non-Feminist Catering to Men: Mary Rodgers[102]

It seems appropriate to end with Mary Rodgers Guettel, for at least two reasons. Nearly all of the women discussed in this chapter wrote lyrics and, in some cases, libretti, whereas Rodgers has almost exclusively written music. Also, as the daughter of Richard Rodgers, she is directly linked to the musical tradition on which all of the other women grew up, and she is the mother of Adam Guettel, one of the fine composer/lyricists who represent the future of musical theatre.

Born in New York in 1931, Mary Rodgers was eager to escape the bonds of childhood and parental influence. She attended Wellesley College, which provided little encouragement for any of its all-female student body to study composition. As a result, Rodgers never felt fully trained to write music; indeed, the family felt that their other daughter, Linda, was the musically talented one, whereas Mary was thought to be good with words.[103] Yet Rodgers enjoyed a respectable, if not extensive, career in musical theatre. An early work that never got very far was *The Lady Or the Tiger*, which Rodgers and Stephen Sondheim had begun in their youth.[104] *The Courtship of Miles Standish* (1957) was likewise never produced, but a year later she wrote lyrics—at her mother's urging—to her sister Linda's music for *Three to Make Music*, a children's work which Mary Martin performed on the road.

During this time she was writing songs for Golden Records, having been hired by Marshall Barer. Her works included the children's album *Ali Baba and the 40 Thieves 40*, which she wrote long distance with lyricist Sammy Cahn. In 1959 Rodgers achieved her greatest success in her first Broadway musical, *Once Upon a Mattress* (460 performances). This adaptation of Andersen's "Princess and the Pea" tale, with its medieval royal family visited by an outsider, reminds one of the elder Rodgers' *Connecticut Yankee* (1927). But while Barer's lyrics never matched the brilliance of Lorenz Hart's wordplay, the younger Rodgers acquitted herself well with an eclectic set of numbers. "In a Little While" is a romantic tune with a lilt reminiscent of such Rodgers & Hart songs as "With a Song in My Heart" and "My Heart Stood Still." It carries, however, an ironic message, given Lady Larken's pregnancy and Sir Harry's insensitivity to her plight. "I'm Shy" adds a faintly Latin beat to the patently false declaration that princess candidate Winifred belts out. "Sensitivity," sung by the insensitive Queen who wants "Fred" to fail the pea-beneath-the-mattress test that will determine her son's mate, carries a modern 5/4 time signature. In "The Swamps of Home," Rodgers mocks Fred's homesickness through a sudden melodic dive into an unexpected minor chord—the musical equivalent of falling into a swamp.

This traditional musical remains a favorite of amateur companies, perhaps in part because Rodgers' music still sounds fresh, over 40 years later. Unfortunately, due primarily to problems with direction and choreography, the 1996 Broadway revival, starring Sarah Jessica Parker, failed to capture the spark of the original Carol Burnett star-making production.[105]

Rodgers' next Broadway effort, *Hot Spot* (1963, 43 performances), was indeed an effort. It involved a Peace Corps teacher, Sally Hogwinder, who is sent to remote D'Hum (pronounced "dumb," or—as Rodgers suggests—"doom," given the show's fate). Rodgers recalls that Barbra Streisand was "dying to do it," but director Morton Da Costa thought she was "too ugly."[106] The show became a classic example of backstage chaos on the road: people exited *en masse*, the producers insisted on a star (Judy Holliday, whose star quality, Rodgers felt, unbalanced the show), people were brought in to help out (Stephen Sondheim wrote two songs), and Da Costa "fled" the production in Washington D.C. Holliday tried to conceal her serious cancer from the producers (Ken

Mandelbaum notes that she had recently undergone a mastectomy[107]); as a result, *Hot Spot* brought new meaning to the show-business term "dying on the road," and it soon faded into Broadway history.

In 1966, Rodgers wrote the score for the outrageously satirical Off Broadway musical *The Mad Show* (871 performances). Marshall Barer wrote the original lyrics; however, when *Mad Magazine* publisher William Gaines, who held control over the material, heard the score, "He thought most of it stank; Marshall fled to Florida."[108] Although six of Barer's songs survived in the original cast recording, Rodgers wrote new songs with several lyricists in a very short time. Best known, thanks to its inclusion in the revue *Side by Side by Sondheim* (1977), is "The Boy From," for which Sondheim pseudonymously provided the lyric. The song is a clever parody of "The Girl from Ipanema." Although at times it follows Antonio Carlos Jobim's melodic structure, it has its own harmonic surprises that engage the listener and make it Rodgers' own. In other numbers, such as "Hate Song," her upbeat melodies add a layer of irony and palatability to disturbingly satiric lyrics.[109]

Rodgers was one of several contributors to *Working* (1978), based on Studs Terkel's interviews with average workers. "Nobody Tells Me How" reveals the difficulty of being a teacher when lofty instructional goals are handed down without means to deal with undisciplined students. The message, as conveyed in the lyric by former teacher Susan Birkenhead, seems even more relevant today. Rodgers' wistful 3/4-time minor-mode music tinges the veteran teacher's reminiscence of bygone days when students were obedient and attentive. Perhaps most importantly for our discussion, Rodgers recalls that director/composer Stephen Schwartz made changes in the song without telling her. He "decided the harmonies weren't contemporary enough, so he changed the harmony. [...] I lost that battle."[110] This happened to a woman who had been in the business for 20 years—twice as long as Schwartz. It is difficult to imagine an experienced male composer facing such a battle with a younger female director. If a song "doesn't work," protocol dictates that the director tell the composer and let him/her decide how to change it.

The previous year Rodgers had adapted her 1972 novel *Freaky Friday*—in which a 13-year-old girl temporarily changes bodies with her mother — into a Disney movie featuring Jodie Foster. In 1992 she adapted it yet again as a stage musical, with lyrics by John Forster. It was staged at Theatreworks/USA and, according to Rodgers, did very well.[111] However, the Broadway failure of *Big*, another film-turned-musical with a similar theme, discouraged any plans to try a more ambitious production of *Freaky Friday*. Nevertheless, "At the Same Time" is a bouncy, infectious song that has justifiably enjoyed a life outside the show, suggesting that the musical may have deserved a wider audience.

Rodgers' forty-year output for the theatre has been relatively sparse, due to a combination of demands on her time and limited songwriting ambition. She is a wife who raised five children, while also serving on the boards of

Juilliard School, ASCAP, and the Rodgers and Hammerstein Organization. Still, Richard Maltby, Jr. had enough available material to assemble a solid 1996 revue of her work, *Hey, Love*, which was presented at Rainbow and Stars nightclub. The cast album allows one to hear four songs from *Hot Spot*, which has no original cast recording.

The album also includes a song, "Once I Had a Friend," from *Member of the Wedding*. During the mid–60s, Rodgers had worked directly with Carson McCullers to adapt her play into a musical. Rodgers feels that "this was probably the best work I ever did." Unfortunately, even though Hal Prince wanted to produce the show, there was no contract and McCullers' agent and lawyers blocked the rights. The show later opened with a different producer and composer, closing in one week. This experience made Rodgers turn to writing children's books, and she has no plans to write again for the musical theatre.[112]

Looking for a pattern in the work of Mary Rodgers, one sees a tendency to write about young, intelligent outsiders, especially females, who struggle to mature. Her music may lack the harmonic sophistication of her longtime friend Stephen Sondheim, but within a narrower vocabulary, she finds ways to surprise us harmonically and to choose a song form that adds an additional layer — often ironic — to her collaborator's lyrics. If, as Sondheim has asserted, Richard Rodgers was a man of infinite talent and limited soul, and Oscar Hammerstein the converse, Mary Rodgers lies somewhere between these two men who were close to her. Although she never reached the heights of either man's work, her music combines Hammerstein's fundamental optimism with her father's willingness to break a few harmonic and rhythmic rules for the listener's benefit. In doing so, she "caters" to us all.

Make Someone Happy:
A Few Concluding Observations

At the end of this distaff tour of Broadway's "Golden Age," what can we say about the women who helped gild it? First, it is striking that nearly everyone we have discussed wrote words, rather than music. In a panel discussion titled "Speaking Out: Sisters Gershwin," Mary Rodgers asserted that as she grew up, composing was "viewed as an essentially masculine act," as was playing the piano. Looking at the history of classical music, one finds that both composers and pianists are predominantly male; by contrast, the literary canon of the past 200 years includes numerous fine female poets and novelists, even though many of them had to overcome masculine disapproval of their work. Is this disparity significant?

It may be. Whether at a backer's audition or a rehearsal, a songwriter sitting at a piano commands attention: the instrument is large and heavy, it can be played loudly, and it requires some physical strength to control properly.

Music, moreover, is an abstract art form that works mysteriously on the brain, whereas everyone can communicate by stringing together words. Of course women have shown themselves to be quite capable at the piano, but if we go back 40 or more years, we can imagine a woman with pen and pad being accepted by producers and directors, as long as she was escorted by a man at the piano to "run the show." As Rodgers puts it, "It's partly lifestyle. You can be feminine, but if a woman sits at a piano, it's masculine."[113] Note too that Fields often worked with older brother Herbert, while Comden always collaborated with bombastic Adolph Green. Both these women therefore had a male supporter to see them through any disagreement with their composer or production team.

In addition, music tends to be a more high-profile product than lyrics, and certainly more so than a libretto. People are much more likely to hum a melody of a song they have heard than to remember the lyrics. In the male-dominated environment of musical theatre, therefore, one might expect men to stake out melodic territory, leaving their female collaborator to scribble words on a legal pad — even though lyrics are equally important to a song's success. Given this condition, as well as female literary models dating back to Jane Austen, most women of the Golden Age unsurprisingly gravitated toward the more accepted activity of writing words.

This is not to say that our lyricists are dainty misses. Fields, Comden, and Leigh all wrote sophisticated, candid lyrics that seem indistinguishable to me from comparable work by men. I think the difference is more psychological than stylistic. It is well known, for example, that the musically untrained Frank Loesser would shout at his transcriber and conductor until what was written and played matched exactly what he heard in his head. Mary Rodgers points out that "women can't yell; they can't ask for help" for fear of being seen as either shrill or weak.[114] We have heard, in fact, at least one example of a woman's song being changed against her will because she felt she could not demand her rights as a composer. How many times has this happened to other women writing in the theatre, and to what effect?

But women have sometimes been complicit in the domination against them. For example, in *Three to Make Music*, a show intended to teach children about the orchestra, Mary Rodgers' lyric tells kids that "It takes three to make music [...] the man who writes it, the men who play it, and folks they're playing it for."[115] It no doubt seemed perfectly natural in 1958 for three women (the Rodgers sisters and Mary Martin) to deliver this message to impressionable girls and boys.

Today we probably all agree that drama is drama, and that good writing is good writing. The women of the "Golden Age," however, had to prove themselves in order to be accepted and flourish within what was then a predominantly male profession. Rodgers wryly notes, "my music was called feminine when they didn't like it."[116] It is safe to say that working with the boys may have been difficult at times for the women we have discussed, or it may have challenged them to work harder to prove themselves. Either way, they delivered the goods, and those who love musical theatre should celebrate their vital contributions to an American art form.

Appendix 1: Musicals to Which Dorothy Fields Contributed

Show	Date	b/l*	Collaborator(s)
Lew Leslie's Blackbirds of 1928	1928	l	Jimmy McHugh
Hello, Daddy	1928	l	McHugh
The International Revue	1930	l	McHugh
The Vanderbilt Revue	1930	l	McHugh
Rhapsody in Black	1931	l	McHugh
Shoot the Works	1931	l	McHugh
Singin' the Blues	1931	l	McHugh
Clowns in Clover	1933	l	McHugh
Stars in Your Eyes	1939	l	Arthur Schwartz, J.P. McEvoy
Let's Face It	1941	b	Cole Porter, Herbert Fields
Something for the Boys	1943	b	Porter, H. Fields
Mexican Hayride	1944	b	Porter, H. Fields
Up in Central Park	1945	b,l	Sigmund Romberg, H. Fields
Annie Get Your Gun	1946	b	Irving Berlin, H. Fields
Arms and the Girl	1950	b,l	Morton Gould, H. Fields
A Tree Grows in Brooklyn	1951	l	Schwartz, Betty Smith, George Abbott
By the Beautiful Sea	1954	b,l	Schwartz, H. Fields
Redhead	1959	b,l	Albert Hague, H. Fields, Sidney Sheldon, David Shaw
Sweet Charity	1966	l	Cy Coleman, Neil Simon
Seesaw	1973	l	Coleman, Michael Bennett

*wrote book (b), lyrics (l), or both (b,l)

Appendix 2: Musicals to Which Betty Comden and Adolph Green Contributed

Show	Date	b/l*	Collaborator(s)	Setting/summary
On the Town	1944	b,l	Leonard Bernstein	NYC/ sailors on the town
Billion Dollar Baby	1945	b,l	Morton Gould	NYC/pre–Crash days
Bonanza Bound!	1947	b,l	Saul Chaplin	Alaska/1898 Gold Rush

Show	Date	b/l*	Collaborator(s)	Setting/summary
Two on the Aisle	1951	b,l	Jule Styne	Revue
Wonderful Town	1953	l	Joseph Bernstein Jerome Chodorov Fields	NYC/life in Greenwich Village
Peter Pan	1954	l†	Styne	Never Never Land/fantasy
Bells Are Ringing	1956	b,l	Styne	NYC/telephone romance, bookies
Say, Darling	1957	l	Styne et al.	NYC/creating a musical
Do Re Mi	1960	l	Styne, Garson Kanin	NYC/jukebox business
Subways Are for Sleeping	1961	b,l	Styne	NYC/street people
Fade Out-Fade In	1964	b,l	Styne	LA/the movie business
Hallelujah, Baby!	1967	l	Styne, Arthur Laurents	Various/ entertainment, racism
Applause	1970	b	C. Strouse, L. Adams	NYC/Broadway
Lorelei	1973	l§	Styne	Various/husband hunting
On the Twentieth Century	1978	b,l	Cy Coleman	Chicago–NYC/ Broadway
A Doll's Life	1982	b,l	Larry Grossman	NYC, Norway/ play-within-play
Singin' in the Rain	1985	b	songs by Nacio Herb Brown & Arthur Freed	L.A./the movie business
The Will Rogers Follies	1991	l	Coleman, Peter Stone	Various/show business

*wrote book (b), lyrics (l), or both (b,l)
†added songs to original score by Carolyn Leigh and Moose Charlap; no one credited for libretto
§added songs to original *Gentlemen Prefer Blondes* score by Styne and Robin

Notes

1. From "Another Op'nin', Another Show" in *Kiss Me, Kate*. The author wishes to thank the staff of the New York Public Library for the Performing Arts, David Hummel of the Archives of the American Musical Theatre, Anne Croswell, and Mary Rodgers Guettel for their assistance, as well as the University of Wisconsin–La Crosse for financial support.

2. Qtd. in Walter Meserve, *An Outline History of American Drama* (New York: Feedback Theatrebooks & Prospero Press, 1994) 205.

3. For a book-length account of Fields's life and career, see Deborah Grace Winer, *On the Sunny Side of the Street: The Life and Lyrics of Dorothy Fields* (New York: Schirmer Books, 1997).

4. Producer Leslie felt that the show's attendance surge could be traced primarily to the fact that everyone in America seemed to be singing "I Can't Give You Anything But Love." See Allen Woll, *Black Musical Theatre: From Coontown to Dreamgirls* (New York: Da Capo, 1989) 126. This cannot be proved, nor can the oft-cited assertion that jazz great Fats Waller sold songs, including this one, to Jimmy McHugh for drink money. Since Fields usually wrote lyrics to an existing melody, this questionable transfer of artistic property could have happened without her being complicit.

5. Winer 32.

6. Jimmy McHugh and Dorothy Fields, *Lew Leslie's Blackbirds of 1928*, LP, Columbia OL 6770, 1968 (1932–33).

7. Winer 60.

8. Winer 119–20.

9. Theodore Strauss, "Easy Did It, for a Nice Change: The Career of *Let's Face It* Was Almost Casual from the Idea To the Subsequent Hit," *New York Times* 16 November 1941: IX:2.

10. Strauss IX:2.

11. Brooks Atkinson, rev. of *Let's Face It*, *New York Times* 30 October 1941: 26. Although the show seems rooted in its historical time, in 1976 a letter from attorney/agent Albert DaSilva indicated that a revival was being contemplated. See Dorothy Fields, Papers, 1911–1977, New York Public Library, Performing Arts—Theatre, n. pag.

12. *Something for the Boys*, liner notes, CD, Music Box Recordings MBR 42001, 1997.

13. Lewis Nichols, rev. of *Mexican Hayride*, *New York Times* 29 January 1944: 9.

14. Lewis Nichols, "Pair of Good Ones: A Note or Two on 'Mexican Hayride' and 'The Cherry Orchard,'" *New York Times* 6 February 1944: II:1 .

15. For a perceptive analysis of this song as well as others in the Fields canon, see Lehman Engel, *Their Words Are Music* (New York: Crown, 1975) 81–91.

16. Note from the Editors: The author's article originally included an excerpt of lyrics from *Up in Central Park*; however, we were denied permission from Hal Leonard Corporation to reprint the lyrics.

17. Qtd. in Winer 144. The real-life drama behind *Annie Get Your Gun* is well known: after Mike Todd passed on the project, Rodgers and Hammerstein agreed to produce the show. Dorothy and Herbert were to write the book, and Dorothy would write the lyrics to Jerome Kern's music. But when Kern suddenly died in 1945, Irving Berlin took over songwriting duties, and Dorothy graciously stepped down as lyricist. The title, incidentally, was a variation on the original title of *Something for the Boys*, which was *Jenny Get Your Gun* (*Something* CD liner notes).

18. A 1966 revival with Ethel Merman proved popular, as was the 1999 revisal starring Bernadette Peters, although some have criticized the revised book as being far too politically correct.

19. In fact, a straight play version, with songs excised, was released in 1949 for amateur groups lacking the budget to mount a musical. See Herbert and Dorothy Fields, *Annie Get Your Gun. As a Straight Play without Music* (Chicago: The Dramatic Publishing Co., 1949).

20. Herbert and Dorothy Fields, *Annie Get Your Gun* (New York: Irving Berlin Music Corp, 1966) 14.

21. Brooks Atkinson, rev. of *Arms and the Girl*, *New York Times* 3 February 1950: 28.

22. Atkinson, rev. of *Arms and the Girl*.

23. In fact Smith was an experienced playwright trained by George Pierce Baker, whose other students included Eugene O'Neill and a number of other fine playwrights of his generation. See Betty Smith and George Abbott, *A Tree Grows in Brooklyn* (New York: Harper, 1951) dust-jacket notes.

24. Winer 168.

25. Note from the Editors: The author's article originally included a close analysis of the lyrics of several songs from *A Tree Grows in Brooklyn*; however, we were denied permission from Universal Polygram International Publishing, Inc. to reprint the lyrics.

26. In 1957, Herbert and Dorothy worked on "A Smiling Spring," a musical adaptation of O'Neill's *Ah, Wilderness!* that would presumably have been another traditional musical comedy set in the early 1900s. The adaptation instead became *Take Me Along* (1959), with score by Bob Merrill.

27. Had Comden and Green's 1947 *Bonanza Bound* (see Comden section) not expired on the road, it would have marked chorus girl Gwen Verdon's Broadway debut. See n. 46 below.

28. Dorothy Fields, liner notes, *Redhead*, LP, RCA Victor LSO-1104, 1959.

29. Tom had earlier sung "She's just not enough woman for me," echoing Frank's complaint in *Annie Get Your Gun*.

30. Fields, Papers n. pag.

31. Dorothy Fields, liner notes, *Redhead*.

32. Neil Simon and Dorothy Fields, *Sweet Charity* (New York: Random House, 1966), 39.

33. Compare this to *The King and I*'s "I Whistle a Happy Tune," in which Anna tries to mask her own fear by encouraging her frightened son when they arrive in Siam.

34. Simon and Fields 74.

35. Fields, Papers n. pag.

36. Fields, Papers n. pag.

37. Dorothy Fields and Michael Bennett, *Seesaw* (New York: Samuel French, 1973) 12.

38. Irving Drutman, "I Meet Dorothy And She Says...," *New York Times* 17 April 1966: II: 12.

39. Various birth years between 1915 and 1919 have been listed for Comden. Because she reviewed Robinson's manuscript (see n. 44 below) for accuracy, I assume the date given by her is correct. Betty Comden died 23 November 2006.

40. Readers interested in detailed biographical information should consult Alice M. Robinson, *Betty Comden and Adolph Green: A Bio-Bibliography* (Westport, CT: Greenwood, 1994). See also Comden's memoirs, *Off Stage* (New York: Simon & Schuster, 1995).

41. Note from the Editors: The author's article originally included an analysis of the lyric from "Lonely Town"; however, we were denied permission from Alfred Publishing Co., Inc. to reprint the lyric.

42. In fact Morton Gould was chosen as a replacement "composer" when Bernstein followed his mentor Serge Koussevitsky's advice to abandon Broadway in favor of "serious" music. Schuyler Chapin, videotaped interview with Comden & Green, 17 June 1980 (New York Public Library, Performing Arts—Theatre on Film & Tape Collection).

43. Betty Comden and Adolph Green, *Billion Dollar Baby*, unpublished 1945 libretto (New York Public Library, Performing Arts—Theatre) 1-3-10.

44. The music for this dance can be heard on *Jerome Robbins' Broadway*, CD, RCA Victor 60150-2-RC, 1989.

45. Robinson 60. Readers seeking more information on any of C&G's shows can find complete plot summaries, production credits, and encapsulated reviews in Robinson's bio-bibliography.

46. Chapin interview.

47. Betty Comden and Adolph Green, *A Party with Betty Comden and Adolph Green*, CD, DRG 94768, 1977. One of the more intriguing aspects of this largely forgotten work is that the score was recorded, but the cast album was never released commercially because the show expired on the road. Collectors continue to hope that the master sits in an RCA/BMG vault somewhere and will miraculously see the light of day on compact disc. Until then, the amusing "Inspiration" is available on this "Party" compact disc. Due to a 1945 strike *Billion Dollar Baby* was never even recorded, despite running an entire season. The score was recently recorded after a brief Off Broadway production: Morton Gould, Betty Comden, and Adolph Green, *Billion Dollar Baby*, CD, Original Cast Records OC-4304, 2000.

48. *New York Musicals* 113–14. Bud Coleman reminds me (personal communication) that the historical reference is incorrect: the triple play described actually occurred during the fifth game of the 1920 World Series.

49. C&G describe the process engagingly in *A Party with Betty Comden & Adolph Green*.

50. Mark Charlap and Carolyn Leigh. *Peter Pan*, LP, RCA Victor LSO-1019(e), 1959 (1954).

51. *New York Musicals* 214.

52. C&G stated that Kanin's friend Thornton Wilder was brought in "to help out with the

jokes." See Jule Styne, Betty Comden, and Adolph Green, liner notes, *Do Re Mi*, CD, DRG 94768, 1999, n. pag.

53. Those interested in the behind-the-scenes process of creating the original score should listen to the interview recorded on the day of the 1960 original cast record, which is included on the 1999 concert album of *Do Re Mi* as a bonus track (CD, DRG 94768, 1999).

54. Robinson 73.

55. A similar device had been employed in Lerner and Weill's *Love Life* (1948). It should also be noted that the part of Georgina was originally intended for Lena Horne, who bowed out (as she had in *Two on the Aisle* sixteen years earlier). The role was also offered to Diahann Carroll before Uggams was finally chosen.

56. Cecil Smith and Glenn Litton, *Musical Comedy in America* (New York: Theatre Arts Books, 1981) 261.

57. Robinson 112–13.

58. "An Interview with Betty Comden," Sept. 1995, 14 June 2000, <www.nsmt.org/about/round95/comden.html>.

59. Betty Comden, Adolph Green, and Lee Adams, *Applause* (New York: Random House, 1971) 70.

60. Comden et al., *Applause* 86.

61. "An Interview with Betty Comden."

62. Comden et al., *Applause* 147.

63. "An Interview with Betty Comden."

64. Although not identified as such on the cast album, the four songs by C&G are "Looking Back," "Paris, Paris," "I Won't Let You Get Away," and "Lorelei."

65. "An Interview with Betty Comden."

66. As far back as 1939, C&G's Revuers act included an opera spoof about the Baroness Bazooka.

67. Interestingly, Coleman and Morton Gould both wrote scores with Comden, Dorothy Fields, and Carolyn Leigh.

68. Cy Coleman, Betty Comden, and Adolph Green, *On the Twentieth Century*, CD, Sony Music SK 35330, 1991 (1978).

69. Although screenwriters Hecht and MacArthur were responsible for it, the name "Oscar" is an ironic choice for a theatre man who despises Hollywood and film.

70. Larry Grossman, Betty Comden, and Adolph Green, *A Doll's Life*, LP, CBS Special Products P 18846, 1985 (1982).

71. Robinson 89.

72. Viewing the New York videotape confirmed my memory that the 1982 production was dimly lit and not terribly engaging. See *A Doll's Life*, videocassette of the 1982 Broadway production, New York Public Library, Performing Arts, Theatre on Film and Tape Collection.

73. Robinson 128–29.

74. "An Interview with Betty Comden."

75. Cy Coleman, Betty Comen, and Adolph Green. *Will Rogers Follies: A Life in Review*, CD, Columbia Records CK 48606, 1991.

76. Mark Charlap and Carolyn Leigh, *Peter Pan*, LP, RCA Victor LSO-1019(e), 1959 (1954).

77. Styne later said, "I told Mary [Martin] that we can't improve on 'I'm Flying.' It's damn good!" See "What's New on the Rialto? 'Never Never Land,'" 14 June 2000, <www.talkinbroadway.com/rialto/past/1999/4_4_99.html>.

78. *The Musical Adventures of Peter Pan*, CD, Varèse Sarabande VSD-5722, 1996. Note from the Editors: The author's article originally included lyrics from the song mentioned in this paragraph; however, we were unable to obtain permission from Alfred Publishing Co., Inc. to reprint them.

79. She was reportedly not pleased by the arrival of Comden and Green.

80. Barry Kleinbort, "Not Sorry, Wrong Number," liner notes, Sara Zahn, *Witch Craft: The Songs of Carolyn Leigh*, CD, Harbinger Records HCD 1702, 1999, n.pag.

81. Cy Coleman and Carolyn Leigh, *Wildcat*, LP, RCA Victor LSO-1060, 1960.

82. The latter song also contains such off-putting anachronisms as "fink," and as performed on the original cast album, it ends with Ball's trademarked wail. One almost expects to hear Ricky Ricardo say, "Now, Lucy."

83. The show was revived yet again in 1999 with Martin Short and Faith Prince. See a videotaped performance of this production, New York Public Library, Theatre on Film and Tape Collection.

84. Bill Rosenfield, liner notes, *Little Me*, CD, RCA Victor 09026-61482-2, 1993, 13.

85. Note from the Editors: The author's article originally included lyrics from the songs mentioned in this paragraph; however, we were unable to obtain permission from Alfred Publishing Co., Inc. to reprint them.

86. Here is a list of projects Leigh is known to have worked on with various collaborators: *Gatsby, Caesar's Wife,* and *Flyers* (all with Lee Pockriss); *Enter Juliet* (Morton Gould); *Rain* and *The Heartbreak Kid* (Coleman); *The Mouse That Roared* (Harold Spina); *Roman Holiday* (Richard Adler); *Smile* (Hamlisch); *Hellzapoppin'* (three songs with Styne; closed Boston, 21 January 1977); *Forty-Eight; You're Nobody Til Somebody Loves You;* and *King from Ashtabula* (Carolyn Leigh, Papers, 1944–1985, New York Public Library, Performing Arts— Theatre, n. pag.).

87. Max Shulman and Carolyn Leigh, *How Now, Dow Jones* (New York: Samuel French, 1968).

88. Leigh, Papers n. pag.

89. Leigh also wrote several songs with Gould for *Something To Do*, a Bicentennial show semi-staged at the Kennedy Center in 1976. Three songs have been recorded; see Morton Gould and Carolyn Leigh, *Songs from* Enter Juliet, CD, Premier Recordings PRCD 1016, 1991.

90. Carolyn Leigh, *Smile*, Unpublished MS, 11 July 1983, New York Public Library, Performing Arts, Theatre, n. pag.

91. Leigh, *Smile* n. pag.

92. "Lyrics and Lyricists," lecture, for 92nd Street Y, 23, 24 March 1980, New York Public Library, Performing Arts, Theatre, typewritten notes, n pag.

93. Allen Woll, *Black Musical Theatre: From Coontown to Dreamgirls* (New York: Da Capo, 1989) 147.

94. Victor Young and Stella Unger, *Seventh Heaven*, LP, Decca DL 9001, 1955.

95. Anderson was originally engaged to write *Wonderful Town*, but he was replaced at the last minute by Leonard Bernstein. See Comden and Green section above.

96. Gerald Bordman, *American Musical Theatre: A Chronicle*, expanded ed. (New York: Oxford University Press, 1986) 609.

97. Note from the Editors: The author's article originally included lyrics from this song; however, we were unable to obtain permission from Alfred Publishing Co., Inc. to reprint the lyrics.

98. Tommy Wolf and Fran Landesman, *The Nervous Set*, LP, Columbia OL 5430, 1959 (remastered on CD, DRG Records, 2002).

99. The two chose this material chiefly because it was in the public domain and thus fair game for adaptation (interview with author, 1984).

100. Having seen the show, I can attest that it works as a whole, not just as a string of entertaining songs on the cast album.

101. Lee Pockriss and Anne Croswell, liner notes, *Tovarich*, CD, Angel ZDM 0777 7 64893 2 2, 1993 (1963) 7.

102. Rodgers labeled herself thus in a videotaped panel discussion during which one of the panelists described herself as "a feminist catering to men." "Speaking Out: The Sisters Gershwin," videotaped panel discussion moderated by Deborah Grace Winer, New York Public Library, Theatre on Film and Tape Collection.

103. Indeed, she has written several popular books for young people, including *Freaky Friday*.

104. Their touching song "Once I Had a Friend" can be heard on Mary Rodgers et al., *Hey, Love: The Songs of Mary Rodgers*, CD, Varèse Sarabande VSD-5772, 1997.

105. Rodgers says of the finished product, "We were all terribly disappointed [...] it just plain was a mistake" (interview with author, 2000). I found the production moderately entertaining, with Parker eager to please, if perhaps not given a way to fulfill that desire fully.

106. Mary Rodgers, telephone interview, 24 July 2000.

107. Mandelbaum 64.

108. Rodgers interview.

109. The editors were unable to obtain permission to print a lyric example from "Hate Song."

110. Rodgers interview.

111. Rodgers interview.

112. Rodgers interview.

113. Rodgers interview.

114. Rodgers interview.

115. Mary and Linda Rodgers. *Three to Make Music*, LP, RCA Victor LPM-2012, 1959.

116. Rodgers interview.

Designing Women

TISH DACE

A Broadway theatregoer in the twentieth century's waning months might have concluded that women do not design Broadway musicals. Depending on which new shows she selected, a spectator could have seen several without encountering a program listing any women designers. Fifteen American musicals opened on Broadway during the 1999–2000 season; eight did not employ a single female designer, while the others boasted no women set designers, no women sound designers, three women lighting designers (one of them co-designing with a man) and only four women working in what many take for granted is a woman's domain —costume design.

Bobbi Owen's trilogy surveying Broadway designers from 1915 to 1985 or 1990 (depending on the volume) lists many more men than women, but she does turn up numerous female credits for the years between 1915 (when design began to be thought of as an activity distinct from scene painting) and 1935. Her notes on the women pioneers, both in musical and non-musical theatre, make fascinating reading; they show more women-designed sets on Broadway in the early days than in recent years, a sad commentary on the status of women's equality by the millennium.[1]

If employed outside the home, many women designers throughout the century tended to work in theatrical venues away from Broadway or to design a bit and then marry and stop. Marriage and especially children could limit or preclude a woman's success as a theatrical designer. Some have found balancing family and a design career difficult, some have chosen not to have families, and some have managed the combination but have avoided calling attention to their family status for fear that male prejudice would damage their opportunities.

Despite the substantial roadblocks to success for women designers, particularly in the arena of musical theatre, some talented women have achieved recognition. Twentieth-century theatrical design would have been diminished without the settings and costumes of Aline Bernstein and Lucinda Ballard or the lighting designs of pioneers Jean Rosenthal and Peggy Clark, of the remarkable Tharon Musser — who lit so much on Broadway during the 50s, 60s, 70s, and 80s — and of a younger generation comprising of Jennifer Tipton, Beverly Emmons, Natasha Katz, and Peggy Eisenhauer. Jean Eckart and Franne Lee enjoyed distinguished careers in multiple design roles while collaborating with their husbands. Although female scenic designers have experienced especially virulent discrimination, a few other women, including Heidi Ettinger (previously known as Heidi Landesman), Marjorie Bradley Kellogg, Adrianne Lobel, and Wendall K. Harrington have dazzled spectators with their Broadway musical settings. Women sound designers have not been so fortunate, and even among costume designers, the place where gender stereotyping might actually assist women to find employment, men today dominate the profession. Yet some female costume superstars managed to become household names: Irene Sharaff, Patricia Zipprodt, Ann Roth, Theoni V. Aldredge, Florence Klotz, Jane Greenwood, Willa Kim, Toni-Leslie James, and Julie Taymor.

Broadway Pioneers

Because she began designing Broadway shows before the union in 1936 created the separate costume category, Aline Bernstein avoided the fate suffered by other women designers who could do both scenery and costumes but got shunted off into the supposedly "women's work" of costume design. Yet even she got her first Broadway design jobs in costuming. Only after she had designed on Broadway regularly for ten years (the first eight years solely as a costumer) was she admitted to United Scenic Artists after a two year battle. The union had never before admitted a woman set designer, but they had begun to give an exam in 1924. After she passed it, they could not claim incompetence, and she already had a decade's Broadway experience. Her fellow Local 827 members recognized her anomalous position and undeniable talent by addressing her as "Brother Bernstein."

Bernstein had received an early career boost from the Neighborhood Playhouse where she worked as a staff designer. Two women, sisters Alice and Irene Lewisohn, ran it. They did not suffer from the misconception that only men could design for the theatre because they designed, as well as acted, directed, and created stage adaptations for the Playhouse.[2]

Bernstein designed costumes for *Grand Street Follies* in 1925 and both sets and costumes for every other edition of this musical review from 1926 through 1929. With that exception, however, producers rarely hired her for musicals, which entailed bigger budgets than straight plays. Yet at the end of her career when she finally won a Tony, she achieved that honor for costuming a musical, Marc Blitzstein's *Regina* (1949). In 2001, The Theatre Development Fund (TDF) gave Bernstein its Irene Sharaff Posthumous Award, ironically also a costuming honor.

Unfortunately students of American cultural history will more often know her name because of her role in Thomas Wolfe's career. During the years when they lived together, she urged him to write fiction, supplied him with material from her own childhood, and helped him to obtain a publisher for *Look Homeward, Angel*, which he dedicated to her. Nevertheless, Bernstein had a greater impact on history by her pioneering work as the first woman to have a long and distinguished career as a Broadway designer of sets as well as costumes. What happened to women shunted out of scenic design into costume design after Bernstein's career represents backsliding from the progress Bernstein made.

Lawrence Robinson, unofficial historian of United Scenic Artists, observes:

> The women who came into this union in the early days had a very, very difficult time because it was a man's world. It was not until 1918 that a woman, scenic artist Mabel Buell, was allowed to join a union that had existed since 1891. An excuse was made that you had to go up the ladder, stay all day, and use a bucket to pee. It was regarded as no place for a lady.[3]

Robinson believes the fact that Bernstein had assisted Norman Bel Geddes helped her to finally wear down those preserving United Scenic Artists as a men's-only domain. Milia Davenport, who also gained admittance as a designer in 1926, similarly had the advantage of having worked as Robert Edmund Jones's costume assistant.

Once the union in 1936 recognized costume design as a separate category, women who could do both were generally hired exclusively for costumes. Thus Lucinda Ballard, one of the pioneers prominent in the 40s and 50s, designed a couple of Broadway sets, but she established her reputation in costume design, including a few well-known musicals: *Annie Get Your Gun* (1946), *Show Boat* (1946 revival), *Silk Stockings* (1955), and *The Sound of Music* (1959). Ballard won the very first Tony for costuming in 1947 for *Happy Birthday*, *Another Part of the Forest*, *Street Scene* (musical), *John Loves Mary*, and *The Chocolate Soldier* (musical revival). Towards the end of her career, she won her second Tony for the musical *The Gay Life* (1961). Known especially for her designs of straight plays, Ballard helped to create several of Tennessee Williams' best-known characters in the original productions of such plays as *The Glass Menagerie* (1945), *A Streetcar Named Desire* (1947), and *Cat on a Hot Tin Roof* (1955).

Lighting Designers

The next women to make a name for themselves chose as their specialty lighting design. Indeed, Jean Rosenthal and Peggy Clark are often said to have invented the field. During the century's early decades, one designer had created a production's entire look. Robert Edmund Jones felt strongly that no distinction should be made among a production's visual aspects. If the designer did not care much about lighting, he left it to his electrician. But in 1932 a

Broadway theatre program bore the first separate credit, "lighting by Abe Feder." Since so many designers took responsibility for all aspects, or at least sets and lights, Feder did not get all the work he wanted and eventually branched out into industrial design, which soon absorbed most of his time. As producers began to like the idea of designing lighting for a production instead of just illuminating actors and sets, they began to turn more and more to two women who had gained experience creating mood and ambiance by designing for dance.

Jean Rosenthal had been studying acting and dance at the Lewisohn sisters' Neighborhood Playhouse when she fell down a flight of stairs and injured her back — conveniently, for she did not enjoy these activities — and therefore became faculty member Martha Graham's technical assistant instead. (She would continue lighting Graham's dances right up until Rosenthal's own death in 1969.) Having found her calling, Rosenthal went to Yale to study with Stanley McCandless at what evolved into the Yale Drama School. When she left Yale with a certificate in 1933 she began to work for the WPA Federal Theatre Project. In less than a year she became a technical assistant to John Houseman and Orson Welles' Project 891 of the WPA. Abe Feder served as lighting designer for that theatre. The next year, when Houseman left to produce Leslie Howard's *Hamlet* in New York and on tour, he took Rosenthal with him as second assistant stage manager in charge of feeding the lighting cues to the electrician.

Rosenthal got her chance as a lighting designer by coming through this back door. When the man responsible for setting up the lighting system failed to show up, Rosenthal suddenly became Electrical Technical Director. After she and Houseman returned to New York in 1937, he and Orson Welles established the Mercury Theatre. There she openly designed the lighting for his eight shows. Welles received credit for the entire design as well as direction, while he billed her as Production Manager. But, as Rosenthal herself records, people in the business knew she had designed the lighting for these famous Welles productions, so they launched her renowned career.

In the musical theatre, she designed, among others, the Gian-Carlo Menotti operas *The Telephone* and *The Medium* (1947), *The Consul* (1950), and *The Saint of Bleeker St.* (1954), *Show Boat* (1954 & 1966 revivals), *Carousel* (1954 revival), *The King and I* (1956 revival), *Kiss Me, Kate* (1956 revival), *Jamaica* (1957), *West Side Story* (1957), *The Sound of Music* (1959), *Redhead* (1959), *Take Me Along* (1959), *Destry Rides Again* (1959), *A Funny Thing Happened on the Way to the Forum* (1962), *Hello, Dolly!* (1964), *Fiddler on the Roof* (1964), *Baker Street* (1965), *The Apple Tree* (1966), *A Time for Singing* (1966), *Cabaret* (1966), *I Do! I Do!* (1966), *Ilya, Darling* (1967), and *Dear World* (1969). Of course she also designed many non-musical plays, as well as plays away from Broadway, dances and operas.

Her career cut short by cancer, Rosenthal died at 57 in 1969 after a long illness. Her Broadway lighting career spanned just over thirty years, from *Danton's Death* in 1938 through *Dear World* the year she died. She also opened the design and supply company Theatre Production Service (TPS) and Jean Rosenthal Associates architectural design company, responsible for, among others, the American Shakespeare Festival theater in Stratford, Connecticut, and the Juilliard School in New York City.

A small woman with enormous eyes and a soft voice, by the time she became established as a lighting designer Rosenthal got along famously with the male electricians, her "boys." She called them "darling" or "honey" and commanded the respect of the IATSE (International Alliance of Theatrical Stage Employees) technicians. Winthrop Sargeant, writing in *The New Yorker*, noted in 1956, "Not only do they concede that Jeanie knows everything there is to know about switches, dimmers, and interplugging systems, and how many ellipsoidals to hang on No. 1 pipe, but they also regard her as a boss of infinite forbearance and understanding."[4] Sargeant quotes an electrician's praise: "'Jeanie [...] don't argue and she don't shout. Jeanie is tops.'" One of her friends said of her unusual ability to get exactly what she wanted from the technicians who strove to please her, "She's so little that you can't possibly object to her, and it would be downright inhuman to try to push her around[....] The result is that she nearly always gets her way."[5]

But Rosenthal did not always command that sort of respect. When she applied for membership in United Scenic Artists Local 829 (the eastern U.S. local) in 1947, the year she had her first U.S.A. contract, she was voted down. "It took two votes," recalls Lawrence Robinson.[6] After the union had rejected her, somebody protested and spoke on her behalf. Then when, on the same night, another vote was taken, she got in.

Mary Callahan Boone has studied further evidence of the uneven playing field where Rosenthal trod carefully because the odds favored the male designer. In her "Jean Rosenthal's Light: Making Visible the Magician," Boone notes her "highly tactful mode" of functioning within her profession: "Her role as lighting designer required avoiding the appearance of authority over the men working for her, something she accomplished through the curious fiction of being 'without temperament.'"[7] Boone observes that Rosenthal cultivated "a professional persona that echoed traditional expectations for ladylike behavior." She then provides a detailed account of two parallel instances in 1958 when designers faced a violation of their rights to control and receive compensation for their designs if reproduced in another production. Jean Rosenthal did not obtain justice or even the representation of her union lawyer and adjudication of her complaint at arbitration. Abe Feder, in an identical situation, did win union legal representation, review by an arbitration board, and a finding in his favor. Rosenthal's case involved her design for *West Side Story*, used illegally in London, while Feder's arose over the identical unauthorized London use of his lighting for *My Fair Lady*.

John Houseman, who worked with her early in her career, suggests Rosenthal adopted her quiet, non-confrontational, and meticulously polite demeanor as a method of surviving in a profession hostile to her sex:

Jean's quality of tranquil impersonality was not real. It was self-protective. She had a hard time in the theatre. There was constant and long-term and even violent opposition to her from the electricians because she was a woman [...] and show business is death on women, especially in the technical end. She had to weather it, so she cultivated a great invulnerability, along with her courtesy, to deal with this.[8]

Rosenthal herself has left us an account of this problem which closely corresponds to Houseman's, although she exercises greater tact, as was her way. In *The Magic of Light*, she says in the 30s the theatre did not accept women in technical fields, which "had remained a closed male world." She continues:

To overcome rude prejudice, I used courtesy, on which my mother had insisted since my birth. I also cultivated a careful impersonality, which disregarded sex. [...] My only real weapon, though, in the battle for acceptance, was knowledge. I did know my stuff, and I knew that the technicians knew theirs. I honored, truly, their knowledge and prerogatives. And gradually they came around [...] to honor mine.[9]

Lighting designer Beverly Emmons suggests that Rosenthal derived the confidence to function successfully in a male world, in which her gender worked against her, from Martha Graham's initial support:

Graham gave women permission to think for themselves and to do, to take charge and make decisions. So Jean took control, and the stagehands loved how polite she was, the way she always said "please" and "thank you." Men run in wolf packs, where one top dog is ordering another top dog. But Jean didn't threaten them because she said "please" and "thank you." Then the men even quit cursing when she was around. That politeness is part of our language now as lighting designers. Everything is always "please" and "thank you."[10]

Rosenthal developed a style which emphasized large colored washes from side and back lighting. Although she favored realistic lighting for plays, she took another approach to musicals: "For the spoken parts of the musical's 'story,' realism in the lighting is vital to belief. For the musical and dance sequences, it is unimportant, and mood takes over, along with movement."[11] Despite this distinction she made between spoken and musical segments, she emphasized coherence of both styles into a unified whole.

Above all, Rosenthal thought of light as a sculptor thinks of clay. When she put her hand into the light, her tactile response also suggested she was reacting to water flowing through her fingers. Partly because of her work for Martha Graham's dance company, her understanding of how to sculpt dancers in light and how to respond to dancers' movement with the movement of lighting revolutionized lighting of dancers in musical theatre.

In *Actors, Directors and Designers*, Arnold Aronson sums up Rosenthal's impact on the profession by observing, "By the time of her death in 1969 she had lit some 4000 productions and architectural projects and there were years when as many as one third of the productions on Broadway were designed by her."[12] Jean Rosenthal is the only American woman who designed for the theatre represented in Aronson's enormous book.

Peggy Clark joined United Scenic Artists in April 1938, the year in which she received her M.F.A. from Yale. The same year, she made her Broadway debut as costume designer for *The Girl from Wyoming*.[13] She designed costumes for five more Broadway shows between 1942 and 1945. She even designed a Broadway set before she landed the job in 1946 of lighting *Beggar's Holiday* and filed the very first union lighting contract. Producer/designer Oliver Smith had hired her for that show; thereafter, she designed dozens of other Smith productions. Director George Abbott also hired her repeatedly.

For 25 years following *Beggar's Holiday*, the prolific Clark regularly lit Broadway shows, over 100 in all. Many were musicals, including *Brigadoon* (1947), *High Button Shoes* (1947), *The Rape of Lucretia* (1948), *Love Life* (1948), *Along Fifth Avenue* (1949), *Touch and Go* (1949), *Gentlemen Prefer Blondes* (1949), *Bless You All* (1950), *Paint Your Wagon* (1951), *Of Thee I Sing* (1952 revival), *Pal Joey* (1952 revival), *Maggie* (1953), *Wonderful Town* (1953), *Kismet* (1953), *On Your Toes* (1954 revival), *Peter Pan* (1954), *Plain and Fancy* (1955), *Mr. Wonderful* (1956), *New Faces of 1956* (1956), *Bells Are Ringing* (1956), *Brigadoon* (1957 revival), *Flower Drum Song* (1958), *Say, Darling* (1958), *Juno* (1959), *Billy Barnes Revue* (1959), *Bye, Bye, Birdie* (1960), *The Unsinkable Molly Brown* (1960), *Sail Away* (1961), *Show Girl* (1961), *The Girl Who Came to Supper* (1963), *Bajour* (1964), *Darling of the Day* (1968), and *Jimmy* (1969). The last Broadway musical she lit, in 1980, was the flop *Musical Chairs*. Late in her career, in 1960, Clark married theatrical electrician Lloyd R. Kelley. She died in 1996.

Clark favored realistic lighting rather than openly theatrical effects that called attention to themselves. Yet producers and directors appreciated her remarkable skill. Her importance as a designer led to her election in 1968 as the first woman president of United Scenic Artists Local 829, after previously serving as Recording Secretary and as Trustee. Her stature and her clout also can be measured by the fact she became the first lighting designer to receive credit on a poster advertising a play.[14]

Tharon Musser, who received her MFA from Yale in 1950, led the next generation of lighting designers of either gender. Prospective members of United Scenic Artists still needed to take an exam which covered all aspects of technical theater. Only ten percent of the questions covered lighting, so Musser took five years and four attempts before passing this exam. From 1950 through 1955, she designed for dance, sometimes assisting Jean Rosenthal. Years later she told Jeremy Gerard in the *New York Times*, "Jeanie and I had very different points of view about lighting. I'm a Leko person: I like sharp. And fresnels I find very little use for."[15] Nevertheless, with musicals Musser did use big washes of light similar to Rosenthal's.

After finally earning a passing mark on the union exam, Musser made a splash in her Broadway debut with her moody lighting for *Long Day's Journey into Night* (1956). Because her career spanned the latter half of the Twentieth Century, it overlapped the period after the birth in 1970 of the lighting Tony Award, which she won for *Follies* (1971), *A Chorus Line* (1975), and *Dreamgirls* (1981).

Among other Broadway musicals, Musser designed *Shinbone Alley* (1957), *Once upon a Mattress* (1959), *Here's Love* (1963), *Kelly* (1965), *Flora, the Red Menace* (1965), *Mame* (1966), *Hallelujah, Baby!* (1967), *Tonight at 8:30* (1967), *Maggie Flynn* (1968), *The Fig Leaves Are Falling* (1969), *Applause* (1970), *A Little Night Music* (1973), *Good News* (1974 revival), *Mack and Mabel* (1974), *Candide* (1974), *The Wiz* (1975), *Me and Bessie* (1975), *1600 Pennsylvania Avenue* (1976), *Pacific Overtures* (1976), *The Act* (1977), *Ballroom* (1978), *They're Playing Our Song* (1979), *42nd Street* (1980), *Jerry's Girls* (1985), *Teddy & Alice* (1987), *Welcome to the Club* (1989), *The Secret Garden* (1991), and *The Goodbye Girl* (1993).

Musser introduced to Broadway computerized lighting with a memory board with *A Chorus Line* (1975), in which she also piled on so much wattage, mostly from side lighting, that she made the dancers sweat convincingly. On 8 May 2000 Tharon Musser received the Broadway Theater Institute's Lifetime Achievement Award. She has also been inducted into the Theatre Hall of Fame.

Rosenthal, Clark, and Musser earned such high reputations that sometimes people assume women dominate lighting design. Yet few other women working on Broadway during the last century have made names for themselves in lighting. Producers have declined to hire other women to light musicals, which have bigger budgets because they typically require at least twice as many instruments as non-musical plays. Such producers fear women cannot handle a large budget, an assumption which has also damaged the careers of women set designers.

Musser says the playing field is not level for women and men in theatre design despite the fact that in the beginning lighting was a woman's field.[16] Musser illustrates what happens to women with an incident in Rosenthal's career. Musser recalls how on one show "Jean was brought a bill for things she had not ordered because the electrician assumed she would be fired and had ordered what *he* wanted." Musser says she has also had to prove herself to stage hands.[17]

When she first entered the profession, Musser explains, "Lighting design was women's work. There was just no money there, and women could live with that better than men. Lighting is still the bottom of the barrel. I've been fighting the low pay for years." Yet she concedes that eventually, "when you get the reputation to just name your own price, then it can be okay. But it used to be like going into a hardware store; the owner didn't believe a woman knew what she was doing."[18]

Musser also suggests, for an established designer, that being a woman occasionally can seem an advantage:

You have to prove yourself to the stage hands, prove you know what you're doing. The guys knock you down by asking for details that aren't really needed just to see if you know, not taking what you say at face value, testing you. Some of the older electricians assume you don't know what you're doing. But then, once you've proven yourself, you can get preferential treatment. Then they aren't as willing to knock you down.[19]

Musser protégé Jennifer Tipton, a generation later, began as a dance student and then designed dances for Paul Taylor and Twyla Tharp as well as other modern and ballet companies. She often prefers to design for regional theatres, for opera companies and in Europe, but she has won Tonys for *The Cherry Orchard* (1977) and *Jerome Robbins' Broadway* (1989), as well as numerous other awards. Other Broadway musicals include *Rex* (1976), *Happy End* (1977), *Runaways* (1978), *Billy Bishop Goes to War* (1980), *Pirates of Penzance* (1981), *Sophisticated Ladies* (1981), *Singin' in the Rain* (1985), and *James Joyce's The Dead* (2000). She also designed the Broadway-bound *The Baker's Wife* (1976), which never made it into New York.

Tipton says she suspects producers feel that "women cannot handle big budgets" and of course

big Broadway musicals are very high budget. There was a woman lighting designer in the past five years who was squeezed off a musical and the job given to a man. Her life was made unpleasant. It's also difficult for women to make their way in set design, again because producers are very leery of letting women handle a big-budget show. Traditionally it was the director who chose the team, but more and more it's the producer who mandates who the director can work with, which means not only will there be fewer women but there will be fewer individuals doing the shows. The playing field is not level. Women have to be perfect. You have to do what you do, plus shmooze. And men are provided more assistants to do the leg work.[20]

Tipton, who teaches at the Yale Drama School, notes it seemed hard for women when she was getting started, then got better, but "now it seems to be going the other way, getting worse." By century's end, lighting design students at Yale were mostly men. Asked if Julie Taymor's Tony Awards for directing and designing a musical on Broadway will make a difference for other women in theatre, she responds, "No. Obviously she can handle a large budget, but I don't think it will make producers think more about hiring women designers."[21] Producers' prejudices appear to her to be too entrenched.

In hers and earlier generations, women lighting designers have not had children because "I can't imagine that I could have had a family and have done what I've done. And financially lighting designers are low on the totem pole." Tipton points out that Beverly Emmons, the first prominent woman to try to raise children while working as a lighting designer, "solved the problem by having a hometown job and not working freelance as much as I do." But for Tipton and many others, any desire they might have had for children has been set aside as incompatible with a professional theatrical design career.[22]

Beverly Emmons took the job as Artistic Director of the Lincoln Center Institute in order to stay close to her family and occasionally to design shows in New York City. She describes the routine of a working lighting designer as preventing a mother from being at home,

> except for pit stops. You can't be there for a child's birthday. If you suddenly have to work all night, you must. It's hard to have a family under those circumstances. The actors work at max ten or twelve hours, yet you're there at 8 A.M., work until midnight, then the director wants a quick meeting, and then you're back for crew call at 8 A.M. To get to be a premier designer you need to do ten years of that, but for women that's the prime baby-making years.[23]

Like most lighting designers, Emmons first designed for dance and still does so. Her Broadway musicals have included *A Day in Hollywood/A Night in the Ukraine* (1980), *Reggae* (1980), *Is There Life After High School?* (1982), *Little Me* (1982), *Doonesbury* (1983), *Passion* (1994), *Chronicle of a Death Foretold* (1995, co-designed with Jules Fisher), *Jekyll & Hyde* (1997), and *Annie Get Your Gun* (1999 revival). Emmons has received six Tony nominations. Equally at home in tiny theatres using a handful of instruments or employing hundreds of instruments and thousands of light cues in a mammoth Broadway house, Emmons employs strategies ranging from highly realistic motivated lighting to subtle presentationalism to splashy theatrical effects.

Jennifer Tipton's Tony-award winning career is proving that lighting design *can* be women's work (Beatriz Schiller).

Like Musser, Emmons has perceived a certain advantage to being female when working with the stage hands and electricians. "It's easier on the social structure," she reasons.

> I'm here on the ground, while you guys are the ones who're doing it. They can rise to the occasion of helping out the little lady, whereas a man telling them what to do becomes a sort of class thing. But nobody expects a lady to go up the ladder. In places where I have felt there was going to be a gender difficulty, I've used a different strategy, to come in as an advisor. Once they saw I knew what I was doing and didn't insult them, but rather chose to collaborate with them about how to deal with a difficult director, and I'll help them, and

together we'll figure this out, then they were eating out of my hand. The only time I've had any problem with crew is when the chief — and this has been very rare — has been an incompetent bully who discovers right away I'm going to find him out; then he runs away, leaves the theatre.[24]

Emmons speaks particularly glowingly about Rosenthal, with whom she studied, and laments the fact that "there are fewer women designers now." She accounts for the heyday of women designers — Rosenthal, Clark, and then, overlapping with them, Musser — as occurring because

> when the men figure out you can't make any big bucks in this business, the men go elsewhere. That's when the women take over. In American culture, the jobs that become women's jobs are those that pay less. So men gravitated to scenic design, which traditionally pays double what lighting does. Now, you could argue that mediocre men make it when a woman has to be fabulous to get over the hump. But if you're good, you'll get there.[25]

Natasha Katz, who got her start with the Pittsburgh Civic Light Opera, entered the profession a generation behind Emmons. She assisted several Broadway designers and served as Jules Fisher's associate on the national and world tours of *La Cage aux Folles*. Her first independent designs of large-scale Broadway musicals, *Gypsy* (1989 revival) and *Shogun* (1990), *Peter Pan* (1990 revival), *A Grand Night for Singing* (1993), and *My Fair Lady* (1993 revival), preceded her relationship with Disney's theatrical producing organization, which hired her for *Beauty and the Beast* (1994, Tony nomination) and *Aida* (2000, Tony winner). Her other Broadway musicals include *State Fair* (1996), *The Scarlet Pimpernel* (1997), *The Capeman* (1998), *Seussical* (2000), *The Rhythm Club* (2001), *Sweet Smell of Success* (2002, Tony nomination), *Flower Drum Song* (2002 revival), *Urban Cowboy* (2003), and *Taboo* (2003). Katz excels at magical, other-worldly effects and enhancing scenic designers' phantasmagoric sets, yet she has lit a wide range of musicals in diverse styles.

Katz recalls "the good old days" in the 70s and 80s when Broadway shows were lit equally by women and men. She cites Arden Fingerhut, Tharon Musser, Marilyn Rennagel, Peggy Clark, Pat Collins, Marcia Madeira, Jennifer Tipton, and Beverly Emmons. "For whatever reason," she laments,

> our business is weighted against women. I don't talk about my kids very much, and I would never bring them on a job because people would wonder how I can be working and have children. My husband, sound designer Dan Schreier, could bring them on his job. Lighting designers also spend a lot of time away from home. The traveling can be hard. You have meetings all day in New York, then land in L.A. in the middle of the night, get a car, and drive to your hotel in the middle of nowhere. That's somewhat unnerving. And it's so hard to make a living as a lighting designer, especially starting out. You have to take jobs other than theatrical lighting. [...] Women from the day we're born work harder professionally. You have to work 150 percent to make it. I have a three year old daughter who wants to be Superman next Halloween. That's the symbol of power — not Superwoman. Women who want to make it must completely understand the technical aspects of lighting. You also must keep up with the new equipment.[26]

Designer Duos

Peggy Eisenhauer began designing at fifteen and received valuable mentoring from several designers, particularly Jules Fisher. She has focused throughout her career on musical works, including the concert stage, where she has designed for such artists as Chita Rivera, Cyndi Lauper, Bob Dylan, Michael Jackson, and Whitney Houston. Typically, she designs in partnership with Fisher, although she designed *Dangerous Games* (1989) and *Catskills on Broadway* (1991) alone and co-designed with Mike Baldassari the 1998 *Cabaret* revival (Tony nomination). She and Fisher have designed such musicals as *Tommy Tune Tonite!* (1992), *A Christmas Carol* (1994), *The Best Little Whorehouse Goes Public* (1994), *Victor/Victoria* (1995), *Bring in 'da Noise, Bring in 'da Funk* (1996, Tony winner), *Street Corner Symphony* (1997), *Ragtime* (1998, Tony nomination), *The Gershwins' Fascinating Rhythm* (1999), *Marie Christine* (1999, Tony nomination), *The Wild Party* (2000, Tony nomination), *Jane Eyre* (2000, Tony nomination), *Amour* (2002), and *Gypsy* (2003 revival). They employ cutting-edge technology and innovative approaches to lighting which is exciting for its own sake. The Vari*Lites for *Street Corner Symphony*, for example, did such a dazzling dance that this lighting team deserved a Tony nomination for best choreography.

Working with male design partners has doubtless spared Eisenhauer some of the struggles recounted by other women. She also acknowledges she could not have had children and still accomplish what she has. "I'm in complete awe of the designers who have kids, especially the mothers" reports Eisenhauer. "My career takes personal sacrifice, so I can only imagine the stress and anxiety it must take to need to be in two places at once and those inevitable circumstances when one needs to choose. It's absolutely daunting."[27]

Asked whether her gender has affected her obtaining work, Eisenhauer says,

> It takes a certain progress of successes to get to the point where the playing field is more even for women. There was resistance to hiring me when I seemed not to have enough experience. It gets easier the more successes you have. There are some who come to any experience with a kind of gender issue or hangup. There are certain organizations that are more difficult. It's related to the backgrounds of the people who have the main say. It might be the producer, the director, or one of the other designers.[28]

Eisenhauer suggests women should look upon their gender as an asset rather than a liability. She includes using your smile, wearing what you look best in — traditional feminine notions — but also exploiting others' appreciation for the feminine sensitivity. "Some part of the creative team has realized on many of my shows," she reports, "that their entire audience isn't going to be male, so there should be some worthwhile contribution to the show from a woman. They want to use a woman on the team."[29]

Eisenhauer and Fisher are not the only famous male-female design duo. William and Jean Eckart, and Eugene and Franne Lee designed together on Broadway, respectively, from 1951–1974 and from 1972–79. The Eckarts, who both earned M.F.A.s from Yale, took joint responsibility for scenery, sometimes lighting, and also occasionally costumes as well. Among their musicals were *The Golden Apple* (1954), *Damn Yankees* (1955), *Li'l Abner* (1956), *Copper and Brass* (1957), *The Body Beautiful* (1958), *Fiorello* (1959), *Once upon a Mattress* (1959), *The Happiest Girl in the World* (1961), *Let It Ride* (1961), *She Loves Me* (1963), *Here's Love* (1963), *Anyone Can Whistle* (1964), *Fade Out–Fade In* (1964), *Flora, the Red Menace* (1965), *The Zulu and the Zayda* (1965), *Mame* (1966), *Hallelujah, Baby!* (1967), *The Education of H.Y.M.A.N. K.A.P.L.A.N.* (1968), *Maggie Flynn* (1968), and *The Fig Leaves Are Falling* (1969). After their 1974 collaboration on all three design aspects for *Of Mice and Men*, Jean Eckart stopped designing and went to graduate school at the University of Texas at Arlington, where in 1976 she received her Master of Science in Social Work. She worked as a therapist until 1986, while occasionally still lecturing on theatre design. The Eckarts had two children, putting Jean Eckart in the small group of women designers who managed to combine motherhood with a design career. Jean Eckart died in 1993.

Franne Lee (M.F.A. University of Wisconsin)—also a mother—collaborated with her then husband Eugene Lee. Their truly joint ventures involved the scenery for the ill-fated musical *Dude* (1972) and for *Candide* (1974). Otherwise, she created the costumes and he the sets for *Sweeney Todd* (1979) plus three plays. Franne Lee also designed costumes for *The Moony Shapiro Song Book* (1981) and *Rock 'n Roll! The First 5,000 Years* (1982). She designed additional costumes and supervised the costumes for the 1993 *Camelot* revival. Both Lees won Tonys for their separate work on *Sweeney Todd*, while for *Candide* they shared the scenic design Tony and she also won the costume design award. She has spent the bulk of her design career in theatre designing costumes away from Broadway and in television and film.

Scenic Designers

The Tony Award in Scenic Design has been given since 1947. Before 1960, no women were nominated. Throughout the 60s the only woman nominated was Jean Eckart, with her husband William, in 1960 for *Fiorello!* and in 1966 for *Mame*. Although several women from abroad received nominations between 1970 and 1990, the only American women were Franne Lee, with her then husband Eugene, for *Candide* in 1974, and Heidi Landesman for *Big River* in 1985. Both Landesman, now known as Heidi Ettinger, and the Lees, won. No other American women won during the 20th Century except Ettinger, who did so again in 1991 for *The Secret Garden*. The only other American woman nominated in the 20th Century was Julie Taymor, with G.W. Mercier, in 1997 for *Juan Darien*.

In the latter half of the twentieth century, Jean Eckart, Franne Lee, Heidi Ettinger, Marjorie Bradley Kellogg, and Adrianne Lobel have designed sets for multiple Broadway musicals. In addition, Ursula Belden, Jane Musky, Helen Pond, Nancy Winters, and Alison Yerxa each have a Broadway musical credit. Only a small number of other women designed sets on Broadway for non-musicals during this period. This contrasts to the over 50 women who designed Broadway sets before mid-century.

After United Scenic Artists created the separate costume design category in 1936, some women who previously had designed sets seem to have been restricted to costumes, and the number of women designing sets fell sharply. But something more may have caused producers to consider only male scenic designers. The bulk of a show's budget goes to scenery, so some designers theorize that explains why women design scenery for only a fraction of big-budget shows. They figure producers trust that men will handle money more prudently.

Heidi Ettinger received a Tony Award for her first Broadway musical design, *Big River* (1985), which she co-produced. Equally at home with imaginative presentational designs and more realistic sets, Ettinger has also designed the musicals *The Secret Garden* (1991, Tony winner; also co-producer), *The Red Shoes* (1993), *Smoky Joe's Cafe* (1995), *Triumph of Love* (1997), *The Sound of Music* (1998 revival), and *The Adventures of Tom Sawyer* (2001, Tony nomination). She also designed Disney's *The Hunchback of Notre Dame* (Berlin, 1999). She mentions in her program bios the energy required to raise her three sons while pursuing her design career.

Ettinger believes that the playing field is not "altogether level," in part because of the stereotype that women lack mechanical skills. She finds this prejudice especially prevalent with regard to

> designing musicals, which are complicated mechanically. Producers believe women are less skillful at figuring out mechanical problems or handling hard materials, steel and heavy-duty construction. This is a uniquely American prejudice. In Europe and Japan, far more women design sets. Maybe we have a more macho society. It doesn't make sense. But as the financial stakes rise, there are fewer women involved. Producers tend to be a conservative bunch, less willing to take what they perceive as a risk when it involves a big chunk of change.[30]

The versatile Marjorie Bradley Kellogg began her design career as an assistant to Ming Cho Lee. She began independently designing sets on Broadway in 1974 with the musical revival *Where's Charlie*. Although she has accumulated an extensive array of credits on Broadway and in regional theatres, television and films, she has only two other Broadway musical credits, *The Best Little Whorehouse in Texas* (1978) and *Spokesong* (1979). Kellogg grew up knowing, from her father and grandfather, how to use hammers and saws but has noticed that some people do not expect women to understand how to do construction. Kellogg believes that for women set designers

> the glass ceiling becomes a problem at mid-career. They're happy to have you work at the lesser-paying jobs. The entry level is pretty open. Women are very good assistants, or not any worse than men, and there's no barrier at that level. And stage hands are wonderful to women designers. The problems are not at the process level, they're at the hiring level. Producers feel more comfortable giving the big-money jobs to the guys. Money is a symbol of power. Yet I know so many wonderful women set designers who are very responsible with money. They must be, because in the situations where they work they have to make their money go much farther. This prejudice doesn't wreck your career; it just limits your access to certain work. You're not supposed to say these things. I've done two dozen Broadway shows, so I shouldn't complain.[31]

Adrianne Lobel graduated from the Yale Drama School in 1979 and since then has designed extensively in regional theatres and with many of the world's most famous experimental directors. She has also designed successful Broadway musical sets for *My One and Only* (1983), *Passion* (1994), *On the Town* (1998 revival), and *A Year with Frog and Toad* (2003). Each set employed its own highly distinctive style suitable to the show. Lobel married in 1995 but does not have children, and she acknowledges, "It would be hard to have children and work in this field."[32]

As for any possible hindrance from her gender, Lobel prefers to look on the bright side. "Maybe I would have gotten along faster in the commercial arena if I had been a man," she reasons,

> but then I wouldn't have done the fascinating things I've done in Europe. I just didn't let it become a hindrance for me. And if you're good at what you do the shop guys will bend over backwards for you because you're a pretty little woman. They'll do things for you that they might not do for a man. But you have to know what you're doing. If they smell for a second that you don't know what you're doing, then you're in trouble.[33]

Another woman who emphatically agrees with Lobel about that, projection designer Wendall K. Harrington, reports, "Most people don't know I'm a woman. They read my name and assume I'm a man." As a youngster she believed that women could do scenery because of another apparently gender-neutral name: "I mistakenly thought Ming Cho Lee was a woman."[34] Harrington has suffered from having invented a design specialty for which no category exists. She creates a major scenic component, projections, yet United Scenic Artists does not regard her as a set designer, and she cannot receive Tony nominations. John Arnone therefore took home the scenic design Tony for *The Who's Tommy* (1993), despite the fact that what everybody thought of as that show's set consisted of Harrington's projections. Indeed, when they both won American Theatre Wing Design Awards for that rock musical, Arnone acknowledged this during the ATW Working in the Theatre Seminar (28 October 1993). Other

Broadway musicals which Harrington has designed include *They're Playing Our Song* (1979), *The Moony Shapiro Songbook* (1981), *My One and Only* (1983), *The Will Rogers Follies* (1991), *Catskills on Broadway* (1991), *Beauty and the Beast* (1994), *Company* (1995 revival), *Steel Pier* (1997), *The Capeman* (1998), *Ragtime* (1998), *The Civil War* (1999), *A Christmas Carol* (1999), and *Putting It Together* (1999).

Although she predicts, "in another fifteen years gender will be a non-issue," Harrington reports a double standard of excellence in design:

> I have to be smarter. I have to know what I'm doing. I can't make a mistake. The boys may cover for the boys in a way they won't cover for the girls. Even now that I'm working with more liberal stage hands, on every show I start all over proving myself to them. A lot of that is about being a woman. When you get to the technical issues, that's where there's prejudice, the "don't worry little woman; I'll handle this for you." Stage hands particularly are guy guys, but they must take orders from me. You learn to flutter your eye lashes. It's part of how you work to get things done.[35]

But producers need Harrington.

> I invented what I do. I had no competition. There was no guy who was going to come in and do it. When I began, I was creating a new technology. I was the person in the room with the most experience, but I was a thirty-year-old woman, and that didn't make for a high comfort level in the over-fifty guys. Not only didn't they know anything about what I was talking about, but they had to learn it from me.[36]

About the economics of working as a woman in her field, Harrington reports,

> Of course, I don't make as much money as a scene designer. The set designer makes the most money, followed by the costume designer, followed by the lighting designer — except for Jules Fisher, who makes more money than God. I've been fighting for parity with the lighting designer. Being a woman is part of it; you've got to get along, so you settle for less. I hope later generations will not feel it is as necessary to go along to get along. But I've believed you should pick your fights. Sometimes winning is actually losing if you end up getting a reputation as aggressive.[37]

The Missing Sound Designers

Not a single woman designed sound for any twentieth century Broadway show, musical or otherwise, as far as sound designer Janet Kalas knows. Kalas, who has pioneered the field for women at such Off Broadway theatres as Playwrights Horizons, the Public Theatre, the Vineyard Theatre, and Circle Repertory Company, knows of only five other women sound designers nationwide and refers to sound designers as "a boys' club."[38]

Talking to *Back Stage* in 1998, Kalas, who initially had aimed for a career as a scientist, noted:

Men more often than women go into technical fields. The technology changes regularly, so it's a lot about keeping up with that. I'm fascinated by the technology. I went into it at a time women were encouraged to do what they wanted. That's changed. I [...] graduated from college in 1981 [...] and we defied traditional roles. I also grew up without a father, so I saw my mom raise four kids by herself. I still carry that attitude: women can do anything. Today women aren't as encouraged to pursue technical fields. I'm disappointed to see few women in the universities looking at such fields as an option. So the playing field is slanted. The people on that field are men. My peers are men.[39]

Kalas tried set design first and encountered the same expectations there that this was a man's field. "With scenery you need to read ground plans and know how to build a set, which is traditionally male." She ended up in sound not because of such notions, however, but because she loves "to make a house sound beautiful."[40] That passion and her excellence at her craft eventually did take Kalas to Broadway in February 2003 when *Take Me Out* (not a musical) moved there from the Off Broadway Public Theater. Nevertheless, no woman has yet designed sound for a Broadway musical.

Costume Designers

A different situation has existed in costume design. There, many women have designed for at least one or two American Broadway musicals. Among those who have not become household words but have created highly original designs which have enhanced their productions are Catherine Zuber, Ann Hould-Ward, Carrie F. Robbins, Judith Dolan, Nancy Potts, Patricia McGourty, Jennifer Von Mayrhauser, Marjorie Slaiman, Susan Hilferty, and Elizabeth Montgomery, the partner in "Motley" responsible for most of their Broadway designs.[41]

Irene Sharaff, the earliest of the costume design superstars, began designing for the theatre even before Lucinda Ballard and kept designing long after her. After assisting Aline Bernstein from 1928 through 1930 and co-designing with various others for five more years, this legendary costumer began designing on her own in 1937 with *Virginia*. Among her other Broadway musicals were *On Your Toes*, *White Horse Inn*, and *The Boys from Syracuse* (all 1938), *The Streets of Paris* (1939), *Lady in the Dark* (1941), *Banjo Eyes* (1942), *By Jupiter* (1942), *Bonanza Bound!* (1945), *Michael Todd's Peep Show* (1950), *The King and I* (1951), *A Tree Grows in Brooklyn* (1951), *Of Thee I Sing* (1952 revival), *Me and Juliet* (1953), *By the Beautiful Sea* (1954), *On Your Toes* (1954 revival), *Shangrila* (1956), *Happy Hunting* (1956), *Candide* (1956), *West Side Story* (1957), *Flower Drum Song* (1958), *Juno* (1959), *Do Re Mi* (1960), *Jennie* (1963), *The Girls Who Came to Supper* (1963), *Funny Girl* (1964), *Sweet Charity* (1966), *Hallelujah, Baby!* (1967), and *Irene* (co-designer, 1973). Her designs last appeared on Broadway in 1989 in *Jerome Robbins' Broadway*. She has been inducted into the Theatre Hall of Fame.

Sharaff spent some of her career in Hollywood; she received sixteen Academy Award nominations and won five Oscars. Yet the numbers show her allegiance to Broadway; she designed more than thirty movies but more than sixty Broadway shows, over half of them musicals. She won a Tony Award for *The King and I.*

Sharaff had created sets as well as costumes for Aline Bernstein. Ann Roth, who assisted Sharaff on several occasions, recalls, "Irene told me when I started with her that she had wanted to be a scenic designer but that it was not all that easy. This must have been in the 30s and 40s. There was a problem, resistance against her doing it."[42] Nevertheless, Sharaff created both sets and costumes for Eva Le Gallienne's *Alice in Wonderland* and won her first Academy Award for both scenery and costumes for the dream ballet sequence of the 1951 MGM film *An American in Paris.* She also received an Oscar nomination for her "Born in a Trunk" scenery and costumes in *A Star Is Born* (1954).

Noted for her preference for muted reds, oranges, and pinks, Sharaff invented fishnet stockings for *On Your Toes.* She ordered Yul Brynner to shave his head and introduced Thai silks to the U.S. for *The King and I.* Sharaff strove for authenticity in her period costumes in an era when that was uncommon yet also invented imaginative garb when appropriate.

Between the late 50s and the mid 60s six extraordinary women began designing costumes on Broadway. Patricia Zipprodt debuted in 1957, eventually receiving ten Tony nominations and winning three: *Fiddler on the Roof* (1964), *Cabaret* (1966), and *Sweet Charity* (1986 revival). She has been inducted into the Theatre Hall of Fame, and in 1997 the Theatre Development Fund (TDF) presented her with its Annual Irene Sharaff Lifetime Achievement Award. Her other Broadway musicals include *She Loves Me* (1963), *Anya* (1965), *Pousse-Cafe* (1966), *Zorba* (1968), *1776* (1969), *Georgy* (1970), *Pippin* (her particular favorite, 1972), *Mack and Mabel* (1974), *Chicago* (1975), *King of Hearts* (1978), *Fiddler on the Roof* (1981 revival), *Sunday in the Park with George* (with Ann Hould Ward, 1984), *Big Deal* (1986), *Cabaret* (1987 revival), *Into the Woods* (1987), *Jerome Robbins' Broadway* (1989), *Dangerous Games* (1989), *Shogun* (1991), *My Favorite Year* (1992), and the *My Fair Lady* revival (1993). Late in life Zipprodt married and moved to Virginia. She continued to design in Washington and Baltimore until her death in 1999.

Few prominent women designers have had children. Zipprodt said about her own choice, "I would not have known how to raise children and be a designer. I figured out I would need twice as much money as I was making. You have to be ready to replace yourself completely. Having children determines what kind of work you can take. Working as a designer is not 9 to 5. You never know what your hours are going to be."[43]

Zipprodt speculated that the other differences between a male and a female designer involved "what they felt they could pay you" and the necessity to be better than a man "in order to hold your own. That's a general rule in any profession. You have to work harder and be more patient. There certainly has been discrimination."[44]

Ann Roth graduated from Carnegie Tech with a scenic design major. She had been painting scenery for the Pittsburgh Opera since her sophomore year, and she continued to do that after graduation. A couple of years later, while working in the scene shop at the Bucks County Playhouse, she met Irene Sharaff, who told her scenic design was a tough career for a woman and urged her to change to costumes. Roth did that and became Sharaff's assistant both on Broadway and in Hollywood.

Among Roth's Broadway musicals were *I Had a Ball* (1964), *Gantry* (1970), *Purlie* (1970), *Purlie* (1972 revival), *Seesaw* (1973), *The Best Little Whorehouse in Texas* (1978), *They're Playing Our Song* (1979), and *Singin' in the Rain* (1985). Roth has a gift for helping actors to create their characters. She gravitates to realistic costumes, whether period or contemporary. Although she chooses to serve the show rather than create costumes which call attention to themselves, she has received three Tony nominations and an Oscar (*The English Patient*, 1997). In 2000, she won TDF's Irene Sharaff Lifetime Achievement Award.

Roth has a daughter and reports that combining career and motherhood "was hard. It gives you a guilt you can't get over. We lived in Pennsylvania, and I tried to get home every night. That was a seventy-four mile drive. It just wasn't easy. I think my kid suffered from it. And I suffered from it." And, of course, she was discouraged from pursuing a career as a scenic designer. Otherwise, Roth reports no problems as a costume designer which she can trace to her gender.[45]

The prolific Theoni V. Aldredge designed her first Broadway shows in 1959, two years after she arrived in New York from Chicago, where she began designing as a student at the Goodman Theatre in 1950. In 2002 she received TDF's Irene Sharaff Lifetime Achievement Award. She has designed over 200 Broadway shows and has been nominated for 13 Tony Awards. She has been inducted into the Theatre Hall of Fame, and she has won an Academy Award—for *The Great Gatsby*—and three Tony Awards: *Annie* (tie, 1977), *Barnum* (1980), and *La Cage Aux Folles* (1984). Her other Broadway musicals include *I Can Get It for You Wholesale* (1961), *Anyone Can Whistle* (1964), *Skyscraper* (1965), *A Time for Singing* (1966), *Ilya Darling* (1967), *Billy* (1969), *Two Gentlemen of Verona* (1971), *Nash at Nine* (1973), *A Chorus Line* (1975), *The Threepenny Opera* (1977 revival), *Ballroom* (1978), *The Madwoman of Central Park West* (1979), *I Remember Mama* (1979), *42nd Street* (1980), *Onward Victoria* (1980), *Woman of the Year* (1981), *Dreamgirls* (1981), *Merlin* (1983), *The Rink* (1984), *Dreamgirls* (1987 revival), *Teddy & Alice* (1987), *Chess* (1988), *Gypsy* (1989 revival), *Oh, Kay!* (1990 revival), *Nick and Nora* (1991), *The Secret Garden* (1991), *The High Rollers Social and Pleasure Club* (1992), *Annie* (1997 revival), and *Follies* (2001 revival).

Aldredge prefers generally subdued colors, and she strives to avoid calling attention to the costume unless the musical requires it. She has stressed that actors must feel comfortable in their costumes and that the costumes must suit the actors. She agonized more over the rehearsal clothes which the cast of *A Chorus Line* must wear until the finale than she did over more complicated garb. She attended rehearsals for the workshop for six months, taking Polaroids of the performers, and then created costumes much like what they had worn there. Yet for *Dreamgirls* and *La Cage aux Folles* she created elaborate outfits appropriate to the singers' slow rise to stardom in the former and to the drag queens at a Saint-Tropez nightclub in the latter, and she prefers period shows to contemporary plays. She drops by each of her Broadway shows once a week to check her costumes for wear. Her *42nd Street* used 400 costumes, and in December 1982 she had six shows running on Broadway simultaneously — which set a record for a costume designer.

Aldredge reports:

> When I went to New York it was a men's era, just as a lot of male designers are popping up again. All my assistants have been men. It's a profession in which you must literally work your butt off, and never make a fortune, and never have a private life, because you're always on call, like a doctor. You cannot plan on anything, not even a vacation. You can make a living only if you have an enormous hit. Your life is not your own. If you don't want to give up everything, don't touch it. Yet I don't regret one minute of it. You're part of a magical moment. There's nothing more exciting than the curtain going up. You forget the pain.[46]

Aldredge has expressed dismay over losing control of her costumes. In an article she wrote for *Theatre Crafts* in 1969, she laments her designs being changed without her knowledge or permission: "How many times the curtain goes up on a show that I have designed and I don't recognize it as mine! [...] What I object to is the interference of people who know nothing about costumes and much less about theatre."[47]

Shortly after Aldredge designed her first Broadway shows, Florence Klotz made her own debut with two plays in 1961. She had previously assisted such designers as Irene Sharaff and Lucinda Ballard; the latter pushed her to begin working independently. By the time she retired after *Whistle down the Wind* folded in Washington, D.C. in 1997, Klotz had won five Tony Awards—for *Follies* (1971), *A Little Night Music* (1973), *Pacific Overtures* (1976), *Grind* (1985) and her 1994 triumph with a *Show Boat* revival, for which she designed a record 550 costumes. Her other Broadway musicals include *It's a Bird, It's a Plane, It's Superman* (1966), *Side by Side by Sondheim* (1977), *On the Twentieth Century* (1978), *A Doll's Life* (1982), *Jerry's Girls* (1985), *Rags* (1986), *Roza* (1987), *City of Angels* (1989), and *Kiss of the Spiderwoman* (1993). She has been inducted into the Theatre Hall of Fame.

Klotz tends to avoid designing for chorus lines, and even when she designs for performers other than the principals she strives to create a distinct character for each member of the ensemble. Although she often creates smart, stylish outfits, she has also produced unfashionable costumes for the prisoners in *Spider Woman*, the low life in *Grind*, and the immigrants in *Rags*. She usually strives for realism achieved through careful research of the periods, but she has also delved into her imagination for the outlandish costumes worn by the Spider Woman/Aurora. In two shows she garbed those characters who are not "real" in black and white — the ghosts of the past in *Follies* and the film's cast in *City of Angels*. Yet she also became famous for her bright colors— as well as for her designs' wit.

Klotz recalls her career with satisfaction:

> I worked mostly for Hal Prince, so I had the best director. I had no husband or children, so I had no problems. I came and went as I pleased. When I started, there were mostly men designing, and then women slowly came in. That's the reverse of fashion design; there it was mostly women when I started, and then it was mostly men. 7th Avenue pays better than theatre. And theatre design is a hard job now, and very stressful. And then there were only a couple of producers, David Merrick and Hal Prince; now there are six hundred. I can't cope with that. And *Show Boat* killed me. I got all my medals. I have no more wall space. I even got a statue from the NAACP when I did *Show Boat*. I've had it. So I've retired.[48]

In 1963, Jane Greenwood designed her first Broadway play. More assignments followed, but not until 1971 did she design a Broadway musical, probably because the understated realism which she has so successfully mastered does not suit those musicals which require glitter and spangles. *70, Girls, 70* (1971) and *That's Entertainment* (1972) did not bring her immediate attention since they ran only 44 performances and nine performances respectively, but after the ensuing decades saw her win more and more acclaim — including twelve Tony nominations— she finally designed several more musicals where her particular strengths were wanted: *She Loves Me* (1993 revival), *Passion* (1994), *Once Upon a Mattress* (1996 revival), *The Scarlet Pimpernel* (1997), *High Society* (1998), and *James Joyce's The Dead* (2000). Greenwood won TDF's 1998 Irene Sharaff Lifetime Achievement Award.

Asked if the playing field is level for women designers, Greenwood replies, "Not exactly. There is a men's club. But there are men's clubs in every walk of life. Women set designers especially have a much more difficult time. But costume designers have been diminished. So often the women are treated like dress makers, yet our work has nothing to do with sewing." Greenwood speaks frankly about the impact of her career on her family life:

> My career is all-consuming. Costume designers must be around more than the other designers, so raising children was very difficult. That was in the early 60s when fathers weren't as willing to help. I had a wonderful husband — wonderful once our daughters were able to put on their own shoes and socks. He was a set designer, Ben Edwards, so I would be away, and then he would be away. There were always dramas. One of my daughters broke her arm when we both were out of town, and the housekeeper was sitting at St. Vincent's hospital waiting to reach one of us to get permission to set the arm.[49]

Korean-American Willa Kim joined this group of grande dame designers on Broadway in 1966, but, again, she did not design a musical until *Goodtime Charley* in 1975. *Dancin'* followed in 1978, *Song and Dance* in 1985, *Sophisticated Ladies* in 1981 and *The Will Rogers Follies* in 1991; all five received Tony nominations and the latter two won. She has also designed *Legs Diamond* (1988), *Tommy Tune Tonite!* (1992), the 1994 revival of *Grease, Busker Alley* (which closed out of town, 1995), and *Victor/Victoria* (1995). She has continued to design numerous ballets. In 1999, Kim won TDF's Irene Sharaff Lifetime Achievement Award.

Kim reports that she never had children, but

> my marriage fell apart early in my career because I was working Off Off Broadway, where I had to do a lot more work. I've slept in theatres at night. When I was doing *Dynamite Tonight* (1964)— I was doing scenery as well as costumes— it was easier to stay there. I slept in Barbara Harris's dressing room. I just spread out on the floor and slept. With children it would have been even more difficult. There's no limit to the hours a designer has to put in. I figured out once I was making ten cents an hour. I became intolerant of my husband's interference with my time and attention. Women who marry must divide their allegiances.[50]

Kim's then husband, illustrator William Pene du Bois, who disliked the division, moved to France.

The designer, who sacrificed her personal life to this extent, introduced stretch fabrics to dance design as part of her pioneering efforts to create costumes which would move as the body moves. Noted for her brilliant colors and witty outfits, she likewise developed costumes which suggest the appropriate period without weighing down dancers with unnecessary material. She spends endless hours on fittings to guarantee that costumes work for performers. Her uncompromising perfectionism about getting details right annoyed *Sophisticated Ladies'* producers but earned her the Tony.[51]

What women, if any, will replace these prolific costume designers remains to be seen. Two who have attracted favorable notice, Toni-Leslie James and Julie Taymor, are not designing for the theatre full-time.

Costume designer Willa Kim was recipient of the Irene Sharaff Lifetime Achievement Award in 1999 (Chong-Gwon Park).

African-American James has two children,

> so it's been beneficial for me to work on a soap, *As the World Turns.* This way, I
> don't have to travel out of town, and it's only five days a week. My husband,
> David Higham, is a lighting designer who teaches at a private school. The most
> difficult time is when I have tech week. Then we drop off our children and I
> don't see them till the next morning. It requires an extraordinarily supportive
> partner.[52]

Despite the demands of television and her other theatre work, James has
designed six Broadway musicals: *Jelly's Last Jam* (1992), *Chronicle of a Death
Foretold* (1995), *Footloose* (1998), *Marie Christine* (1999), *The Wild Party* (2000),
and *One Mo' Time* (2002 revival). In 1996, James won TDF's Irene Sharaff Young
Master Award.

James, who finds costuming a welcoming field "because there's this mind-
set that costumes are women's work," believes if more women produced, more
women designers would have jobs. Margo Lion hired her for her first Broadway show, *Jelly's Last Jam* (1992), and she has continued to benefit from working for women producers. James points out that many women designers end
up in educational theatre rather than struggle for work in the commercial arena.
She also shrewdly notes that in England more women design sets because there
"the same person often designs both sets and costumes."[53] This suggests the
American union's creation of a separate costume design category in 1936 might
actually have hurt women by steering them into the "women's work" of costuming.

Julie Taymor, primarily a director, never designs costumes for others and
indeed for the Broadway production of *The Green Bird* (2000) turned that
responsibility over to Constance Hoffman. Taymor, who refers to herself as "a
theatre maker" and "a play maker" says, "I never wanted to be a designer. I just
am."[54] She won the Tony for designing the costumes for *The Lion King* (1997)
in 1998, the same year she became the first woman to win a Tony for directing
a musical. She also co-designed the remarkable masks and puppets. She co-
designed the set and costumes and designed the masks and puppets for *Juan
Darien* (revived on Broadway in 1996), which she also wrote and directed. Taymor designs in a strictly imaginary realm: "I don't do clothes," she explains. "I
design costumes. No one would ask me to do a contemporary modern drama.
I create worlds."[55]

Like most other women designers, Taymor does not have children, but she
does have a partner, composer Elliot Goldenthal, who also often collaborates
with her professionally. "He's totally supportive," she remarks. "We understand
each other's responsibilities and as a result don't make demands on each other.
We're one of the lucky couples."[56] This sort of understanding, which some other
women designers' partners lack, has made possible for Taymor the intense
focusing on a project for which she is famous.

As the century waned, more than half the costume design members of

United Scenic Artists were women, but few of those were designing Broadway musicals, an arena which male designers had come to dominate. Many women scenic and lighting designers, and even a few sound designers, likewise wait in the wings for gender barriers to topple. May a new century and a new millennium see talent unequivocally prevail.

Notes

1. Bobbi Owen, *Scenic Design on Broadway: Designers and Their Credits: 1915–1990* (New York: Greenwood, 1991); *Costume Design on Broadway: Designers and Their Credits: 1915–1985* (New York: Greenwood, 1987); *Lighting Design on Broadway: Designers and Their Credits: 1915–1990* (New York: Greenwood, 1991).

2. Bobbi Owen, *Scenic Design* 113.

3. Lawrence Robinson, telephone interview, 5 July 2000.

4. Winthrop Sargeant, "Please, Darling, Bring Three to Seven: A Profile of Jean Rosenthal," *New Yorker* 4 February 1956: 33.

5. Sargeant 59.

6. Robinson.

7. Mary Callahan Boone, "Jean Rosenthal's Light: Making Visible the Magician," *Theatre Topics* (March 1997): 78.

8. Qtd. in Jean Rosenthal, and Lael Wertenbacker, *The Magic of Light* (Boston: Little, 1972) 35.

9. Rosenthal 35.

10. Beverly Emmons, telephone interview, 27 Feb. 1998.

11. Rosenthal 75.

12. Arnold Aronson, *Actors, Directors and Designers: International Dictionary of Theatre*, ed. David Pickering, vol. 3 (Detroit: St. James, 1996) 673.

13. Bobbi Owen, *Costume Design* 22.

14. Beth Howard, "Designstyle: Direct from the Past," *Theatre Crafts* February 1990: 20.

15. Jeremy Gerard, "Bringing a Stage to Light," *New York Times* 3 August 1987.

16. Tharon Musser, telephone interview, 1 March 1998.

17. Musser.

18. Musser.

19. Musser.

20. Jennifer Tipton, telephone interview, 19 June 2000.

21. Tipton.

22. Tipton.

23. Beverly Emmons, telephone interview, 27 Feb. 1998.

24. Emmons.

25. Emmons.

26. Natasha Katz, telephone interview, 27 Feb. 1998.

27. Peggy Eisenhauer, telephone interview, 1 March 1998.

28. Eisenhauer.

29. Eisenhauer.

30. Heidi Ettinger, telephone interview, 4 March 1998.

31. Marjorie Bradley Kellogg, telephone interview, 1 March 1998.

32. Adrianne Lobel, telephone interview, 1 March 1998.

33. Lobel.

34. Wendall K. Harrington, telephone interview, 1 March 1998.

35. Harrington.

36. Harrington.

37. Harrington.

38. Janet Kalas, telephone interview, 7 March 1998.

39. Quoted in Tish Dace, "Designing Women," *Back Stage* 20 March 1998: 32. Some quotations from the 1998 designer interviews first appeared in this article and are republished by permission from BackStage NNU.

40. Kalas.

41. Owen, *Costume Design* 115.

42. Ann Roth, telephone interview, 26 June 2000.

43. Patricia Zipprodt, telephone interview, 1 March 1998.

44. Zipprodt.

45. Roth.

46. Theoni Aldredge, telephone interview, 30 June 2000.

47. Theoni Aldredge, "Costumes and the Budget," *Theatre Crafts* Nov.-Dec. 1969: 34.

48. Florence Klotz, telephone interview, 3 July 2000.

49. Jane Greenwood, telephone interview, 7 March 1998.

50. Willa Kim, telephone interview, 26 June 2000.

51. Beth Howard, "Willa Kim," *Theatre Crafts* March 1989: 29–33, 56.

52. Toni-Leslie James, telephone interview, 4 March 1998.

53. James.

54. Julie Taymor, telephone interview, 26 June 2000.

55. Taymor.

56. Taymor.

Helburn, Dalrymple, and Lortel

A Triumvirate of Great Producers

BUD COLEMAN

Almost completely neglected in written histories of the theatre is the work of female producers. Suffice it to say, it often seems like producers share the same perceived caste as critics and agents: unfortunately necessary, but definitely a lower life form than the artists who act, write, compose, and/or design. Yet without producers providing the funding and assembling various constituencies together into a cohesive team of creators, there would be no finished product, only some great ideas bandied about in lonely rooms. The many women who produced professional theatre in nineteenth century America is fairly well documented, and as per the organizational structure of the time, they were actor/managers: Laura Keene, Jesse Bonstelle, Charlotte Cushman, Elizabeth Blanchard Hamblin, Helen Dauvray, Catherine Sinclair, Mrs. D.P. Bowers, Matilda Vining Wood, and Louisa Lane Drew.[1] In the male dominated world of early twentieth century theatre, the emergence of female producers who did not first establish themselves as star performers took longer than their male counterparts. This chapter will look at three such women who distinguished themselves as producers of musical theatre: Theresa Helburn, Jean Dalrymple, and Lucille Lortel. Part of the management team of the Theatre Guild for forty years, Helburn (1887–1959) helped to realize *The Garrick Gaieties* (which ushered in the era of little revues), *Porgy and Bess* (the most produced American opera), and *Oklahoma!*, the inaugural production of the Golden Age of Musical Theatre. While theatre history celebrates the important careers of Cheryl Crawford (Group Theatre and the Actors Studio), Hallie Flanagan (Federal Theatre Project), Eva Le Gallienne (Civic Repertory Theatre), and Margaret Webster (American Repertory Theatre), little is written about Jean Dalrymple (1902–1998), the actress, publicity agent, playwright, director, and producer who played a major role in the creation and success of the New York City Center of Music and Drama, the home of New York City Ballet, New York City Opera, New York City Center Theatre Company, and New York City Center Light Opera Company. As Off Broadway proved its legitimacy in the 1950s with milestone productions like *Summer and Smoke* (1952) and *The Iceman Cometh* (1956), Lucille Lortel (1900–1999) successfully made the case that musicals could be presented in smaller venues (and with smaller budgets) than their well-heeled musical cousins on Broadway.

A Paradoxical Genius: Theresa Helburn

While the groundbreaking innovations contained in the musical sensation *Oklahoma!* are well known, it is arguable that this unlikely project would have been realized if it had not been for producer Theresa Helburn. Due to World War II, the unknown quality of a Rodgers and Hammerstein collaboration, and the universally despised subject matter of ranchers in a western territory made raising the modest capitalization of $83,000 for a new musical not just difficult, but impossible. Out of desperation, Helburn approached playwright S.N. Behrman, many of whose plays had been produced by the Theatre Guild. "Sam, you've got to take twenty thousand dollars of this because the Guild has done so much for you." Helburn admitted she was blackmailing the playwright; nevertheless, she got her money, and Behrman eventually made $660,000 off his investment.[2]

As the Theatre Guild only had about $30,000 in the bank in 1943 when co-director Lawrence Langner gave his go ahead to Helburn to pursue the musicalization of *Green Grow the Lilacs*, he dubbed the project, "Helburn's Folly."[3] But Helburn pursued her vision, since she felt she had the right property "for the fulfillment of my dream, the production of a totally new kind of play with music, not a musical comedy in the familiar sense but a play in which music and dancing would be aids to and adjuncts of the plot itself in telling the story."[4] But musicals in the 1940s did not have a murder during the second act, and Richard Rodgers' choice of Oscar Hammerstein II as a collaborator was a lyricist who had had ten successive flops since writing *Show Boat* (1927). But faith in her convictions was one of many qualities which guided Theresa Helburn as she crafted a brilliantly successful career for herself as a producer, director, and playwright. As Langner noted about his friend and colleague, "if her appearance was soft and comfortable, her nerves were like whipcord and her will power like steel[...]."[5]

If geography is destiny, then it would be no surprise that Theresa Helburn would make a life in the theatre, as she was born on West 45th Street in New York City, in the heart of the theatre district. But when she was four years old her family moved to 90th and Columbus Avenue, and as the theatre was not frequented by the Helburn family, it became an illusive concept. Although contemporary theatre was not studied at Bryn Mawr College (where she was majoring in English and Philosophy), Helburn took it upon herself to produce plays. "I knew nothing about producing, directing, casting, staging; but then, neither did any of the other girls. So, as I was to do so often afterwards, I rushed in where angels fear to tread."[6] Helburn immersed herself in the world of writing, directing, acting, and producing school plays, finding this to be the most stimulating work of her time at Bryn Mawr.

Helburn was determined to become a writer, so she enrolled at Radcliffe in 1909 in order to participate in George Pierce Baker's 47 Workshop at Harvard, describing this as "one of the most important decisions I ever made."[7] There she met future associates Lee Simonson, Philip Moeller, Maurice Wertheim, and budding playwrights Eugene O'Neill and Philip Barry. Although Helburn was to devote several years to writing poetry (published in *Century, Harper's, New Republic, Poetry*) and plays (some of which played briefly on Broadway in the 1940s)—even eventually becoming the dramatic critic of *The Nation*—it was not as a writer that she was to make her mark in the American theatre.

While struggling as a writer, Helburn taught drama at the Merrill Finishing School in New Rochelle, counting Katherine Cornell as one of the students under her tutelage. She joined a play reading group with many alums from Baker's 47 Workshop, some of whom eventually formed the Washington Square Players in 1915. With the purpose of producing the work of new playwrights, they also were unique in advocating a noncommercial subscription ticket model. Lawrence Langner wanted Helburn to act in his one-act play *Licensed*, being produced by the Players, but she withdrew since her family regarded the play's subject matter of birth control as "immoral."[8] Content not to be an actress, Helburn stayed on

Influential producer Teresa Helburn was part of the management team of the Theatre Guild for forty years (courtesy Billy Rose Theatre Collection, The New York Public Library for the Performing Arts, Astor, Lenox and Tilden Foundations).

as a play reader and playwright, seeing her one-act play, *Enter the Hero*, produced by the Washington Square Players in 1917.

The last production of the Washington Square Players closed in May 1918,
and later that year Langner organized the first meeting of the group that was
to form the Theatre Guild. The mission of the Guild was to be a professional
theatre which produced "great plays" supported by a subscription audience. The
resulting Board of Managers was composed almost completely of alumni from
the Players (including Langner, Helburn, Rollo Peters, Philip Moeller, Helen
Freeman, Helen Westley, Justus Sheffield, and Lee Simonson); establishing a new
organization protected its members from creditors, who were owed thousands
of dollars spent by the Players.

At the creation of the Theatre Guild, Helburn was given the title of Play Representative. As Lawrence Langner was to recall in his autobiography, "Had we
realized the outstanding talents of Theresa Helburn at this time, she would
undoubtedly have been made a member of the original Board of Managers. As
it was, this took place later at a time of crisis."[9] From its founding in 1919 to 1939,
the Guild operated by consensus of the Board which almost proved its undoing;
thereafter Langner and Helburn were named co-administrative directors.[10]

The Theatre Guild began producing work in the Garrick Theatre in 1919,
and by 1925 they were so successful that they built their own theatre on 52nd
Street (now called the August Wilsen Theatre). Along with introducing New
York audiences to George Bernard Shaw, Henrik Ibsen, Georg Kaiser, Ernst
Toller, Ferenc Molnar, Luigi Pirandello, and Ivan Turgenev, the Guild also
championed local talent such as Sidney Howard, William Inge, Walter Kerr,
Eugene O'Neill, S.N. Behrman, Philip Barry, Maxwell Anderson, Robert Sher-
wood, William Saroyan, Sophie Treadwell, and Tennessee Williams. During its
first decade of existence, the Guild presented forty-seven plays from abroad,
earning it the moniker of the "House that Shaw built." But by the 1933–34 season, only one of its offerings was written by a non–American author.[11] Mark
Fearnow contends that while it cannot be said that the Guild was wholly responsible for the "flowering of serious American drama that occurred in the 1920s
and 1930s," it is reasonable to concede that the production of unconventional
plays, innovative musicals, and new design aesthetics meant that American theatre makers could see their work reach the stage.[12] That a group of producers
would be more dedicated to artistic innovation than to the bottom line surprised producers like George M. Cohan. Writing in 1930, he marveled,

> I found, for one thing, that Miss Helburn was an intelligent and shrewd
> woman and that her associates also knew their way around. They are peculiarly
> stubborn people and often will produce a play they know is going to lose a lot
> of money simply because they think it ought to be produced, and they are as
> independent as theatrical firms come.[13]

While Helburn took a sizable gamble with the team of Rodgers and Hammerstein in 1943, this was not her first association with one half of the team.

In 1925 she had been introduced to two young men who had been writing shows for Columbia University when they performed some of their material at a private party. Richard Rodgers and Lorenz Hart were hired to write the first *Garrick Gaieties* for the Theatre Guild, giving the world such tuneful melodies as "Manhattan" and "Mountain Greenery."[14] *The Garrick Gaieties* was only scheduled for two performances (matinee and evening) on 17 May 1925. The Guild had no money to pay Rodgers and Hart, so it was arranged that they receive a small percentage of the gross, plus a weekly salary if the revue were to have an extended run (which no one had any reason to think would happen). But the first performance of *The Garrick Gaieties* was a hit — ten curtain calls — whereupon Rodgers approached Helburn before the then final performance and pleaded for a longer run. Four matinees were announced and quickly sold out, at which point the Guild announced *Gaieties* for an open run. Even in the summer's blistering heat, the lively revue took audiences by storm and ran for a total of twenty-five weeks (211 performances). "Rodgers and Hart each received about $50 a week from their percentage of the gross; in addition, Rodgers was earning a handsome $83 a week, union scale, for being the show's conductor. It was the first actual wages either of them had earned from their work on musicals since the day they joined forces nine years before."[15]

The Guild commissioned a second edition of *The Garrick Gaieties* from Rodgers and Hart, which opened 10 May 1926. Lightning rarely strikes twice and this edition of the revue proved only moderately successful, running forty-six performances. A third and final edition of *The Garrick Gaieties* in 1930 did not feature any songs by Rodgers and Hart. (Even though Helburn would not work with Richard Rodgers for another seventeen years, the Theatre Guild eventually produced three more of his musicals: *Oklahoma!, Carousel,* and *Allegro.*) The success of *The Garrick Gaieties* spawned other intimate revues, notably Leonard Sillman's six *New Faces* productions (1934 to 1968). As for the Theatre Guild, they never found success with the form after the first *Gaieties. Parade, a Satirical Revue* (1935) boasted music by Jerome Moross with dance numbers staged by Robert Alton, but ran only thirty-two performances.

As if running a large theatre organization were not enough, Helburn directed briefly for the Theatre Guild. First she staged John Howard Lawson's *The Pure in Heart* (1932), which after poor notices in Baltimore, Pittsburgh, and Cincinnati for Guild subscription audiences, was pulled before it reached New York. Helburn made her Broadway debut as a director with Maxwell Anderson's *Mary of Scotland* (1933), starring Helen Hayes and Helen Menken. Produced by the Theatre Guild, this acclaimed production ran for 236 performances. With *Mary of Scotland*, "Helburn thus became one of the few women stage directors in the history of the American theatre who was not first and foremost an actress."[16] But after the artistic failure of directing Ferdinand Bruckner's *Races* (1934) — which also closed before it reached New York — Helburn determined that directing was not her strong suit. Instead, in 1934, Helburn took a leave of absence of nine months from the Guild to accept an offer with the motion picture industry. As an executive at Columbia Pictures, she was appointed the director of the Bureau of New Plays. Set up by seven Hollywood film studios, the Bureau of New Plays offered scholarships to young playwrights who submitted their work in a play contest whereupon the studios got first crack at their play. Due to Helburn's Hollywood connections, several future Guild's productions were optioned for film adaptations; in the 1936–37 season, for example, Paramount Pictures financed up front four of the Guild's productions to the tune of $90,000 (two at $25,000 and two at $20,000).

In 1929, George Gershwin signed a contract with the Metropolitan Opera to compose a new opera based on the Jewish folktale "The Dybbuk," to be performed in 1931. When Gershwin learned the musical rights already belonged to the Italian composer Lodovico Rocca, he abandoned the project. Instead, he returned to a previous idea, an operatic adaptation of DuBose Heyward's novel *Porgy*, which George had read in 1926. Even though the Theatre Guild had presented it as a play — also titled *Porgy* by Dorothy and DuBose Heyward — in 1927 (217 performances), George convinced the Heywards that the story was so rich it could support both a play and an opera.[17] Alas, the musical rights to *Porgy* were also tied up, as Heyward had sold them to Al Jolson, who wanted to play the title role in blackface. But Jolson let his option lapse, whereupon the Theatre Guild signed on in 1933 to produce this folk opera, and so George was back at work on *Porgy and Bess*, turning down a $5000 offer from the Met to present its premiere.[18]

The original 125 consecutive performances of *Porgy and Bess* on Broadway in 1935 is the "longest uninterrupted run ever achieved by a serious opera in the history of music."[19] With a cast of seventy and a forty-five piece orchestra, this was a huge undertaking for the Guild; indeed, the production was a financial disaster, losing its entire capitalization. But during the first eighteen years of its existence, the Theatre Guild had produced few events more momentous than this musical folk tale, which many now regard as the "first American opera of any real importance."[20]

By the early 1940s, the Theatre Guild was staring at bankruptcy even though at their peak they had 75,000 subscribers in six cities besides New York. They leased their theatre out as a radio station and faced the very real possibility that this noble experiment had come to an end. Some, like designer (and former Theatre Guild Board member) Lee Simonson, placed the blame squarely on the co-directors: "Langner and Helburn convinced each other that they alone knew how to cast a play, select a director, supervise him, run a theatre, and manage its finances, although every season we continued to lose money, prestige, or both on productions that missed fire and for which they were no less responsible than any other members of the Board."[21]

But Helburn's faith in *Oklahoma!* pushed her to find its necessary backing, a drive which literally saved the Guild. *Oklahoma!* played for over five

years on Broadway and set an all time record in London at the Drury Lane Theatre with 1548 performances. National companies criss-crossed the country and
it played around the world. At its 10th anniversary, the lucky few who had
invested $1500 in 1943 had been paid back more than $50,000 for their gamble on this folk tale.[22] Indeed, without *Oklahoma!*, Helburn and Langner would
not have had the sufficient capitalization to launch a new Guild season. The
profits of *Oklahoma!* allowed them next to provide American audiences with
Margaret Webster's provocative interpretation of *Othello* featuring Paul Robeson, José Ferrer, and Uta Hagen, and O'Neill's *The Iceman Cometh* in 1946.

During the 1940s, the Guild continued to offer plays, but the output was
uneven, and the box office was soft. After a valiant attempt to duplicate *Oklahoma!*'s success with Walter Kerr's play with authentic American folk music,
Sing Out, Sweet Land!, the next substantial hit came from none other than
Rodgers and Hammerstein: *Carousel* (1945). But the failure of *Allegro* (1947)
and other financial disappointments led to the selling of the Guild Theatre in
1950 to the American National Theatre and Academy (ANTA). When Helburn
died in 1959, the Theatre Guild had produced 190 productions in 11 cities
(including London), and had earned numerous awards, including seven Pulitzer
Prizes for drama. An obituary in *The New York Times* described Helburn as "a
short, indomitable woman" who held the Theatre Guild "together with charm,
toughness and business sense," to become "one of the strongest influences in
the American Theatre from the Nineteen Twenties to the Fifties."[23] Helburn's
high energy level was noted by her contemporaries, no strangers to workaholics
and larger than life personalities in the theatre. Even the perfectionist Richard
Rodgers recalled that Helburn had "more drive than a football player."[24]

Speaking at her funeral service, Oscar Hammerstein II observed that Helburn guided the Guild for more than forty years with a "deft and diplomatic
hand"[25]:

> A producer is a rare, paradoxical genius: hard-headed, soft-hearted, cautious,
> reckless. A hopeful innocent in fair weather, a stern pilot in stormy weather, a
> mathematician who prefers to ignore the laws of mathematics and trust intu-
> ition, an idealist, a realist, a practical dreamer, a sophisticated gambler, a
> stage-struck child. That's a producer. That was Theresa Helburn.[26]

The Dynamo Behind City Center: Jean Dalrymple

During the bulk of the twentieth century, the number of independent
female producers presenting on Broadway has been very small: Cheryl Crawford, Jean Dalrymple, Lucille Lortel, Irene Selznick, and Margaret Webster. On
the other hand, the last fifteen or twenty years have seen an explosion of women
producing musical theatre on Broadway: Mary Lea Johnson (*Grind, On the
Twentieth Century, Sweeney Todd, A Doll's Life, La Cage aux Folles, March of*

the Falsettos, Chicago); Margo Lion (Jelly's Last Jam, Annie 2, The Triumph of Love, The Garden of Earthly Delights, Hairspray); Rhoda Mayerson (Big River, Into the Woods, The Secret Garden, Smokey Joe's Cafe, The Producers); Kim Poster (Grand Hotel, Busker's Alley); Anita Waxman (Cabaret revival, The Wild Party, The Music Man revival), Fran Weissler (My Fair Lady revival, Busker's Alley, Grease revival, South Pacific 2001 tour, Chicago revival, Jane Eyre, Seussical), etc. This recent influx of successful women producers gives the lie to the supposition that producing is not "women's work," despite the macho, cigar-chewing, ruthless, conniving aura surrounding this field.

Like Hallie Flanagan, Jean Dalrymple (1902–1998) found herself in the not-for-profit world (New York City Center of Music and Drama), presenting not only theatre, but also opera, musical theatre, concert, dance, and recitalists. Joffrey Ballet artistic director Gerald Arpino reflected, "The City Center has given birth to so many great innovative movements, it is really a theatre of history,"[27] a history which would not have happened without the inspired stewardship of Jean Dalrymple.

A native of Morristown, New Jersey, Dalrymple's first sign of genius was writing. Before the family moved to Washington Heights and young Dalrymple was enrolled in the 8th grade, she had already earned several hundred dollars from newspapers and magazines publishing her short stories. Education was not valued in her family, so when she graduated from junior high, her father announced her schooling was over. Fortunately, a family friend gave the sixteen year old $100 which she used to enroll in a business college, lying on the application that she was eighteen and had a high school diploma.[28] Upon graduation, she was offered a secretarial job at a prestigious firm on Wall Street.

Although she was only a teenager, she discovered an immediate affinity for the world of finance.[29] Dalrymple's first employer on Wall Street told her father that "she intimidates me," and that was when she was seventeen years old.[30] Despite two great jobs on Wall Street, the nineteen year old Dalyrmple horrified her family by accepting a job as an actress in a touring one-act vaudeville play. After less than six months on the road as an actress, she co-wrote a one-act play with a fellow vaudeville actor which proved to be a big success on the Keith circuit.[31] This led to commissions to write for the new medium of sound motion pictures (James FitzPatrick Pictures), which she did, in addition to casting them with vaudeville entertainers she had met on the road.[32]

She and co-author Dan Jarrett then sat down to write a full-length play, On the Chin, which in very short order was optioned by the Broadway producer John Golden. Golden had carved a niche on Broadway by producing wholesome family plays, including the blockbuster Lightnin' (1918), which ran for 1291 performances. When Golden realized that most of the writing of On the Chin was done by Dalrymple, he collaborated with her on the rewrites to the Jarrett/Dalrymple play — now called Salt Water — which opened a month after the stock market crash. Starring Frank Craven, Salt Water was a modest success, running eleven weeks after receiving mixed reviews from the critics.[33] Regardless of the show's soft performance at the box office, Frank Craven and John Golden both recognized Dalrymple's talent.

That's Gratitude, a comedy co-written by Craven and Dalrymple, opened on Broadway in 1930, running for 197 performances (an excellent run for a light comedy in the Depression). This show also marked Dalrymple's debut as a press agent, as she was lured into service by producer John Golden when his in-house man left unexpectedly.[34] Despite having co-authored two Broadway plays, her name was not in either program as the men she wrote with did not want her name known. Dalrymple did receive her share of royalties, but not public credit for her co-authorship of these two plays.

While working in the John Golden office as his publicist, she began a courtship with Ward Morehouse, theatre columnist for the *New York Sun*. As Morehouse did research for his column, "Broadway After Dark," Dalrymple met every important producer, director, press agent, newspaper critic, and performer on the Great White Way. Although their 1932 marriage lasted only five years, the contacts she made during her time with Morehouse served her well for decades.

In 1937, the recently divorced Dalrymple began her free-lance career as a publicist, concert manager, and personal manager; her roster of clients included the Spanish pianist José Iturbi, opera star Grace Moore, Leopold Stokowski, and Mary Martin. In addition to creating publicity for individuals, Dalrymple was soon approached by Broadway producers to promote their plays and musicals. Some of her Broadway hits include *Mr. and Mrs. North* (1941), *One Touch of Venus* (1943), and *Anna Lucasta* (1944). As she was getting her free-lance business established, Dalrymple became one of the founding members of the American Theatre Wing in 1939, serving as its first publicity volunteer. During the late 1930s, Dalrymple was also having an affair with the powerful magazine publisher Henry R. Luce (*Time, Fortune*), even though he was very married to Clare Booth Luce. Certainly any one of these activities would have kept most mortals busy, but Dalrymple not only managed to do them all (and well), she also agreed to be part of a daring new theatrical adventure.

In 1943, when Mayor Fiorello La Guardia proposed a center for the performing arts which would be affordable to the working class, Broadway ticket prices averaged about $2.50.[35] In the 1940s a waiter made $16 dollars a week, bookkeepers $25, and pharmacists $50, and even a ten-inch string of cultured pearls secured by a gold clasp could be yours for $10 at Bloomingdales. In this economic climate, few people could afford the luxury of attending theatre, opera, or concerts, since the top Broadway ticket to a musical was $4 to $5.50.

To realize his dreams of a center to present plays, musicals, and operas at popular prices, Mayor La Guardia turned to a recent city acquisition, the Mecca Temple, located on 55th Street between Sixth and Seventh Avenues. Built in 1924 for the Ancient Order of Nobles of the Mystic Shrine (the "Shriners"), this

$3.5 million mosque-like building was reminiscent of many grand, fanciful movie palaces built in the 1920s. But the Depression hit the building hard, and the Shriners lost it to the city of New York in 1942 for non-payment of taxes. After assembling a blue chip panel to realize La Guardia's dream, the City Center of Music and Drama was born.

One of the first hires was Jean Dalrymple as press director. And it was Dalrymple who convinced the board to hire their first managing director, someone she knew as a capable and insightful manager, Harry Friedgut of the Mosque Theatre of Newark, New Jersey. Dalrymple wasted no time producing events in City Center, even though the new foundation was no where close to providing its own programming. The winter of 1942 she presented six concerts for the Treasury Department in the Mecca Temple, events to sell to the public Treasury stamps and bonds for World War II,[36] and just as importantly, to introduce New Yorkers to arts programming at City Center. The official opening of "New York City Center of Music and Drama, Inc." happened a year later, with a concert given by the New York Philharmonic Orchestra on 11 December 1943. Two days later, Gertrude Lawrence opened in a revival of Rachel Crothers' *Susan and God*, directed by Jean Dalrymple.

Despite the recent financial failure of the New Opera Company (1941–2) it was decided that City Center's first performing unit would be an opera company. When City Center opened in 1943, New York

Renaissance woman Jean Dalrymple — actress, publicity agent, playwright, director, and producer — played a major role in the creation and success of the New York City Center of Music and Drama (courtesy Billy Rose Theatre Collection, The New York Public Library for the Performing Arts, Astor, Lenox and Tilden Foundations).

had three resident operatic organizations: the Metropolitan, the Mascagni Opera Guild, and Alfredo Salmaggi's popular-price company (at the time named the "99-cent Grand Opera Company"). "The Mascagni and Salmaggi groups were immediately dismissed as being below the desired standards" of City Center.[37] The Hungarian-born conductor László Halász (1905–2001) was selected as the Artistic and Musical Director of City Center — once again, he came with the recommendation of Dalrymple, as she knew of his work conducting concerts featuring some of her singing clients.[38]

Aware of music critic Harold C. Schonberg's observation that "the human mind has not yet conceived a way to spend money faster than sponsoring a season of opera,"[39] Halász nevertheless succeeded in assembling an opera company whose mission was to present opera at inexpensive prices. New York City Opera soon became well known in America — they were featured on the cover of *Life* magazine on 11 April 1949 — and abroad because of the great variety and the quality of their productions, even though they were produced at a fraction of the budgets for the Met's productions.

Concurrent with her job at City Center, Dalrymple continued her work as a free-lance publicist. In the mid to late 1940s, Dalrymple's office was not only the press representative for individual performers and plays, but also produced approximately one play a year. Her staff of twenty-two kept all these balls in the air, in addition to concerts at Lewisohn Stadium and bookings for several summer theatres.[40]

Back at City Center, New York City Opera was soon joined by New York City Drama. Initially this division of City Center presented revivals of plays and musicals. One of the ingenious ways that Dalrymple devised to save money was to get sets and costumes from touring companies which had come off the road; therefore, her revival of *My Fair Lady* featured the original Broadway costumes. Also, all of the actors were paid the same; there were no star salaries at City Center. Dalrymple justified this on two grounds: first, City Center was not employing a company of actors, rather actors were hired for individual productions, so City Center Drama did not have to support actors in the long term. Second, Dalrymple believed that "the knowledge of this— eliminating all inherent personal quirks in competitive greed — allows each artist involved subconscious freedom to display his talents for his own inner satisfaction and for the benefit of the whole."[41]

After World War II, Lincoln Kirstein and George Balanchine established a new dance company, Ballet Society. Aside from their offices on 56th Street and using rehearsal space at the School of American Ballet, Ballet Society had no home. After renting performance space all over Manhattan, a life-saving offer came from City Center in 1948 to become a fellow constituent with New York City Opera, the City Center Orchestra, and City Center Drama. According to biographer Lynn Garafola, this invitation to join City Center saved Ballet Society from "economic collapse."[42] Like NYCO, NYCB rapidly grew to be a major company in its field. Indeed, for many arts patrons, "It is impossible to consider dance in New York City without considering City Center."[43] Not only had it been the home of New York City Ballet before it moved to Lincoln Center in 1964, it also has been the home base for the Joffrey Ballet, Alvin Ailey American Dance Theatre, as well as the primary stomping grounds for numerous other dance troupes, especially before the Joyce Theatre opened its doors in 1982.

While the excellent acoustics of City Center made it an appealing home for opera and musicals, it was not a natural home for dance.[44] For example, wing space was severely limited, especially stage right. If you were exiting stage right with any sort of run or flying leap, you had better have a fellow dancer or stage hand present to cushion your body so that it would not encounter the stage right brick wall of the theatre with full force. Second, before City Center's renovation in 1982, the sightlines from the orchestra seating area were notoriously bad for dance: you could not see the dancer's feet. In 1986, the stage right wing space was finally expanded, along with renovations to the dressing rooms and updates to the theatre's equipment.

The City Center board decided in 1953 to expand its theatre program and appointed Dalrymple director of the New York City Center Theatre Company. To inaugurate this division, she convinced José Ferrer to commit to an eight week season of *Cyrano de Bergerac*, *The Shrike*, and *Charley's Aunt*, all directed by and starring Ferrer; the season ended with the Margaret Webster staging of *Richard III*, starring Ferrer, Vincent Price, and Maureen Stapleton. All the actors, including Ferrer, received only Actors' Equity minimum ($85.00) a week; the season netted $80,000 profit for City Center, pulling it out of the financial doldrums.[45] Highlights of Dalrymple's stewardship of the New York City Center Theatre Company included Helen Hayes in *What Every Woman Knows* and *The Wisteria Trees*, Orson Welles in *King Lear* (1956), and Tallulah Bankhead in *A Streetcar Named Desire* (1956).

Dalrymple returned to playwriting in the 1950s, collaborating with Charles Robinson on *The Feathered Fauna* (produced in Dallas and Denver) in 1955, and writing *The Quiet Room*, produced in London in 1958.

The seemingly indefatigable Dalrymple was handed another challenge in 1957 when she was appointed director of the New York City Center Light Opera Company. Initial productions included revivals of *The Beggar's Opera*, *Brigadoon*, *The Merry Widow*, *South Pacific*, *The Pajama Game*, and *Carousel*. The revivals presented by Dalrymple's New York City Center Light Opera Company proved to be so popular that their profits helped subsidize other City Center companies. Some artistic highlights of the Light Opera productions were the 1960 revival of *The King and I* (starring Barbara Cook and Farley Granger), two revivals of *Pal Joey* (1961, 1963), both starring Bob Fosse as Joey, and the Frank Loesser Festival in 1966.

Given her expertise in many genres of arts presentation, it is hardly surprising that Harold Clurman — high commissioner of the United States for the

1958 World's Fair in Brussels—asked Dalrymple to be his co-coordinator of the Performing Arts Program. Some of the events Dalrymple arranged (from April to October) included the world premiere of Menotti's opera *Maria Golovin*, the NYCO production of the opera *Susannah*, the musicals *Carousel* and *Wonderful Town*, the play *The Time of Your Life* (directed by Dalrymple), and performances by American Ballet Theatre, Jerome Robbins' Ballets U.S.A., Van Cliburn, Leontyne Price, Eleanor Steber, Isaac Stern, Harry Belafonte, and the Philadelphia Orchestra under the direction of Eugene Ormandy.[46] Dalrymple concluded this could be done on a budget of $3 million; even after she was told she would only be given $500,000, she managed to present all the events she had scheduled without going into debt. In appreciation for her inspired programming, she was awarded the Knight, Order of the Crown, from the Belgium government.

In many ways, City Center became a victim of its own success. After years of negotiations, it was finally decided in 1966 that City Center would assume full operating responsibility of the New York State Theatre at Lincoln Center, the future home of New York City Ballet and New York City Opera.[47] Without two of its shining jewels—NYCB and NYCO—and with the impact of New York City's financial crisis, the 1970s would be very hard on City Center. No endowment to help fund its programming meant the death knell to the City Center Light Opera Company and the City Center Theatre Company. Faced with increasing financial instability, the board decided to cede City Center from City Center Music and Drama (the parent company of NYCO and NYCB), in order to make it a self-sustaining entity separate from its illustrious off spring, now housed at Lincoln Center. This was a fundamental shift in ideology for City Center, as it now became primarily a rental house (producing only Encores!).

Even before the reorganization of City Center in the 1970s, Dalrymple—as was her norm—had her hands in many projects. As producer-director of the television WNTA "Play of the Week" series, this television pioneer presented *The Cherry Orchard*, *Crime of Passion*, and *Reunion at Vienna* (Producer's Showcase, NBC) in 1959. In 1960, she was appointed Executive Producer for Paramount's International Telemeter Company (pay television), for which she presented Menotti's opera *The Consul*, the 4th Street Theatre's production of *Hedda Gabler*, *A Country Scandal*, *The Second City Revue*, and the first live transmission of a Broadway show, *Show Girl*, in 1961 from the Eugene O'Neill Theatre, starring Carol Channing. While her independent projects still found success, Dalrymple's last venture with a theatre company dedicated to popular priced entertainment did not prosper.

The Light Opera of Manhattan (LOOM), established in 1974—America's only year-round operetta company—lost its theatre space in 1984. The closing of the Eastside Playhouse was disastrous for the troupe, known primarily for their Gilbert and Sullivan repertory, forcing them to close their doors in 1986. Dalrymple had been president of LOOM since 1984, and simply could not find enough ways to keep the company afloat financially. Now in her 80s, Dalrymple did not slow down. In 1990 she was inducted into the Theatre Hall of Fame, and until 1991 she served as one of the thirteen nominators for the Tony Awards. She also appeared often on cable television as the creator and co-moderator of the American Theatre Wing's "Working in the Theatre" seminars.

As *Variety* reported upon her death in 1998, "The founding of City Center in 1941 began Dalrymple's lifetime career."[48] Even though the original mandate of City Center, to create its own programming at affordable prices, changed in the 1970s, there is no doubt that Dalrymple's leadership in the first three decades of City Center gave the world several lasting institutions—New York City Opera and New York City Ballet—and stirring revivals of some of the gems of American musical theatre. Like many women who earned management positions in the 1950s and 1960s, Dalrymple was often described in ways which discussed her physical appearance, an approach which would never have been used in profiling a male. Concerning the "Mother of City Center," producer Robert Whitehead remarked: "She always had a kind of serenity about her. She had a great determination to get things done, but she was always very feminine, very pretty. She was an extraordinary person."[49] A reporter for the *Cleveland Plain Dealer* saw a slightly different side of Dalrymple, noting she was "as fragile as a Fragonard painting but hep and with a sense of timing like a Garand rifle."[50] But perhaps Isabelle Stevenson, chair of the board of the American Theater Wing, said it best, declaring that her long time friend and board member "was the most knowledgeable person in theater that I knew."[51]

The Queen of Off Broadway: Lucille Lortel

While Broadway is often synonymous with the musical, Off Broadway and Off Off Broadway have sometimes been the starting place for productions which moved to Broadway for long runs—i.e., *Hair, A Chorus Line, Rent*—or for productions which stayed in their original location: *The Fantasticks, The Threepenny Opera, Little Shop of Horrors*. Running for seven years, *The Threepenny Opera* helped legitimize Off Broadway, and due to the success and commitment of its producer to theatre not headed for the Great White Way, Richard Coe of *The Washington Post* dubbed Lucille Lortel "The Queen of Off Broadway" in 1962.[52]

Born Lucille Wadler in Manhattan in 1900, her brother Mayo was a violinist and child prodigy, which enabled the family to travel twice to Europe on his concert tours. Even though Lucille studied acting in Berlin with Arnold Korff and Max Reinhardt, and in New York at the American Academy of Dramatic Arts, her family did not support her desire to pursue acting as a career. But Lortel seemed to have a magical magnet which drew her into situations where she would be working alongside the best in American theatre. As a young actress she appeared in summer stock with the future distinguished playwright S.N. Behrman. In 1925 — the year of her Broadway debut — she appeared in three Broadway plays, including the inaugural outing of the Guild Theatre: George Bernard Shaw's *Caesar and Cleopatra* starring Helen Hayes, Helen Westley, and Harold Clurman.

After appearing in several more stage plays and films, Lortel was wooed by wealthy chemical engineer Louis Schweitzer, who had made his fortune manufacturing cigarette papers. Schweitzer made it clear when they married in 1931 that he wanted his wife at home in the evenings, but within a year she was back on Broadway with *The Man Who Reclaimed His Head*, starring Claude Rains and Jean Arthur; this short-lived production was Lortel's last performance on Broadway.

While Lortel may have given up her acting career, she was by no means through with the theatre. In 1947 she began to produce readings of experimental plays by American and European playwrights in the barn of the couple's summer estate in Westport, Connecticut. She wanted the White Barn Theatre to be a refuge, safe from the marketplace economics of commercial theatre. Full productions of plays began in 1949 when she installed a stage in the second floor of the barn. The third offering at the White Barn Theatre was the musical *No Casting Today* (1947); other musicals which premiered at Lortel's White Barn Theatre include the Cy Coleman and A.E. Hotchner musical *Welcome to the Club* (which premiered at the White Barn as *Let 'Em Rot*, 1987). When asked about the founding of the White Barn Theatre, Lortel quipped she had originally thought of buying horses: "But the war was on. It was difficult to get feed."[53]

Eight years after Lortel started producing at the White Barn, Schweitzer, growing tired of never seeing his wife in New York City due to her theatre in Connecticut, presented her with the Theatre de Lys on Christopher Street in Greenwich Village as a 24th wedding anniversary present. She reopened the 299-seat theatre with the Marc Blitzstein adaptation of *The Threepenny Opera* in 1955; it ran for 2707 performances, winning the only Tony Awards ever awarded to an Off Broadway production. *Threepenny* helped put Off Broadway on the map, in addition to sparking renewed interest in the musical plays of Brecht/Weill.

While the seven year run of the inaugural production of the Theatre de Lys more than validated Lortel as a viable producer in New York, *The Threepenny Opera* was also a nuisance in that she wanted to present more theatrical works in her theatre. Lortel begged the American National Theatre and Academy (ANTA) to support a matinee series at the de Lys as a "laboratory for innovation." Lasting over twenty years, the Tuesday afternoon series lived up to its mission as Lortel introduced to American audiences dance dramas by Anna Sokolow and May O'Donnell, and performances of rarely seen plays by Albee, Inge, Ionesco, O'Casey, and Tennessee Williams. Even though the relatively small size of the Theatre de Lys was not the most economically viable space to produce musicals, Lortel nevertheless presented—in addition to *Threepenny Opera*—the musicals *Trixie True, Teen Detective* (1980) and *Falsettoland* (1991), as well as the revues *Put It In Writing* (1963) and *Sprechen Sie Brecht?* (1985).

In 1988, *The New York Times* called Lortel a "den mother and angel to [the] hundreds of playwrights, directors, actors" she had worked with in her 500+ productions she produced or co-produced,[54] introducing American audiences to Jean Genet, Athol Fugard, Samuel Beckett, and contemporary American playwrights such as Terrence McNally and Adrienne Kennedy. She was nominated for five Tony Awards, including one for the South African musical, *Sarafina!* (1988), her 499th production.

In 1962, Lortel received the first Margo Jones Award, the Lee Strasberg Lifetime Achievement Award (1985), and was inducted into the Theatre Hall of Fame in 1990. Two permanent exhibits celebrate her career at the New York City Public Library's Performing Arts Library at Lincoln Center and at the Westport Public Library, and the official name of the Theatre de Lys was changed to the Lucille Lortel Theatre in 1981.

A generous patron of the arts, Lortel established the first theatre chair for a woman, the Lucille Lortel Distinguished Professional Chair in Theatre at the City University of New York. She also established the Lucile Lortel Fund for New Drama at Yale University (August Wilson's *Fences* was the fund's first production) and The Lucille Lortel Fellowship in Playwriting at Brown University (1996). The Lucille Lortel Awards for Outstanding Achievement Off Broadway were created in 1985 by the League of Off Broadway Theatres & Producers (which had been established in 1959). Previous winners include the musicals *Urinetown* (2002), *Bat Boy* (2001), *James Joyce's The Dead* (2000), *Violet* (1997), *Floyd Collins* (1996), *Wings* (1994), *Forbidden Broadway* (1993), *And the World Goes Round* (1992), *Falsettoland* (1991).

Producer Lucille Lortel was dubbed "The Queen of Off Broadway" (courtesy Billy Rose Theatre Collection, The New York Public Library for the Performing Arts, Astor, Lenox and Tilden Foundations).

"Honey, I've got a one-track mind and it's theatre, theatre, theatre," Lortel once said. "I have no time for anything else."[55] For a biographical entry printed in 1976 for *Notable Names in the American Theatre*, Lortel listed her recreation as "theatre." Before she died on 4 April 1999 at the age of 98, she had left instructions that her tombstone be inscribed:

Lucille Lortel

Theatrical pioneer, patron of the arts,
Loving mentor to all who worked for her
HER THEATRES WERE HER CHILDREN

Having grown up in an era when a woman's worth was often determined by the success of her father, her husband, and her children, Lortel may have wanted this tombstone to silence any future biographers who might be moved to suggest that she was incomplete because she did not give birth to nor raise any children. In her last "press release," Lortel purposely embraced the roles of teacher and mother — not producer or theatre owner — for she wished to be remembered not for the money she made (or lost) but rather for being a "pioneer" who brought ambitious new work to her audiences. Did fellow (male) producers George Abbott or David Merrick leave such a tombstone? In a word: no. Once she had left acting, Lortel was very aware of crafting a new public persona. Having married into a life of privilege, Lortel often had to battle not only misogyny but also classism in her quest to be taken seriously as a theatrical producer. Yet even when she established herself as a thoughtful and risk-taking producer, Lortel chose not to act like "one of the boys." She enjoyed the moniker of being the "Queen of Off Broadway," and realized that her goal of bringing new work and new theatres into the world could be framed in a way — mentor and mother — that made people (mainly men) more comfortable with the notion of a "lady" producer.

The combined legacies of Theresa Helburn, Jean Dalrymple, and Lucille Lortel encompass the worlds of producing organizations dedicated to giving place to new voices in the theatre (Theatre Guild), to establishing theatres where quality dance, opera, and musical revivals were available to the public at reasonable prices (City Center), and to musicals being presented in the Village in the early days of the Off Broadway movement. It is telling that all three of these women created careers for themselves on the fringes and margins of professional theatre. By working outside of the mainstream of traditional Broadway or regional theatre, they were able to make a living (and leave a legacy) in high-risk arenas which were not attractive to their male counterparts. Each one of these women blazed new trails and created new institutions which not only had an impact while they were alive, but shaped the course of musical theatre in America. Without their creative work as producers, musical works like *Oklahoma!*, intimate reviews like *The Garrick Gaities*, and *Porgy and Bess* might never have come to be (or at least would not have been realized in the form that was presented). Dalrymple's work at City Center in many ways created the canon of the Golden Age of American musical theatre as her revivals bolstered the popularity of confirmed hits, or provided a venue for the re-evaluation of under-appreciated works like *Pal Joey*. Lortel not only produced musicals while she was alive, but her endowments at Yale, Brown, and the Lucille Lortel Awards for Outstanding Achievement Off Broadway mean that her support of new artists and their work will continue for generations to come.

We are right to keep in mind what Milly Barranger wrote in her biography of Margaret Webster — an admonition which applies to all the women discussed in this book — "[her] achievements cannot be overestimated in a profession that continues to favor men as producers, directors, and managers."[56] How much richer the American theatre is for the artistry and brilliance of Theresa Helburn, Jean Dalrymple, and Lucille Lortel.

Notes

1. Faye E. Dudden, *Women in the American Theatre: Actresses & Audiences, 1790–1870*, (New Haven: Yale University Press, 1994) 123–124.

2. Meryle Secrest, *Somewhere for Me: A Biography of Richard Rodgers* (New York: Alfred A. Knopf, 2001) 254.

3. Theresa Helburn, *A Wayward Quest* (Boston: Little, Brown, and Co, 1960) 282.

4. Helburn, *Wayward*, p. 282.

5. Lawrence Langner, *The Magic Curtain: The Story of a Life in Two Fields, Theatre and Invention by the Founder of the Theatre Guild*, New York: E.P. Dutton & Company, Inc., 1951) 126.

6. Helburn, *Wayward* 10.

7. Helburn, *Wayward* 13.

8. Langner 97.

9. Langner 121.

10. Langner 158.

11. Roy S. Waldau, *Vintage Years of the Theatre Guild, 1928–1939* (Cleveland: Case Western Reserve University, 1972) 189.

12. Mark Fearnow, "Theatre Groups and Their Playwrights," *The Cambridge History of American Theatre, Volume Two: 1870–1945*, Don Wilmeth and Christopher Bigsby, eds. (New York: Cambridge University Press, 1999) 359.

13. Qtd. in Waldau 87.

14. Langner 205.

15. Meryle Secrest, *Somewhere for Me: A Biography of Richard Rodgers* (New York: Alfred A. Knopf, 2001) 64.

16. Waldau 167.

17. Edward Jablonski, *Gershwin: A Biography* (New York: Da Capo Press, 1998) 251.

18. Jablonski 250.

19. Waldau 223.

20. Waldau 222.

21. Qtd. in Waldau 335.

22. Waldau 386.

23. "Theresa" 29.

24. *Notable Names in the American Theatre* (Clifton, New Jersey: James. T. White Company, 1976) 932.

25. Qtd. in "Tribute" 21.

26. Qtd. in "Tribute" 21.

27. Qtd. in Beth Howard, "City Center," *Theatre Crafts* 10:22 (December 1988): 41.

28. Jean Dalrymple, *September Child: The Story of Jean Dalrymple by Herself* (New York: Dodd, Mead & Company, 1963) 24.

29. Dalrymple, *September* xii.
30. Dalrymple, *September* 29.
31. Dalrymple, *September* 77.
32. Dalrymple, *September* 109.
33. Gerald Bordman, *American Theatre: A Chronicle of Comedy and Drama, 1914–1930* (New York: Oxford University Press, 1995) 399.
34. Dalrymple, *September* 111.
35. Martin L Sokol, *The New York City Opera: An American Adventure* (New York: Macmillan Publishing Co., Inc., 1981) 2.
36. Dalrymple, *September* 218.
37. Sokol 32.
38. Sokol 34.
39. Qtd. in Sokol 33.
40. Dalrymple, *September* 235.
41. Dalrymple, *September* 299.
42. Lynn Garafola, *Dance for a City: Fifty Years of the New York City Ballet* (New York: Columbia University Press, 1999) 6.
43. Howard 41.
44. Howard 62.
45. Dalrymple, *September* 279.
46. Dalrymple, *September* 289.
47. Edgar B. Young, *Lincoln Center: The Building of an Institution* (New York: New York University Press, 1980) 235.
48. "Jean Dalrymple," *Variety* 23 November 1998: n. pag.
49. Qtd. in Richard Severo, "Jean Dalrymple, Persuasive Dreamer Who Brought Theater to City Center, Dies at 96," *The New York Times* 17 November 1998: C30.
50. Qtd. in Severo, p. C30.
51. Qtd. in Allan Wallach, "Jean Dalrymple, 96, Producer, Writer, Publicist for Theater," *Newsday* 17 November 1998: A65.
52. Richard L. Coe, "Off Broadway Is Her Realm," *Washington Post* 3 April 1962: n. pag.
53. Qtd. in Jesse McKinley, "Queen of Off Broadway Is Remembered," *The New York Times* 26 May 1999: C21.
54. Alice M. Robertson, Vera Mowry Roberts, and Milly S. Barranger, Eds. *Notable Women in the American Theatre: A Biographical Dictionary* (New York: Greenwood Press, 1989) n. pag.
55. Qtd. in Enid Nemy, "Lucille Lortel, Patron Who Made Innovative Off Broadway a Star, Is Dead at 98," *The New York Times* 6 April 1999, p. A25.
56. Milly S. Barranger, *Margaret Webster: A Life in the Theatre* (Ann Arbor: University of Michigan Press, 2004) 2.

"Open a New Window, Open a New Door"

Women Directors Take the Stage

ANNE FLIOTSOS

Many famous musicals owe a debt to the creative talent of their directors, who provided a vision and artistic path for the production and fused the many creative efforts into an artistic whole. Great directors of Broadway musicals come easily to mind: George Abbott, Michael Kidd, Gower Champion, Jerome Robbins, Bob Fosse, Hal Prince. But who are the women? Certainly Susan Schulman, Graciele Daniele, and Julie Taymor have all received recognition for their directing on and off Broadway, but almost exclusively in the last decade and a half of the twentieth century. Other women have paved the way for this recent batch of women directing on Broadway, although most of them remain "unsung."

Studies have addressed the history of women in directing,[1] but none have focused on the particular challenges associated with musical theatre: staggering budgets (requiring staggering returns) and large creative teams that can be unwieldy. The result is a plethora of details requiring careful attention; success is crucial, and the stakes for the producer are staggering. Traditionally, this crucial leadership role has gone to men, but several women have struggled to prove themselves as well. It is commonly agreed that fewer women than men direct musical theatre professionally, but little data exists to explore the width and character of this gender gap. Therefore, this study begins with an examination of the number of women directing musicals in a variety of professional venues: Broadway, Off Broadway, Regional, and National Tours. An overview of data highlights some of the changes during the twentieth century in each venue and illuminates the discrepancy between the number of men and women hired to direct musical productions.

The numerical data from the study suggests a structure for the remainder of the essay. In terms of chronology, women directors of musicals divide into "waves" or groups: that of the early pioneers (before 1960), of later pioneers (with a resurgence of women directing in the 1960s), and of successful working professionals at the end of the century. This essay examines each group, or generation, of directors, highlighting the careers of women who have been instrumental as professional directors of musical works, including Dorothy Raedler, Mary Hunter, Vida Hope, Lucia Victor, Vinnette Carroll, Sue Lawless, Julianne Boyd, Graciela Daniele,[2] Susan Schulman, and Julie Taymor. The study concludes with a reevaluation of the inroads made by women directors of musicals over the century, in part to answer the question, "How far have we come?"

Although women have been directing for over a century, it was not until the advent of the women's movement that studies on women directors were undertaken in order to determine if sexism lie in the path of their success. In 1976, six women conducted a study entitled "Action for Women," to explore employment discrimination against women playwrights and directors in non-profit theatres. Their results were telling in terms of Broadway hiring as well. The authors of the study discovered that unlike their male counterparts, women who tried to climb the ladder of success hit a "glass ceiling" or found a "broken ladder" when it came to directing productions on Broadway. They reported that

> certain trends [were] apparent in directors' resumes: the women had exceptional theatre training — degrees from prominent universities or professional training programs. Many had worked for several years as assistants to highly regarded male directors and while there were instances of regional theatre, Off Off Broadway and Off Broadway credits, there was very little Broadway work.[3]

A subsequent study of women directors' and designers' careers from 1977 to 1982 found that although women could find work directing for a small stipend of $100–$300, "once a woman director enters the paying job market, directorial positions become scarce."[4] When women were hired, it was perceived as limited tokenism, especially in high-paying regional theatres.

Although the causes of discrimination are not the central goal of this study, these findings clearly indicate that women have had significant difficulty working as directors compared to their male counterparts. A numerical comparison of women versus men directing musicals is especially telling of the "glass ceiling" syndrome. The charts that follow provide an intriguing look at the pattern of women directing in major venues (Broadway, Off Broadway, Regional Theatres, and National Tours) in relation to the total number of directing positions. The criteria for "musicals" are used liberally in this study: operettas, opera, revues, and musical theatre are all included.[5] Data was gathered from *Theatre World*, an annual record of theatre productions that was published beginning in 1944 under the title *Daniel Blum's Theatre World*. The publishers describe *Theatre World* as "the authoritative statistical and pictorial record."

Accuracy of the data in this study is bound by the accuracy and limitations of *Theatre World.*[6]

Broadway is one of the most interesting categories to examine, in part because the statistics go back the furthest and in part because the "glass ceiling" syndrome is particularly significant in this venue. The small percentage of women directing on Broadway bears out the assumptions stated in previous studies: although women have worked on Broadway in each decade, their numbers are woefully low in comparison to their male counterparts.

Broadway

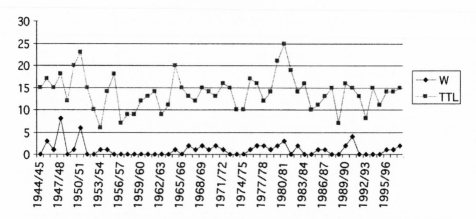

Figure 1. Musicals/opera/operetta/revues opening on Broadway, directed by women.

At first glance, there is a noticeable flurry of activity in the late 1940s that suddenly ceases in the later 1950s. The early spikes in the late 1940s represent the multiple operettas directed by D'Oyly Carte's Anna Bethnell and Eleanor Evans, two British women. There is an entire decade of inactivity between 1954–55, with Vida Hope's *The Boy Friend*, and 1964–65, with Joan Littlewood's production of *Oh! What a Lovely War.* It is less surprising to see a lull in the employment of women in the 1950s, the decade of women at home, than in the 1960s, an era famous for feminism and protest. Two of the seven musical productions directed by women in the 1960s were Yiddish revues directed and performed by Mina Bern: *Sing, Israel, Sing* and *Let's Sing Yiddish.* Others directing in the late sixties and early seventies included: Lucia Victor, Agnes de Mille, Lee Theodore, and Onna White. DeMille and White were well-known choreographers. Victor was an assistant of Gower Champion's who went on to restage some of his famous musicals (notably *Hello, Dolly!*) on national tours and on Broadway, but she also directed Broadway musicals on her own, such as *Heathen!* (1971–72) and *Ari* (1970–71). Note that women who had already made a name for themselves as actors or choreographers are those who succeed in directing on Broadway as well. In other words, producers were willing to take a gamble on a woman director if she already had a proven record of success and substantial name recognition.

Another three years without women stretches from the 1972–73 season to 1975, when Victor directs the all-black version of *Hello, Dolly!* with Pearl Bailey. At this point a second generation of directors, still pioneering, make some inroads directing on Broadway: Vinnette Carroll, Elizabeth Swados, Julianne Boyd, and Sue Lawless. A few more sporadic years ensue, with choreographers Twyla Tharp and Patricia Birch making their Broadway directing debuts before we come to a further cluster of women directors: Graciela Daniele, Susan Schulman, and Julie Taymor among others. The total number of women directing musical works on Broadway from 1944 to 1998 was a mere 7.5 percent, or a total of 56 out of the 751 musical productions.

Off-Broadway

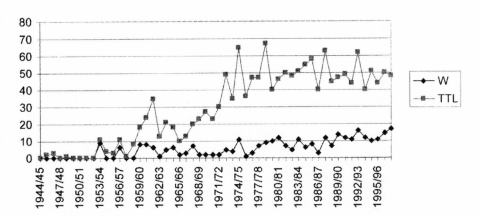

Fig. 2. Musicals/opera/operetta/revues opening Off Broadway, directed by women.

Women fared much better directing Off Broadway, but the number of women directing musical works was only 19.3 percent out of 1596 titles reported. As Figure 2 reveals, the first decade displays very little activity. All of the Off Broadway work in the 1950s (and much of the work in the 1960s) was by Dorothy Raedler, directing the operettas of Gilbert and Sullivan. As would be expected, most of the same pioneering women who were directing on Broadway were busy Off Broadway as well.

Theatre World does not include a substantial amount of data on regional theatres until 1980, as Fig. 3 demonstrates, yet it is the most complete source of data available for this study. This data is limited, as many regional theatres did not report specific data on directing, but it still gives us some insight into the proportion of women to men directing in regional theatres at the end of the twentieth century.

Regional Theatre

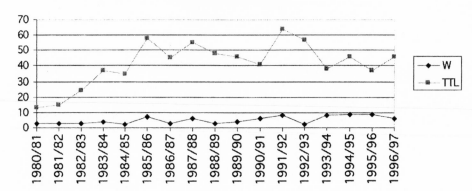

Fig. 3. Musicals/opera/operetta/revues opening in regional theatres, directed by women (from limited data in *Theatre World*).

Women seem to be directing more consistently in regional theatres than on or off Broadway. For example, there are no years without women directors, nor are there large, sudden spikes in the data for women, as with Broadway productions. Women represented 12.4 percent of the directors of musical works in this venue, almost double the percentage directing on Broadway.

The data reveal that one of the worst venues for women to direct musical works has been national tours. As with Broadway, it is likely that the cost, size, and high risk of the productions has deterred producers from hiring women over the decades. Figure 4 shows the pitiful history of women's representation

National Tours

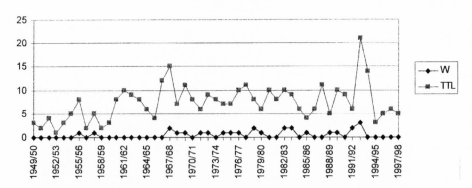

Fig. 4. Musicals/opera/operetta/revues beginning national tours, directed by women.

in this venue. Although Broadway producers have a poor track-record of hiring women, with 7.5 percent of musical works directed by women, national tours are slightly worse, with 7.3 percent. Because most Broadway directors are also the directors of the touring productions, the close correlation makes sense. However, directors like Lucia Victor and Ruth Mitchell, who were assistants to Gower Champion and Harold Prince, may in fact be under-represented in the data; it is impossible to tell how many national tours may have been re-staged by the assistants, yet credited to the original Broadway directors. Of the women who have directed on Broadway, Lucia Victor and Susan Schulman have been among the most successful in the touring venue.

Further data from *Theatre World* suggest that a number of women directors took on additional roles in the productions they directed, such as choreographer, writer, composer, lyricist, designer, and producer. Perhaps this trend is a reflection of starting their careers in another area, then becoming directors in order to get their work staged. Interviews with women playwrights reflect this phenomenon. For example, playwright Sandra Perlman became a director "because it just had to happen that way or it [her play] wasn't going to be done."[7] In addition, this propensity for multi-tasking may show a different relationship between the women and their works—that they are willing to collaborate on a number of levels and take on several roles to get the work produced. Some women took on as many as four roles at a time, yet the majority (53.3 percent) functioned as directors only. It is interesting to note how rare designer/directors such as Julie Taymor are (1.4 percent) compared to more traditional director/choreographers (17.1 percent). Although similar statistics for male directors of musicals are not available for comparison, these statistics give some indication of how women directors are incorporating their talents to accomplish their goals.

Table 1

Musical productions directed by women (Broadway, Off Broadway, Regional, National Tours) by function of the director, from *Theatre World*, 1944–1997.

(Additional) Function	*Number of Productions*	*Percentage*
Director only	262 of 492 productions	53.3%
Choreographer	84 of 492 productions	17.1%
Writer/creator	65 of 492 productions	13.2%
Producer	56 or 492 productions	11.4%
Composer and/or Lyricist	25 of 492 productions	5.1%
Performer	7 of 492 productions	1.4%
Designer	7 of 492 productions	1.4%

One additional source of data that illuminates the career paths of directors comes from the professional directors union, the Society of Stage Directors and

Choreographers (SSDC, founded in 1959). Considering the gap between men and women who direct professionally, as evidenced in figures 1–4, it comes as little surprise that SSDC membership at the end of 1999 echoes the trend. Of the 946 members who identified themselves as directors, 82 percent were male and only 18 percent were female. In contrast, the majority of members identifying themselves as choreographers (58 percent) were women. Those choosing the label director/choreographers were 71 percent men and 29 percent women. Clearly, the number of women identifying themselves as choreographers, where they have traditionally been accepted, is much higher than those who claim directing as their chief occupation.

The numerical data reveal that although women have made some inroads into the professional direction of musicals, their paths have been difficult and slow. Several historical studies have examined the earliest pioneers of directing in order to help us understand the careers of these women and the obstacles they faced.

Shirlee Hennigan's study of women directors (of both plays and musicals) was one of the first to delve into their murky history.[8] Hennigan reported that in the first quarter of the twentieth century, some actresses managed to direct and even produce theatre, but the number dwindled as directors became distinct specialists in the field rather than actor/directors or producer/directors. She also found that following World War II, women directors had a much harder time in the profession; by the fifties, almost no women were directing at all. After studying the careers of women in the professional theatre, Hennigan concluded that sexual discrimination and social ideas about women's obligations to family were among the primary culprits in deterring women from professional careers in directing.[9]

A slightly different telling comes from Tamara L. Compton in "The Rise of the Woman Director on Broadway, 1920–1950." Her statistical count of women directing both straight plays and musicals on Broadway shows a fairly strong presence from 1920 up to 1950; thereafter the number falls dramatically. Compton argued that women of the 1910s and '20s had a difficult time finding work as stage managers, the traditional training for directing. Furthermore, she cites a shift from a technical emphasis in directing to one of artistic emphasis around 1930, thus opening doors for women who were not seen as technically-minded. Other factors that contributed to the growing number of women directing on Broadway could be "the influence of the female audience, the feminist involvement in establishing clubs and networking, the rise of the Little Theatre Movement [...] and the experiments in repertory theatre."[10]

Typically, the women who directed in the first half of the twentieth century incorporated directing into their careers along with acting, choreography, or writing (book, lyrics, or music). For example, Hennigan noted that Agnes Morgan directed, acted, and wrote book and lyrics for five editions of *The Grand Street Follies* at the Neighborhood Playhouse in New York, all before 1927.

Morgan is credited with book, lyrics, and staging of the next two years of *The Grand Street Follies* (1928, 1929) at the Booth Theatre, and wrote and directed *If Love Were All* at the Booth under the pseudonym Cutler Hatch.[11] My own review of data from *Theatre World* confirms a connection between directing and other creative contributions, especially in the early years. The pioneering women who were entrusted to direct musicals had first made a name for themselves as an actress or choreographer, fields which had been more accepting of women. For example, choreographers Agnes de Mille and Katherine Dunham are both credited with staging musicals in the 1940s, as is actress Stella Adler.[12]

Several women stand out in the late 1940s to mid–1950s for directing musical works on Broadway. Oddly enough, it was two British women who gained early credits because of their work with Gilbert and Sullivan operettas: Anna Bethnell and Eleanor Evans of the touring D'Oyly Carte Opera (directing in 1947–48 and 1950–51, respectively). Bethnell directed seven productions in repertory and Evans four. Bethnell, also known as Mrs. Sydney Granville, was appointed director of the famous D'Oyly Carte Opera in 1947, but evidently held that post for only a short period. She joined the chorus of the company in 1909, and after serving an apprenticeship, moved on to leading roles before stepping in as a director. Although both women were traveling with touring productions and both directed operetta rather than musical comedy, they deserve mention as early women directors whose musical works appeared on the Broadway stage.

The American counterpart to Bethnell and Evans was Dorothy Raedler, who directed and produced some sixty productions (again, in repertory) of Gilbert and Sullivan operettas Off Broadway and at the New York City Center. Raedler formed an amateur Gilbert and Sullivan company while studying at Hunter College in 1936. The group turned semi-professional, and finally became The American Savoyards in 1952, when it became an Off Broadway Equity troupe. Before her death in 1993 she helped establish the St. Croix School of the Arts in the U.S. Virgin Islands, where she spent the last twenty-five years of her life. Although Raedler's work was not limited to Gilbert and Sullivan, nor to productions in New York City, they have become her legacy.

Operetta aside, who are the women who directed more traditional musical comedy at the time? Another British woman gets the credit for directing a "hit" Broadway musical in the 1950s. Vida Hope, an actress turned director, had success in London with Sandy Wilson's *The Boy Friend* and directed the Broadway version in the 1954–55 season. Hope started her stage career as an actress, making appearances at the Old Vic with Lawrence Olivier and working in film. According to her obituary, Wilson asked Hope to direct two of his Water Gate revues, which lead to her direction of *The Boy Friend* as well.[13]

A photo essay in New York's *Journal-American* (25 Sept. 1954) depicts Hope at rehearsals and illustrates the novelty of women directing a Broadway musical. It depicts a woman who is a peacemaker in a highly stressful collaborative process. The first caption reads:

> The day of the theatrical director who grew bald through tearing his hair out over temperament is gone according to Vida Hope, first woman to stage a musical in many a year. Her forte is calmness, keeping everybody happy and ... most important ... getting what she wants out of the cast and principals.[14]

Additional captions provide insight into Hope's directing style, or at least the newspaper's perception of her style. In addition, these quotations reveal some interesting discrepancies between journalists' treatment of men and women. For example, newspapers traditionally refer to men by their last names once the full name has been reported. Here, Hope is referred to by her first name, in a more familiar manner. The tone of the writing is brisk and light, and the photographs feature her in a skin-tight outfit, revealing a curvaceous figure.

> She discusses, never argues a point[...]. A bundle of energy, she sets the pace for the rest of the gang[...]. She's a stickler for detail and somehow gets it, without upsetting the attitude of the cast.... Vida, a perfectionist, gives her personal attention to everyone on stage, from prop man to chorine, to star and producer.

At the end of the photo essay, a picture depicts her discussing the play in close quarters with four male colleagues. The caption highlights her collaborative spirit. "Vida's a great believer in the 'huddle' after a day's work: 'There's always something I might have missed and I've always figured five heads are better than one.'"[15]

Although the press made rehearsals look rosy, what was hailed as a celebration of a woman directing quickly became a tale of infighting and insecurity. Three days after the photo essay appeared, the producers of *The Boyfriend* barred Hope and Wilson from rehearsals, only a week and a half before opening night. Cy Feuer, Earnest Martin's co-producer, stepped into the role of director when the disagreement erupted about "how the show should be presented here."[16] Two cast members were replaced, and Hope reportedly returned to London, but retained credit for the direction of the Broadway production and the United States national tour. Hope was announced as the director of another New York musical, *My Royal Past*, but apparently was replaced. She continued to direct in England until at least 1960. She died at the age of forty-five in an automobile accident; it is difficult to know whether her directing career was just beginning or had played itself out by her untimely death in 1963.

Mary Hunter also deserves mention as an early pioneer on Broadway, both as a leader and as a director. In addition to directing, Hunter was associate producer for the Theatre Guild, helped originate the Society of Stage Directors and Choreographers, and was known as a great educator. Born in 1904 in Bakersfield, California, Hunter studied art history at Wellesley College and anthropology at the University of Chicago, where she got her first opportunity to direct for a group called The Cube Theatre. A job at Chicago's radio station WGN led her to audition and accept a role on the radio show "Easy Aces." When the show moved to New York, Hunter studied acting in order to understand directing, first with Maria Ouspenskaya and later with Tamara Daykarhanova, both former actors at the Moscow Art Theatre. She considered this period, along with one year as Russian actor Andrius Jilinsky's assistant, to be the most influential in her training.[17]

Hunter directed for the American Actors Company until 1944, then directed the Horton Foote play *Only the Heart* at Provincetown Playhouse; it moved to Broadway, but floundered there. Her first musical on Broadway, *Carib Song*[18] (1945), starred Katherine Dunham (who also choreographed the production) and was not financially successful. She was signed to direct *High Button Shoes*, but was replaced by George Abbott two weeks before opening. The producers argued that they needed a hit and could only get it with Abbott's name.[19] Unlike Hope, Hunter brought the matter to arbitration for breach of contract. Under the scrutiny of the court, the producers declared that she was replaced for incompetence. Fortunately for Hunter, glowing reviews for her next production came out during the trial, making the charge of incompetence seem contrived, at best. The board awarded Hunter "the full extent of her contract, to the letter."[20] Although she originally asked for only her director's fee of $2,000 and a percentage of the gross, she was awarded $40,000 at a time when there was no director's union.[21]

Hunter continued directing musicals, both on Broadway (*Great to Be Alive!* 1949–50) and in Dallas, where she spent two summer seasons as the first female director at the State Fair Casino, directing *Maytime, Brigadoon, Roberta, Desert Song, Annie Get Your Gun, Where's Charley?, Song of Norway, Texas Li'l Darling, I Married an Angel, Miss Liberty*, and *The Merry Widow*. According to Compton, she left after two seasons "because she found the routine and the long planning time tedious."[22] Back in New York, she co-created an additional folk-musical called *Musical Americana*, based in part on material from her previous work, *American Legend*. It opened in New York in 1953, then toured for two years, with a few selected performances the third year.

As with Vida Hope, the newspapers described Hunter's work ethic as one of calm demeanor and open collaboration rather than strong, autocratic leadership — almost to the point of making her sound diminutive. John Rosenfield, theatre columnist, called her method of working with actors "evocative rather than didactic." He described her as a "tiny little woman with a deliberately unobtrusive personality and the quietest of voices," with "a rare knack of divining the core quality of a musical play."[23] Another columnist noted, "She has always been persuading singers and dancers to learn acting and actors to learn to sing and dance."[24] It was her philosophy of crossing disciplines that inspired her work with Agnes de Mille (a childhood friend), Katherine Dunham, and Jerome Robbins. Of her own work, Hunter commented, "I don't try for any 'style' or trademark of my own; I think that ought to be in accord with the script."[25]

The earliest pioneers, Raedler, Hope, and Hunter, among others, are gone now, but some of the next crop of women directing musicals have talked extensively about their careers and contributions to musical theatre. They, too, are pioneers, establishing many "firsts" for women in the field, thus paving the way for a new group of directors. The following biographical sections, with excerpts from interviews, help chronicle this second wave of women's direction of musical theatre and give these women an opportunity to delineate their careers in their own words.

Vinnette Carroll holds the distinction of being the first African-American woman to direct on Broadway. Born in New York, but with roots in the West Indies, Carroll attended Long Island University and New York University, where she earned a degree in psychology. She was a psychologist for several years before succumbing to the temptation of theatre at the age of twenty-six. Carroll took night classes to rid herself of a West Indian accent and won a scholarship to Erwin Piscator's Dramatic Workshop at the New School for Social Research in 1948. She was then invited to study at the Actors Studio as a free pupil. Although she began her theatre career as a successful actress, she later turned to directing, explaining, "As one gets older, you begin to want to see the whole picture and to collaborate with the playwright."[26]

Carroll considers her major influence as Piscator and his colleagues, but also has been affected by the teachings of Stanislavsky, via Lee Strasberg and Stella Adler from her work at the Actors Studio. In keeping with their influence, she enjoys working one-on-one with actors and uses sense-memory in her rehearsals, believing the actors must find the characters from within. Yet, whereas many Method-trained actors and directors turned to the naturalistic style, Carroll's directing is more presentational in approach. She credits this to several factors: her training with Piscator, the style of music in her work (gospel-inspired), and the choreographers with whom she collaborated. She explained, "the choreographers learned from Piscator-like people — how to use it to forward the piece."[27]

Carroll began directing plays in 1958 and had early successes directing Langston Hughes' *Black Nativity* (1961) and *The Prodigal Son* (1965) Off Broadway. However, shortly after her auspicious beginning as a director, Carroll found it difficult to find material for Black casts and began creating her own works. After successfully directing Off Broadway, directing with the Inner City Repertory Company, and teaching at New York's High School for the Performing Arts, Carroll became a founder and Artistic Director of the Urban Art Corps, established in 1967 as part of the Ghetto Arts Program of the New York Council for the Arts. It was there that she began a legendary collaboration with musician Micki Grant. Their first major hit, *Don't Bother Me, I Can't Cope* (1970, Urban Arts Corps; 1972 Playhouse Theatre), went Off Broadway and toured nationally. Mel Gussow, critic for *The New York Times*, called it a "hand-clapping, foot-tapping, sky-reaching, body-swaying, ear-splitting musical revue."[28] Their next hit was *Your Arms Too Short to Box with God*, based on the Gospel of St. Matthew, which premiered in 1975 and played both on and off Broadway before going on national tour. Carroll and Grant collaborated on several other musical plays, including *The Ups and Downs of Theophilus Maitland* (an adaptation of a West Indian folk tale, 1976), *But Never Jam Today* (adapted from the works of Lewis Carroll, 1969; Broadway 1979–80), *Croesus and the Witch* (1971), and *Step Lively Boy* (1972, later entitled *The Boogie-Woogie Rumble of a Dream Deferred*, an adaptation of Irwin Shaw's play *Bury the Dead*, with music added).

Carroll achieved incredible validation of her work as a director and creator when *Your Arms Too Short to Box with God* opened at the Spoleto Festival in Italy, then moved to Broadway in December of 1976. She was directing on Broadway at a time when very few Black men had achieved that status. She recalls, "Lloyd Richards got a break with *A Raisin in the Sun* (1959) — then he just kept working. But I wasn't preoccupied with that."[29] Richard's success was undisputed; in the years following *A Raisin in the Sun* he worked steadily in New York, directing *The Long Dream* (1960), *The Moon Beseiged* (1962), *I Had a Ball* (1964), *Amen Corner* (1965), *Who's Got His Own* (1966), and *The Ox Cart* (1966), all of which earned him exposure through reviews in *The New York Times*. Carroll's focus has been on creating her theatre pieces for black actors and audiences and not necessarily on commercial success, although the success was certainly welcome.

Carroll's work is characterized by a unique combination of music, dance, acting, and ritual all coming together, often with a Biblical or spiritual text as a basis for the celebration of the human spirit. Gospel music is also central to Carroll's musicals. She credits Langston Hughes with that influence, recalling, "When I went [to church to hear a choir] with Langston, boy, that would be GREAT! That made a big difference, and I began to love, love, love that music. I thought, 'This is so theatrical and should be in theatre.'" She not only absorbed the music, but also the movement in the church. She explains, "We started to do something that was new — absolutely new then — having the actor come down the aisle[...]. If the theatre was going to be the church, then the actors come in to be the choir."[30] She reports that she relies heavily on the actors for their creative contributions. In an interview for *The Daily News* in 1976, she gave insights into her creative process with collaborator Grant and her casts:

> What we usually do when starting a play is set up an idea, a scene and some music[...]. Then we bring in the actors and improvise from that. So we need actors who have freedom, who won't get locked into theatrics.[31]

Carroll is passionate about her art, but is also a realist about living the life of a director. No doubt, paving the way as a Black woman only intensified the struggle that is faced by any aspiring director. She explains:

> Had I known what I know now, I wouldn't have done any of it. I think it's an enormously difficult pursuit. All the things you read about are lies. All the things you think are going to happen to you if you work hard are lies[...]. There are so many "ifs" and "buts" and all these things. But occasionally something happens, and you meet a few people who are just marvelous.[32]

Many actors and collaborators would attest that Carroll herself is "just marvelous." Not only has she had an award-winning career as actor, director, and playwright, but also she has led the way for women and African-Americans to direct and create their own art. Along the way she has mentored those under her and helped launch the careers of Jonelle Allen, Marvin Felix Camillo, and Sherman Hemsley, among others.[33]

Sue Lawless is another remarkable woman with a string of "firsts" in more than thirty years as a director. Like Carroll, Lawless started as an actor, much to the chagrin of her mother, who was reduced to tears by the decision. From the beginning of her career, Lawless dealt with an inner struggle about her new vocation, because she was raised Roman Catholic and found that the League of Decency condemned a life in the theatre when she was growing up in the 1940s and '50s. It was not until she had begun her career as an actor that she approached the issue with a priest at Saint Patrick's Cathedral. His counsel was very clear: she must choose between the Roman Catholic Church and theatre. She made her choice.

Lawless earned a bachelor's degree in physical education before leaving her hometown of Chicago to pursue acting in New York in 1957. With very little money, and even less experience, Lawless worked her way through the actor's training program at the American Theatre Wing and was fortunate to start a successful acting career at the age of twenty-four. She became very involved in the early regional theatre movement as well as working Off Broadway.

In the late 1960s, Lawless got an invitation to direct at the Equity Library Theatre (ELT), a great starting ground for both directors and actors. Although she had never directed before, George Wojatsik, managing director at ELT, offered her an opportunity to direct a revival of Charles Gaynor's revue *Lend an Ear*, because she "knew all the best comics in New York."[34] Lawless recalls her reasons for taking the offer to direct:

> At that age, it wasn't really in my mind [to direct], but I did want to know a sense of the overall. And the second thing has to do with being a woman. At that point I had worked under a lot of directors, and only one female director, and I didn't understand why they were so sadistic. [...]. I thought, "What is there about this position that would make people attack?" And, of course, the answer I found out was that it has nothing to do with anything except personal insufficiency and a need for power and control.[35]

Lend an Ear proved to both Lawless and her colleagues that she made an excellent director, and soon the offers came streaming in from her previous contacts. For several years she worked as both an actor and director, then she met her husband, had a child, and continued to direct because she could take her daughter to rehearsals and control her hours somewhat. She traveled where the work was and reports that she was the first female director at all the regional and stock theatres in which she directed, including The Actor's Theatre of Louisville, The Goodspeed Opera House, The Walnut Street Theatre, The Cleveland Playhouse, The Coconut Grove Playhouse, and The Pennsylvania Stage Company, among others.

Although many of the musicals and revues Lawless directed were revivals, she also directed several original musical works Off Broadway, starting with *In Gay Company* in 1974–75 (Drama Desk nomination for Best Director of a Musical) and continuing with *Sterling Silver, Tip-Toes, Potholes, Chase a Rainbow, The Rise of David Levinsky, Cutting the Ribbons,* and *Body Shop.* She got a brief stint on Broadway, directing *The Five O'Clock Girl* in the 1980–81 season.[36] Although the production closed as quickly as it opened, Lawless revels in the fact that she actually made it to Broadway. "I made it. I got there. And I loved it! It didn't frighten me for beans. I wanted to be there from then on."[37]

In talking about her own work, Lawless says it is definitely shaped by her sense of humor, her comic physicality, and a certain pace. Even when she's tackled heavy pieces, "it's imbued with that [humorous] outlook." She trusts her instincts at auditions, finding that "you take somebody's mettle in the first eight seconds they walk in the door." She also looks for that sense of humor and finds comedic actors to be "the biggest stinkers and the deepest feelers. I'm pretty sure they'll have a sense of me and feel at ease with me."[38]

Lawless learned quickly how *not* to direct based on her own experiences as an actress with authoritarian male directors, whom she labeled "sadistic." She found such men pleasant enough in social circumstances, but in the rehearsal hall they became "foul-mouthed tyrants." Choosing a nurturing rather than adversarial role, Lawless likes to work "moment to moment," with actors. She does not always come in with preconceived notions on the first day of rehearsals, but instead tells actors, "We'll find it together." Likewise, she loves designers who are flexible and able to see the flaws in their own work, rather than relying on someone else to point them out.[39]

Now that she has over three decades of experience in the theatre, Lawless looks back at her substantial career and wonders at her initial naivete.

> Julianne [Boyd] and all those people were substantially younger when those of us who were doing it finally came crashing through for them. And I didn't know you had to have money. I didn't know you had to have contacts. It never entered my mind! [...] I didn't know there was a glass ceiling. I didn't know I wouldn't get to direct [more] on Broadway because I wasn't a guy. At one point I was optioned to direct three Broadway shows, but they couldn't raise money on *one.* Now I understand that.[40]

After Carroll and Lawless had started their directing careers, Julianne Boyd made her mark by creating and directing a musical revue based on the music of Eubie Blake. It is striking that when *Eubie!* opened on Broadway to critical acclaim in 1978, it provided Boyd her first paying job as a director.

Like Carroll and Lawless before her, Boyd's fascination with theatre began with acting, but an interest in directing was soon to follow. After obtaining a Bachelor of Arts degree at Beaver College and a Master of Arts at Adelphi University, Boyd studied theatre at City University of New York (CUNY), working on a doctoral degree because she did not consider directing a true vocational option for women. As she was studying, raising two children, teaching in the CUNY system, and directing Off Off Broadway, she realized she had to make a choice between finishing her doctorate and having a professional career. Her drama professor from college gave her valuable advice: "You know how you become a director? You say 'I AM A DIRECTOR' [...] and then you go out and find a project that you own or that a playwright wants you involved in[...]. You know, theatre's a business, something that someone wants to buy." Boyd recalls thinking, "My God. It's taken me this long to figure this out."[41]

Boyd was directing Off Off Broadway for no pay when she stumbled upon an archival recording of Blake's *Shuffle Along* in the summer of 1977. She wanted to direct a revue-version of the show, for the book was considered racist by 1970s standards. She eventually got permission to perform her revue at a tiny Off Off Broadway theatre (Theatre Off Park) that was looking for something for Black History Month. It opened on Blake's ninety-fifth birthday. As the lights were going down that night, Blake stated, "Now we're all the same color," a comment that Boyd, as a white woman, says she will never forget.[42] The newspaper critics were impressed, and immediately Boyd sought the rights to the rest of Blake's music and got offers from twelve producers to pick up the project. Months later, in September, *Eubie!* opened on Broadway. Boyd recalls, "Oh, I loved it. Broadway wasn't like it is now. It was a home, a great place[...]. And you took chances on shows. I was thirty-three years old!"[43] Quickly, several national tours were launched as well.

Boyd's subsequent musical project, *Onward Victoria*, played Off Broadway in the 1978–79 season, then opened and closed on 14 December 1980 on Broadway. *Onward Victoria*, with book and lyrics by Charlotte Anker and Irene Rosenberg, is the story of 19th-century suffragist Victoria Woodhill. Critics of the musical took pleasure at lambasting it. *New York Times* critic Frank Rich found fault with nearly every detail, from the book and lyrics, to the orchestrations, to the direction. Lest anyone accuse him of sexism, Rich was equally negative about the contributions of the male set and lighting designers, and called the male choreographer's work "lame." His introduction to the review advertised his lack of interest in the evening's entertainment: "You want a good night's sleep? Pay your money and rest in peace."[44]

Surprisingly, the failure of her feminist musical did not deter Boyd from her next project: a new feminist musical revue, for which she became part of the creative team. By now her name was well-known in New York, both for her success and her failure on Broadway. Her career lay in the balance, and Boyd needed to prove herself once more. Her collaboration with Joan Micklin Silver on *A ... My Name is Alice* garnered her the positive attention she needed. She explains the reason for her belief in that project: "Things about women hadn't been funny things, where women could make fun of themselves. Up until *Alice* all the women's stuff was like, 'He beat me, he left me, and I'm miserable.' It was negative stuff." Boyd and Silver requested friends to write songs which reflected a modern woman's experience in America. To their amazement, the women wrote more negative songs, "because that's what they were used to writing. That's what sold. That's what the market could bear."[45] They opened up the writing to both women and men, looking for a more positive reflection of womanhood. Their comical, musical revue benefited from a lengthy workshop at the Women's Project of the American Place Theatre. Success was theirs when it opened Off Broadway in the 1983–84 season, requiring an extended run and later a sequel, entitled *A ... My Name is Still Alice.*

In the 1980s, Boyd became the first woman president of the Society of Stage Directors and Choreographers, a post she held for six years. She also served her profession by co-authoring "Directors and Designers Report on Sex Discrimination in the Theatre" in 1983, under the auspices of the new League of Professional Theatre Women (of which she was a founding member). Her findings give a good idea of what women directors were going through in the early 1980s:

> There were a few regional theatre directors, but even those were few and far between. There were more women who had started their own theatres as artistic directors, like Lynne Meadow. And one of the things that it said was that one woman's success is her own success; one woman's failure is every woman's failure. So my success was, "Oh, great! She did a show. Wasn't that nice?" Had it been a flop, it would have been, "That's why you don't hire a woman."[46]

Boyd eventually followed in the footsteps of Lynne Meadow and became the artistic director of The Barrington Stage Company, in the Berkshires, in 1995. Two years later her production of *Cabaret* was so popular that it transferred to Boston, where it received two Boston Critics Awards and four Outer Boston Critics Awards (including Best Director and *Boston Globe*'s Best of 1997 List).

Women like Carroll, Lawless, and Boyd were still novelties as directors when they began — women operating in a man's world. There were many others, of course, and often they were women who wore two or more hats. For example, Elizabeth Swados wrote, composed, and directed her own musicals on and off Broadway for several decades, starting in the mid–1970s. Patricia Birch, a noted Broadway choreographer, began directing Off Broadway in the 1980s.[47] Other names may be less familiar: Pamela Hunt, another choreographer-turned-director, has made a living directing musicals both Off Broadway and in regional theatres. Miriam Fond has worked professionally directing musicals over the past thirty years and is known for her direction of the comic revue *What's a Nice Country Like You Doing in a State Like This?*

In interviews, women directors comment that their gender has made their career paths more challenging. For example, Hunt recalls a male colleague who sat her down to tell her which theatres might hire women; Boyd recalls being asked if she could handle the stage hands; Lawless recalls her male manager forcing her to wear a dress to all interviews; Fond recalls how her short stature and her gender worked against her. ("I'm this little under five foot woman and these big guys go, 'I'm going to trust my millions to her?!'") But the six women interviewed for this article are definitely seeing a change: women are now accepted as directors, although the competition to direct, be it man or woman, is extremely tough, and the primary starting place, the Equity Library Theatre, is now gone. ELT, "one of the premiere showcase theatres for directors," was one of the few theatres that existed in order to produce the works of beginning theatre artists and was extremely important for opportunities in musical theatre.[48] Although Off Off Broadway is now an option for new directors, the opportunities in musical theatre are not as rich. Furthermore, no Off Off theatre serves as the one-stop showcase for up-and-coming talent as ELT did.

A new group of directors took the spotlight on Broadway as the century drew to a close. Starting in the 1980s and continuing into the 1990s, the names Graciela Daniele, Susan Schulman, and Julie Taymor all appeared in Broadway *Playbills*. Daniele was already an award-winning choreographer when the artistic director at INTAR suggested she try her hand at directing as well. The result was *Tango Aspasionado* (1987), and Daniele has gone on to direct a number of musicals on and off Broadway. Her work as director and choreographer for *Once on This Island* (1990–91) won her two Tony nominations and helped secure her career as a new director. Now a resident director at the Lincoln Center Theatre, she has continued directing new works, including *Hello Again* (two Drama Desk nominations, 1993–94), *Chronicle of a Death Foretold* (Tony nominations as director, choreographer, and co-author, 1995), *A New Brain* (1998), and *Marie Christine* (1999). In a completely different vein, she also directed the Broadway revival of *Annie Get Your Gun* (1999), staring Bernadette Peters and Tom Wopat, although she admits that her passion is for original works. "Personally, I don't like doing revivals. There's not enough freedom, I think" (Daniele). Despite that lack of freedom, Daniele's production of *Annie Get Your Gun* won the Tony Award for Best Revival, a tribute to her great talent.

Like most directors of musicals, Daniele has directed non-musical plays as well. When asked what makes directing a musical different, she provided a splendid metaphor:

> I say directing a play is like having a nice dinner for six at home. Very elegant, very quiet, with Mozart playing in the background, and quiet conversation. Directing a musical is like going for a picnic in the summer at the beach in Italy — with the cousins, and the aunts, and the children, and the sausages, and

the wine — everybody's talking at the same time. It's maddening! You have to listen to everybody, but it can drive you crazy sometimes. Because it's "Me, me, me, me, me!"[49]

Like Daniele, Susan Schulman reports that she began in theatre as a dancer, but from there her career path and training have been quite different. After attending New York's High School of Performing Arts, where Vinnette Carroll was teaching, Schulman attended Hoftstra University and then applied to the directing program at Yale. She got the same response as Lynne Meadows (Artistic Director of the Manhattan Theatre Club): Yale was not accepting women into the directing program in the late 1960s. Schulman explains, "They didn't want to invest the time and money training a woman who, in their view, would get married, ultimately have a family and drop out of the profession."[50] She needed a scholarship, and having published a play at age sixteen, found the playwriting program at Yale more receptive. While at Yale, Schulman studied both playwriting and directing (under Nikos Psacharopoulos); she cites both Psacharopoulos and Carroll as important influences on her early work. Mostly, however, she says she has learned from "just going to theatre" as she grew up in New York.[51]

After Yale, Schulman managed to get a directing job fairly quickly. Like Carroll and Lawless, she was working as an actress when the opportunity to direct came about. She explains,

> I went to a theatre in Buffalo as an actress, and they lost a director when I was there, so I got a chance to direct, which was definitely just coincidental. I always knew I wanted to be a director, but I felt there was no place to go to do it.[52]

She decided she was not cut out to be an actress, and proceeded with a directing career. Like Lawless and other beginning directors, she did some early work at the Equity Library Theatre, where she "camped out" and pestered them into letting her direct. She firmly believes that you have to do whatever you can to be seen, even if it's a project in someone's living room. She explains her own auspicious beginnings, stating,

> I got my biggest break doing a show on 42nd Street before it was Theatre Row. A group of us got together, and I did *Look, We've Come Through*, the Hugh Wheeler show. We rented a space on 42nd Street and invited everyone we could. Hugh Wheeler heard it was being done. He came and saw it, because it was a show of his that wasn't done very often. He loved the production. Later, when I was asked to do *Company* at the York Theatre, he said to Stephen Sondheim, "Oh, I know her. She's great." And I wouldn't have been asked if Hugh hadn't said that. I could connect the dots, because from *Company* came *Sweeney*—I mean, you just go all the way. And had I not made that happen, that little production, nothing would have happened after that.[53]

But Schulman bumped her head on the glass ceiling associated with Broadway. In the mid-eighties, after serving as principal director of Civic Light Opera in

Pittsburgh for a number of years, she almost gave up directing, stating, "I had to come to terms with the fact that I might never direct a Broadway play[...]. Once I accepted that fact [...] a big weight was lifted from me. I suddenly felt freer to take theatrical risks. And perhaps that even opened doors for me."[54]

In the 1988–89 season Schulman directed an Off Broadway production of *Sweeney Todd* at the York Theatre that earned rave reviews from *New York Times* critic Frank Rich, among others. At first, when asked to direct a small-scale version of the production, she just laughed. But when she reread the play, she realized that although Hal Prince's production was lavish and physical, with an eye to the industrial, *Sweeney Todd* could also work on a smaller scale with a different, psychological focus. "This is a man's story. This is a man's obsession," she reasoned.[55] Heralded as a new, "human" telling of the tale, with less emphasis on politics and more attention to Mrs. Lovett and the woman street beggar, this downsized version was intimate and compelling. Critic Rich tried to account for the woman's touch, writing,

> It is not that the director set out to create a feminist interpretation — which the text cannot support in any case — but that she gives equal weight to female characters who originally came off as stylized slatterns in a man's story. It may be simply that she sees the play's women more fully or has more compassion for them.[56]

The production transferred to the intimate Circle in the Square the following year and was soon dubbed "Teeny Todd" by spoof-master Gerard Alessandrini of *Forbidden Broadway* because of its small scale.

Once the glass ceiling was broken for Schulman, she garnered attention for her direction of the new musical *The Secret Garden* (1990–91). When Schulman took over the project, the backers had fled, and the project was in real need of revision under a director with vision; Schulman provided that leadership, along with the tenacity to get the show funded and staged in New York.[57] According to book writer Marsha Norman and set designer/conceiver Heidi Landesman (now Ettinger), the previous director, a male, had never "spoken their language" or understood the world of the play. Whereas the previous director spent his time with dramaturgy, trying to rewrite the book, Schulman's approach was more collaborative, and she began by discussing imagery. She asked Norman and Landesman how they saw the story, then focused on some of Norman's descriptions and decided that the central image for the production might be through ghosts, specifically the ghosts of Mary's parents. Norman and Landesman agreed and were further encouraged when Schulman picked up the book of the musical and said, "Let's just decide the order of events in the story."[58]

Together, the creative team of women discovered that a minimalist approach, as used in a previous workshop, did not work for the gothic saga. It needed to be steeped in the period: from design, to dialects, to emotional depth. Landesman admits that they were afraid of the sentimentality at first, but had to learn to embrace the gothic tradition and be true to the period. The idea of personal perspective became crucial as well. Schulman explained,

> Heidi and I started talking very soon about seeing it through a child's eyes. How do children see things? And that led us to Victorian games, and that led us to picture books, and that led us to the toy stage[...]. But the first thing [impulse] was very emotional, which I think it always is. And my emotional feel was that we were seeing it through Mary's emotions, her perceptions, and that things would be out of scale.[59]

With money raised primarily from family and friends, this trio of women set off to produce a "do or die" workshop of *The Secret Garden* in New York. According to Schulman, the production team was excellent, the cast was emotionally committed, and the chemistry was extraordinary. They continued to rework the show in rehearsals and all breathed a collective sigh of relief after the first preview, when the audience "buzz" began to spread that they had a winner. Although it received some mixed critical reviews, *The Secret Garden* was an audience-pleaser.

Once the Broadway run ended, after 709 performances, *The Secret Garden* surprised its creators by becoming a cult show of sorts at colleges. Reflecting on the phenomena, the creators believe that the story "makes people not feel helpless." Mary, the protagonist, gives the audience a sense of empowerment. Although a mere child, Mary has the ability to effect change through her actions; she is able to make one person well and make one garden grow. It is this feeling of empowerment, they believe, that helped make the musical such a favorite with audiences.[60]

In the 1990s Schulman continued to work steadily, directing national tours of *The Secret Garden* (1990–91, 1991–92), *Annie Get Your Gun* (1992–93), and *Sunset Boulevard* (1998–99). She also worked Off Broadway and in regional theatres directing several new works before returning to Broadway with a revival of *The Sound of Music* (1997–98). When approaching revivals, she believes in starting fresh, with the text in front of her and preconceived notions behind. "I don't think of them as revivals," she states. "I think of them as new musicals. I think how I would approach the show if it were being done today for the first time."[61] Like Daniele, she enjoys directing new works, but admits that the more commercial jobs help pay the bills. "But for me the greatest thing is to just keep working. And to be challenged continually."[62] Fortunately for Schulman, she has proceeded to accomplish both.

The last woman to leave her indelible thumbprint on Broadway in the twentieth century was Julie Taymor, winner of the 1998 Tony Award for Direction of a Musical (*The Lion King*). Women could be particularly proud that year, as two women swept the directors' awards, with Garry Hynes winning for Direction of a Play (*The Beauty Queen of Leenane*). Never before in the fifty-one year history of the award had a woman won a Tony Award for direction. Ironically, the Tony, or Antoinette Perry Award, is named for a woman who was an actor, director, and producer.

Born and raised in the suburbs of Boston, much of Taymor's inspiration came from her experiences traveling to Sri Lanka, India, and Indonesia as a young adult. She explains, "The four years in Indonesia were almost a rebirth for me. It's where I got rooted in what I wanted to do in the theatre and where I started to create my own pieces and work as a director."[63] Unlike the other women represented in this essay, Taymor's art, both in terms of direction and design, has been well chronicled with two books, yet she is relatively new to mainstream theatre, surfacing Off Broadway in the late 1980s. She received high critical acclaim with her musical piece, *Juan Darien* (Obie Award, 1988) which transferred to Lincoln Center and was nominated for Tony Awards in the 1996–97 season.

In addition to her travels, Taymor's study of folklore and mythology at Oberlin College is evident in her approach to the text. Consider her language as she describes her work: primitive, symbolic, ritual, human, physical, spiritual, musical, ancient, timeless, cinematic, and archetypal.[64] It is this focus on the mythic which helped her take *The Lion King* from animated cartoon to stage in a compelling, human way. Her approach was to emphasize the image of the circle as a metaphor for nature's cycle of birth, death, and rebirth; focusing on the universal or archetypal in the text enables her to transcend a more literal interpretation of the story.

Taymor's insight carries through her design work and use of puppetry as well, for she finds the power of transformation in the use of puppet and mask. She explains that the exaggerated form of the puppet expresses something fantastic and at the same time very human. "You are exposing, in an almost cubist way, the inner emotion in an external form."[65] It is the actor's use of the body and tilt of the head that make the audience perceive a change in attitude or expression, as in the Chinese and Japanese theatre. When casting, Taymor says she looks not for puppeteers, but for "inventive actors who move well. A strong actor gives an idiosyncratic performance, because he infuses the puppet character with his own personality instead of relying on generic puppet technique."[66]

Because she invests so much time and energy into the design process of costumes and masks, one might think that Taymor is not actor-oriented. Untrue, according to her assistant director for *The Lion King*, Dan Fields. "As a director, Julie is very interactive. She allows—sometimes insists—that the actors bring ideas into the rehearsal room, that they develop moments and business[...]. At the same time, when she has something in mind that she's trying to achieve, she's very eager to get to it."[67] Because of the intense physical work required, Taymor gets the actors on their feet right away, experimenting. Conceptually, she asks performers to find "ideographs," a concept first introduced to her in the late 1970s under the tutelage of experimentalist Herbert Blau. She explains:

> In the visual arts, an example of an ideograph would be a Japanese brush painting of a bamboo forest: just three or four quick brush strokes capture the

whole. In the theatre, an ideograph is also a pared-down form — a kinetic, abstract essence of an emotion, an action, or a character.[68]

She also pays close attention to style, not wanting the production to be so abstract that it alienates the audience, yet not so naturalistic that it becomes bland. Her answer is a "juxtaposition of highly stylized gestural moves with the more naturalistic ones."[69] Such a juxtaposition might be expected in performance art, but not in a Broadway musical. As a risk-taker, that is what Taymor wants, to push the envelope and open new realms. As Vincent Canby framed it, "she is quite capable not only of meeting the demands of the commercial theatre, but also of setting new standards for it."[70]

Looking back at the twentieth century, women directors have had many benchmarks of accomplishment: from Vida Hope directing *The Boyfriend* on the West End and on Broadway in the mid-fifties, to Vinnette Carroll's bringing a black woman's voice to musical theatre, to Taymor and Hynes winning dual Tony Awards for Direction in 1998. Susan Schulman said the field was now open for women directors, "more open right now than it ever has been."[71] The newest concern is that although things are better for women, they are tougher for new directors, in part, because the competition is fierce. Sue Lawless sees one problem is that beginning directors are unwilling to start at the bottom and work up. "They don't want to wait tables. They want to have a personal life."[72] Her personal philosophy is that true artists will find the work. Schulman concurs, stating, "If they hear it's good, they will come. It really is the truth." Pamela Hunt, who directs primarily in regional theatres, also sees this as a "great time" for women directors. Her advice to newcomers is to assist and observe an established director, something she never got to do. Graciela Daniele agrees that observing is key, citing her learning experience through assisting Bob Fosse and Michael Bennett. "The beliefs that they instilled in me were so crucial. They are constantly present inside me."[73]

Despite a tough market, women's names are ever-present in the data for the 1990s: Schulman, Daniele, and Taymor continued to direct on Broadway and in other venues. Off Broadway, several names appear in the data three or more times in the 1990s, including Lisa Brailoff and Helen Butleroff. Regionally, women with established careers continued to direct frequently, including Dyanne Earley, Marcia Milgrim Dodge, and Pamela Hunt. The entrance into the new millennium was encouraging, considering two Tony Award nominations for direction for Susan Stroman (nominated for both *Contact* and *The Music Man*)[74] and the Broadway debut of another choreographer-turned-director, Lynne Taylor-Corbett (*Swing!*) in the 1999–2000 season. Both women received excellent press for their accomplishments. Reviewing *Contact* in the *New York Times,* critic Ben Brantley raved about Stroman's contributions to musical theatre, writing,

> Ms. Stroman [...] has created the unthinkable: a new musical throbbing with wit, sex appeal and a perfectionist's polish. Brimming with a sophistication that is untainted by the usual fin-de-siecle cynicism, *Contact* restores the

pleasure principle to the American musical. It's the kinetic equivalent of Rodgers and Hart.[75]

Although she did not win the Tony Award for Best Director, *Contact* won the Tony Award for Best Musical in 2000. In 2001 she built upon her excellent reputation by directing the mega-hit *The Producers*, winner of 11 Tony Awards including Best Director and Best Musical. (However, her subsequent Broadway production, *Thou Shalt Not*, was much less successful.)

In addition to American women's accomplishments on Broadway, the British women made their presence known with musicals imported from London's West End: Arlene Phillips with *Saturday Night Fever* (1999) and Gail Edwards with *Jesus Christ Superstar* (2000).

Most women I spoke with, as was true in previous studies, did not want to be considered for their gender, but for their work. At the same time, all of those asked admitted to encountering discrimination based on gender. Schulman thinks the idea that women cannot handle big budgets is over. Perhaps she summed up the situation best:

> You know, it's interesting, because I still get asked about it. Julie Taymor, Graciela [Daniele], and myself—we're still the "women directors." At some point, you just want to be "one of the directors." Then it would be great. Then you would know it's over. Then you'd know it's done. But I certainly think it's opening up now—Susan Stroman is directing a musical on Broadway—and that's great. All of that helps. Makes it no big deal. I've always said, "Either you can do it, or you can't." And sex doesn't make a bit of difference[...]. You're either talented or you're not.[76]

Notes

1. Tamara Compton's master's thesis focuses on women directors on Broadway, 1920–1950, and covers the entrance of women in directing through the role of actress-manager. Compton's thesis shows that of the nine women who directed during 1920–1950 on Broadway, only one, Mary Hunter, directed musical theatre in that venue. See Tamara Compton, "The Rise of the Woman Director on Broadway, 1920–1950," thesis (Kansas State U, 1985). Both Shirlee Hennigan's and Rebecca Adams's dissertations concern gender issues of women directing in the professional theatre. No distinction is made for musical theatre. Wendy Vierow's dissertation is concerned only with women directors of non-musicals. See Shirlee Hennigan, *The Woman Director in the Contemporary, Professional Theatre*, diss., Washington State University, 1983. Ann Arbor: UMI, 1983. 8315227; Rebecca Adams, *Perceptions of Women Stage Directors Regarding the Influence of Gender in the Artistic Process*, diss., University Oregon, 1993. Ann Arbor: UMI, 1993. 9238890; Wendy Vierow, *Women on Broadway: 1980–1995*, diss., NYU, 1997. Ann Arbor: UMI, 1997. 9808349. Several other dissertations, articles, and books address specific careers of prominent directors such as Eva LeGallienne, Antoinette Perry, Margaret Webster, Margo Jones, and Zelda Fichandler.

2. Graciela Daniele has been a force on Broadway, both as a choreographer and later as a director; her career is only touched upon in this essay, as it is more fully examined elsewhere in this anthology.

3. Julianne Boyd and Kay Carney, "Directors and Designers Report on Sex Discrimination in the Theatre: Directors," unpublished report, League of Professional Theatre Women, New York, 8 Mar. 1983, 1.

4. Boyd and Carney 3.

5. One person shows, concerts, and one night events were excluded from the data. Plays with music were also excluded when stated as such; often the line between a musical and a play with music was difficult to determine.

6. See *Theatre World* [Alternately titled *Daniel Blum's Theatre World* and *John Willis's Theatre World*] (New York: Crown, 1944–).

7. Qtd. in Anna Kay France and P.J. Corso, *International Women Playwrights* (Metuchen, NJ: Scarecrow, 1993) 47.

8. For a thorough review of the entrance of the stage director, see James P. Cochran, *The Development of the Professional Stage Director* (Diss. University of Iowa, 1958); Robert T. Hazzard, *The Development of Selected American Stage Directors from 1926 to 1960* (Diss. University of Minnesota, 1962); Charles Cox, *The Evolution of the Stage Director in America* (Diss. Northwestern University, 1957); or David G. Schaal, *Rehearsal-Direction Practices and Actor-Director Relationships in the American Theatre from the Hallams to Actor's Equity* (Diss. University of Illinois, 1956).

9. Hennigan 83.

10. Compton 53.

11. Hennigan 28.

12. I use the term "staging" because it was used in *Theatre World*. In the early part of the twentieth century, the terms directing and staging were sometimes used interchangeably (no other director is cited). Stella Adler is credited with staging *Polonaise* in the 1945–46 season and de Mille with *Allegro* in the 1947–48 season. Agnes de Mille is again credited with staging in 1950–51 for *Out of This World*.

13. "Vida Hope Dead; British Actress," *New York Times* 25 Dec. 1963: 33.

14. "The Lady is a Director," *Journal-American* 25 Sept. 1954: n. pag. Clipping: Vida Hope.

15. "The Lady."

16. "Not Even Standing Room," Unidentified clipping: Vida Hope, New York Public Library, Billy Rose Theatre Collection, 28 Sept. 1954.

17. Paul Moor, "Lady on Her Way," *Theatre Arts* 33 (1949): 54.

18. *Carib Song*, "a musical play of the West Indies." Book and lyrics by William Archibald and music by Baldwin Bergersen. Production staged by Katherine Dunham and Mary Hunter; book directed by Hunter; choreography by Dunham; produced by George Stanton at the Adelphi Theatre.

19. Moor 54.

20. Moor 54.

21. Compton 171–72.

22. Compton 182.

23. John Rosenfield, "The Passing Show: Stage Directing Musicals," *The Dallas Morning News* 21 Feb. 1952: III, 4.

24. Arthur Pollock, "Theater Time: Mary Hunter Stages Musical, and About Time," *The Daily Compass* 13 Feb. 1956: 22.

25. Qtd. in Moor 54.

26. Vinette Carroll, Interview with David Diamond, Stage Directors and Choreographers Foundation, New York, 9 Nov. 1999.

27. Carroll.

28. Mel Gussow, theatre review, *New York Times* 8 Oct. 1970: 60.

29. Carroll.

30. Carroll.

31. Qtd. in Patricia O'Haire, "She Came a Long Way," *Daily News* 10 May 1976: 26.

32. Carroll.

33. Jo A. Tanner, "Carroll, Vinnette." *Notable Women in the American Theatre: A Biographical Dictionary*, eds. Alice M. Robinson, Vera Mowry Roberts, and Milly S. Barranger (New York: Greenwood, 1989) 113.

34. *Lend an Ear* was originally directed by Gower Champion on Broadway and helped make Carol Channing a star.

35. Sue Lawless, interview with the author, New York, 16 Mar. 2000.

36. *In Gay Company*, music and lyrics by Fred Silver; *Sterling Silver*, music and lyrics by

Frederick Silver; *Tip-Toes*, music by George Gershwin, lyrics by Ira Gershwin, book by Guy Bolton and Fred Thompson; *Potholes*, book and lyrics by Elinor Guggenheimer, music by Ted Simons; *Chase a Rainbow*, book, music, and lyrics by Harry Stone; *The Rise of David Levinsky*, book and lyrics by Isaiah Sheffer (based on a novel by Abraham Cahan), music by Bobby Paul; *Cutting the Ribbons*, music by Cheryl Harwich and Mildred Hayden with additional music by Nancy Ford, lyrics by Mae Richard; *Body Shop*, book, music, and lyrics by Walter Marks; *The Five O'Clock Girl*, book Guy Bolton and Fred Thompson, music and lyrics, Bert Kalmar and Harry Ruby.

37. Lawless.

38. Lawless.

39. Lawless.

40. Lawless.

41. Julianne Boyd, interview with the author, New York, 14 Mar. 2000.

42. Boyd.

43. Boyd. *Eubie!* closed 7 Oct. 1979 after a successful run of 439 performances. Although Boyd's memories of *Eubie!* are happy ones, the show was plagued by two issues in the press. The producer, Ashley Springer, was brought up on charges for not paying back investors. In addition, choreographer Billy Wilson claimed to the *Village Voice* that he deserved credit for directing the production. Within a week of that interview, he was fired.

44. Frank Rich, "*Onward Victoria*: A Woman's Freedom Fight," *New York Times* 15 Dec. 1980: C 15.

45. Boyd.

46. Boyd.

47. See additional essays in this volume for further information on Swados and Birch.

48. Susan Schulman, telephone interview, 23 March 2000.

49. Graciela Daniele, telephone interview, 25 Mar. 2000.

50. Qtd. in Horowitz, "Inside the Secret Garden: Women Directors Make Inroads on Broadway," *TheaterWeek* 10 Feb. 1992: 22.

51. Schulman.

52. Schulman

53. Schulman

54. Qtd. in Horowitz 25.

55. Qtd in Mervyn Rothstein, "Does the Demon Barber Have a Human Face?" *New York Times* 10 Sept. 1989: II, 1.

56. Frank Rich, "On Stage, the Feminist Message Takes on a Sly and Subtle Tone," *New York Times* 19 Apr. 1989: C 15.

57. "Dialogue with Marsha Norman, Susan Schulman, and Heidi Landesman." Videocassette, Theatre on Tape and Film Archive, New York Public Library, Billy Rose Theatre Collection, 1992.

58. "Dialogue."

59. Schulman.

60. "Dialogue"

61. Qtd. in Rothstein.

62. Schulman.

63. Qtd. in Robert Brustein, "Recapturing the Fantasy in Our Lives," *New York Times* 16 Apr. 2000: II: 18.

64. Eileen Blumenthal and Julie Taymor, *Julie Taymor: Playing with Fire*, updated and expanded ed. (New York: Harry Abrams, 1999).

65. Qtd. in Hilary DeVries, "Julie Taymor: Giving Theater a Touch of Cross-Cultural Whimsy," *Christian Science Monitor* 31 Oct. 1986: 26.

66. Julie Taymor with Alexis Greene, *The Lion King: Pride Rock on Broadway* (New York: Hyperion, 1997) 136.

67. Qtd. in Taymor 137.

68. Taymor 139.

69. Taymor 143.

70. Vincent Canby, "'The Lion King' Earns Its Roars of Approval," *New York Times* 23 Nov. 1997: II: 5.

71. Schulman.

72. Lawless.

73. Qtd. in Robert Armin, "Graciela Daniele," *Playbill*, Special Issue: 14th Annual "Mr. Abbott" Awards 1998: N. pag.

74. *Contact* was billed as "a dance play" by Susan Stroman and John Weidman; written by Mr. Weidman; directed and choreographed by Ms. Stroman. Presented by Lincoln Center Theater, under the direction of Andre Bishop and Bernard Gersten. At the Mitzi E. Newhouse Theater, Lincoln Center. Opened 7 October 1999.

75. Ben Brantley, "Musical Elixir Afoot," *New York Times* 8 Oct. 1999: E1.

76. Schulman.

Social Consciousness and the "Search for New Directions"

The Musicals of Gretchen Cryer, Nancy Ford, and Elizabeth Swados

JUDITH SEBESTA

Right off Michigan Avenue, in the heart of Chicago's "Miracle Mile" Shopping District, sits the "American Girl" store and theatre. Young girls and their mothers (as well as an occasional father) flock to this doll shop, making pilgrimages from all across the country to bask in a sort of American Girl theme-park and, hopefully for its owners, spend lots of money on the books (which spawned this retail phenomenon), dolls, doll clothes and matching outfits for the girls. An escalator takes visitors down to the American Girl Theatre, where they can pay $25 to watch their favorite character/doll come to life in *Circle of Friends*, the second musical by Gretchen Cryer, lyricist/librettist, and Nancy Ford, composer, based on the phenomenon.

Both *Circle of Friends* (premiered 2001) and its predecessor, *The American Girls Revue* (premiered 1998), depict strong young women making their way in America, both past and present and in a variety of American cultures, celebrating the characters' triumphs over societally imposed limitations. Their messages are not so different from the ones Cryer and Ford penned two decades earlier in their quintessential 1970s "feminist" musical, *I'm Getting My Act Together and Taking it On the Road*. Stanley Green, writing in 1980, called the team the "foremost exponents of the women's experience in the musical theatre today."[1] Cryer and Ford might modestly agree with Green's assessment; however, the lyricist and composer have stressed that while the show *is* feminist theatre, its concerns are applicable to both women *and* men.[2]

Interestingly, a contemporary of Cryer and Ford's, composer and lyricist Elizabeth Swados, has also chosen children and strong women as the subjects of some of her theatrical works. The resemblance between Swados's work and the work of the team of Cryer and Ford does not end there. Their work in musical theatre arguably peaked with a single seminal show during the 1970s, both developed at Joseph Papp's Public Theater; social consciousness has been at the heart of their musicals; they have attempted to move beyond the conventional book musical with their shows; and they often utilized rock music at the heart of their musical "rebellions" against traditional form. Although there are some important differences, these similarities suggest that a comparison of the musical theatre aesthetics of Cryer and Ford with those of Swados, from the roots of their work, to the success of their respective shows *I'm Getting My Act Together* and *Runaways*, to their most recent work at the turn of the twenty-first century, is a worthwhile pursuit, particularly in order to gain a better understanding of the work of female composers/lyricists who were creating at the height of the women's movement.

Strong Women in the Making

Cryer was born Gretchen Kiger on 17 October 1935 in Dunreith, Indiana, a tiny country town near Indianapolis. Although she had never seen a live theatre performance and did not even really know what a play was, Cryer spent the long Indiana winters putting on shows for her family. Unlike Cryer, Ford was exposed to considerably more culture at an early age. Born in Kalamazoo, Michigan, on 1 October 1935, Ford composed her first music at the age of four and a year later organized a glee club, for which she served as both director and composer. Looking back on her childhood, Ford admits, "My fantasy idea was to be a musical comedy star, but my reality idea was to get married."[3]

Cryer and Ford met when they both arrived at DePauw University, a small Methodist school in Greencastle, Indiana, in 1953. They lived in the same dorm and were introduced when a boy suggested that the three of them write a musical.[4] Cryer, an English major, had never even seen a musical; Ford, who was studying music, had seen only two: *South Pacific* and *Oklahoma!* Undaunted, they collaborated on their first show, the sophomore musical. *For Reasons of Royalty* concerns a princess from Europe who comes to America dressed as a boy. She becomes a lumberjack to learn the technology of woodcutting to take back to her kingdom in Europe. Meanwhile, the princess falls in love with a fellow lumberjack, who discovers that she's a girl. When he professes his love for her, she leaves him to take her new knowledge back to her own country. Twenty years later Ford joked, "You see, it was really ahead of its time. It was about a woman giving up her love for her career."[5]

Their first musical might have been ahead of its time, but Cryer and Ford knew that they still had a lot to learn. Cryer began performing summer stock in all kinds of musical theatre, and Ford continued to study music. The budding collaborators wrote their next show, about the slums of New York, for their senior musical. However, at this point, their attentions turned elsewhere. As much as Cryer and Ford enjoyed their new-found talent, the women "were programmed to think of finding husbands first and doing a line of work that would fit in with our husbands.'"[6] Ford married at the age of twenty-one, and Gretchen Kiger married David Cryer on the day that he graduated from college. Both women chose husbands who planned to be ministers, and their lives continued on similar paths. The two couples traveled east to New Haven, where the men attended Yale Divinity School. They all lived in the same apartment house, and both Cryer and Ford worked as secretaries to support their husbands. The women continued to work on their musicals as a hobby.

Oddly enough, the women's desire to do theatre spread to their minister-husbands, who both decided to take up theatre for a living. They abandoned divinity school, and soon the two couples were moving again, this time to Boston. While the men studied theatre, Ford continued to work as a secretary, and Cryer earned a Master's degree in English at Radcliffe. Soon she began teaching, an occupation that she felt would accommodate her husband's. Meanwhile, Cryer and Ford managed to write another musical, about love between a college professor and a student, which was directed by David Cryer for his Master's thesis.

Then for the third time the Cryers and Fords experienced life-changing upheavals. Nancy Ford, at the age of twenty-five, divorced her husband; David Cryer was drafted. The women decided that now was their best chance to pursue what they loved best, deciding to move to New York City and try to get one of their musicals produced. In New York, both women worked once again as secretaries while auditioning for anything in theatre. Cryer sang

Lyricist, librettist and actress Gretchen Cryer wrote for *and* performed in *I'm Getting My Act Together and Taking it On the Road* (photograph courtesy the subject).

in the chorus of *Little Me* and *110 in the Shade*; Ford played the piano for *The Fantasticks* and *Brecht on Brecht*. Soon they began to work on the musical that would be their first produced Off Broadway.

This background became a personal basis from which Cryer and Ford would write their musicals. Growing up in a society and at a time when women often shaped their lives to fit a man had a great impact on these two women. They protested the social norm by deciding to develop lives of their own. Cryer and her husband divorced after eleven years of marriage, although she stresses that he was a supportive husband. But as she reached thirty, the strain of her life became too much: "I was a physical wreck because I had been working all that time, I had two kids; I was trying to be the perfect wife and mother and have some kind of career.... I was so exhausted I started getting sick all the time."[7] Although Ford later remarried, both women agree that the main force in their lives since those early marriages has developed not from their marital status but from how they have seen themselves in a male-oriented world.

Elizabeth Swados grew up in a world quite different from the Midwestern milieu of Cryer and Ford's upbringing. Swados was born in Buffalo, NY, in 1951, to a Jewish family of writers, musicians, and singers. Her grandmother, a concert pianist, had had a lobotomy; her second cousin was a prominent novelist, Harvey Swados. She has described her family as eccentric, passionate, moody, and dramatic. "You had to be careful." She recalls a lonely, independent childhood, and frequently she ran away, leaving home permanently at the age of sixteen to attend Bennington College. In 1974, her mother committed suicide. "What an unusually spiteful, horrendous act! A parent leaving a legacy that life is no good, that the solution to problems is to die. The world began to look like that parent. I was mad at everybody."[8] At Bennington, Swados, who played the piano at five, the guitar at ten, and performed as a folk singer by the time she was twelve, began composing at the age of seventeen. She studied under Henry Brant, a "dark, intense, wild-eyed" professor who reminded her of the White Rabbit.[9] Even for the notoriously free and liberal college, Swados was a self-admitted "black sheep" in the music department, which focused primarily on classical composition.[10] Her first "symphony" was an overture in which thirty actors posed as a Balinese monkey chorus.[11] While still at Bennington, she began working at Ellen Stewart's La Mama ETC in New York City, where she first worked with director Andrei Serban — with whom she formed a long-lasting collaboration — on a production of *Medea*, one of the many background scores she wrote for Serban's productions. Her collaborations have been efforts to combat her personal feelings of fragmentation, as well as metaphorical searches for more functional families to replace her own dysfunctional one: "Every time I thought I was putting on a play, I ended up with a family. It always has to do with family."[12] Although she left school before graduation, she submitted the score for *Medea* in completion of her degree and graduated in absentia in 1972.

For the next few years, Swados continued her work as a composer, collaborating with Serban on *Electra* and *The Trojan Women* among other productions, touring Europe and the Middle East with Serban, and Africa with Peter Brook and his company, preparing the performance piece *The Conference of the Birds*. According to Mel Gussow of *The New York Times*, "Africa brought her closer to animals; birdcalls became her musical trademark."[13] Her travels also exposed her to an eclectic range of musical styles, from Nigerian drumming to Indian ragas, and this eclecticism, like the birdcalls, became a hallmark of her work. From her early work on, Swados has been committed to combining eastern and western, high and low art, classical and popular forms, battling elitism in the arts. "I would love to do a workshop with the New York Philharmonic," she was quoted during the run of *Nightclub Cantata*, "to make them talk to their instruments, throw their instruments across the stage. They really need to loosen up."[14] By her own admission, her work is derivative, borrowing and blending from a wide range of sources.[15]

While deeply touched by their own personal experiences, all three women found themselves influenced as artists by the turbulent 1960s/70s society around them. Cryer describes theatre as an experience that "offers people the opportunity to see their lives on stage — a sense of community of the human condition."[16] Swados criticizes artists who "have a tendency to ignore whatever lies beyond the narrow boundaries of their own experience."[17] With these attitudes it is not surprising that Cryer, Ford, and Swados looked to the contemporary human condition for the inspiration for their musicals. What they found was war and war protests, draft-dodging, a generation gap, child prostitution, drugs, technology gone awry, and growing civil and women's rights movements. These artists began writing musicals during a period in the history of musical theatre that Gerald Bordman labels "Exhaustion and a Search for New Directions." He describes a lawless society that was led by an even more lawless government. Just getting to the theatre could be difficult. The Vietnam War caused inflation that "created havoc on both sides of the footlights."[18] That havoc indirectly caused three major developments in the American musical theatre: the emergence of increasing numbers of African-Americans as both creators and playgoers; more reliance on librettists, lyricists, and directors; and the use of rock music.[19] It was the latter that Cryer, Ford, and Swados would use as their stepping stone to communicating the discord of a society.

The musicals of Swados and Cryer and Ford are rooted in the personal experiences of these women and the society which influenced these experiences. It was on this foundation that they pursued their goals in theatre, which Cryer expressed as the following: "What I want to communicate is the power of the individual to transform himself or herself, so the audiences feel it — that people can change and grow and are not necessarily tied into old patterns, bound by old behavior."[20] Swados has stated similar goals: "Music can't change political trends, but it can be a strong provocative force."[21] Their musicals would become a protest against the "old patterns" and "old behavior," "provocative force[s]" against both social ills and the "ills" of conventional, Golden Age musical theatre, as these women perceived them.

Into the Mainstream

Cryer and Ford's first two professional musicals, *Now Is The Time For All Good Men* and *The Last Sweet Days of Isaac*, were timely pieces about, respectively, war resistance and the numbing effects of new technologies. *Now Is The Time* (1967) reveals Cryer and Ford's budding desire to work against traditional, "Golden Age" musical theatre aesthetics. It is a small, intimate show about a conscientious objector to the Vietnam War; the ending is far from happy; some of the music is in the style of early rock-and-roll, relying on perceptions of this style as inherently "rebellious"; the characters are three-dimensional, whose morality is far from clear-cut, whose strengths and weaknesses are both clearly drawn. The lead female character eschews the more traditional, male-supportive role of women in Golden Age musicals by leaving her safe life — and a safe man — behind at the end of the show. Still, their rebellion against traditional musical theatre forms was only nascent in this early show; Cryer admits that the show was "very much in the Rodgers and Hammerstein vein, as were the musicals we wrote in college. Even though the show had a very gritty story, it had a very romantic score."[22]

Cryer and Ford took more than three years to write the show; they were working on and off in New York City, and as Ford puts it, "Gretchen was busy having babies."[23] *Now Is The Time* opened on 25 September 1967 and ran for 111 performances; in spite of the relatively small production costs ($40,000), it "didn't make a cent," as Cryer put it. And the investors lost all of their money.[24] It had a London production the following year, and a fourteen-performance run revival in 1971. Musical theatre historians are less-than-favorable about Cryer and Ford's first major musical effort. Gerald Bordman describes it as "perhaps more preachy than entertaining,"[25] and Stanley Green reiterates the preachiness of the show and points out the conventional nature of the score. But he sees more in the show, recognizing that "the work won applause for daring to grapple with a serious contemporary issue."[26] With this musical, the team began to realize their vision of musical theatre with a message. They continued their work on this vision, moving further away from the constraints of conventional musical theatre, with their next show, *The Last Sweet Days of Isaac*.

Isaac is a musical in two parts. The first is titled *The Elevator Play*, and it is about a thirty-three-year-old "life poet" named Isaac who is trapped in an elevator with a secretary named Ingrid. The second part, *I Want to Walk to San Francisco*, is about a nineteen-year-old boy, Isaac (who may or may not be the same Isaac as the first), and a young girl, Alice. Both are trapped in jail cells after being arrested at a demonstration. Cryer described the message of the piece as follows:

> Ultimately, my message in *Isaac*, was that one's humanity is diminished in direct proportion to the extent to which she/he relates to once-removed images as if they were the things themselves. [...] *Isaac* had to do with the change in human sensibility from the primitive one where there is direct contact — one-to-one with a person or object — to the present society which deals with images as if they are the real thing.[27]

The music of the show reinforces this message, primarily through the use of "soft rock" and "folk rock," as described by Ford.[28] The rock music conveys a modern sound that complements the modern technological society conveyed in Cryer's book and lyrics. Cryer and Ford also use music played on a tape recorder to further demonstrate the extent of technological extension.

With *Isaac*, Cryer and Ford attempted to move away from any kinds of conventional musical theatre forms. Cryer explains that she wanted to explode the Rodgers and Hammerstein form of her previous show and search for new structural methods.[29] More specifically, she

Nancy Ford, composer, has collaborated with Gretchen Cryer for over fifty years (Rahv Segev).

had to find other ways to use music that wasn't sung dialogue. Now, the way we did that was by having the convention that Isaac was thinking of his life as a piece of art. Sometimes he would imagine music underscoring his life. So we used that convention as though it was music in his head. When he sang things, it was that he was trying to heighten the moment of his life-art by using music.[30]

Cryer's libretto contains two storylines, each of which occupy a tightly knit time span and, unlike the previous show, contains no subplot, a technique that focuses the musical on one specific situation. The characters are not uniquely individualized, probably because they are meant to be universal. However, they might not invite empathy from everyone in the audience. The issues at work in this musical are complex and hard to grasp; structural weakness hinders sustained audience interest from beginning to end, something that some of its critics have affirmed.[31] Nonetheless, *Isaac* ran for 485 performances and won an Obie for best musical, as well as Drama Desk, Outer Critic's Circle, and *Variety*'s Poll Awards. Cryer and Ford believe that the reviews were the kind that they would never see again in their lifetimes. Walter Kerr called it his "favorite rock musical thus far"; Clive Barnes praised the book and lyrics, calling them the best of the offerings Off Broadway; and Martin Gottfried raved that Isaac was "an especially important theatre event" and "terribly intelligent and supermodern, very funny, pertinent and impertinent."[32] However, Cryer felt that the critics failed to pick up on the themes and political implications of the show. Nevertheless, *Isaac* was an auspicious second musical for the two women. With *Isaac*, the team was attempting to break the conventional mold of musical theatre; they were searching for new ways to integrate the music and libretto while avoiding sung dialogue. However, what they were doing was not that different from what was going on Off Broadway at that time. The main difference is that they were doing it better.

The next year, they created one more musical on themes of technology, *Shelter*, their only Broadway show. The show depicts a man who lives in a television studio, deluding himself into believing that his fabricated existence is real.[33] Self-delusion is the central theme of the show, but the musical, like *Isaac*, is also about the nature of reality and the difficulty of distinguishing between image and reality. Unfortunately, the show closed less than a month after it opened. Edwin Wilson of *The Wall Street Journal* praised the honest, fresh lyrics and the solid music but concluded with a statement of disappointment that Cryer and Ford failed to "strike a formidable blow for women" because they allowed the main character to dominate the three women in his life who visited him at the studio.[34] Kevin Sanders of WABC in New York failed to find anything redeeming in the show, bluntly asserting that *Shelter* was "one of the all-time lousy Broadway musicals" and thus should not even be discussed. However, he did discuss it, and although he acknowledged that the show may reflect some women's point of view that he could not understand, he called the show "an utterly pointless, inane, inept waste of time, money, and talent."[35] Perhaps the lessons learned from the failures of *Shelter* paved the way for the overwhelming success of their next musical, *I'm Getting My Act Together And Taking It On The Road*.

Elizabeth Swados's theatrical journey before *Runaways* took a decidedly different path than Cryer and Ford's, since she worked primarily as a composer writing music to underscore "straight" plays. Swados's first major success creating a show on her own came with a revue based on the work of Pablo Neruda and other poets, such as Sylvia Plath, Isabella Leitner, and Muriel Rukeyser, called *Nightclub Cantata* (1977). With it, Swados was already revealing her penchant for combining high art with low: "I set out to do a piece that would have the seriousness of a cantata and the frivolousness of a nightclub."[36] The cast of four women sang, danced, and even performed comic acrobatics to the poems set to music. Described by Clive Barnes as "the most pleasurable form of night-club entertainment I have ever encountered," he also described the actresses in the show as "perfect, and there is, appropriately, a very womanly touch of feminism about the whole show."[37] Martin Gottfried was not so impressed; although he admitted that the show was "more professional than most avant-garde and the skill of its production creates a magnetic interest of sorts," his chauvinist slip was showing with "it still plays like women's college art in the days before liberation."[38] On their way to success, all three women seemed to be faced with critics who expected certain things of their shows because they were women. In a way, the next musicals by Cryer and Ford and Swados seemed to answer those expectations.

After the failure of *Shelter*, Cryer and Ford formed a cabaret act and made two albums of their songs. During this hiatus from musical theatre composition, Cryer and Ford began to realize that they wanted to write a musical based on their own "personal odyssey" as women in a male-oriented society.[39] They felt that the time was ripe for such a musical. In 1972, Congress passed the ERA, and in 1973, Roe vs. Wade and Doe vs. Bolton gave women the right to a legal abortion.[40] The United Nations declared 1975 the International Year of the Woman, and in 1976 male chauvinism was certified a psychiatric illness by the American Psychiatric Association.

In writing *I'm Getting My Act Together*, Cryer claims to have been influenced by Simone de Beauvoir's *The Second Sex*, which she read at the age of nineteen. That is when her feminist leanings began.[41] But Cryer stresses that, although the show *is* feminist theatre, it is more about self-realization —for women *and* men. She believes that women's concerns should be universal concerns and explains that *I'm Getting My Act Together* is "about what happens when the ground rules are knocked out from under you," whether you're a woman or a man.[42] The show is based in part on Cryer and Ford's personal experiences as women who were raised on a set of ideals, only to discover that those ideals no longer seem right. They molded these experiences into the central character of the show, Heather Jones, around whom three themes revolve: relationships, transition, and the desire to drop all disguises and be honest with yourself, or self-celebration. Jones, on a comeback in her singing career after acting in soap operas for several years, is auditioning her new cabaret act for her manager, Joe. She is attempting to express in her music her new feminist attitudes toward age, relationships, self-sufficiency, and honesty. But Joe, who is struggling with a failing marriage, rejects Heather's music and her attitudes; he wants things to remain the way they were. In the end, the two business partners and friends cannot reconcile their differences, and Joe leaves.

Cryer and Ford carefully crafted the form of *I'm Getting My Act Together* to convey the themes and reveal the characters and their relationships. The authors have moved farther away than ever before from the concept of sung dialogue; the show, like the second act of *The Last Sweet Days of Isaac*, is actually a play punctuated by songs. Cryer does follow some of the conventions of musical theatre in her libretto. The storyline is simple and easy to follow, and it occupies a very tightly knit time span. The characters, however, are three-dimensional with both strengths and weaknesses, although Joe does occasionally come across as a stereotypical male chauvinist. And there is no subplot; the story focuses on one situation and never strays from it. As is usual with the team's controversial shows, the amount of empathy *I'm Getting My Act Together* receives would depend on the audience. Certainly the show would elicit strong reactions, both positive and negative, from the audience. The humor injected liberally into the show would aid in its acceptance, as would the catchy tunes. Cryer and Ford discarded the conventional division of musicals into two acts and made the action continuous; this technique helps the audience feel as if they are actually sitting in on an evening in Heather's life. Furthermore, the creators paid little attention to the convention of liberal contrast within the musical sequence. Ballads follow ballads, rhythm songs follow rhythm songs. The emphasis in this musical is on reality, since the songs are all a part of Heather's act; any attempt to build a contrived musical sequence in the interest of contrast would have failed.

When Cryer and Ford conceived the idea for the show, they originally planned to write a conventional musical. At the time, both women were performing in their cabaret act. One night, in the middle of a performance, Cryer thought, "I'm getting my act together and taking it on the road."[43] She later decided that that thought would be a perfect metaphor for an unconventional show written in the form of a cabaret act. With only two main characters and a rock band, *I'm Getting My Act Together* was, financially, an extremely feasible show, and Cryer and Ford had no difficulty in finding a producer for it Off Broadway: Joseph Papp, under the auspices of his New York Shakespeare Festival Public Theater. Next came the problem of casting Heather. No one seemed as right for the role as Cryer herself. Cryer had no intentions of stepping into the lead at first, but she finally conceded after much persuasion by Papp.

I'm Getting My Act Together and Taking It On The Road opened at the Public/Anspacher Theater Off Broadway on 14 June 1978. During the previews, the audience response was emphatically positive. Hopes were high on opening night, but the hostile critics soon dashed those hopes. Although Richard Eder of *The New York Times* admitted that some of the music was agreeable, he pointed out that the show had "some freshness of inspiration but none of achievement." He called Cryer's perception about aging and feminine identity "off" and declared that the show's affliction was "self-celebration." He closed his review with the statement, "'I'm Getting My Act Together and Taking It On The Road' is not so much a title as a pious hope."[44] Two weeks later, Walter Kerr dealt his blow to the apparently doomed show. Admitting from the start that he was a chauvinist, Kerr admonished Cryer for making a weak case for women's liberation, "or making it wrongly." He did praise Cryer for being "lyrically intelligent" and "self-assertively bold," but he claimed that although Heather gained her freedom as a woman in the show, she was still miserable with a permanent frown. Kerr even went so far as to criticize Cryer's hair and wardrobe, saying that "she also, quite deliberately, looks terrible." Finally, he asked how anyone could possible sympathize with Heather.[45]

The show faired little better under the pens of the few female critics. Edith Oliver found the show disappointing in light of Cryer and Ford's earlier success with *The Last Sweet Days of Isaac*. She called the team's newest musical "a lexicon of all those awful words and phrases [...] that are the jargon of the nineteen-seventies—'relate,' 'relationship,' 'confrontation,' 'cleaning lady,' 'manipulating,' 'sick,' and, worst of all, 'celebrating me.'" Although she recognized Cryer's courage in playing the lead, she did not think that Cryer pulled it off.[46]

When the show opened, Cryer and Ford had no premonition of the hostility of the critics. At first they were crushed, and they were sure that the show would close, even though the house was full every night. But Kerr's review was the last straw for Cryer, filling her with indignation and determination. She later commented, "That review was so personal! You never get descriptions of a male actor's physical looks in a review."[47] The morning Kerr's review came out, Cryer read it, laughed, and went back to sleep. A little later, Papp sent Cryer an article from the *New York Times* that stated that there were 500,000 single women in New York. Papp wrote Cryer, "This is our audience." Together, they began to beat the critics.

I'm Getting My Act Together completed a seven-month run of 226 performances at the Public then moved to Circle in the Square, also Off Broadway, where if ran for three years. It closed on 15 March 1981 after 1,165 performances. Cryer played the lead for a year. A variety of actresses, including Betty Buckley, Nancy Ford, and Phyllis Newman, took over the role during the run, and Cryer returned as Heather for the last five performances of the show. The show toured for three years, and as it toured, the popular musical was placed in larger and larger theatres. The original production had played in the 299-seat Circle in the Square, and the first theatre (in Chicago) on the tour seated 850. The show played the 1,100-seat proscenium house of the Huntington Hartford in Los Angeles and a 1,600 seat theatre in San Francisco.

By the time the London production opened in 1981, the show was playing in a total of twenty international cities. In the United States, regional theatres had already begun their own productions, and the motion picture rights were being negotiated. Jill Clayburgh, Shirley MacLaine, Carol Burnett, and Cher all reportedly wanted to play Heather, but although Dolly Parton was eventually signed on with TriStar Pictures to do the movie, the project was eventually dropped and never picked up again.

I'm Getting My Act Together would never have had a long production history if Cryer, Ford, and Papp had listened to the critics. When critics claimed that the show did not say anything that had not already been said, Cryer replied, "Well, the show's not saying, 'Here's a new piece of information.' It's about the difficulty of dealing emotionally with this stuff that we all know."[48] In other cases, Cryer thought that the critics viewed the show with a distorted perception: the "temper of the times" caused male critics to be irritated by the show. However, Cryer's reasoning does not account for the female critics, such as Oliver, who also were annoyed by the show.

It was the audience response that was crucial to Cryer and Ford, and that response was overwhelmingly positive. During the original run, women *and* men kept coming back to see the show repeatedly. People would rush backstage after the performances to talk about the show. This response became so overwhelming that Cryer and Ford began holding discussion sessions after Wednesday evening performances. The topics ranged from the politics of feminism to Cryer and Ford's personal experiences that led them to write the show. Most of the women commented on how the show had touched their lives, helping them to make major decisions. The male response was strong and varied. Many men claimed that they identified with Heather. Few men were willing to admit that the identified with Joe. One man bluntly dismissed Joe as absurd. Later, he sent his picture to Cryer and Ford with a letter that read, "On second thought, I've decided I'm just like the guy in the play — and I want to audition for the part."[49] Another night after the show, Cryer overheard a man who had just looked at his program exclaim, "My God! Those two girls wrote all that themselves."[50] The strongest negative response came from a man who told Cryer at a Wednesday night discussion that he wanted to blow her away with a shotgun. When Cryer and the audience laughed, he solemnly explained, "I'm not kidding. I feel very hostile. Don't you realize that you women are causing a lot of problems in the world? You're trying to change things too fast."[51]

This kind of strong reaction is a part of the greatest achievement of *I'm Getting My Act Together*— its influence on the audience. Cryer and Ford had gained a small following from their previous shows, especially *The Last Sweet Days of Isaac*. But with their newest musical, the team was influencing more people than ever before; women were even bringing the men in their lives to the show as a relationship test to see how they reacted.[52] By the 1990s, Cryer believed that the issues at work in the show were still pertinent, but she did not think that an audience for the show continued to exist, since most people, women and men, by that time mistakenly believed that the problems depicted had been solved.[53] Cryer is probably correct. *I'm Getting My Act Together* was successful at targeting an audience during a specific moment in time.[54] Ken Bloom admits that although it was not the best show ever, "it did speak to a lot of people and was actually topical, something rare in musical theatre."[55] Stanley Green gives the show and its authors this high praise: "Its success is testament that the catharsis Gretchen Cryer and Nancy Ford have experienced through their songs can also be felt by a wide spectrum of women today, no matter their divergence in background or interests."[56] Cryer and Ford will likely be remembered mainly for this show. Although their days as musical theatre writers are far from over, *I'm Getting My Act Together and Taking It On The Road* has become a tough act to follow.

Runaways is not so clearly "woman-centered" as Cryer and Ford's show, since it revolves around both female and male runaways. But it could arguably be labeled feminist in its attempts to deal with marginalized stories in unconventional — to the Broadway musical stage — ways. The show is based on Swados's own itinerate life and unstable childhood; she ran away from home the first time at the age of five, leaving behind a note stating a litany of grievances. Although she soon returned home, it was only the first in a string of sudden departures from her home, culminating in her permanent departure at the age of sixteen. Mel Gussow claims that *Runaways* "did not come from contemplating ghetto children, but from her own life and her feeling of 'fragmentation.'"[57] She also wanted to do a piece about adolescence, partly in order to utilize pop/rock music, which she viewed as perfectly appropriate to the subject. To prepare, Swados read *Weeping in the Playtime of Others*, a book about abuse by Kenneth Wooden, and Tom Wicker's *A Time to Die*; she also interviewed numerous adolescents and hung around schoolyards observing children.

In this relentlessly hard-hitting piece, young actors deliver songs and soliloquies on such issues as growing up, child abuse, divorce, neglect, homelessness, and child prostitution. It began life at the Public, and like that other famous Public transfer to Broadway of the time, *A Chorus Line*, it is a "chamber musical" of personal stories from the characters. Swados utilized a few professional actors but mostly inexperienced amateurs, students she auditioned at local public schools and even several runaways.[58] In her book *Listening Out Loud*, Swados describes the nonprofessional performers as "instruments":

> My "orchestra" included a tough black boy who could hustle his way through anything; a monosyllabic child of sixties parents, rendered numb by relentless freedom; a driven show-biz kid; a Hispanic boy who felt responsible for his family's economic problems; a young black woman, old before her time; a rich smart-ass filled with self hatred; the guilty child of a manic family who wanted to be all things to all people. These were kids from broken homes, kids who had seen their parents commit crimes, kids worried about their sexuality. Some of these "instruments" had a hard edge and weren't perfect in pitch, nor were the harmonies perfect; but once again, I chose these voices to expand the conventional vocal types of musical theatre performance.[59]

Swados did not want the audience to be lulled by the typical beautiful voices of Broadway; she felt that this would have undermined the meanings of the musical.

She worked with these "instruments," ranging in age from eleven to twenty, to develop the piece collaboratively over ten months, employing an unconventional rehearsal process that incorporated a variety of physical, vocal, and emotional exercises devised by Swados. Mel Gussow, who observed rehearsals, describes the process:

> The transition from workshop to full production was organic. Actors were given songs, dances, monologues. Roles were switched and expanded. Songs were dropped and new lyrics written. The show took the natural shape of the participants. For example, with the presence of Bernie Allison, a skateboard champion, in the cast, there was no doubt that there would be skateboard choreography. Tony Butler's prowess as a graffito artist assured that he would paint "multicolored curses" during the show. One day, John Fine brought in his violin; he now plays it on stage.[60]

The show was finalized at over three dozen monologues/numbers, ranging from the light-hearted, as in "The Basketball Song," to the satiric, as in "Where Are Those People Who Did 'Hair'?," to the brutally honest, as in one monologue about a girl who smashed the television to get her parent's attention, only to be given a scalding bath and scraped with the broken glass as punishment. The music is a characteristic, for Swados, melding of styles: pop, rock, salsa, country, disco, punk, blues. Several sources labeled the form of the show a "collage."[61] Swados received some criticism for laying the blame for the runaways' plights squarely on the shoulders of neglectful parents, undergirding the children's complex pain with too-facile causes. The author's own relationship with her parents could have contributed to this perspective.

Runaways did extremely well at its downtown home. Jack Kroll of *Newsweek* effusively proclaimed: "To call it far and away the best musical of the season is to insult it. 'Runaways' seizes your heart, plays with your pulse, dances exuberantly across the line that separates entertainment from involvement."[62] Mel Gussow, who seems to have been a champion of Swados's early work, claims that the show "is the first musical since 'Hair' to unite, successfully, contemporary popular music and the legitimate theater," and he called *Runaways* "an eloquent and mature vision, a musical that touches our hearts."[63] Richard Eder suggested that "it is in its beauty, its wit, its sad gaiety, its unexpectedness that the real pain and wonder of 'Runaways' take possession of us."[64] But when it moved to the Plymouth Theatre on Broadway on 13 May 1978, Walter Kerr took the opportunity to pan the show, causing a furor amongst fans of the show and an avalanche of letters to the editor of *The New York Times*, where the review appeared. Kerr criticized Swados for not allowing her performers to show emotion, accusing her of turning them "bland, non-committal, muted, evasive, in some cases stony cold. [...] The performers' neutralization neutralizes us."[65] Joseph Papp, experts on child abuse, parents, and others wrote to the paper defending the "authenticity" and appeal of the show. Clearly *Runaways* had struck a chord in audiences and most critics, and it was nominated for five Tony Awards. But, unlike its sister show, *A Chorus Line*, it enjoyed only a brief run on Broadway. It has had a life, albeit somewhat limited, after its Broadway run, particularly in schools; one controversial 1984 production at a high school in Vermont was banned by the school board for being "inappropriate" for the school.[66] In spite of its brief Broadway run, *Runaways* proved that children were an appropriate subject for a musical, and that, as in *Hair* before it, rock music could certainly be an appropriate medium in which to work in mainstream musicals, and social consciousness was not anathema to that milieu. Furthermore, like *A Chorus Line*, it experimented with alternative, more collaborative development strategies, and moved away from the linear book musical that had become the norm toward a more "postmodern" collage.

Far From Over

Since *I'm Getting My Act Together*, Cryer and Ford have yet to see another of their original musicals produced on or Off Broadway in New York. However, they have created several more shows, and both have been busy with their own individual projects. Cryer acted in a number of productions throughout the eighties and has written some non-musical pieces, including educational plays for various pharmaceutical companies. She also created a company, "Food from Home," that provides mail-order, frozen food, inspired by her experience trying to care long-distance for aging parents in Indiana. Ford has worked mainly in soap operas, writing scripts, not music, for such shows as *As the World Turns*. She laughingly admitted, "That has kept me off the streets."[67]

While working on their own projects, the team has continued to work together in a partnership that spans almost fifty years. With Richard Maltby, Jr., they co-wrote a revue of women's songs called *Hang on to the Good Times*, which ran for almost a month at the Manhattan Theatre Club Off Broadway in 1985. For years they worked on a musical about the life of Eleanor Roosevelt that was never produced. And most recently they created *The American Girls Revue* and its sequel for American Girl Place in Chicago. But even if they fail to see another of their musicals produced on or Off Broadway, Cryer and Ford will be remembered as the first female lyricist-composer team to write for the Broadway stage. But this is rather misleading considering that their best work was done Off Broadway. Their intimate, socially conscious musicals were well-suited to the Off Broadway stage, and despite Cryer's claims that she and Ford searched for and discovered new forms, their musicals were typical of the Off Broadway shows. However, both *The Last Sweet Days of Isaac* and *I'm Getting My Act Together And Taking It On The Road* were more significant in their impact than the usual Off Broadway fare. With these works, the creators attempted to alter the musical comedy formula, and they were quite successful. Although their attempts have been less influential than those of, for example, Stephen Sondheim, Cryer and Ford made an impact with their "state of the art" music theatre theory, their continual search for new directions, their unfailingly original ideas, and their sensitive understanding of a certain segment of society: women.

Cryer considers her major achievement her search for new forms to eliminate sung dialogue. She claims, "I've always known that I've been breaking rules, searching for other forms for the musical."[68] However, Cryer hasn't exactly broken rules; instead, her development of interesting methods for combining music and dialogue is a continuation of the experimental process in musical theatre, a process in which writers like Sondheim, William Finn, Adam Guettel, Jeanine Tesori, and Jason Robert Brown have had a hand. In 1991, Ford expressed her belief that she herself had not achieved much in musical theatre: "I guess the only contribution I have made are some shows that maybe people enjoyed and music that sometimes touched people in some way." Ford does think that perhaps it is "something" that she has written what she wanted to write in the style that she wanted to write it.[69] Ford takes musical styles, such as rock and folk, and makes them her own. She does not write rock, but her own idea of rock, never parodying rock. And, like Sondheim, Ford never assumes musical associations, writing a slow, lovely melody to undercut Cryer's biting lyrics, or using a quick tempo melody in a minor key for lyrics about love.

Austin Pendleton's blunt opinion concerning the achievements of the team are that they simply contributed "two really fine musicals and two interesting, unsuccessful ones" that are "provocative pieces with lovely music."[70] But even with their less successful shows, Cryer and Ford brought their own integrity and originality to the musical theatre. Stanley Green reflects this point of view: "They have never been, not are they ever likely to be, creators who can adapt themselves to concepts other than their own; their songs and librettos have all shown marked originality in both subject matter and viewpoint as they have consistently reflected the collaborator's mutual attitudes and deep concerns."[71] Cryer stated that when theatre is "real and true," it allows insight into the human condition and is a transforming experience.[72] By delving into their own experiences and questioning the human condition, Cryer and Ford have written musical theatre that is original, controversial, and "real and true."

Elizabeth Swados has been considerably more prolific post–*Runaways* than Cryer and Ford after *I'm Getting My Act Together*. She seemed to find a permanent new "family" at the Public, where she continued to work after *Runaways*, with shows like *Alice In Concert* (1978), *Lullabye and Goodnight* (1980), and *Dispatches* (1979), a rock musical about the Vietnam War based on Michael Herr's highly acclaimed book. Detractors apparently criticized her for attempting a musical about Vietnam; Swados's response was: "I'm not doing Vietnam, I'm doing the book. [...] I wanted to do it *because* I'm a woman [Swados's emphasis]. I wanted to know what men are subjected to. The book told a lot about them, not about intellectuals but about men who fight wars—the grief, the pain and poetry of here-and-now men. It's set within a very masculine context. War is very macho, but the book showed the sensitivity."[73] She cast three women in the show, explaining paradoxically their presence as a symbol of war, since war is a "sensual and sexual experience."[74] Richard Eder was extremely critical of this choice in his review of the show, although his biases are clear from the lede of the review: "An artist needs to know what he can do. An artist cannot do whatever he wants; only what he can do." He goes on to cite the "rhetorical convenience" of the use of the word "he" and admits its inaccuracy in this case, but the damage has been done in the odd lede.[75]

Swados's eponymous 1983 musicalization, with Garry Trudeau, of Trudeau's comic strip *Doonesbury*, had the distinction of being included in Ken Mandelbaum's *Not Since Carrie: 40 Years of Broadway Musical Flops*. Mandelbaum lays much of the blame for the show's failure on Swados's "usual non-music," as well as the lack of integration of the songs into the script.[76] Swados and Trudeau continued their collaboration the next year with *Rap Master Ronnie*, a revue that attacks the administration of then–President Ronald Reagan. For both of these shows, Swados continued to utilize an eclectic mix of musical styles, and this stylistic variety pleased some critics and annoyed others. In *Swing* (1987), Swados returned to her work with children, crafting a collage of dance, drama, and music based on themes similar to those in *Runaways*; "swing" refers to "swings of fate, swings of mood, swings of luck, and swings of fashion," in addition to swing music.[77] Swados admits, "I stop what I'm doing every couple of years to do a show with kids. There's no suffering competition going on, but I had a really bad growing-up myself, so we can almost relate instantly — these are basically the people I hang out with."[78] Religious themes also pervade a number of the Jewish creator's works: *Esther: A Vaudeville Megillah* (1988), *Job: A Circus* (1991), *Jerusalem* (1992), *Jonah* (1989), and *Missionaries* (1997).

Swados continues to write music for the theatre, and she is also a prolific author of books, including a number of award-winning children books. Her most autobiographical book is *Listening Out Loud: Becoming a Composer*, in which she gives advice to young people seeking a career as a composer. The book includes a lengthy section criticizing contemporary (circa 1988) musical theatre, arguing that "to begin to innovate, we clearly must move beyond the structural confines of the 'book' musical."[79] Even more interesting for the purposes of this essay is the chapter "Writing as a Woman," in which Swados reveals strong opinions, some contradictory, about being a woman in a largely male profession. Generally, Swados sees clear cut differences between men and women, engaging in a certain amount of essentializing about both sexes. She argues that in "visible positions of power," equity between men and women has increased, but in less visible activities, such as composing, less pressure exists to include women. She decries the "long-standing sexist mythology" that has dictated the kinds of emotions women would be likely to express in music and engages in the now-too-familiar lament that when a man is aggressive, he's "assertive," while an aggressive woman is viewed as "bitchy": "What would be called adventurous for a man was careless for me; prolific for a man was facile for me; opinionated, passionate, strong for a man was schoolmarmish, hectoring, strident for me."[80] Yet she argues that women tend "to recover more quickly than men" from things like bad reviews[81] and that when women lead a rock and roll rhythm section of all males, "the gender differences are as palpable as they would be if you tried to quarterback a football team."[82]

Most telling is Swados's admission that "a portion of almost every day of my working life is also devoted to some struggle with sexism, and every woman composer I know has to cope with anxiety and depression because the jobs and funding, already so scarce, are almost unavailable to them."[83] She suggests several strategies for combating this sexism: behave professionally, adopt a stinging wit, avoid being cornered into playing roles, and be proactive. Certainly Swados has lived by this last piece of advice, for in spite of the sexism that she perceived in the musical world, she has carved out a long, diverse career for herself in music and theatre as a composer, lyricist, playwright, and director.

Feminist Musical Theatre?

At the height of their careers in musical theatre, Cryer, Ford, and Swados were writing during a time when feminism was coming to the forefront of American society's cultural imaginary, thanks to the increasingly visible women's rights, or "women's liberation" movement; they came of age in a time when women were clamoring for their voices to be heard, understood, and validated. Certainly *I'm Getting My Act Together* is the show most visibly influenced by feminism, labeled as such by its creators. Yet in their caveat that the show is about issues concerning both women *and* men is the reminder that "feminism" is a difficult term to define, and the variety of belief systems that fall under its rubric are more appropriately termed "feminisms." But all these feminisms involve the promotion of equality among the sexes, the refutation of culturally imposed gendered identities, and the opportunity for increased representation of women throughout all segments of society. Cryer, Ford, and Swados were all promoting these ideals— if not explicitly through the subjects of their shows, then implicitly through their processes in creating the musicals. Each fought for the chance to work outside the box of the then-dominant book musical, with its "romantic" music and tangential social consciousness, if present at all. They resisted categorization, playing various roles in the collaborative, creative process that is theatre, music, and musical theatre, and paving the way for a new generation of female composers and lyricists.

Notes

1. Stanley Green, *The World of Musical Comedy*, 4th ed. (London: Tantivy, 1980) 357.

2. Al Kasha and Joel Hirschhorn, *Notes on Broadway: Intimate Conversations with Broadway's Greatest Songwriters* (New York: Simon, 1985) 83.

3. Qtd. in Jeff Sweet, "Their Songs are for Women — and Men," *Newsday* 16 Nov. 1975 (Located in NewsBank [Microform], Performing Arts, 1975, 77: A12–13, fiche).

4. In an interview with Jeff Sweet, Ford later revealed that she suspected that the boy chose Cryer because he wanted to date her. He soon dropped out of the picture (A13).

5. Qtd. in Sweet A13.

6. Qtd. in Joan Connely, "The Act is Together and Thriving: Cryer and Ford are a Double Success," *Horizon* Jan. 1979: 60.

7. Qtd. in Barbara Kantrowitz, "How One Lyricist Got Her Own Act Together," *Philadelphia Inquirer* 4 Oct. 1981 (Located in NewsBank [Microform], Performing Arts, 1981, 56: G6–7, fiche): G6.

8. Qtd. in Mel Gussow, "Elizabeth Swados— A Runaway Talent," *New York Times* 5 Mar. 1978: sm5.

9. Elizabeth Swados, *Listening Out Loud: Becoming a Composer* (New York: Harper, 1988) 20.

10. Gussow, "Runaway" 5.

11. Swados also was the first woman at Bennington, which admitted men in 1969, to live with a male roommate, a distinction that landed her on the cover of *The New York Times Magazine*.

12. Qtd. in Gussow, "Runaway" 22.

13. Gussow, "Runaway" 5.

14. Qtd. in Mel Gussow, "Elizabeth Swados Writes Cantata for Cabaret," *New York Times* 7 January 1977: 40.

15. Gussow, "Writes" 40.

16. Qtd. in Betsy Harris, "Her Act's Together and on the Road," *Indianapolis Star* 5 February 1981. (Located in NewsBank [Microform], Performing Arts, 1981, 106: G6–7, fiche).

17. Swados 86.

18. Gerald Bordman, *American Musical Theatre: A Chronicle*, 2nd ed. (New York: Oxford University Press, 1986) 642.

19. Bordman 643.

20. Qtd. in Kasha 87.

21. Swados 122.

22. Qtd. in Kasha 77.

23. Qtd. in Beatrice Berg, "From School Days to Sweet Days," *New York Times* 15 Feb. 1970, sec. 2: 3.

24. Gretchen Cryer, telephone interview, 5 Dec. 1990.

25. Bordman 654.

26. Green 357.

27. Qtd. in Kathleen Betsko and Rachel Koenig, *Interviews with Contemporary Women Playwrights* (New York: Beach, 1987) 104.

28. Nancy Ford, telephone interview, 9 Feb. 1991. In my interview with Ford, she called the music "almost baroque rock." Paul Taylor refers to baroque rock as popular music with over-ornate arrangements; however, Ford's music simply has a baroque sound because of the use of a harpsichord-like instrument or synthesizer, especially in the song "A Transparent Crystal Moment." Folk rock is a term for songs that are lyrically intelligent with political or protest themes using folk-style harmonies and electric instruments. See Paul Taylor, *Popular Music Since 1955: A Critical Guide to Literature* (Boston: Hall, 1985) 484.

29. Betsko 103.

30. Cryer, telephone interview. Cryer refers to sung dialogue as the technique of bursting into song when the emotion becomes too great to be spoken. This technique involves lyrics that are similar to dialogue; in other words, the songs are merely dialogue set to music.

31. See Clive Barnes, rev. of *The Last Sweet Days of Isaac*, by Gretchen Cryer and Nancy Ford, *New York Times* 27 Jan. 1970: 49; Martin Gottfried, rev. of *The Last Sweet Days of Isaac*, by Gretchen Cryer and Nancy Ford, *Women's Wear Daily*, *New York Theatre Critics' Reviews* 31 (1970): 292; and Walter Kerr, "'My Favorite Rock Musical Thus Far,'" rev. of *The Last Sweet Days Of Isaac*, by Gretchen Cryer and Nancy Ford, *New York Times* 8 Feb. 1970, sec. 2: 1+.

32. Kerr 1; Barnes 49; Gottfried 292.

33. Cryer and Ford's plot considerably predates similar ones used in the films *EdTV* and *The Truman Show*.

34. Edwin Wilson, "What's Needed: A Bit More Women's Lib," rev. of *Shelter*, by Gretchen Cryer and Nancy Ford, *Wall Street Journal* 8 Feb. 1973: 12.

35. Kevin Sanders, rev. of *Shelter*, by Gretchen Cryer and Nancy Ford, WABC, New York. 6 Feb. 1973, *New York Theatre Critics' Reviews* 34 (1973): 372.

36. Qtd. in Gussow, "Writes" 40.

37. Clive Barnes, rev. of *Nightclub Cantata*, by Elizabeth Swados, *New York Times* 10 Jan. 1977: 22.

38. Martin Gottfried, rev. of *Nightclub Cantata*, by Elizabeth Swados, *New York Post* 10 Jan. 1977.

39. Kasha 83.

40. Before 1973, more women died from abortions in this country each year than American men were killed in Vietnam; see Peter N. Carroll, *It Seemed Like Nothing Happened: The Tragedy and Promise of America in the 1970s* (New York: Holt, 1982).

41. Kasha 80.

42. Qtd. in Kasha 83.

43. Qtd. in Kasha 83.

44. Richard Eder, rev. of *I'm Getting My Act Together And Taking It On The Road*, by Gretchen Cryer and Nancy Ford, *New York Times* 15 June 1978, sec. 3: 17.

45. Walter Kerr, "Two Women, Both Alone, Two Moods," rev. of *I'm Getting My Act Together And Taking It On The Road*, by Gretchen Cryer and Nancy Ford, *New York Times* 9 July 1978, sec. 2: 3.

46. Edith Oliver, "Lady Sings the Blues," rev. of *I'm Getting My Act Together And Taking It On The Road*, by Gretchen Cryer and Nancy Ford, *New Yorker* 26 June 1978: 54.

47. Qtd. in Betsko 102.

48. Qtd. in Kantrowitz G7.

49. Qtd. in Betsko 102.

50. Qtd. in Kantrowitz G7.

51. Qtd. in Judy Klemesrud, "She's Got Her Act Together Again," *New York Times* 16 Dec. 1978: 48.

52. *I'm Getting My Act Together* was the *Vagina Monologues* of its time.

53. Cryer, telephone interview.

54. Indeed, in his review of a 2002 production in Seattle at the Liberty Deli Dinner Theatre, critic Steve Wiecking concurs that while a lot of Cryer's concerns are still "sadly relevant," the show now feels "sticky and pedantic." Steve Wiecking, "Ms. Musical: It's a '70s thing," rev. of *I'm Getting My Act Together and Taking It On The Road*, by Gretchen Cryer and Nancy Ford, 11–17 July 2002. 15 February 2003. <http://www.seattleweekly.com/features/0228/arts-wiecking.shtml>.

55. Ken Bloom, *American Song: The Complete Musical Theatre Companion*, 2 vols. (New York: Facts, 1985) 341.

56. Green 358.

57. Mel Gussow, "Runaway," 22.

58. One of the experienced young actors was Diane Lane, who soon left the stage for a film career and in 2002 was nominated for an Academy Award for her work in *Unfaithful*.

59. Swados 47

60. Gussow, "Runaways," 52.

61. See, for example, John Beaufort, rev. of *Runaways*, by Elizabeth Swados, *Christian Science Monitor* 15 March, 1978. *New York Theatre Critics' Reviews* (1978): 282; and Edwin Wilson, rev. of *Runaways*, by Elizabeth Swados, *Wall Street Journal* 30 March, 1978. *New York Theatre Critics' Reviews* (1978): 281.

62. Jack Kroll, "Babes Up in Arms" rev. of *Runaways*, by Elizabeth Swados, *Newsweek* 27 March 1978. *New York Theatre Critics' Reviews* (1978): 280.

63. Mel Gussow, rev. of *Runaways*, by Elizabeth Swados, *New York Times* 10 Mar. 1978: C3.

64. Richard Eder, rev. of *Runaways*, by Elizabeth Swados, 22 Mar. 1978: C17.

65. Walter Kerr, "'Runaways' Runs Into Trouble," rev. of *Runaways*, by Elizabeth Swados, *New York Times* 21 May 1978: D5, 9.

66. "Vermont Students Fight School Ban on Presenting 'Runaways' Play," *New York Times* 21 Feb. 1984: A15.

67. Ford, telephone interview.

68. Qtd. in Betsko 103–4.

69. Ford, telephone interview.

70. Austin Pendleton, telephone interview, 24 Jan. 1991.

71. Green 357.

72. Qtd. in Kasha 87.

73. Qtd. in Mel Gussow, "A Rock Musical About Vietnam," *New York Times* 8 April 1979: D1.

74. Qtd. in Gussow, "Rock" 9.

75. Richard Eder, Rev. of *Dispatches*, by Elizabeth Swados, *New York Times* 19 April 1979: C17.

76. Ken Mandelbaum, *Not Since Carrie: 40 Years of Broadway Musical Flops* (New York: St. Martin's, 1991). This is a common criticism of Swados's work. But like Cryer and Ford, Swados was experimenting with musical forms, moving away from the Golden Age integration of book and song. However, she and Cryer and Ford have found popular acceptance from audiences as evidenced by long runs and sales of recordings of their work.

77. Qtd. in Patricia Leigh Brown, "'Swing'" Songs of Innocence and Experience," *New York Times* 18 Oct. 1987: 5.

78. Qtd. in Ariel Levy, "Child's Play," *New York* 5 October 1998: 93.

79. Swados 123.

80. Swados 185.

81. Swados 182.

82. Swados 179.

83. Swados 182.

The Rise of the Female Director/Choreographer on Broadway

MARY JO LODGE

"We found that in general, women could get just so far as
directors, then they'd run up against what we called the
broken-ladder syndrome. Women can direct in regional theatres,
Off Broadway or Off Off Broadway, but when it comes to large
commercial Broadway productions, producers are not willing
to put their millions of dollars, as well as their faith and
belief in a woman director."
— Julianne Boyd[1]

Helen Krich Chinoy, in her essay "Women Backstage and Outfront,"
quoted Julianne Boyd, co-coordinator (with Kay Carney) of a 1983 study by
the League of Professional Theatre Women, on their findings concerning conditions in the early 1980s for professional female theatre directors. In the nearly
twenty years since that study was conducted, the so-called "Broadway-barrier"
has begun to crumble, as is evidenced by Julie Taymor's 1998 Tony Award win
for Best Direction of a Musical for Disney's *The Lion King.* Taymor's win, as
well as Garry Hynes' 1998 Tony for Best Direction of a Play for *The Beauty
Queen of Leenane,* made for an unprecedented female sweep of the directing
categories that year and marked the first time that women won the coveted
directing statuettes. That recognition may be indicative of the growing numbers of successful women directors on Broadway, and certainly demonstrates
female progress in the male dominated Broadway production world. Marilyn
Stasio of *Variety* says, in reference to the 1998 Tony Awards:

> And that about explains why so many women are thrilled about the Tony hon-
> ors— not because a couple of women finally got noticed but because two
> women directors won commercial success by doing their work their way. And

221

in Taymor's extraordinary case, because she maintained her artistic integrity with an $11 million monkey on her back.[2]

The 1998 Tony Awards recognized what many working theatre women across the country already know — women can successfully direct at every level of American professional theatre. Boyd's "broken ladder" is showing signs of repair and now, more than ever, female directors are becoming a force to be reckoned with on Broadway and in other major theatre venues in New York and across the country.

While the recognition of Taymor and Hynes marked a milestone for female directors everywhere, the 1999–2000 New York theatre season, in many ways, demonstrated an even stronger feminine presence in control of the boards, particularly in the area of musical theatre. In that season, women broke through the barriers keeping them from one of the few remaining exclusively male jobs in show business: the professional director/choreographer. Prior to that time, professional female director/choreographers had been, as Lawrence Thelan points out in his text *The Show Makers*, "few and far between throughout the latter half of the century."[3] During the 1999–2000 season, however, four female director/choreographers created Broadway productions, while two others headed major Off Broadway works. These six women — Graciela Daniele, Patricia Birch, Lynne Taylor-Corbett, Ann Reinking, Susan Stroman, and Kathleen Marshall — have made the treacherous climb up the "broken ladder" to create a diverse body of musical theatre pieces. Certainly other female director/choreographers are creating musical theatre throughout the country, but these six have emerged as the most visible and prolific in major New York theatres. They are developing and creating original work on Broadway and Off Broadway, as well as in films and on concert stages, and have firmly established themselves as director/choreographers. They have joined the "boy's club," to quote Graciela Daniele, and they stand as pioneers among professional female director/choreographers, with only the legendary Agnes de Mille, who directed and choreographed *Allegro* in 1947, to blaze a trail for them. The ultimate acknowledgement of their success came with the 2001 Tony awards, when Susan Stroman became the first woman in history to win both the direction and choreography awards for her work on a single production, namely her smash hit, *The Producers*.

Stroman's wins may finally herald a new era of professional recognition for female director/choreographers, whose work until now has garnered little acknowledgement and even less academic attention. The work of the six groundbreaking female theatre artists examined in this chapter, for example, has gone largely unstudied, even though they are reshaping the role of the director/choreographer and indeed, the current musical theatre world. An exploration of the lives, thoughts, experiences and perspectives of these six pioneers may shed new light on the evolving role of the director/choreographer in American musical theatre. (Unless otherwise noted, quotations come from original in-person interviews conducted with the six female director/choreographers.)[4]

Of the group, Graciela Daniele stands as the first female director/choreographer of the "modern" era, and in fact, is the first female director/choreographer to work on Broadway since Agnes de Mille. Daniele's winding path to New York took her to several countries on several continents. She was born in 1939 in Argentina and says of her training, "I became a professional (ballet dancer) at fourteen. It is a very different kind of training. I don't really have an academic background. What I have is an experience background, which is very valuable." Daniele did not come from a theatrical background, but she describes her family as "very musical," and says that they enjoyed "singing and dancing and playing music." Her start in dance was for practical, rather than artistic, reasons:

> I started dancing when I was seven years old, and the reason was that I had some problem with the arch of my foot. I mean, it wasn't flat, but there was some muscle that wasn't really developed. My mother took me to an orthopedic doctor, thinking that he was going to give me special shoes and the doctor said, "Why don't you put her in ballet? Take her to ballet class, because the work will develop this muscle, and in six months or a year, she will be fine." That was the beginning of it all.

Ballet lessons were a hardship for the working class Daniele family, so Graciela's mother "very intelligently and very courageously" took her to audition for lessons at the premiere Teatro Colón in Buenos Aires. The Teatro Colón housed elite opera and ballet companies, as well as a premiere ballet school. All three were government subsidized, and the ballet school and company, in particular, had a world famous reputation. Daniele says that at the time she enrolled at the school, "in 1947 or 1948," it was "an extraordinary school" and the corps de ballet there rivaled the world famous Russian company, the Bolshoi Ballet. The training at the Teatro Colón (in the Ballet Estable del Teatro Colón) was rigorous and competitive:

> They got you in at seven and you graduated at fourteen if you were alive. It was some of the roughest, roughest training! You could continue your schooling, your grammar school and everything, aside of the theatre, but it was extremely hard because the first class in the Teatro Colón was at six o'clock in the morning. The curriculum wasn't only ballet. We had to study other forms, and character and all that, plus music, plus one language, plus we were used as extras in the performances of the operas and ballets.

Though she started with eighty classmates, the program had an exceptionally high rate of attrition, since students were required to audition each year and to take periodic performance tests. For some, the intense training was simply too much. As she says, "When I was fourteen, we graduated five students. It was really hard. For me, it was just practicing and I loved it!"

Graduation from the Teatro Colón launched Daniele's dancing career and at age fourteen, she became a soloist in the Teatro Colón Ballet Company. Her professional career took off immediately: "I was very good. I was a major ballerina. I got a contract to be the prima ballerina in a company that was forming in Brazil. My mother and I went there. The contract was for about three months, and I never went back. From then on, I just continued traveling!" As a very young professional, Daniele's performing opportunities took her from Argentina to Brazil and then to Europe, where she was "immediately accepted into the Opera Ballet of Nice."[5] It was in Europe that she saw a live performance of *West Side Story*, an experience that altered her future: "The show completely changed my life. I left the theatre and walked the streets of Paris by myself, overwhelmed by what I had seen. I decided I would have to go to New York to learn how to tell stories through dance."[6]

Graciela Daniele moved to New York City in 1964, at age 25, to learn American "jazz" dance and to study the musical theatre style of storytelling dance. She had intended to start out in beginning jazz dance, since her impressive ballet resume had not prepared her for this other form of movement. She says of those early days, "When I came here, though I was a very good ballerina, I didn't know what jazz was and I had never learned it." She went in search of "the best jazz teacher," and as she says, she was "very lucky," because she began lessons with Matt Mattox, who was a disciple of the legendary dancer Jack Cole. She enrolled in a low level class, but when Mattox saw her "in the beginner level, he said, 'You're a great dancer, you shouldn't be in the beginner class. Let me help you!'" She started working closely with Mattox, who at that time had just landed a job choreographing the 1964 musical *What Makes Sammy Run?*, the show in which Daniele made her Broadway debut. Daniele admits that her appearance on Broadway after only one month in the country was unusual:

> I was very lucky. I've been very lucky. Matt Mattox was choreographing *What Makes Sammy Run?* and he said, 'There is a little role in it for a Latin American or South American bombshell who is also the leading dancer in a nine minute ballet. Would you like to audition?' I said, 'OK!' I didn't even know what to do! I didn't even speak English very well! I spoke three or four languages, but not English. I auditioned and within a month, I was on Broadway, which is unheard of! It was really unheard of! I mean, it was unbelievable!

Her appearance in *What Makes Sammy Run?* led to a long string of Broadway performances. Daniele also started "studying voice and English and all that." As she says, "I started going from show to show and almost immediately I got to work with Michael Bennett. I became his female assistant." Her career was, in fact, fostered by several established director/choreographers, most notably Bennett, whom she assisted on several shows, including 1969's *Coco*, 1971's *Follies* and 1973's *Seesaw*.[7] She also assisted Bob Fosse on the original production of *Chicago*, which was the last show in which she appeared as a performer, when she was thirty-five.

Daniele began working as a choreographer in the late 1970s. Her first job was on a popular industrial show of the 1960s and 1970s, *The Milliken Show—* which was "about fabrics, Milliken fabrics." Daniele says that in its heyday, it was "a huge event in New York" that was "really a fashion show, but instead of models, they used dancers." She got started performing in the show when Michael Bennett was choreographing it, around the same time that she was working with him on *Promises, Promises* (1968). The complex show featured several production numbers, and required a great deal of dancing from its per-formers, as well as numerous speedy costume changes. It was held at the Wal-dorf-Astoria and attracted "the best dancers in America" and "extraordinary stars." After a year as a performer, Daniele assisted Bennett and later assisted his successor Alan Johnson. After several more years, Daniele inherited the choreographic responsibilities for the show. She credits Bennett with getting her the job: "Michael recommended me. He said, 'She's ready to choreograph it herself.'" In 1975, she choreographed the show on her own. *The Milliken Show*, for Daniele, was "a great training ground" which forced her "to learn how to really construct and structure a number." She worked on the show sev-eral years until it was no longer produced, in the early 1980s, due to rising pro-duction costs. The show, which had one performance open to New York theatre professionals during its run, was a valuable showcase for young talent, and Daniele credits it with opening many doors for her: "The moment that I started doing it, I started getting offers to choreograph outside of New York, on Broad-way and everything! My career just picked up immediately, because of this showcase."

Building on the opportunities that *The Milliken Show* created for her, Daniele began choreographing in and around New York City. Today, her chore-ographic resume is filled with a diverse range of theatre and film, including 1981's *Pirates of Penzance*, 1985's *The Mystery of Edwin Drood*, 1998's *Ragtime* and three Woody Allen films, *Mighty Aphrodite*, *Everyone Says I Love You* and *Bullets Over Broadway*.[8] It was, however, a show that she created with a small Latin organization in New York called INTAR that started her career as a direc-tor/choreographer.

Daniele was giving a seminar at INTAR when the artistic director, Max Ferra, offered her the chance to create an original piece. The offer surprised her:

> Even though I was an established choreographer, when people called me to do a show, they sent me scripts or music. Nobody had asked me that question, which is really, "What would you create from nothing?" So that opened up a new world of possibilities!

Working with Jim Lewis, the dramaturg of INTAR, she chose to use the music of fellow Argentinean Astor Piazzolla, who created "the new tango," or tango music mixed with rock and jazz. She and Lewis adapted short stories of Argen-tinean writer Jorge Luis Borges to create *Tango Apasionado*, which translates to "tango with passion." The poorly funded project was a labor of love, but a successful workshop led to support from corporate giant AT&T for a limited downtown engagement. Daniele believes that project was instrumental in positioning her as a New York director:

> The interesting thing about it is that although I had never directed, because I just went and did it and it was artistically successful, a lot of people saw it and believed I was a director. They just still don't know that I am not. [Laughs] I've fooled them! I learned a lot from it. It opened a window into direction for myself and for other people.

Daniele's first major Broadway production as a director/choreographer following *Tango Apasianado* was 1990's *Once on this Island*. Since then, she directed and choreographed several shows as resident director at Lincoln Center including *Hello Again* (1994), *Chronicle of a Death Foretold* (1995), *A New Brain* (1998) and *Marie Christine* (1999), an update of the classical Greek tragedy *Medea*. In addition, she directed and co-choreographed (with Jeff Calhoun) the Tony Award winning Best Musical Revival of 1999, *Annie Get Your Gun*. Her theatre work thus far has been recognized with nine Tony nominations, six Drama desk nominations, and the Fosse and Ovation awards.[9] Daniele, proud of the fact that she recently entered her sixties, seems likely to gain more accolades as she continues in her prolific career as a director/choreographer.

Patricia Birch, like Graciela Daniele, is a veteran of the Broadway stage, and a long time performer, choreographer and director. Unlike Daniele, Birch was born not far from New York City, in Englewood, New Jersey. Her earliest training was with modern dance choreographer Merce Cunningham. Cunningham saw promise in Birch and encouraged her to train at both the School of American Ballet (George Balanchine's School) and at the Graham Studio (with modern dancer and choreographer Martha Graham). Early on, Birch realized that she would have to choose between classical ballet and modern dance, since the styles stood at odds with one another: "I loved the ballet a whole lot, but it was clear I was never going to be a Balanchine ballerina. I decided to pursue the Graham stuff." Birch continued with some ballet training, but focused more on Graham's style and joined Graham's company as a young dancer. She moved into a leading soloist position with Graham and continued to work with her over the years, though, as she says, she was drawn to dance on Broadway.[10] Her training, while well suited to concert work, was unusual for a Broadway dancer: "I didn't have the usual Broadway line that a lot of these people do. My background was concert [dance]. I'd always been pulling over [to Broadway style dance] because I liked it." Like Daniele, she was drawn to Robbins' choreography for *West Side Story* and she "switched to Broadway early on to play the gamine role of Anybodys."[11] Birch found time to earn a B.A. degree at Bennington College, and continued performing on Broadway, where she appeared in several shows including revivals of *Brigadoon*, *Oklahoma!* and *Carousel*.

Birch tells an amusing story of her initial foray into choreography:

The start of the choreographing was really kind of funny, because they were doing *West Side Story* in some god-forsaken place in New Jersey. I'd been in it in New York, so I wasn't really interested in doing it badly somewhere. [But] they promised me if I would do my Anybodys part in *West Side Story*, they would let me do *Irma La Douce*. Now how could a girl turn that down? There I was with the short hair and ready to go, except that the place closed down before we ever did *Irma La Douce*! [Through that experience] I met Arthur Whitelaw, who was producing [the original Off Broadway production of] *You're a Good Man, Charlie Brown* [in 1967] and he asked me if I wanted to play Patti and I said, "No. Lucy or nothing." They weren't very interested in that and I said, "All right, then I'll tell you what I'll do, I will choreograph and assist Joe Hardy [the director] and I'll understudy Lucy, and maybe I'll get to be Lucy." And so I did just that. And indeed, I did go on for a weekend as Lucy and I lost my voice immediately and a funny thing happened. I was backstage and I really enjoyed the applause for the numbers I'd choreographed as much as I enjoyed being out there.

After *Charlie Brown*, producer Arthur Whitelaw asked her to choreograph her first Broadway show, *Minnie's Boys*, in 1970. Unfortunately, after a turbulent rehearsal period due to the fact that Larry Cornfeld, the show's "wonderfully gifted alternative director" (according to Birch) would disappear for days at a time, Birch was removed from the show. In the director's absence, however, she had taken on greater responsibility for the show, and she credits this as the first time she's ever done a project on such a large scale. After her work on *Minnie's Boys*, she rejoined the Graham company and returned to concert work: "I directed her company and danced for them, even after *West Side Story*." Around that time, she also worked with Agnes de Mille on a few revivals. Of de Mille, Birch says: "She kind of plucked me out, when I was in the Graham company and I had these little babies and I needed a job. I wrote her a letter and she was very aware that I was the baby of Martha's company, the very pregnant baby, at that point."

Birch's next Broadway choreography endeavor was *The Me Nobody Knows*. She describes that show as "much more [her] kind of territory." The "rock and roll" inspired show opened the door to her first huge hit, *Grease* (1972). Following her success with the Broadway choreography for *Grease*, Birch again returned to the Graham company. She says, "I mean, I didn't solely do [the Graham Company], but I was back there helping out and directing and performing again with [Martha Graham]." She continued working on Broadway, as well, and followed up her choreography success with *Grease* with *A Little Night Music* the following year. That production began her long association with highly acclaimed director Hal Prince. She went on create the choreography for Broadway's *Candide* in 1974 and 1997 (with Hal Prince directing both) and for other Broadway productions including *Over Here* (1974), *The Happy End* (1977), *They're Playing Our Song* (1979) and *Parade* (1999). She created the choreography for the phenomenally successful 1978 *Grease* film and directed and choreographed its sequel, *Grease 2* (1982). Those projects started her association with Hollywood, where she has created many memorable film moments, including Tom Hanks' famous piano dance in the film *Big* (1988) and the triumphant closing dance for the stars of *First Wives Club* (1997). She has been on staff for television shows ranging from *The Electric Company* to *Saturday Night Live*, where she created the memorable "Dancing in the Dark" number made famous by comedians Steve Martin and Gilda Radnor. Her eclectic resume crosses mediums from music video to opera with ease and includes such diverse pieces as *Salomé* at the New York City Opera and music videos for rock musicians ranging from Cyndi Lauper to The Rolling Stones. In the 1999–2000 theatre season, Birch emerged as the director/choreographer of both the Off Broadway *Exactly Like You* and Broadway's *Band in Berlin*, which she directed, choreographed and co-conceived. Birch holds numerous awards for her work, including two Emmys and five Tony nominations. She also holds the distinction of having her choreography seen in three different Broadway shows running simultaneously (*Grease*, *A Little Night Music* and *Candide*). As for the future of her work, Birch says, "Even though I've been doing it for so long, I pride myself on being one of the people who always is coming up something new." It is this originality that insures that Birch's work will continue to break new ground and explore new territory.

Lynne Taylor-Corbett, like many of her fellow female director/choreographers, is a veteran dancer and choreographer with experience in many different mediums. She was born in Colorado and comes from a musical family. She says, "My mother had trained as a concert pianist at Julliard." Taylor-Corbett's father worked as an educator and a vice-principal in the public school system, while her mother worked as a church organist and choir director. As part of her work for the church, Taylor-Corbett's mother accompanied the ballet classes offered in the church basement and enrolled five-year-old Lynne in lessons. That marked the beginning of Taylor-Corbett's aspirations of being a professional dancer. She says, "It really was an assumption of mine from that moment that I would be a dancer. I mean, that was just such a given. There was really never any other thing I wanted to do." Though she started training early, Taylor-Corbett acknowledges that "it was not a very privileged background" and that her dancing school, while "full of love," was short on technique.

When Taylor-Corbett was a teenager, Constance Garfield and her husband, both dancers from the New York City Ballet, started a school in the area. The arrival of these well-trained technicians was an awakening for Taylor-Corbett, "The light came into my eyes and I saw that I was very badly trained and I began to go [to class] every day. They could see my talent, but obviously, I had not had the correct training or enough of it." The Garfields convinced her that New York was the place for her if she intended a serious career in dance, and at seventeen, Taylor-Corbett packed her things. Sadly, thirty-two year old Constance Garfield died of cancer just prior to Taylor-Corbett's departure, an event that she said "double propelled" her to move to New York.

In New York, the financially struggling Taylor-Corbett took a job for two years as an usherette at the State Theatre where the New York City Ballet performed. She credits her experiences of watching the dancers as formative in her career:

> I think I gained a lot of my wisdom about the structure of dances through literally being high in the balconies, where I initially ushered, and seeing the structure on the floor. That was a huge part of my training.

Following her work at the State Theatre, where she dreamed of performing in ballets by Robbins or Balanchine, she was accepted as an apprentice at Harkness House, a place dancer Rebecca Harkness had established for, as Taylor-Corbett describes it, "the worship of dance." There, she trained with famed dancers like Jack Cole, and she made connections that would have an impact on her future:

> Just coincidentally, Alvin Ailey was there. I think he was using some of the space. People told me about his company and how exciting it was, and I auditioned for it and to my astonishment, I got that job! I was the only non African-American in the company. I toured with him all over Africa and Europe, and then in the United States for a year and a half and then I quit.

After her return from the Alvin Ailey tour, she returned to study dance briefly with Anna Sokolow, before crossing over to the more theatre oriented experimental groups The Living Theatre and The Open Theatre. By then, Taylor-Corbett was married to a man "in the record industry" and she returned to dance to "make some money." She was cast as a dancer in *Promises, Promises* (1968) and *Seesaw* (1973) on Broadway and describes herself as "a Michael Bennett person."[12] In addition to her extensive dance training, Taylor-Corbett was also a singer who had studied opera. Broadway seemed suited to her multiple talents:

> When there would be small parts, I would get them, because I was more interesting looking and wasn't the typical chorine. I also had studied acting. I don't think I understood how talented I really was. Interestingly, even if an agent would come back and say, "You should come to my agency," I would be afraid. I don't know why, really.

She attributes her apprehension with agents to coming to New York at such a young age, with "no preparation."

After her Broadway work, she decided to start a concert dance company called Theatre Dance Collection with several other people. She describes her company as "rather successful," since they participated in a now defunct touring program sponsored by the National Endowment for the Arts. She credits her experiences with Theatre Dance Collection as starting her on the road to choreographing: "I think we really developed as choreographers. We danced in each other's works, so I got to be finished with the frustrated dancer in me." Her company struggled, however, after what Taylor-Corbett calls an "ill timed" appearance in the Brooklyn Academy of Music series, because they produced story-oriented dance in "a mostly postmodern era." As she says, "We just got killed [by the critics]. I mean, it was just the wrong context and it was the end of our company, even though we tried to do a couple more concerts." Fortunately, in spite of the demise of her company, Taylor-Corbett continued to get choreography work.

Her first big break as choreographer came in 1980, when she staged a ballet for the workshop of American Ballet Theatre II, called *Sequels*.[13] Mikhail Baryshnikov, then the Artistic Director for the American Ballet Theatre, commissioned her to do a ballet for ABT that resulted in her highly successful *Great Galloping Gottschalk* (1982). That ballet landed her a job choreographing the film *Footloose* (1984), which led to other film work, including *My Blue Heaven* (1990). While Taylor-Corbett had some additional theatre successes around that time, directing such pieces as the Off Broadway *Mona Rogers in Person* (1987), and the Broadway production of *Chess* (1987), she was unable to focus completely on her career because a divorce gave her increased responsibilities as a single mom. As she says, "Unfortunately, I became single and it was better to do hamburger commercials and dance commissions, because the entry-level director that I was, was not going to get the fees, plus I didn't know people." She concedes that she has done much more directing and choreographing for the theatre now that her child is grown, including such diverse pieces as 1996's *Twentieth Century Pop*, a New York City cabaret featuring rock legend Marianne Faithfull, and the 1997 Broadway musical *Titanic*. She was nominated for two Tony Awards for the direction and choreography of her 1999 Broadway endeavor, *Swing!*, a high energy show featuring swing dancing. She continues to choreograph for ballet companies across the country. In spite of her work as a director/choreographer, Taylor-Corbett has not ruled out appearing in front of the footlights again "if it were a crazy situation or a cameo." As she says, "I'd totally do it again, but that hasn't come up." She says of her eclectic career, "It's an interesting balance that I've been able to achieve in my life and I also hope to achieve it in my theatrical career as well and so far have, for the most part." That "interesting balance" continues to inspire her highly innovative choreography and direction for theatre, film and concert dance.

Ann Reinking, probably the most famous professional dancer of the women in this essay, gained renown in part because of her long association and then love affair with Broadway legend Bob Fosse. Also, she is the only one of the six women profiled who is still an active performer. In March of 2001, she joined the company of *Fosse* for a limited engagement as the star of the Broadway production that she also co-directed and choreographed.

Reinking, who hails from the Seattle area, got a relatively late start in dance, when she was in sixth grade. As she tells it:

> We had a talent show. I had a classmate, Carla Sealander, who was really precocious in dance. She was exceptionally gifted. She was already on scholarships with the Ford Foundation [at the San Francisco ballet] — that's how good she

was. Well, for her piece, she had a tutu and pointe shoes and she did the "Sugar Plum Fairy" variation from *The Nutcracker*. I was smitten! I had never seen ballet, let alone really good ballet, so I just completely fell in love. She and another little girl in sixth grade gave me tights and a leotard and some of their old slippers and stuff. They taught little variations and steps to me on the playground, like "The Four Swans" in *Swan Lake*.

Reinking's parents, however, were not as taken with ballet. Money was tight and they tried to persuade her to take up tap dance or swimming instead. To convince them of her genuine interest in ballet, she "auditioned" for her parents, aunts and grandparents. She danced the "Four Swans" variation that her friends Carla and Lori had taught her in the schoolyard. Her "audition" was successful, and as she says, "For my eleventh birthday, my only request for a present was ballet lessons. I asked if they could pool their money together so I could go once a week." The young Reinking indeed began dancing, and she recalls that one time a week she would "travel on a bus to Seattle, with a little suitcase and red tights."[14] She credits her excellent teachers with her quick improvement and says of them, "My teachers were two Russians, who were from the Kirov. They had gone to school with Balanchine." Once Reinking turned fourteen, her friend Carla, who already spent her summers on scholarship with the San Francisco ballet, suggested that Reinking audition for a scholarship for two months of summer training there:

She told me where to go and when. I auditioned, but I didn't get [the scholarship] then. Carla said, "Go down and do a month," since I could afford a month from my savings. She said, "Do the first month and then ask if they will give you a scholarship for the second month, because by that time

Ann Reinking — director, choreographer and dancer — continues an active career as a performer (photograph courtesy the subject).

> they'll know you better and you won't be nervous and all that." So I did it, and indeed, they gave me a scholarship in the middle of the two-month program.

Reinking's scholarship was renewed for the following two summers, in 1964 and 1965. After her third year, however, she says she lost her scholarship because she was "a little heavy. They had to subtract some people, because they had some cutbacks, and I was one of them."[15] As a double blow, her close friend Carla, who had been a guiding force in her training, "got into this San Francisco flower-child thing" and "died of an overdose at nineteen."[16] After coping with "the two hardest times during [her] young life — rejection and loss" things turned around a bit for Reinking and she won a Joffrey Ballet Scholarship.

As she says, "At that time, in my amateur work, I had, no pun intended, one foot in plays and musicals and the other foot in concert work in the Seattle area." The time was coming for her to make a decision about which world to concentrate on. Ballet groundbreaker Joffrey would prove instrumental in her decision:

> Robert Joffrey and Gerald Arpino are from Seattle, so they had started this summer program for local talent to be groomed at Pacific Lutheran University. I got a dance scholarship to that program. After we had our classes, everybody would do improvs. Everybody was always dancing and doing ballet and when it was my turn, I always sang. Well, Joffrey had gotten wind of all of these improvs and he was observing off to the side and he came up to me and said, "You know, Ann, if you want a career in ballet, you can have it. It is within your grasp. You would have to work very hard, but it's within your grasp. You've got something that you can't teach, which is heart and you are good! But you know, Ann, you really sing well. You've got a good personality. You're a good actress. If you do go in to ballet, they're probably going to make you a dramatic or comedic person — you're going to get the story roles, because you've got that in you." He said, "You've got the accoutrements for a musical theatre performer." He respected musical theatre, so I felt that he wasn't giving me a line.

During her work with Joffrey, Reinking was working in Seattle trying to save money to move to New York to pursue her dreams. She wrestled with the decision over whether to pursue concert dance or musical theatre: "I really was giving serious thought to what I wanted to do, because I knew I had to go to New York with one direction and one goal." She chose the musical theatre route, though when she arrived in New York at age eighteen, her first job (which she got after only two weeks in the city) was dancing in the now defunct corps de ballet at Radio City Music Hall.[17]

From there, she landed a chorus dance role in an Equity bus-and-truck tour of *Fiddler on the Roof*, supervised by Hal Prince:

> It was hands on. Hal Prince was there and so was Tommy Abbott, who was Mr. Robbins' associate. I didn't realize how lucky I was to be in that particular company. I got my Equity Card, which was exceptionally lucky, and I got to work with people who were obviously gifted.

Her turn in *Fiddler On the Roof* caught Prince's attention and when the tour ended, she was asked to audition for a role as a Kit Kat girl in the Broadway company of *Cabaret*. She got the role and her turn in *Cabaret* marked her Broadway debut and set her on a road toward continued success:

> Well, one thing leads to another and the dance captain [of *Cabaret*], Bonnie Walker, was also going to be the dance captain for Michael Bennett on his Broadway show called *Coco*, starring Katharine Hepburn. I went to the Equity call, but it was huge because everybody wanted to be in this show. They had to type. Of course, I looked like a little hippie then because that's what everybody did and that was the time and I went in and I got typed out. Bob Avian [Bennett's associate] did the typing. Michael Bennett wasn't there. Bonnie said, "How did it go?" I said, "Well, I got typed out." She said, "Look, I know that they're going to have another general call. The next time you go, put your hair up in a bun and look like a Chanel model. You can do this." I went and they were typing once again, but this time, Michael Bennett and Bob Avian kept me. Bonnie was there, so I'm sure she pointed me out in the line. Then I was on my own. The auditions lasted for three days! We actually got paid for one day. We learned practically the whole show by the time we were done. We did singing, reading and everything and I got it, out of hundreds and hundreds of dancers, and that was a real break. That was my first original Broadway show, and then I was *in*. I was in "the" group on Broadway for ensemble dancers [Reinking's emphasis].

Coco (1969) gave Reinking her first speaking role on Broadway and set her on a mission to move herself up through the ranks from chorus member to leading player. Her transition to leading lady did not happen as quickly as she'd hoped, though Reinking credits her time in the chorus with teaching her "a lot more about my craft and about the ups and downs of theatre." The next show she was cast in, *Wild and Wonderful* (1971), flopped on opening night, but it opened the door to *Pippin* (1972) and began her association with Bob Fosse. In fact, her chorus role in *Pippin* also propelled her into her first principal part:

> I got *Pippin* and that was amazing! In *Pippin*, Bob [Fosse] utilized the ensemble so well. We did all of the backup singing, demi-solo singing and all of the small parts, as well as the dancing. Pat Birch saw it and called to ask if I would audition for *Over Here*. She fought for me — I must've been in there to audition three or four times, too, doing everything. She definitely wanted me. That was my first principal role, and I got all this attention, and then that lead to my first starring role opposite Joel Grey in *Good Time Charley*, which was my first [Tony Award] nomination.

Of course, *Good Time Charley* (1975) closed after only a few months on Broadway. The show taught Reinking another hard lesson:

> I realized you have to be good, you have to be a principal, but the show also has to be good. I had figured out how to get out of the ensemble, thanks to Bob Fosse and Pat Birch and people who believed in me, so it wasn't like it was bad, because now I was recognized as a solid person for principal roles.

Agents were now interested in Reinking and her work, but after some disappointments in Hollywood, she accepted an offer from Michael Bennett to replace Donna McKechnie as Cassie in his hit *A Chorus Line*. From there, at Fosse's request, she replaced Gwen Verdon as Roxie Hart in the original Broadway company of *Chicago*, a role she revived on Broadway twenty years later. As she says, "Here I was replacing two legendary women on Broadway!" She appeared in *Chicago* for eight months in 1977 and moved directly from there into her starring role in Fosse's dance extravaganza, *Dancin'* in 1978. Finally, she says, "I did all of the pre-production work for *Dancin'* and then there I was in an original show that was a hit." Following *Dancin'*, she appeared as the Fosse character's girlfriend in his highly autobiographical movie, *All That Jazz* (1979), a role that mirrored her turbulent real life relationship with the director/choreographer. She appeared in other movies, including *Annie* (1982) and *Micki and Maude* (1984), and she continued to perform in musicals and plays in various venues around the country.

While she had no real aspirations of becoming a choreographer at that time, she was choreographing dances for herself and for her friends. When she performed at the 1986 Williamstown Theatre Festival in *Summer and Smoke*, director Nikos Psacharopoulos saw some numbers she had staged for herself and some friends in a cabaret there and he asked her to choreograph the musical *Eleanor* for him. In one week, she "put together seventeen numbers with non-dancers" and the show was a success. That landed her a job choreographing *Pal Joey* at Chicago's Goodman Theatre, after which she took a hiatus to give birth to her son, Christopher. Choreography offers continued to come in, and Reinking landed a job choreographing a production of *Chicago* at the Long Beach Pacific Light Opera in 1992. That production, which starred Juliet Prowse and Bebe Newirth, earned her the L.A. Drama Critics Award for Choreography. In 1995, Reinking took over the choreographic responsibilities for the Encores! production of *Chicago* presented at New York's City Center. At age 46, she choreographed the concert version, and at the urging of director Walter Bobbie again starred as Roxie, a role she reprised when the production moved to Broadway in 1996. In 1997, Reinking's choreography for *Chicago*, which was done in Fosse's style, in accordance with the Encores! mission of retaining the spirit of the original production, won her the "triple crown" of dance: The Tony, Drama Desk and Outer Critics Circle Awards for Best Choreography.[18] On the heels of her success with *Chicago*, Reinking went on to aid Gwen Verdon in creating *Fosse*, a retrospective of Bob Fosse's dances for stage, film and television. Reinking directed and choreographed the show along with veteran revue director Richard Maltby, though it was Reinking who created the show's crucial transitions from song to song. *Fosse* danced away with the Best Musical Tony for 1999 and since then, Reinking has kept busy mounting productions of both *Chicago* and *Fosse* around the world. She has also continued to work on a variety of projects, including the Burt Bacharach review *The Look of Love* (2003) for Broadway. In addition to her professional work, Reinking is also the founder and artistic director of the Broadway Theatre Project, a Florida based arts program dedicated to training young people who have Broadway aspirations, an endeavor that earned her the Governor's Award, Ambassador of the Arts for the State of Florida. Reinking's full dance card is indicative of her talent, and she continues to work prolifically as a dancer, choreographer and director.

Susan Stroman, best known until recently as the Tony award winning choreographer of 1992's *Crazy for You*, emerged as 2000's golden girl, with four Tony Award nominations for direction and choreography of both the revival of *The Music Man* and of the dance driven *Contact*. She took home a statuette, her third, for her choreography of *Contact* (the others are for the choreography of both *Crazy for You* and the 1994 revival of *Show Boat*). She also holds the distinction of having had three shows that she both directed and choreographed running simultaneously on Broadway (*Contact*, *The Music Man*, and 2001's *The Producers*). Stroman's greatest feat to date, however, is her win of the 2001 Tony awards in both direction and choreography for *The Producers*, an accomplishment that made her the first woman ever to win in both categories for a single show in a single year. Stroman has been nominated an astounding eight times for the Best Choreography Tony Award (with the four wins listed above), and three times as Best Director (for *The Music Man*, *Contact* and *The Producers*, with one win for *The Producers*). The many accolades and achievements she has earned have solidified her status as a true groundbreaker for female director/choreographers.

Stroman, who hails from Wilmington, Delaware, had an early interest in music, fostered by her father, who "was and still is a wonderful pianist." Since she "grew up in a house filled with music," she "took piano lessons and guitar lessons." Stroman believes that her early musical experiences shaped her future: "When I was little, part of my thing was that I would visualize music. When my father would play the piano, I would imagine hordes of people dancing through my head. It was more like wanting to be an artist or a painter and paint pictures." Stroman soon realized that her visualizations of people moving to music were far more suited to a career in dance. As she says, "Becoming a choreographer is something that I've always wanted to do." To that end, she began studying dance at a young age at the Academy of Dance in Delaware, with teacher James Jameson. That began her lifelong immersion in dance: "I've been in a dancing school since I was about five. I've danced my whole life." Her primary training was in ballet, though her teacher Jameson, who was in the original Broadway company of *Brigadoon*, was a great fan of theatre dance.[19] She then went on to study at the Delaware Dance Center, where she immersed herself in "all forms of dance: ballet, and jazz and tap."

Her experience with theatre came later, and as she says, "I really learned from community theatre," while an English major at the University of Delaware. While she "took acting classes in college," she never became a theatre major. She came to New York after graduating from the University of Delaware in the late 1970s to continue her training: "I studied acting here. I also studied voice here and studied piano here and studied dance here." Her training was a step-ping-stone toward achieving her career goals:

> I came to New York to be a choreographer, but I knew I couldn't come to New York and just take over, because in New York, you know, it's hard to get started. I came as a song and dance gal, because I could sing and dance, but it was always with the mission to become a creative person and to go on the other side of the table. It's almost like singing and dancing came easy to me, but it was always more of a goal to be someone who creates theatre.

Stroman found early success as a Broadway performer and appeared in such shows as *Chicago*, *Whoopee!*, *Sugar Babies* and *Sweet Charity*.[20] She met frequent collaborator Scott Ellis when the two appeared in a flop called *Musical Chairs* in 1980.[21]

Her first New York success was a 1987 Off Off Broadway production of *Flora, the Red Menace* that Stroman choreographed and Scott Ellis directed.[22] That production was important to her career, because it was the elusive "right show that had connections with other people." In fact, from *Flora, the Red Menace*, Stroman and Ellis established some important New York contacts: "We got to know [John] Kander and [Fred] Ebb and Hal Prince and Liza [Minnelli]." She and Ellis followed up that initial success with the creation of the Kander and Ebb revue, *And The World Goes Round*. Also, Stroman "ended up doing Liza's show at Radio City," because of her connection to Liza from *Flora, the Red Menace*, a show which starred Minnelli in its original production. In addition, Stroman found work with another *Flora* connection, Hal Prince, at the New York City Opera choreographing, among other things, *Don Giovanni*. These various productions helped her secure her highly visible role as the choreographer for the 1992 Broadway production of the musical *Crazy for You*:

> The director and producers of *Crazy for You* were looking for a choreographer, and I happened to have *The World Goes Round* Off Broadway and Liza's show at Radio City. I think it was the extremes of the big production values of Liza and the comedy numbers in *The World Goes Round* that made them think that I would be right for *Crazy for You*. So again, I was lucky with that Catch-22 that when someone wanted to see my work, I happened to have something on. That's how I got *Crazy for You*.

Crazy for You brought her "overnight" success, after fifteen years in New York. She describes the show as "the big thing that exposed me to the masses."

Crazy for You and her subsequent Tony Award for it changed Stroman's life, both professionally and personally. It was on that show that she met her future husband, director Mike Ockrent, whom she married in 1996.[23] Since then, she's choreographed consistently on a wide variety of shows including *Big* (1996), *Steel Pier* (1997) and a Christmas extravaganza, the musical version of *A Christmas Carol* produced annually at Madison Square Garden. Stroman's transition to directing came later, though she admits that she "started early with [directing], because when I decided to go to the other side of the table, I did it as a director/choreographer first." The first productions that she directed and choreographed were "industrial shows and cabaret acts and small venues and some regional theatres." While she choreographed prolifically in New York, she admits that, "other than some club acts and a comedy revue and things like that, the first big thing I directed and choreographed was, of course, *Contact*." She followed up her debut on *Contact* with her direction and choreography of the 2001 *Music Man* revival on Broadway and her mega-hit *The Producers*. While she says that she "had actually been in charge of the whole thing before," she admits with a laugh that none of her previous projects were on the same scale as her current productions. She says, "They were the biggest!"

In addition to her Broadway turns as director/choreographer, Stroman created the choreography for the 1998 London revival of *Oklahoma!* (which transferred to Broadway in 2002) and the teen-oriented dance film *Centerstage*, which she choreographed with Christopher Wheeldon. Unfortunately, her current successes have been tempered by

Susan Stroman became the first woman in history to win both the direction and choreography Tony Awards for her work on *The Producers* (photograph courtesy the subject).

personal tragedy; in December of 1999 her husband Mike Ockrent died after a yearlong battle with cancer. In spite of her personal hardships, Stroman continues to create an enormous volume of work. While her creation of *Thou Shalt Not* (2001), a musical based on the Zola novel *Therese Raquin* and featuring music and lyrics by Harry Connick, Jr., was not as successful as some of her other projects, Stroman continues to be among the most highly sought after director/choreographers in the business. Though Stroman once acknowledged that she "couldn't just come to New York and take over," she now appears to have taken the theatre town by storm. Stroman is at the top of her game and it seems that she will stay that way for years to come.

In comparison with her fellow female director/choreographers, Kathleen Marshall is the "new kid on the block" with an impressive body of work already behind her, though she has not yet turned forty. For all her early success, Marshall got a relatively late start as a dancer. As she says, "I didn't start off wanting to dance. I thought ballet was for little girls on Saturday mornings and I didn't want any part of it." Marshall and her older brother Rob, best known for his direction and choreography of the blockbuster film *Chicago*, grew up in a household that favored the arts: "My parents were great musical theatre fans and theatre fans in general. They took us to everything: symphonies, ballets and operas. They took us to musicals and had a huge LP collection of musicals that we listened to a lot." Though the Marshall children had no professional training, they wanted to perform on stage. As Kathleen says:

> When I was ten and my brother and sister, who are twins, were twelve, we saw that the Pittsburgh Civic Light Opera, the big professional summer stock company, was doing *The Sound of Music*. They were holding auditions. We saw it in the paper, and said, "We want to go down and audition!" All three of us got in! We played three of the Von Trapp children!

After that first taste of the stage, blond and blue-eyed Kathleen returned to the Civic Light Opera to play "a politically incorrect" version of a "Polynesian girl in *South Pacific*." It was those early performances that inspired Kathleen and then Rob to begin dancing:

> I didn't start taking dance until I was thirteen, which is actually relatively late for a dancer, especially for women. Men tend to start later. My brother, Rob, didn't start dancing until a year after me, when he was sixteen.

Her early training was in ballet and tap, which was "a package deal" at the studio where she studied. She says that, "Even though I was only interested in ballet, I started taking tap as well, which was good, because it's actually been useful." She believes that much of her dance training, though, came from her onstage experiences, "For theatre dance, most of my experience, like most people's, is from performing, rather than from the classroom." Marshall's vocal training was less formal. She sang in choirs in school and choirs in college and she didn't start private vocal coaching until she came to New York.

Marshall went on to Smith College as an English literature major but "took a lot of dance classes and some theatre and acting classes." As Marshall tells it, she picked Smith specifically because:

> There was a woman named Gemze deLappe, who was one of Agnes de Mille's main dancers and assistants and who was teaching there. She taught not only ballet but also musical theatre and musical theatre choreography classes. In a dance concert at Smith, we did the *Carousel* ballet and she taught me the role of Louise [the principal dancer in the ballet]. Now I realize how incredible that experience was, because she had been one of the Louises along the way [on Broadway] and she had been taught by de Mille.

Marshall performed frequently at Smith in dance concerts, plays and musicals. She returned home in the summers to Pittsburgh and landed a job in the adult singing and dancing chorus of the Civic Light Opera where she had started performing as a child. As she says, "I got into the ensemble right after my freshman year, when I was eighteen, and [Broadway director] Susan Schulman was the director." Marshall has continued her long association with Ms. Schulman and in 1996 she choreographed the musical *Violet*, which Schulman directed.

Throughout her college years, Marshall returned home to work at the Civic Light Opera:

> It was an incredible experience, because it was one of those summer stock companies where you would do six musicals in eight weeks. I got to do all these different musicals! No one would necessarily cast me in *Fiddler On the Roof* anywhere else, but I could do *Fiddler On the Roof* there. One week we did *Brigadoon*, the next *West Side Story*, the week after that *Kiss Me, Kate*, the week after that *The Student Prince*. I mean, it was great! I think that's how I know so much about older shows.

Her experiences at the Pittsburgh Civic Light Opera earned her an Equity Card. After graduation from college, she did a tour of the musical *George M!*, based at the Civic Light Opera, and she then moved to New York City in 1986.

From Encores! to Broadway, Kathleen Marshall is amassing an impressive body of work as a director/choreographer (photograph courtesy the subject).

Once in New York, she landed a role in the national tour of *The Mystery of Edwin Drood* and then toured with the musical *Cats* for about a year and a half. She describes her early work in New York: "I auditioned and went up through the ranks— ensemble, swing, dance captain, assistant choreographer— classic progress."[24] By that time, her brother Rob had started choreographing and he asked her to assist him on the new Broadway musical *Kiss of the Spider Woman* in 1993, less than a year after she left the company of *Cats*. She stopped performing at that point, and assisted Rob both on *Kiss of the Spider Woman* and again later in 1993 on his Broadway production of *She Loves Me*. She got her first big break choreographing a 1994 musical revue:

> The first thing I choreographed on Broadway was a little musical revue called *Swinging on a Star*. I had already worked with my brother on *Kiss of the Spider Woman*. The director of this little revue, *Swingin' On A Star* at The George Street Playhouse in New Brunswick was friends with John Kander [the composer of *Kiss of the Spider Woman*] and had lost his choreographer. He called

Kander and said, "Who do you recommend?" John Kander recommended me, even though I hadn't done anything on my own. I think he'd seen me work with my brother. That's how it came about. I mean, who knew it was going to end up in New York?

The success of *Swinging on a Star* got Marshall a job choreographing *Call Me Madam* for the relatively unknown Encores! series at City Center. She went on to choreograph several more shows for Encores! and when Walter Bobbie resigned as Artistic Director of the series, Ms. Marshall was "first choice to succeed him."[25] In the four years of her tenure as Artistic Director, Marshall turned the series into one of the most popular New York theatre events, a success that earned it (and her) a special 2000 Tony Award.

Outside of the Encores! series, Marshall assisted her brother on the 1996 revival of *Damn Yankees* on Broadway. On her own, she choreographed the 1997 revival of *1776* at Roundabout Theatre Company, which transferred to Broadway. She also created choreography for the 1999 play *Ring Around the Moon* at Lincoln Center. Marshall was nominated for a Tony award for her choreography of the 1999 revival of *Kiss Me Kate*. Marshall has created choreography for 2000's *Seussical*, the 2001 revival of Sondheim's *Follies* and the 2003 Broadway premiere of the Off Broadway sensation *Little Shop of Horrors*.

She transitioned into the role of director/choreographer for the Off Broadway production and New York premiere of the first Sondheim musical, *Saturday Night*, in 2000. That was her first fully realized venture into directing and choreography (in her Encores! concerts, in contrast, the actors perform with minimal sets and scripts in hands). She has also directed and choreographed additional productions for Encores!, including *Babes in Arms* and *Wonderful Town*. Though she has stepped down from her Artistic Director position at Encores! to dedicate more time to her Broadway work, she directed and choreographed the final show of the Encores! 2001 season, *Hair*. Marshall is in great demand as a Broadway choreographer as she works toward her goal of becoming a Broadway director/choreographer. As the youngest member of this elite group of professional New York director/choreographers, she is poised on the threshold of a long and productive career.

These six women — Daniele, Birch, Taylor-Corbett, Reinking, Stroman and Marshall — bring unique training and attributes to the identity of the director/choreographer. While differences in their backgrounds and training are evident and they took different routes to filling the director/choreographer position for major New York productions, similarities do emerge in their backgrounds, training, and even appearances. For example, all six women are rather petite and slender and have retained their dancer figures. All but Daniele, who is a Latina, are Caucasian. All studied ballet and took to other forms later. In addition, all six can be classified as "triple threat" performers, that is, performers with skills in dancing, acting and singing, since the various roles that they've portrayed have required all of those skills. All six women performed professionally before turning to choreography and all choreographed first before directing. Also, nearly all are closely associated with a mentor figure, with the exception of free-spirit Lynne Taylor-Corbett, though she did do a good deal of her performing on Broadway under the tutelage of director/choreographer Michael Bennett. Daniele, Birch, Taylor-Corbett and Reinking began their careers in the concert dance world, which is not unusual, since they emerged as Broadway dancers in the late 1950s and 1960s, a time when concert dance paved the route to Broadway for many dancers. The other two, Stroman and Marshall, geared their careers more specifically toward musical theatre dance, a much more established field by the time they started in New York in the late 1970s and late 1980s respectively.

The career paths of these groundbreakers reiterate that these female director/choreographers have much in common. All tend to trace their career progress in three stages. These women find that in the first stage influential people, predominantly men, inspired them to explore their talents. In the second stage, the women embarked upon their careers, often with the aid of established theatre artists, and sought to develop their artistic identities. Only Susan Stroman set out to be a director/choreographer, while the others aspired to the position later in their careers. Most often, the women worked first as performers, then earned their way into each greater level of responsibility: dance captain, assistant choreographer, choreographer and director/choreographer. Most assert that they emerged as director/choreographers when they created their own projects and won positive critical responses. Also, now that their own careers as director/choreographers are established, these women prioritize not only their own continued creative growth, but also, the nurturing of future artists. They urge aspiring talent to work as frequently as possible in whatever venues are available and to assist as many established artists as they can.

The various stages of career development through which these women have moved have required them to carefully consider their views on their styles and strengths, as well as their opinions concerning the position of the director/choreographer. For the most part, the women find their own styles difficult to catalogue because they strive for diversity in their work, though Ann Reinking acknowledges that she is associated with the "Fosse" style and Kathleen Marshall admits that she is known for re-conceiving vintage dance. Most of the women prefer to work as director/choreographers for the musical theatre stage because of the level of control the director/choreographer can exert over a production. All continue, however, to serve in other capacities on various productions in a wide range of mediums, since they find that the position may not be the right one for them to hold on all projects. Pat Birch argues that directors and choreographers have different strengths and skills, and that not all choreographers make good directors, while the other women in this elite group find that their directing abilities grew out of their skills as choreographers.

When asked for their opinions concerning the role of the director/choreographer, these women believe that the position is still in development. At one extreme, they find that director/choreographers have become "visionaries," in Pat Birch's words, responsible for every aspect of a production, while at the other end of the spectrum, some director/choreographers simply serve the librettist, composer and lyricist on a given production. Such diversity in the position raises the question of what the modern director/choreographer's role in musical theatre is and where the position is headed. Initially, the director/choreographer was known for creating musical theatre pieces in which dance played a primary role in the storytelling. Today, however, the director/choreographer seems to be moving toward becoming a director/choreographer/conceiver or a "visionary" director/choreographer. The male predecessors of these women provide a model that reinforces this view, since by the ends of their careers, director/choreographers George Balanchine, Jerome Robbins, Bob Fosse and Michael Bennett were focused on conceiving ballets and dance oriented productions that were under their total control. Because none of these six women have, as yet, filled the role of director/choreographer for an extended period of time, it is difficult to determine the eventual direction their work will take. Certainly Susan Stroman's *Contact* suggests that she is following the path of her predecessors, as she has created a dance-focused show that she directed, choreographed, wrote and conceived. Also, while none of these women have, as yet, chosen to leave the theatre world entirely to create works for dance companies, the example of Balanchine and Robbins suggests that that could be the ultimate destination of the director/choreographer.

The unique marriage of these women to the role of the director/choreographer in the theatre has resulted in their personal artistic processes. These processes govern the way they create work and break down into four distinct steps: selection, development, casting and rehearsal of a project. Though the final two steps are much more visible to observers, the women agree that the first two steps— selecting a project and preparing it for production — are the most critical. These artistic processes which focus on "research and development" may indicate that director/choreographers have become the true innovators and groundbreakers in the musical theatre arena. This "new" female director/choreographer, whom these women agree is a collaborative, compassionate and visionary artist dedicated to the creation of new works and the re-envisioning of classic ones, may embody the culmination of the director/choreographer position, or may simply mark another step toward the development of the ultimate musical theatre creator.

Notes

1. Julianne Boyd, qtd. by Helen Krich Chinoy in "Women Backstage and Outfront" in *Women in American Theatre*, Revised & Expanded Edition, ed. Helen Kritch Chinoy and Linda Walsh Jenkins (New York: Theatre Communications Group, 1987) 359.
2. Marilyn Stasio, "Broads Make Boards or Do Two Tonys Really a Trend Show?" *Variety* 14 Sept. 1998: 48.

3. Lawrence Thelan, *The Show Makers* (New York: Routledge, 2000) 43.

4. Personal in-person interviews were conducted by the author with the six women included in this paper on the following dates: Pat Birch (Nov. 10, 2000); Graciela Daniele (Nov. 9, 2000), Kathleen Marshall (Jan. 15, 2001), Ann Reinking (Jan. 17, 2001 & Mar. 17 2001); Susan Stroman (April 27, 2001) & Lynne Taylor-Corbett (Sept. 19, 2000). Unless otherwise indicated, quotes are from these interviews.

5. Rose Eichenbaum, "Faces in Dance: Graciela Daniele," *Dance Magazine* Sept.1999: 64.

6. Eichenbaum 64.

7. Thelan 39.

8. Eichenbaum 65.

9. Eichenbaum 64.

10. Svetlana McLee Grody and Dorothy Daniels Lister, *Conversations with Choreographers* (Portsmouth, NH: Heinemann, 1996) 16.

11. Hilary Ostlere, "Patricia Birch on Broadway's Seesaw," in *Dance Magazine* Aug. 1999: 42.

12. Liz Williamson, "Eclectic Dancers," *The Journal for Stage Directors and Choreographers* 1.9 (1983): 27.

13. Terry Trucco, "Lynne Taylor-Corbett: Dance's All-Purpose Freelancer," *Dance Magazine* May 1997: 46.

14. Tony Stevens, "Ann Reinking: Forget the Before, Forget the After," *The Journal for Stage Directors and Choreographers* 11.2 (1997): 22.

15. Stevens 22.

16. Stevens 22.

17. Kevin Boyd Grubb, *Razzle Dazzle: The Life and Work of Bob Fosse* (New York: St. Martin's Press, 1989): 168.

18. Hilary Ostlere, "Reinking Winds Triple Crown" *Dance Magazine* Aug. 1997: 27.

19. Sylviane Gold, "Choreographer Stroman makes *Contact* with a vision in yellow," *Dance Magazine* Feb. 2000: 67.

20. Gold 67, and Hilary Ostlere, "Susan Stroman, It's Her 'Big' Year," *Dance Magazine* Apr. 1996: 63.

21. Jesse McKinley, "Susan Stroman's Full Dance Card," *New York Times* 21 May 2000, Arts & Leisure: 4.

22. Gold 67.

23. McKinley 4.

24. Hilary Ostlere, "Kathleen Marshall: Taming the Musical," *Dance Magazine* Dec. 1999: 84.

25. Jesse McKinley, "Kathleen Marshall: She's Fast on Her Feet and Full of New Steps," *New York Times* 6 Feb. 2000, Arts & Leisure: 2.

From Revolution to Revelation

Women Performance Artists and the Transformation of American Musical Theatre

WOODROW HOOD

I've always believed that music theatre, like film,
in its integrative, inclusive nature can perfectly reflect
the perceptual richness and complexity of our lives.[1]
— Meredith Monk

Certainly the idea of performance art has been around longer than the term — to combine or recombine many artistic modes of expression into one work through experimental and self-reflexive practices. Precursors just in the twentieth century include the work of Oskar Schlemmer, Walter Gropius and other Bauhaus artists in Germany who staged a number of experimental performances involving music, dance, theatre, and visuals in the 1920s. The same type of experimental hybridization of artistic disciplines continued with the work of Josef and Anni Alpers at Black Mountain College in North Carolina and at the New Bauhaus in Chicago in the 1930s. John Cage's compositions and Merce Cunningham's choreography broke the rules of art in the 1940s and continued to do so for decades to come. Allan Kaprow's "happenings" in the late 1950s and 1960s would seek to minimize the gap between art and life. By the late 1960s, new experimentations would lead to what we now call performance art and to a handful of performance artists who would question, transform, and expand the definition(s) of musical theatre.

These new performance artists sought to co-opt the techniques of the modernist school, move beyond them, and use them to explore and create new works. Many of these artists were women who were entering a previously male-dominated art world. These women performance artists were generally college-educated; many majored in studio/fine art. Initially performance art was easily accessible to women. Little capital was needed other than a gallery space and a few materials for the performance. Grant agencies like the National Endowment for the Arts were also interested in non-represented artistic groups like women and minorities so funding was available. These factors seem to have created an inroad for a unique aesthetic means of cultural critique — questioning the dominant from within.

Performance artists like Laurie Anderson, Meredith Monk, and Diamanda Galás, three of the most well known and high profile performance artists who appropriate musical theatre elements in their work, question American cultural norms and present a multiplicity and diversity of perspectives. The multimedia means of expression available to performance artists allow them to articulate viewpoints that have been previously marginalized because of gender, race, and sexual orientation. Their work is important not only because of their commitment to social and political issues but also because they work within a cultural framework in order to root out cultural tendencies that favor particular groups, classes, or races. They utilize numerous avenues for expression including live performance, audio and video recordings, literature, visual arts, dance, and other artistic mediums.

Previous artists of the avant-garde movements saw themselves as outside of or separate from the institutions they critiqued. By this model, an artist had to always concern herself with "selling out" if she achieved any sense of commercial success. A new breed of performance artists (so-called usually because they were solo performers who mixed a multitude of media and disciplines and performed live) began to emerge who decided to adopt the communication power of mass media to reach their audiences. This emergence was not a break necessarily from the artistic practices of the avant-garde, conceptual, or experimental practices of the artists who came before but simply an expansion of how art can affect and change American ideological practice.

Many members of the current group of performance artists emerged from the pluralist 1970s New York conceptual art scene. Manhattan would become an important center for the exploration of performance events, particularly Soho and Greenwich Village. These areas began to attract actors, painters, filmmakers and musicians because of the abandoned manufacturing spaces that, because of a 1966 law, could be rented cheaply and turned into studio apartments.

Combining various types of artists into a relatively small area created a cross-communication between the various artistic pursuits. A small number of artists soon emerged to forge a new type of inter-disciplinary art that would begin to explore the boundaries between the visual arts, theatre, music, and dance. These performers often worked alone on stage or with a few others. Solo performance is one of the most important aspects of much performance art — every part of the performance in some way originates with the central artist.

Performance artists are difficult to categorize because one of their central tenets is eclecticism — perpetually avoiding any type of pigeonholing. But there are a few remarkable similarities in the various manifestations of performance art. First, performance art places primary importance on the process of how an artwork is created, linking its foundations to the Conceptual and Minimal art movements of the 1960s and 1970s. The emphasis on process, rather than product, can be seen as the first real ideological move away from the dominant mode of aesthetic practice, modernism. This shift to process operates similar to the idea of Brechtian distancing or historicization — if one sees the artistic process in the product then one can observe, study, and analyze the work's contents (as evidenced in the work of Laurie Anderson).

Second, personal identities are no longer fixed but constructed. Performance artists often study the relationship between the social/political and artistic practice, especially regarding marginalized groups of people. Performance pieces in this vein range from the radical (Diamanda Galás) to the more moderate (Laurie Anderson). Often iconoclastic and anti-nationalistic, change is the focus of the work, ranging from a clear call-to-arms to a less polemical cultural awareness. Whether politically or socially radical or more middle-of-the-road, the same ends are in sight — women's performance art offers a feminist critique of dominant institutions and seeks to expose misogynist or racist ideological practice. They operate as critics not by standing outside of the system but by implicating themselves as prone or subject to that system. In the end, women performance artists celebrate difference and seek to undermine any means of expression or existence that naturalizes separateness.

Third, technology is central to the staging of most performance art. Though quite expensive to acquire and use, computers, midi (computer-controlled, electronic) keyboards, video projectors, and other electronic hardware have become a mainstay for many performance artists. Performance artists highlight the process of the artist in the work itself and utilize aesthetic techniques from the past intermingled with current technology. Technology seems key to this change; not only are new (usually digital) technologies employed but the audience is continually reminded and made aware of their use. The performance artist is foregrounded as the instigator and controller of the technology; it is not simply a celebration of technological advance in and of itself as in the Futurist movement. In an article for *American Theatre* magazine in 1995, James Hannaham details Laurie Anderson's techno-wizardry:

> Anderson is waging her revolution from within corporate structure [...] Her clever subterfuge has allowed her to have many cakes and eat them, too. Her techno-saturated vision smacks of the forward-thinking hucksterism so prevalent in the modern age, currently epitomized by the computer industry's promotional blitz on every new piece of hardware. However, like a dutiful

postmodernist, she recognizes that the super-old contains the new — that there is a ghost in the machine, and tech-heads need gods, too.[2]

Anderson along with others can be said to be bringing down the master's house with the master's own tools.

Fourth, fixed models for understanding the universe are brought into question. Performance artists question Newtonian scientific precepts; linear models of time are often abandoned. The postmodern era embraces the less rigid notion of cyclic time, the point where notions of past, present and future disappear. Chance happenings and ambiguity are not only accepted but also embraced. This has led many artists to use video and audio looping in performance to explore and test the perception of time (especially Monk and Anderson).

And finally, performance artists discard the notion of originality and question modes of perception by putting disparate elements or materials together in a new way. By juxtaposing two elements, the artwork not only creates a new way of seeing the materials but also exposes the relationship between them; the binary system itself is revealed. This process of revelation expands and embraces natural ambiguity and seeks to make the perceiver aware of this ambiguity. Questions are created in the perceiver's mind like: "what is dream and what is real?," "what is male and what is female?," and "what is public and what is private?" Many postmodern artists do not seek to manipulate or lead the questions, but ask the perceiver to experience the work in whatever way they want and to find their own answers to these questions.

Three women performance artists especially stand out as long lasting, who continually reinvent themselves, and who continue to hybridize multiple performance disciplines. From their efforts, these three continue to transform music theatre, stretching the very definition of the form and bringing new audiences into its folds. First, the world-touring, multi-media stage shows of Laurie Anderson have probably reached more live audiences than any other performance artist. Arguably the most recognized and popular, Anderson's version of music theatre makes use of cutting-edge technology for some surprising effects. The operatic staging of multi-disciplinary artist Meredith Monk offers a glimpse of the ultimate fusion of all performance media. Song, sound, and dance are extensions of the same action in her world. And Diamanda Galás creates an expressionist music theatre to combat social woes. She transforms the traditional voice recital form into an engaging and inescapable environment where pain, horror, and fear of death are cleansed in vocal fire.

Laurie Anderson

In the past twenty years, Laurie Anderson has become one of the world's most recognizable performance artists. From her early 1970s performances in

the United States and throughout Europe to her magnum opus multi-media piece *United States*, Anderson went from obscure Soho performance spaces to international acclaim. Her performances have run the gamut from song cycles that present material from her record albums (*Empty Spaces*), song cycles that rework her recordings (*United States Live*), to relatively conventional musical plays (*Songs and Stories from Moby Dick*).

Anderson sings and tells stories intermittently during each show, sometimes with comic irony and sometimes with poignant significance. The product is a large-scale, electronic/human performance collage usually performed alone onstage by the cyborg-like (half human, half machine) Anderson. Her work could be described as cyber-art because of its reliance on digital technology.

Laurie Anderson was born to Arthur Anderson and Mary Louise Rowland Anderson in Chicago in 1947, and grew up in Glen Ellyn, a wealthy, nearby suburb. The second oldest of eight children, she always had her hands in the arts, training several years as a violinist and later taking classes at the Art Institute of Chicago.

For college, she briefly attended Mills College in California as a biology major, later transferring to Barnard in New York where she majored in art history, graduating magna cum laude. Barbara Novak's seminar on American landscapes at Barnard would influence her exploration of America in her later works. Also, encounters with Merleau-Ponty's *Phenomenology of Perception* and Wittgenstein's *Philosophical Investigations* would begin her postmodern aesthetic explorations. In 1969, she studied art with Sol LeWitt and Carl Andre at the School of Visual Arts. She then completed an M.F.A. in sculpture in 1972 at Columbia.

After graduating from Columbia, she taught art history at City College, in New York, where she offered courses in Egyptian sculpture and Assyrian architecture.[3] Her interest in semiotics and linguistics was growing and, in 1971, she studied Indian gestures and deaf signing. Experimental artists working in the Soho area of New York in the early and mid–1970s like Philip Glass, Robert Wilson, Vito Acconci, and others began to influence Anderson's work. It was the Glass/Wilson opera *Einstein on the Beach* (1976) that struck Anderson the most.[4] Much of what would become *United States* (1983) shows sharp influence from the Glass/Wilson collaboration in its epic proportions and use of juxtaposed images and sounds.

By the late 1970s, Anderson met William S. Burroughs, one of the key figures of influence on her writing style. She would later work with him on her film *Home of the Brave* (1986). Burroughs was known for his use of cut-up phrases from the media as material to comment upon the way the mass media influences modes of reception.

In the early 1970s Anderson created a well-noted series of art installations and performances in the Soho district of Manhattan, garnering many showings of her photography and drawings. She also began to write some songs for some of her installations and gallery shows. Her first performance piece was created in the summer of 1972. In Rochester, Vermont, Anderson created an orchestra piece for car, truck, and motorcycle horns called *Automotive*. The vehicles were parked around a band shell with the audience seated in the shell. Anderson directed the piece by using color-coded scores. From this point, Anderson began to focus mainly on performance pieces.

Her next performance, *As:If*, was performed in 1975 at Soho's Artist's Space. The piece incorporates word play, songs, and language games with short films and tape recordings. From 1974–1978, she worked on a series of street performance pieces that would first appear in New York City and then in Italy. She called the series *Duets on Ice* (1974–75 version) and in these street theatre events Anderson questioned the intersections of life and art by playing a violin duet with pre-recorded music from a built in speaker in the instrument while wearing ice skates embedded in a block of ice. The melting of the ice controlled the length of the performance; when the ice melted, the performance was over. Not only was Anderson exploring the intersections of life and art, she was beginning to explore notions of time in a performance setting. On a more personal note, the ice signified Anderson's stage fright. She literally had cold feet.

A series of performances followed in various spaces in New York like The Kitchen (*Songs For Lines/Songs For Waves*, 1977), the Whitney Museum and the Museum of Modern Art (*For Instants, Refried Beans*, 1976), and in Europe (*Engli-SH*, 1976 Berlin Festival). In these works, Anderson began to experiment with the use of various electronic media such as video, film, and vocoders (vocal processors). Much of what would become the later performances of *Americans on the Move* (1977) and *United States* (1983) came from these performances. Anderson is known for recycling earlier material into the larger performances.

Anderson continued to write songs. One of these, "It's Not the Bullet That Kills You, It's the Hole" appeared in an installation called *Juke Box* and refers to another contemporary performance artist, Chris Burden, who had shot himself on purpose with a gun during a performance. Another song from *Juke Box*, "Time To Go (For Diego)," is an audio study of the repetitive speech of a museum guard as he cleans people out of the building. Another song from the same period is about a bizarre moment of language confusion Anderson once experienced at a Buddhist retreat. "Juanita" loops the title repetitively as Anderson slowly begins to learn that the monks are not chanting Juanita but the word for ego or self. The *Juke Box* installation was comprised of a total of twenty-four songs composed and recorded by Anderson.

This period is most significant because of Anderson's experimentation with tape loops and a movement away from a linear sense of time. Much like the works of theatre auteur director Robert Wilson, composer Philip Glass, and writer William S. Burroughs, repetition plays a significant role in Anderson's work. With the help of her technology cohort, Bob Bielecki, Anderson began to adapt the violin she played in her songs and during performances into a new instrument. Starting by placing a vinyl record on the body of the violin and a record needle on the bow, she transformed the violin into the Viophonograph. Eventually, this device would move through the Tape-bow violin (incorporating audio magnetic tape) to digital versions that played pre-recorded music samples via an offstage computer. She has continued to create a host of new musical instruments including body suits that contain audio sensor pads which when pressed would produce music and sound.

Americans on the Move may be considered Anderson's first major performance, since it premiered at Carnegie Hall on 11 February 1979. The piece eventually moved to The Kitchen later that year and became *United States, Part I* ("Transportation"). These two shows would be incorporated into her largest stage work to date, Anderson's *United States* (1983). This performance exists as a document of Anderson's creative power and pushes at the boundaries of American music theatre. Over seven hours long, *United States* ponders what it means to be an American and employs a wild assortment of songs and stories. Sporadically during the show Anderson repeats questions like "Do you want to go home now?," evoking a sense of wonder and confusion about how we as Americans define our home. Is it a state of being or a physical place? She never offers a response, implicating the audience by leaving them to answer the question.

United States used many multimedia gadgets for startling special effects; numerous film, slide, and sound effects littered the show. One of the most notable images from the show was a graphic of four large clocks that represented the four different time zones of the continental U.S. At another moment, Anderson appears onstage with bright, headlight-like goggles over her eyes as she walks a plank over the orchestra pit to embody the search for a true American identity. She also used a vocoder or voice processor in *United States* to create what she has called "the voice of authority," representing the voice of oppression, dominance, and even patriarchy. Anderson continues to use various new technologies to manipulate the sound of her voice, creating multiple characters though she is often the only performer on stage. She is then free to create male voices, a chorus of women, and a host of eccentric or unusual entities.

By the first half of the 1980s, Anderson had signed a multi-album recording contract with Warner Brothers Records and book contracts with Harper Perennial, she had made a performance film called *Home of the Brave*, and her concerts had toured around the world. Anderson played to packed houses at Lincoln Center, the Brooklyn Academy of Music, the Royal Festival Hall in London, and in almost every major city in the United States and Europe. Massive touring and noteworthy record sales gave Anderson immediate pop star status by the mid–1980s. Several of her albums went "gold," meaning they sold over 100,000 copies, and she had a top ten pop song in England, "O Superman," which alone grossed over one million dollars. "O Superman" was one of the first videos to premiere on the MTV cable network and is a masterpiece of how semiotics can be employed in a performance piece. In the video, Anderson stands in front of a screen creating a new type of sign language, based on sign language for the deaf and the movement of shadow puppets, to emphasize how language is subjective to every individual; some signs translate from person to person and other signs do not.

She made appearances on "Saturday Night Live" and "The Tonight Show with Johnny Carson," received considerable MTV video play, created commercials for Nike and American Express, was interviewed for features by such mass market magazines as *People Weekly* and *Vogue*, and was examined by academic critics in educational journals like *TDR*. By the late 1980s, Anderson had become one of America's highest profile performance artists, gaining media exposure that few other performance artists have yet achieved. She helped bring performance art out of Soho and into popular culture. In 1995, Jay Leno introduced Laurie Anderson on the "Tonight Show" as "the most popular, highly acclaimed performance artist in the country."[5] That same year, her live performance, *Nerve Bible*, ran in a limited but successful engagement on Broadway.

Anderson's major stage works since *United States* include *Mister Heartbreak* (1984), *Natural History* (1986), *Talk Normal* (1987–88), *Empty Places* (1989–1990), *Voices from the Beyond* (1991), *The Nerve Bible* (1994–95), and an adaptation of Herman Melville's *Songs and Stories from Moby Dick* (1999). These shows have toured throughout North and South America, Europe, Japan, and Australia.

She has published several books as a means of documenting these performances as well as filming *Home of the Brave* (based on the 1984 *Mister Heartbreak* tour). Though they often differ greatly from each other, she has also released several audio recordings to document her live shows: *Big Science* (1982), *United States Live* (1984), *Mister Heartbreak* (1984), *Home of the Brave* (1986), *Strange Angels* (1989), *Bright Red/Tightrope* (1994), *The Ugly One With the Jewels and Other Stories* (1995), and *Life on a String* (2001). She has also scored music for several stages pieces (Robert Wilson's *Alcestis*, Molissa Fenley's *Bridge of Dreams*, Trisha Brown's *Set and Reset*) and two films for Spalding Gray (*Swimming to Cambodia* and *Monster in a Box*). In 1995, she even created a cd-rom based on much of her previous work, called *Puppet Motel*.

Anderson's shows have become even more technology focused in later years. She uses multiple video projectors, digital sound processors and effects, lighting effects, large banks of speakers, and numerous camera and computer effects. By *Songs and Stories from Moby Dick* (2000), everything onstage but the live actors is controlled by computers. All video and sound is computer-controlled and created, including the new musical instrument she created just for this performance — Anderson calls it the "Talking Stick." The Talking Stick is a digital remote-controlled instrument that looks like a long, skinny, metal pole with a moveable sheath on it. The instrument is played by moving hands up and down the shaft, triggering a set of audio samples stored in an offstage six-foot bank of computers, doubly operating as a phallic representation of the patriarchy at play in Melville's novel. The Talking Stick also serves as a harpoon for the actors onstage during the whaling scenes. Unusually, Anderson appeared onstage for this production with five male performers.

With this increased reliance on technology in her staging, Anderson continues to redefine American musical theatre in *Songs and Stories from Moby Dick*. Anderson has turned a critical examination of Melville's book into a work of musical theatre; this performance may exist as the first music theatre book review ever to hit the stage. Anderson creates an expansive space here where her sets are created via digital video and her props are musical instruments. Performance art expert Roselee Goldberg describes the opening sequence of the show:

> [...]Ms. Anderson stands alone, center stage on a raised platform, her back to the audience. A small figure against a large horizontal screen showing a panoramic film of ocean waves crashing slowly at her feet, she plays an electric-violin solo, drawing a bow back and forth across her body in long, steady motions. A deep wailing sound fills the stage and seems to loom over members of the audience, enveloping them viscerally in Ms. Anderson's world.[6]

In her 2000 biography of Anderson, Goldberg quotes Anderson saying that *Songs and Stories from Moby Dick* is "about Americans." She proffers:

> So what does Melville have to say to late–twentieth-century Americans. [...] Obsessive, technological, voluble, and in search of the transcendental, we're a lot like our nineteenth-century forebears. [...] For me, a key question is asked, almost as an afterthought, at the end of Father Mapple's famous sermon, "for what is a man that he should live out the lifetime of his God?" Yes, really. What do you do when you no longer believe in the things that have driven you? How do you go on?[7]

Anderson takes this question into musical form during the show in the song "One White Whale":

> How to find you
> Maybe by your singing
> A weird trail of notes in the water.
> One white whale in all these oceans
> One white whale.
>
> Slipping through the nets of silence
> Under polar ice caps miles down
> You leave your echoes in the water
> One white whale in all these oceans
> One white whale.[8]

The sense of longing for what is lost or missing seems remarkably similar to the lost sense of home that appears in *United States*. A consistent theme in

Anderson's work is the need to uncover how we define ourselves, think about ourselves, and understand ourselves as Americans.

The songs of *Songs and Stories from Moby Dick* are performed in the Laurie Anderson characteristic talk-sing style. Anderson sets her lyrics (monologue and song) against tape loops and ambient music backgrounds. The effect is that of minor key, late 20th century pop songs that rely on timbre and mood more than on clever arrangement of melody. Critic Bradley Quinn described her music this way in *Merge* magazine:

> Ranging from techno to orchestral, the musical score has a contemporary pop base, offset by a fun and funky acid jazz groove. Live instruments compete with pre-recorded electronic music to produce deliberately dissonant harmonies. In the background, bells toll, waves break, water gurgles, and splashes, seagulls call and organs pipe eerily. At times I thought I was hearing Buddhist chanting or an Islamic call to prayer. Anderson plays a range of melancholy tunes on her violin, electronically enhanced to sound like an entire string orchestra.[9]

The beats of the music are very simple yet driving throughout, building and rarely releasing the musical tension as the search for the white whale forges onward.

Laurie Anderson continues to break ground and stretch the definition of performance art and music theatre. In early 2000, she recorded part of the audio book for *The Path to Tranquility*, written by one of her most important influences, His Holiness the Dalai Lama. She also continues to work on creating artworks for the Internet, new sculptural works, and new audio and video pieces. Her 2001 recording on the Nonesuch recording label, *Life On A String*, is a dark recording, full of songs of longing and emptiness.

To date, Anderson has not published most of her music work, thereby prohibiting others from performing pieces like *Songs and Stories from Moby Dick* and *United States*. Anderson's work is possibly too personal and specific to her own life perspective for others to perform — maybe something important to Anderson would be lost in the translation.

Utilizing the media tools available to her, Laurie Anderson's work offers a prime example of how performance artists can work within a market economy and are still able to critique American culture and ideological practice. The results are cutting-edge, beautiful, and full of thought-provoking irony.

Meredith Monk

Fewer artists have boosted experimentation in American music theatre and new opera than Meredith Monk. A composer, singer, filmmaker, author, choreographer, designer, and director, Monk's work has been applauded for its integration of multiple disciplines. Asked by *Dance Magazine* in 2001 if she saw herself as a composer who dances or a dancer who composes she answered: "I never think I am a noun; I always feel like I'm a verb. [...] I've always fought against being categorized. I think everything feeds everything else."[10] Monk has always seemed more fascinated by the fluidity of her artistic identity than interested in finding some fixed, aesthetic position.

Her operas (any large-scale music theatre piece is an opera to her) are often bright, colorful, and aurally and visually dynamic. Monk wants to create an ideal theatrical space for all forms of art to come together, and she often appears in her own work as actor, singer, and dancer. She has performed at such diverse traditional and non-traditional spaces as the Whitney Museum of American Art and the Guggenheim in New York City, the Smithsonian Institute in Washington, D.C., the Houston Grand Opera, and the Brooklyn Academy of Music. She performs at major art, dance, theatre, and music spaces throughout the United States, Canada, and Europe, often creating work that is site-specific for that space.

Highly metaphorical, her productions often become meditations on aesthetic and personal issues and ask the audience members to open themselves (musically, visually, and mentally) to new perceptions. Monk's work edges towards a sense of personal mythology, an attempt to get at the core of personal dreams, aspirations, and fantasies.

Born in 1942, Monk grew up in New York state and Connecticut with music filling her house. Her grandparents on her mother's side, both Russian and German immigrants, were professional classical musicians. Monk's mother was a professional singer who recorded radio commercials in the 1930s and 1940s. Following family tradition, Monk studied music and would later graduate from Sarah Lawrence College in 1964 with a multi-disciplinary arts degree. Her first, post-college work, entitled 16 Millimeter Earrings, premiered in New York City in 1966. The multi-media piece incorporated Monk in a tapestry of film, music, and movement. In 1968, Monk created "The House," an interdisciplinary performance art group that later gave birth to The House Foundation — a non-profit organization that today still oversees her work. However, much of her material (both performance and visual) during the late 1960s and early 1970s focused on her work as a solo artist.

Other Monk works of the late 1960s and early 1970s focused on large-scale, contemporary operas that employed a battalion of vocalists. By 1969 she had created a major music-theatre piece for 85 voices, Juice: A Theatre Cantata in 3 Installments. The piece was performed in three different spaces: The Guggenheim Museum, Minor Latham Playhouse, and The House, New York City. Two more large-scale opera pieces would quickly emerge: in 1970 Monk created Needle-Brain Lloyd and the Systems Kids with a staggering 150 voices accompanied only by electric organ, guitar, and flute, and then followed in 1971 with Vessel: An Opera Epic which employed seventy-five voices. But her Education of the Girlchild in 1972–1973 with only six voices, organ, and piano would begin a new trend in her work — more intimate operas.

Her 1976 work, *Quarry*, used a chorus and prompted Monk to explore the idea of creating works for an ensemble. The work included thirty-eight voices, two pump organs, two soprano recorders, and audiotape. In 1978 she created a vocal ensemble to expand and explore the practice of vocal music and by 1979 they had performed their first major work, *Dolmen Music*, which included parts for six voices, piano, violin, cello and percussion. *The Games* came next in 1983 and featured a dark subject (nuclear holocaust survivors) compared to most of her other work.

Monk would have to wait until 1991 to see one of her grandest pieces ever staged. Commissioned by the Houston Grand Opera, the Walker Arts Center in Minneapolis, and the American Music Theatre Festival, Monk created *Atlas: An Opera in Three Parts* which premiered in Houston. An epic that features a musical score of diverse styles, *Atlas* follows the life of Alexandra (played by Monk) who is a world traveler. Alexandra's excursions with her various companions on a host of realistic and fantastic adventures offer a clear metaphor for a spiritual quest for enlightenment. Guides who eventually take her to a timeless place of light lead Alexandra around the world.

Atlas contains few lyrics and relies heavily on vocalise (wordless melodies). Monk's approach to singing is based in a combination of noise (human, animal, industrial sounds for example), classical music, and world music. She often develops her nonsense lyrics from this oddball combination. In a July 2000 restaging of *Atlas*, *The New York Times* music critic Anthony Tommasini described the singing this way:

> Her sounds range from deep-set bogeyman chest tones to chirping falsetto high notes. She can bend notes and inflect a phrase with the raspy poignancy of a great blues singer like Mississippi John Hurt. And like a Tibetan Buddhist chanter, she can sustain a steady low tone while shaping a floating melody in soft, eerie high harmonics. Movements—bobbing, weaving, arm gestures, leg lifts—are as much a part of the music as sound.[11]

The musical accompaniment alternates between a series of persistent drones, melodic, repetitive musical patterns, and irregular rhythms. Since *Atlas*, Monk has continued to publish music and oratorios (though rarely performed by others) and to release audio recordings.

Not only does Monk work in many fields, she has proved herself a leader in many of them. She has received a string of awards for her work: two Guggenheim Fellowships, three Obies (one for Sustained Achievement), a Bessie award for Sustained Creative Achievement, two Villager awards, sixteen ASCAP Awards for Musical Composition, the 1986 National Music Theatre Award, and the 1992 *Dance Magazine* Award.

In addition, Monk has received several honorary doctorates from schools such as Julliard and Bard College. She has released over a dozen audio recordings and her music has appeared in the feature films *The Big Lebowski* (1998, from Joel and Ethan Coen) and *Nouvelle vague* (1988, written and directed by

A composer, singer, filmmaker, author, choreographer, designer, and director, Meredith Monk's work has been applauded for its integration of multiple disciplines (Massimo Agus).

Jean-Luc Godard). She has also created her own films *Ellis Island* and *Book of Days*; the latter was aired on PBS and released in theatres. Along with Philip Glass, John Cage, and Robert Ashley, Monk was the subject of a video project directed by UK experimental film director Peter Greenaway in the series, *Four American Composers* (1983)—testament to her importance as a 20th century American composer.

Meredith Monk's powerful aesthetic yearning, brilliant compositions, and cutting-edge staging practices will continue to stretch the lines between artistic disciplines. Her work bridges cultures and perspectives across a wide range of creative practice. The result is an unflinching pursuit of the balanced production aesthetic where primacy is not given to any one element in particular but all stand out as unique and discrete units of the whole. Rooted deeply in the conceptual art of the 1960s and 1970s, Monk defies the world of Broadway production and marketing. Process is the product in Monk's universe—the action is the objective with no nicely wrapped package at the end of the pursuit. She is a verb, not a noun.

Diamanda Galás

Diamanda Galás has transformed the concept of the classical vocal recital from that of beauty, elegance, and vocal showmanship to a dark and unforgiving examination of AIDS, death, personal remorse, and deep longing. Horror writer and film director Clive Barker, who penned the introduction to Galás's book, *The Shit of God*, remarks on the powerful impact of one of her performances:

> Her own voice — one moment serpentine, the next a juggernaut — carries her audience on a journey into primal regions, where intellectual analysis and even aesthetic judgments become redundant. All you can do is listen and feel.[12]

Galás uses her four octave vocal range like aural fireworks, screeching, growling, bellowing, and hissing throughout her songs, often making us wonder when her voice will simply give out. Whereas the damaged voices of pop performers like Billy Holiday and Marianne Faithfull were and are simply byproducts of their lifestyles, Galás's vocal damage seems intentional. The voice itself becomes a sort of road map, foregrounding the physical processes and toll that emotional distress (anger, fear, pain, suffering, guilt) can have on the human voice.

Writing and performing her original pieces alone, Galás fuses American Musical performance with German Expressionist style drama to create a dark and ecstatic *mise-en-scène*. Possibly dismissed sometimes as bombastic, self-indulgent, and self-righteous, the power and conviction of Galás's work cannot be denied. The macabre atmosphere of her performances even garnered her the title of "Queen of the Nightmare" from *The Village Voice*.[13]

Raised by Greek Orthodox parents in San Diego, California, she studied keyboards as a child and eventually majored in music at the University of California. A wild youth would lead her to heavy drug experimentation and a brief stint of confounding gender expectations by presenting herself as a drag queen.

As with many other women performance artists who must rely on European festival support of her work, Diamanda Galás's professional singing career would begin to take off in Europe after her first live performance at the Festival d'Avignon in France in 1979. She toured heavily in the 1980s throughout the continent with small, solo pieces like *Medéa Tarántula*, *Wild Women With Steak Knives*, and *Song From the Blood of the Murdered*. Of this period, Galás has said that the music "is concerned with tendencies towards excessive behavior."[14] In 1982 she released her first audio recording, *The Litanies of Satan*, based on writings by French author Charles Baudelair. She followed this with a solo stage performance, *Panoptikon*, about a prisoner facing imminent death and explores issues of injustice.

Returning to San Francisco, she began perhaps her most personal work — a series of performances that would become the trilogy entitled *Masque of the Red Death* (1984). *Masque of the Red Death* would parallel and give a voice to the AIDS epidemic in that town in the mid–1980s. Attacking homophobia and intolerance, Galás began her trilogy with *The Divine Punishment*. It skewers religious, conservative Americans who thought that AIDS was a deserved punishment for homosexuals. Galás followed with similar content in *Saint of the Pit*.

Then she lost her playwright/poet brother, Philip Dimitri Galás, to AIDS; he died in her arms. Completing her trilogy with *You Must Be Certain of the Devil*, she adapted gospel music in a grand theatricalization of fear, loss, and anger. The performance may be read as a spectacular ritual of mourning for her very public and private loss. Her versions of "Swing Low, Sweet Chariot" and "The Lord is My Shepherd" are maniacally angry and powerfully sad. Galás screeches and growls the songs in near animalized fashion. In 1989, she premiered the full *Masque of the Red Death* at Queen Elizabeth Hall in London.

Her work of the 1990s focused heavily upon abandoned or disowned groups of people, specifically AIDS victims and the mentally infirm. She indicts religious institutions as targets, considering them bastions of empty posturing and practices rife with misogyny, homophobia, and other forms of oppression and intolerance. Her work continues to struggle with unearthing social injustice and cultural bigotry.

Technology is a large part of her staging process. Rather than heavily using film or video, Galás utilizes the advances in digital audio technology. She employs multiple microphones, multiple speakers, reverb devices, audio mixers, tape decks, vocal processors, and other effects and techniques to manipulate her voice beyond its utmost physical power. Her use of digital audio technology is evident in her 1990 performance of *Plague Mass* at Saint John the Divine Cathedral in Manhattan. Enacting a dark mass by entering in black robes, Galás was backlit with haunting red light and shrouded in smoke. One song from *Plague Mass*, "There Are No More Tickets to the Funeral," serves as a clear example of Galás's continuation of dark themes and the study of human misery:

> And on that holy day
> And on that bloody day
> And on his dying bed he told me
> "Tell all my friends I was fighting, too,
> But to all the cowards and voyeurs:
> There are no more tickets to the funeral
> There are no more tickets to the funeral.[15]

The song also includes bits of the Roy Acuff song "Were You There When They Crucified My Lord":

> Were you there when they crucified my Lord
> Were you there when they nailed him to the cross
> Sometimes it causes me to tremble, tremble, tremble
> Were you there when they crucified my Lord?[16]

Galás's song conjoins the sentimental Acuff song with what seems to be the voice of her dying brother into a scathing indictment of a society that chose to let her brother die without help. She twists the original referent (the country song) into a darker image of a brutal death by incorporating bits of the spiritual, "Swing Low, Sweet Chariot":

Swing swing
A band of Angels coming after me
Coming for to carry me home
Swing swing
A band of Devils coming after me
Coming for to drag me to the grave[17]

Galás's cultural critique is solidified by her stage appearance. Galás performed most of the piece partially nude and covered in stage blood, a contortion of the Christian image of being washed in the blood of the lamb.

Her next performance, *Vena Cava* (1992), premiered at the Kitchen in New York. Here Galás explores some dark and frightening corners of the mind, using much of her deceased brother's writings as the basis for the work. Following *Vena Cava*, she released a compact disc full of the twisted and tortured versions of gospel songs for which she was becoming known in her live performances. Entitled *The Singer*, the album drew much critical favor. The *Rolling Stone* review of the album summed up the mood of the album well:

> The talented Diamanda Galás has a vision of the world that makes the horror-stricken likes of Edgar Allan Poe and H.P. Lovecraft seem like pink-cheeked Pollyannas [...] Alone on the album, accompanying herself with what can be described only as two-fisted piano playing [...] Each song on *The Singer* is transformed into a howl, a shriek, a rant against life, death, nature, the history of music and the will of God. To close, she simply eats the piano.[18]

She followed this release with a new performance; *Insekta* opened that same year for the Serious Fun Festival at Lincoln Center using expressionistic (creepily elongated) cages inset with harnesses as a backdrop setting.

In 1994, Galás created the radio work *Schrei 27* by intertwining her writings with those of Job and St. Thomas Aquinas. She eventually staged the show as *Schrei 27/Schrei X*, which was performed completely in the dark, allowing the audience to fully imbibe her extended vocal technique. She followed with 1996's *Malediction and Prayer* and 1999's *Defixiones, Will and Testament*.

Like Anderson and Monk, Galás publishes her material in a

Performer Diamanda Galas fuses technology and German expressionism with music theatre (Austin Young).

multitude of forms and has appeared in many different types of venues. Many of her performances are issued on compact disc; Mute Records has faithfully released most of her live performances including *The Divine Punishment, Litanies of Satan, Plague Mass, Vena Cava, Schrei X Live/Schrei 27, You Must Be Certain of the Devil,* and others. She has also worked on recordings with former Led Zeppelin bassist John Paul Jones. Her *Judgment Day* video (1993) features segments of her *The Singer* concerts.

Many other artists have also incorporated her work into theirs. Her audio recordings have appeared in films by Francis Ford Coppola (*Bram Stoker's Dracula*) and British experimental director Derek Jarman (*Last of England*) and recording artists Erasure and others have sampled her voice. A collection of her performance texts and notes can be found in her book, *The Shit of God* (1996). She has been well recognized for her contributions to musical theatre, has received acknowledgments from Ford Foundation and Meet the Composer grants, and has gained a major following around the world. She also maintains a continual recording contract with Mute Records in London.

Diamanda Galás's work continues to surprise and challenge audiences by taking music theatre performance to some very dark and hard-to-take places (pain, suffering, death, loss). All the while, she continues to mark her voice with the history of her own human existence and share it with us in a theatrical setting.

A Multiplicity of Voices

Performance art seems to have matured past a fad to a legitimate and vibrant means of expression for music theatre artists. Like Anderson, Monk, and Galás, many other performance artists continue to struggle with issues of identity, oppression, and the representation of women onstage. African-American performance artists Robbie McCauley and Rhodessa Jones intersect race and performance in a unique blend of songs and monologues. For example, in her 1994 play, *Sally's Rape,* McCauley uses minstrelsy to get at the core of race relations in the U.S.

Not all performance artists use musical theatre elements in their work. Karen Finley, Marga Gomez, Dawn Akemi Saito, and Brenda Wong Aoki add their cultural perspectives in their performance work by exploring issues of race, ethnicity, and the cultural position of women in the U.S. Other strong feminist voices like those of Holly Hughes and Rachel Rosenthal continue to enrich monologue driven performance. Actress/performance artist Ann Magnuson accesses large audiences with her television work. On the international side, French performance artist Orlan often performs in the U.S., surgically mutating her face to mimic famous paintings, commenting on the intersection between artistic and female beauty.

The work of these artists will continue to inspire music theatre practitioners to look towards future potentials, beyond what has been done. With them and their commitments to using all media at hand, multiple voices and perspectives can continue to be articulated. As Laurie Anderson said in *United States*:

> Welcome to Difficult Listening Hour. The spot on our dial for that relentless and impenetrable sound of Difficult Music. So sit bolt upright in that straight-backed chair, button that top button, and get set for some difficult music.[19]

Difficult music may aptly describe the work of Anderson, Monk, and Galás for change is always a difficult process and these three women have been and continue to be instrumental in the changing face of American music theatre. Are you ready for some difficult music?

Notes

1. Meredith Monk in the liner notes to *Atlas: An Opera in Three Parts*, Ecm Records, New York, 437773, 1991.
2. James Hannaham, "Laurie Anderson: Media Masseuse," *American Theatre* July 1995: 48.
3. William Duckworth, *Talking Music* (New York: Schirmer Books, 1995) 368.
4. John Howell, *Laurie Anderson* (New York: Thunder's Mouth Press, 1992) 21.
5. *The Tonight Show*, NBC, New York City, NY, 2 February 1995.
6. Roselee Goldberg, "Hitching a Ride on the Great White Whale," *New York Times* 3 Oct. 1999: 29.
7. Qtd. in Goldberg. *Laurie Anderson* (New York: Harry N. Abrams, 2001) 187.
8. Qtd. in Goldberg, *Laurie Anderson* 188.
9. Bradley Quinn, "Laurie Anderson," *Merge* 1 Nov. 2000: 40.
10. Gus Solomons, Jr., "Meredith Monk: A Voice in Motion," *Dance Magazine* July 2001: 46.
11. Anthony Tommasini, "High or Low, Meredith Monk Bends the Melodies," *New York Times* 24 July 2000: E5.
12. Qtd. in Diamanda Galás, *The Shit of God* (London: Serpents Tail/High Risk, 1996) ii–iii.
13. Kyle Gann, "Queen of the Nightmare," *The Village Voice* 23 Jan. 1996: 54.
14. Galás 1.
15. Galás 41.
16. Qtd. in Galás 42.
17. Galás 42.
18. Brian Cullman, "Recordings—*The Singer*," *Rolling Stone* 25 June 1992: 44.
19. Laurie Anderson, *United States* (New York: Harper/Colophon Books, 1984) 93.

Contributors

Jennifer Jones Cavenaugh is an associate professor of theatre and dance at Rollins College. Her book *Medea's Daughters: Forming and Performing the Woman Who Kills* was published by Ohio State University Press in 2003. She has also published articles in *Theatre Notebook, The New England Journal of Theatre, Theatre History Studies, Modern Drama* and *American Drama*. Her essay on Lizzie Borden and actress Nance O'Neil is in *Passing Performances: Queer Readings of Leading Players in the American Theatre*, published by University of Michigan Press.

Bud Coleman is an associate professor at the University of Colorado at Boulder and Chair of the Department of Theatre and Dance. A former dancer with Les Ballets Trockadero de Monte Carlo, Fort Worth Ballet, Kinesis, and Ballet Austin, he has directed or choreographed numerous productions. He has a Ph.D. in theatre history and criticism from the University of Texas at Austin, and his publications have appeared in the *St. James Press Gay & Lesbian Almanac, www.glbtq.com, The Encyclopedia of Homosexuality* (Garland Press), *New York Native, Theatre History Studies, The Austin American-Statesman, Theatre In Sight* and *Choreography and Dance*. His essay on Loïe Fuller is in *Passing Performances: Queer Readings of Leading Players in the American Theatre*, published by University of Michigan Press.

Tish Dace, Chancellor Professor Emerita at the University of Massachusetts–Dartmouth and winner of its 1997 Scholar of the Year Award, has published over 200 essays, articles and book chapters; reviews of several thousand plays; and several books. She chaired the Maharam Foundation/American Theatre Wing/Hewes theatrical design awards in New York for nearly 20 years, also chaired the ATW "Working in the Theatre" Design Seminars, served six years as a member of the Executive Committee of the American Theatre Critics Association, now serves on its advisory board, and was vice president of the ATCA Foundation. The New York critic for *Plays International* in London, she is a member of the editorial board of the Best Plays series and of the executive committee of the International Association of Theatre Critics. She has published in such periodicals as *The New York Times, London Times, New York Magazine, Ms., Boston Phoenix, Village Voice, Soho News, American Theatre, Vogue, American Poetry Review, New York Daily News, Playbill, African American Review* and *Back Stage*.

Anne Fliotsos is an associate professor of theatre at Purdue University, West Lafayette, Indiana. She has published in *Theatre Topics, Theatre Studies, The Journal of American Culture, Studies in Popular Culture, American Theatre,* and *Research in Drama Education*. She is an award-winning director and has published *Oedipus! A New Musical Comedy* through Baker's Plays. She is co-editor of *Teaching Theatre Today* (Palgrave 2004) and is finishing her second book, *American Women Stage Directors of the 20th Century: A Sourcebook*, for the University of Illinois Press.

Barbara Means Fraser is an associate professor of theatre at Santa Clara University in California. She contributed to *Stephen Sondheim: A Casebook*, edited by Joanne Gordon, and has written articles and presented papers on the body of work by Stephen Sondheim in the United States and Taiwan. Fraser is also a playwright and director. She earned her Ph.D. from the University of Oregon.

Anna Wheeler Gentry made her Lincoln Center solo debut in 2003 on the concert series *Autumn in New York: Vernon Duke at 100*— a centennial celebration of composer Vernon Duke's life and music — where she performed and presented an overview of her work restoring for revival the 1932 Broadway musical revue *Walk a Little Faster* (music by Vernon Duke, lyrics by E.Y. Harburg), which premiered the time-honored standard "April in Paris." Ms. Gentry's expanding areas of published research — including book articles and journal publications with Continuum, Gale Publishers, Routledge, Music Library Association, Western Illinois University, University of Alabama, Hofstra University, and Johns Hopkins University Press—focus on early twentieth-century lyricists, composers and choreographers of the American musical theatre, particularly those who have Russian and Yiddish influences in their work such as E. Y. Harburg, Vernon Duke, Jay Gorney, Harold Arlen, Dimitri Tiomkin, and Albertina Rasch. Her research grants include the 1999 UMKC Women's Council American Multi-Cinema (AMC) Award with Outstanding Merit, the Harriette Yeckel Theatre Award with Outstanding Merit, National Endowment for the Arts, and travel grants from the Yip Harburg Foundation and Society for American Music. Currently on faculty at the Arizona State University School of Music and a stage director for the ASU Lyric Opera Theatre, Ms. Gentry is a member of Actors Equity, American Federation of Television and Radio Artists, the Stage Directors and Choreographers Foundation, and chair of the "Music Theatre Interest Group" for the Society for American Music.

Woodrow Hood is currently the chair of theatre arts and an associate professor at Catawba College in North Carolina. Published in journals such as *Theatre Journal, American Theatre Magazine, The Journal of Dramatic Theory and Criticism, Postmodern Culture, Theatre Forum*, and *PAJ*, Woody is also co-author of *Theatre: Its Art and Craft*. He is a member and a director of the Terra Incognita Theatre Company.

Gary Konas is associate professor of English at the University of Wisconsin–La Crosse. He holds a Ph.D. in English from the University of California–Davis, as well as degrees in mathematics, wine chemistry, and creative writing. He is the editor of *Neil Simon: A Casebook* (Garland 1997). He has published several articles in the areas of American drama and musical theatre.

Mary Jo Lodge is currently an assistant professor of English and theatre at Lafayette College in Easton, Pennsylvania, after four years of teaching and running the Musical Theater program at Central Michigan University. She earned an undergraduate degree in Musical Theatre from Catholic University in Washington, D.C., an M.A. in Theatre from Villanova University and a Ph.D. in Theatre from Bowling Green State University. She concentrated her dissertation research on the emergence of the female director/choreographer on Broadway and continues to research and write on various aspects of musicals and their creators. In addition to her scholarly work, Dr. Lodge is an experienced director, choreographer and actress-singer-dancer.

Korey R. Rothman serves as academic director of the South Carolina Washington Semester Program and is a visiting assistant professor in theatre history at the University of Maryland. Her current research centers on gender and the American musical, particularly in the period before *Oklahoma!*. She is currently researching the career of Nancy Hamilton, a lyricist of intimate revues, and the presence of an "Old Girl's Network" of women lyricists on Broadway.

Judith Sebesta holds a Ph.D. in theatre history and criticism from the University of Texas at Austin and is currently teaching theatre history, criticism, and theory at the University of Missouri–Columbia. Previously she was associate professor and head of Theatre Studies in the School of Theatre Arts at the University of Arizona. She has published articles in such publications as *Studies in Musical Theatre, Theatre Journal, Contemporary Theatre Review, New England Theatre Journal, Theatre Annual, On Stage Studies,* and the *Sondheim Review* and is secretary of the Association for Theatre in Higher Education. She is working on an innovative book/web/dvd learning tool titled *Explore Theatre: A Backstage Pass,* to be published by Allyn & Bacon.

Index